The Pilsen Revolt of 1953

The Pilsen Revolt of 1953

Kindred by Currency

Jakub Šlouf
Translated by Lucie Mikolajková

LEXINGTON BOOKS
Lanham • Boulder • New York • London

Published by Lexington Books
An imprint of The Rowman & Littlefield Publishing Group, Inc.
4501 Forbes Boulevard, Suite 200, Lanham, Maryland 20706
www.rowman.com

86-90 Paul Street, London EC2A 4NE

British Library Cataloguing in Publication Information Available

Library of Congress Cataloging-in-Publication Data

Names: Šlouf, Jakub, 1982- author. | Mikolajková, Lucie, translator.
Title: The Pilsen Revolt of 1953 : kindred by currency / Jakub Šlouf ; translated by Lucie Mikolajková.
Description: Lanham : Lexington Books, [2022] | "The text in this book is a revised English translation of the author's dissertation...published in Czech [in 2016]."—Introduction. | Includes bibliographical references and index. | Summary: "This book examines the Pilsen revolt in Czechoslovakia in 1953, a spontaneous confluence of several individual, mutually incompatible protests, through which different parts of society reacted to the currency reform using different cultural traditions. The author analyzes how each protest brought their own alternative authorities into public space"— Provided by publisher.
Identifiers: LCCN 2021051664 (print) | LCCN 2021051665 (ebook) | ISBN 9781793646453 (cloth) | ISBN 9781793646460 (epub)
Subjects: LCSH: Strikes and lockouts—Czech Republic—Plzeň—History—20th century. | Monetary policy—Czech Republic—Plzeň—History—20th century. | Rationing—Czech Republic—Plzeň—History—20th century.
Classification: LCC HD5372.3.Z9 P66 2022 (print) | LCC HD5372.3.Z9 (ebook) | DDC 331.892/94371—dc23/eng/20211202
LC record available at https://lccn.loc.gov/2021051664
LC ebook record available at https://lccn.loc.gov/2021051665

Contents

List of Figures

Acknowledgments

Translation of the book was funded by the National Archives in Prague.

The original Czech text was reviewed by Dr. Michal Kopeček (Institute for Contemporary History of the Czech Academy of Sciences) and Dr. Jiří Křesťan (National Archives in Prague).

Abbreviations and Glossary of Terms

a. j.	archive unit
CO	Civil Defence Headqurters
CZV	Factory Committee
č.	number
č.j.	reference number
ČSAV	Czechoslovak Academy of Sciences
ČSD	Czechoslovak State Railroads
ČSM	Czechoslovak Union of Youth (nationwide youth organization)
ETD	subsidiary plant Elektrotrakce Doudlevce
f.	archival fonds
inv.č.	inventory number
JNV	Consolidated National Committee (municipal administration authority)
JUDr.	law degree ("doctor of law")
kart.	carton / box
KAV NF	National Front Regional Action Committee
Kčs	Czechoslovak Koruna, CZK (unit of currency)
KNV	Regional National Committee (regional administrative authority)
KS MV	Ministry of Interior Regional Authority
KS StB	State Security Regional Administration
KSČ	Communist Party of Czechoslovakia
KV	Regional Committee
KV KSČ	Regional Committee of the Communist Party
LM	People's Militias (armed units of factory workers, Communist Party members and supporters)

MNB	Ministry of National Security
MV KSČ	Municipal Committee of the Communist Party of Czechoslovakia
NF	National Front (official coalition of all legal political parties and associations)
NMS	new social movement
OAV NF	National Front District Action Committee
ROH	Revolutionary Trade Union Movement
SBČS	Czechoslovak State Bank
sig.	file reference number
SNB	National Security Corps, national police in Czechoslovakia from 1945 to 1991
SOA	Regional State Archive
SNR	National Revolution Union
StB	State Security, secret police force in Czechoslovakia from 1945 to 1990
sv.	document folder
ÚAV NF	National Front Central Action Committee
ÚNV	Central National Committee (municipal administrative authority)
ÚRO	Central Council of Unions
ÚSD AV ČR	Institute of Contemporary History of the Czech Academy of Sciences
ÚSTR	Institute for the Study of Totalitarian Regimes
ÚV	Central Committee
ÚV KSČ	Central Committee of the Communist Party
VB	Public Security (regular, uniformed police force)
ZO KSČ	Factory Organization of the Communist Party
zn.	court file reference number
ZR	Factory Council
ZVIL	The Vladimir Ilyich Lenin Factories in Pilsen (formerly Škoda Works)

Introduction

Between June 1 and 4, 1953, a wave of strikes and protests broke out in Czechoslovakia in reaction to the recently declared currency reform and cancellation of the rationing system imposed during World War II. The reform, announced to the public on Saturday, May 30, 1953, rendered worthless the savings of a large part of the population, reduced certain benefits for industrial workers, and caused nationwide panic due to the fear of a possible supply crisis. One hundred and twenty-nine factories and production plants all over the country joined the strike. In some towns, workers actually tried to take to the streets in protest. The largest and most turbulent protests took place in Pilsen, a city in West Bohemia with a population of roughly 132,000 at the time. On Monday June 1, rioting in the streets caused a temporary collapse of the local party administration and security forces. For a single day, the dictatorship of the Communist Party effectively ceased to exist. The protests were only subdued later that night, with the help of the Czechoslovak military and other security forces summoned from other parts of the country.

The events in Pilsen were very similar to other revolts that occurred in several countries of the Eastern Bloc in the years 1953–1956, when the process of de-Stalinization began. The conflicts were mostly motivated by a combination of various economic, political, national, and religious factors, usually beginning with spontaneous strikes of industrial workers who demanded various social concessions and benefits, and later evolved into mass public protests voicing political demands.

In their final stage, the protests turned into violent riots and clashes with the security forces, with the protesters attempting to seize control of the infrastructure and administrative institutions. This was true not only for the Pilsen revolt of June 1, 1953, but also the subsequent uprising in East Germany (June 17, 1953)[1] and the Poznań protests of June 28, 1956.[2] Slightly different in nature and dynamic was the Hungarian Revolution of 1956 (October 23 to November 10), largely initiated by students who had a political agenda from the outset.[3]

In many respects, however, the situation in Czechoslovakia was different from that in East Germany and Poland. Far fewer people were involved in the Pilsen protests than in the Berlin uprising, and the protesters were far less organized.[4] No strike committees or revolutionary committees were established with the intent to replace the official administrative bodies, save for a few instances where the protesters elected representatives to negotiate with the authorities.

Some of these differences can be explained by the fact that Pilsen was not a large city and that the protests were suppressed before they could escalate any further, but the reasons the events took a different course lay much deeper. After the war, Czechoslovakia was officially part of the winning coalition of countries and was not occupied by the Soviet Union. In May 1945, most people had viewed the Soviets as liberators and key allies that would guarantee the country protection against another possible German attack.[5] The Munich Agreement of September 1938, by which Czechoslovakia's Western allies yielded to the demands of Nazi Germany, was still viewed as an act of betrayal and a source of considerable national trauma. Combined with the lingering Pan-Slavic traditions born in the 19th century, this had led to the idea that Czechoslovakia could become a sort of a bridge between the East and the West, which the Czechoslovak politicians (including members of the non-communist political parties) had actively been trying to promote in the years 1945–1948, with a view of effectively combining the best advantages of democracy and socialism. However, following the onset of the Cold War in 1947, this course had become untenable, and was effectively abandoned after the communist coup in February 1948.

The dictatorship of the Communist Party was initially supported (or at least tolerated) by a good part of the population; compared to the Great Depression of the 1930s and the hardships of World War II, the regime change had actually been beneficial for certain social groups, providing them with much-desired welfare as well as the opportunity for rising on the social ladder at the expense of the former bourgeoisie and the middle classes.

For the above reasons, the Pilsen protests, unlike the East German uprising, were not primarily anti-Soviet, despite voicing some pro-American sentiments. The protesters in Pilsen did not unite against a common foreign enemy and did not use collective national identity as a recruitment tool, centering primarily on social issues. Political issues only played a marginal part and found much less support among the industrial workers and low-ranking party members than in East Germany. Most of them endorsed the protesters' social demands, but generally remained loyal to the communist regime.[6]

The Poznań protests were heavy on anti-Soviet rhetoric, and both the workers and low-ranking members of the Polish United Workers' Party engaged in political protests. The Polish revolt also had strong religious overtones. Compared to Poland, Czechoslovakia had been heavily influenced by the ideas of socialism and secularism in the early 20th century, and religious symbols had no part in workers' protests.[7]

However, the most distinctive difference between the protesters in Pilsen and their East German and Polish counterparts lay in their (un)willingness to resort to an armed conflict. There were many instances where the Pilsen protesters managed to disarm members of the armed forces, but not once did they try to use the confiscated weapons or even threaten to use them; they threw the weapons away or destroyed them instead. Members of the Communist Party of Czechoslovakia (KSČ) also considered the use of firearms unacceptable, mainly for propaganda and ideological reasons. Compared to the protests in neighboring countries, both sides of the Pilsen conflict still considered themselves to be part of a single nation and made a concerted effort to prevent a bloodbath. For all of these reasons, analyzing the Pilsen revolt may increase our understanding of the mechanism of the emergence of public protests under a socialist dictatorship, which may not be as apparent in other revolts. In particular, it may shed light on the process through which a social conflict transforms into political revolt.

The fact is that public protests within socialist dictatorships[8] cannot automatically be construed as attempts to overthrow the establishment. Such a presumption is contradicted by the fact that the protests in Czechoslovakia were joined by many members of the privileged groups (by their material, social, or ideological status) which otherwise remained loyal to the current regime. This indicates that the cause of the protests was far more complex and multifaceted, and economic, social, and cultural aspects played an almost equal role to political motivation. Czechoslovak society had undergone a turbulent transformation during the Stalinist era, and was far from homogeneous, with the interests of various groups often clashing. Besides being a means of putting pressure on the government, the protests also fostered communication between various social groups. Studying the protests can therefore be an important tool for understanding the social dynamic of the time. An in-depth investigation into the causes of the revolt was conducted at the time, which resulted in a wealth of archive material documenting the views of various segments of Czechoslovak society, providing us with valuable insight into ongoing social movements and the differing opinions of the various social groups, which would otherwise remain hidden due to the limitations of personal freedoms.

The present text uses these methodological premises as a starting point. Based on a thorough analysis of archive sources, it examines the Pilsen revolt as a manifestation of certain long-term tendencies within society. Opting for an unorthodox approach, it puts the incident into the context of previous minor protests that had broken out in the region after the communist coup d'état of 1948, up until the year 1953. Comparing these conflicts allows us to outline the development of various protest cultures[9] that had emerged within different social groups and contributed to the emergence and nature of the 1953 revolt, each in their own distinctive way. This has allowed us both to provide a detailed, critical outline of the June protests, but also their cultural origins, thereby uncovering the structure of the primary social movements participating in the revolt, as well as the set of social conflicts that gave rise to it.

Protest is primarily construed in this text as a culturally determined means of social communication.[10] Each such incident therefore stems from a broader cultural background shared by certain segments of the population, taking on the patterns of conduct and experience acquired during previous protests, becoming easily understandable to the general public.[11] The protests are not a series of isolated incidents but a chain of events that brings to the surface certain long-term tendencies and conflicts within society.[12] It is therefore important to study the protests as a continuous phenomenon, focusing less on isolated examples and more on the general protest culture they stem from.

Pilsen, the administrative capital of West Bohemia, provides a particularly convenient ground for this type of research. In June 1953, it was the scene of a wave of strikes and demonstrations provoked by the currency reform. It was also the seat of the world-renowned Škoda Works (renamed Vladimir Ilyich Lenin Factories in 1951), one of the country's most important industrial conglomerates whose employees had enough clout and confidence to organize a series of strikes in the 1950s. Last but not least, Pilsen had been liberated from the Nazis in May 1945 by the American army, which left a lasting impact on the local population. Young people in particular had a strong affinity toward Western culture, which had led to isolated pro-American demonstrations in May 1948, followed by other protests (including that of June 1953). The region was also known for its strong interwar rivalry between the Communist Party and the local social democrats, which had had a considerable impact on regional politics in the years 1945–1948 and caused the communists in West Bohemia much difficulty.[13]

The specific research into the origins of the Pilsen revolt attempts a detailed reconstruction of all the protests occurring in the years 1948–1953. We have analyzed the course of the protests, the mechanisms that have provoked them, the participants' motivations and patterns of behavior, the specific forms of protest, the reactions of the party apparatus and the security forces, as well as those citizens who chose not to get involved. We have specifically chosen to focus on the connections and similarities of the incidents, outlining the way various social groups learned to incite and start protests, as well as the way the security forces and party organizations learned to prevent them, and demonstrating the way social reality changed after each protest and its suppression.

We have chosen to analyze the following protest clusters and conflicts:

- A wave of demonstrations in May 1948, following the anniversary of the city's liberation by the American army;
- Demonstrations following the state funeral of former president Edvard Beneš in September 1948;
- An unsuccessful attempt to incite demonstrations in May 1949, following that year's anniversary of the city's liberation by American army;
- Strikes in the Vladimir Ilyich Lenin Factories in the years 1949–1953;
- Strikes and demonstrations in June 1953, following the announcement of the currency reform.

The structure of the text reflects the various types of protests. The introductory chapter outlines and explains the theoretical models we have chosen to utilize for analyzing the various forms of protests within a socialist regime. It also explains the concepts utilized for researching historical sources, the results of which are presented in the subsequent chapters. The first of these practical sections focuses on the public protests in West Bohemia in the first years of the newly established communist regime (1948–1949). The next section discusses the causes and the chain of events that comprised the workers' strike at the Škoda Works, which grew in intensity over the course of the first Five-Year Plan (1949–1953). The central section of the text then analyses the series of strikes and demonstrations provoked by the currency reform of June 1953, exploring their connection to the previous protests. The final chapter seeks to evaluate and reinterpret the causes and consequences of the Pilsen revolt, and place it within the context of an established tradition of such protests.

Up until now, research into the public protests in Pilsen in the years 1948–1953 has focused almost exclusively on the events following the currency reform of June 1953. However, ongoing protests in the region had been a politically sensitive issue since the early 1950s, first kept a close secret by the government, and later presented with considerable ideological bias. This led, among other things, to an exaggeration of the political aspects of the protests. A typical example of this tendency is an article written by Vladimír Brichta, which views the events of June 1953 as an attempt to reverse the results of the 1948 coup d'état.[14]

In the years 1953–1959, this had actually been the predominant interpretation of the Pilsen protests, with the brief exception of the so-called Prague

Spring of 1968. In this period of political liberalization and loosened restrictions, a number of articles were published in the censor-free press offering a more unbiased, multifaceted view of the Pilsen revolt, even if they were a far cry from any systematically researched view.[15] Attempts were even made to explain the 1953 protests as an ideological precursor to the events of the Prague Spring. Conservative authors, however, tried to curb these tendencies, decrying the persecution of many people who were mere innocent bystanders of the 1953 events, but still maintaining that the demonstrations were an attempt to execute a reactionary putsch. The most extensive text in this vein was written by Josef Brand, whose access to the Communist Party's archives granted him a wealth of detailed factual data.[16]

Valuable attempts at describing and interpreting the Pilsen revolt were published by writers in exile, especially in the form of memoirs, such as the works of Otta Ulč,[17] as well as a well-known study by Pavel Tigrid,[18] which was the first to put the Pilsen revolt into the context of other major revolts in countries within the Soviet sphere of influence.

After the Velvet Revolution of 1989, Zdeněk Štěpánek published his ground-breaking, text, written in the style of a news report, *The Secret Uprising of 1953*.[19] The book provides more factual data than any previous text written on the subject but suffers from the typical post-1989 tendency to simply reverse the ideological poles compared to the previous official interpretations. It does not present any new or more nuanced take on the subject, but merely describes the events, formerly branded as a counter-revolutionary attempt, as the first anti-communist uprising in the Eastern Bloc. Furthermore, it does not make a clear distinction between the various stages of the protests, contains a number of factual errors, and presents certain rumors as facts. A slew of shorter journalistic texts written in the same vein appeared in the 1990s, generally viewing the events of 1953 as a mere precursor to the Velvet Revolution.[20]

A number of studies published after 1989 on the currency reform in general have also touched upon the Pilsen revolt, the most important of these being the joint work of Zdeněk Jirásek and Jaroslav Šůla,[21] or texts by historians Dana Musilová,[22] Karel Kaplan,[23] Jiří Bílek,[24] and Jiří Pernes.[25]

A further shift in perspective with regard to the Pilsen revolts came from two directions. First, regional historians took notice of the fact that the demonstrations had not been nearly as turbulent for their entire duration as the words revolt or uprising might suggest. This stage of research, leading to the creation of a better timeline and structure of events, resulted in an edition of documents compiled by Adam Skála, which for the first time incorporated a wide range of regional sources and connections.[26] Historians researching the history of industrial workers became the second group that helped shift the perception of the Pilsen events. This included especially the works of Peter

Heumos, offering a different perspective of workers as a social and professional group in the 1950s.[27] The Pilsen revolt was now being interpreted using the concepts of social as well as political history. The recent works of Johann Smula[28] and Kevin McDermott[29] have chiefly focused on exploring the changing relationship between Pilsen workers and the socialist government, interpreting the demonstrations as a culmination of long-standing social unrest among them, with certain political demands added once the protests moved outside the factory gates.

The political consequences of Pilsen's liberation by the American army in May 1945 have been discussed in certain ideologically skewed studies since the 1950s, the most notorious of these being the works written jointly by Karel Bartošek and Karel Pichlík.[30] However, even such biased works can still be relevant today due to the wealth of facts they contain. Almost no systematic historical treatises on the issue have been published since 1989, with the exception of the work of Jindřich Pecka[31] and a collection published by the University of West Bohemia, edited by Tomáš Jílek.[32]

Archive documents related to the events in Pilsen are mostly located in the State Regional Archive in Pilsen, especially within the following *fonds*: The West Bohemian Regional Committee of the KSČ in Pilsen (discussions induced by the demonstrations of 1948 and 1953; documents pertaining to the investigation of the incidents); The Regional Court in Pilsen (criminal proceedings initiated in 1948); The National Front Regional Committee in Pilsen (out-of-court sanctions imposed in 1953); and documents from the former Škoda Plzeň Factory Archive (union activities in the factory in the years 1948–1953). Documents covering the criminal proceedings conducted in 1953 are stored in the Pilsen-South State Regional Archive in Blovice (the Regional Court in Pilsen fonds).

Additional information has been obtained from documents stored in the Pilsen City Archive. Summary reports and general context information have been drawn from documents stored in the National Archive in Prague. This includes especially the fonds containing documents produced by the KSČ Central Committee, the Czechoslovak Union of Youth in Prague, Union of Friends of the USA in Prague, and several others. Invaluable information also came from documents stored in the Security Services Archive in Prague, detailing the perspective of the security forces charged with taking action against the protesters and allowing us to piece together the course of the investigation. As an additional source, we have used materials from the Trade Union Archives in Prague, the Czech National Bank Archive in Prague (exchange centers in 1953), and the Military Historical Archive in Prague (actions of the military in 1953).

The text in this book is a revised English translation of the author's dissertation, successfully defended at the Department of Czech History at the

Faculty of Arts of Charles University in 2015 and published in Czech the following year.[33] I would like to express my sincere thanks to everyone who has contributed to the writing of this book with their invaluable advice. My main source of inspiration as to how to tackle the topic came from discussions at the Newest History Seminar at the Department of Czech History, especially from comments and contributions made by Michal Kopeček. Jiří Křesťan from the National Archive provided an invaluable critique as alpha reader. Jiří Jelen from the State Regional Archive in Pilsen and Adam Skála from the Pilsen City Archive have kindly provided me with a wealth of information crucial for putting the issue into the regional context. The National Archive in Prague, with director Eva Drašarová, has funded the English translation. My warmest thanks, however, go to my wife Hanička, who has not only read through every single chapter and provided insightful comments, but who has been forced to endure the demonstrations and strikes of the 1950s far longer and far more intensely than she would have wanted to.

THEORETICAL MODELS FOR ANALYZING VARIOUS FORMS OF COLLECTIVE PROTESTS WITHIN A SOCIALIST REGIME

Were the 1950s strikes and protests a manifestation of anti-communist resistance? Or were they simply a form of defense against any outside factors restricting the participants' personal needs? Were they attempts to overthrow the communist dictatorship, or a way to protect one's identity as an individual within the uniform reality of the regime, a means to finding a renewed meaning of one's existence?[34]

Public acts of protest may be interpreted from various perspectives and through different theoretical models. For understandable reasons, Czech historical science after the Velvet Revolution of 1989 focused primarily on describing the oppressive nature of the state socialist regime, so as to illustrate how markedly different it was from Western democratic systems. For this reason, it adopted the concept of a totalitarian state, inspired by totalitarianism theories, formulated in Western historiography since the 1950s as a tool for comparing and classifying political regimes.[35] Protests against the regime were therefore analyzed using primarily the structural-functional approach.[36]

Structural functionalism interprets social phenomena based on their presumed function within a political system. It posits that one of the system's primary characteristics is the tendency to maintain its existing structure, which means that anti-system protests are viewed as something that disrupts the system's equilibrium.[37] Czech historians also tended to construe the meaning and significance of public protests during the Stalinist era based on their actual impact on the state socialist regime, viewing the protests primarily as potential means to weaken or even overthrow the regime—that is, as manifestations of anti-communist resistance. This perspective corresponds with a significant number of documents issued by the former authorities, because the dictatorship of the Communist Party saw the autonomous public initiatives as hostile acts. With a bit of exaggeration, we may claim that post-1989 historical writing viewed (and indeed was forced to view, due to the sources available) the protests of the state socialism era from the perspective of the system, and therefore interpreted them in much the same way as the former regime.

The pitfall of the structural-functional approach lies in the logic it employs: it tends to focus on the effects on the phenomena it studies on a system, not on their causes (such as the participants' motivation). For a comprehensive grasp of the protest phenomenon, however, we need to examine both the objective consequences (function) of the participants' actions and their subjective motivation.[38] Obviously, people's motives for a certain action may not always result in the desired consequences. Protests that are seen by the political elites as an attempt to undermine their power may be motivated by various reasons, which may not always be directly tied to the structure of the system in the eyes of the participants, and they may have nothing to do with the system's repressive nature at all. If it is the historian's intention to examine political protests as a means of studying both the political regime and the various aspects of social differentiation, a purely functional approach is not the most suitable tool, since it does not sufficiently take into account the participants' subjective motivations.

In the past decade, a heated debate on the theory of totalitarianism has broken out in the Czech historical science community. Critical voices have arisen, perhaps understandably, among social historians, since the prevalent paradigm did not provide sufficient grounds for a detailed analysis of the social and cultural development in Czech society.[39] For this reason, they began challenging the hitherto preferred notion of the dichotomy of power; that is, the ideal-type concept of an all-powerful totalitarian state, exercising complete control over an utterly subdued society which, as a mere passive object, has only two choices: put up resistance, or adapt. Social historians have also challenged the one-sided categorization of the various participants resulting from this concept, which presents human beings as one-dimensional entities with no inner contradictions, whose motives are reduced merely to their stance toward the ruling regime (the rebels, the undecided, and the collaborators).[40]

As a theoretical basis, this group of historians chose the social constructionist approach, which centers on the notion that rather than an objective, unchangeable fact, social reality is a dynamically developing result of various social interactions and communication.[41] They find inspiration in German historiography describing the two German dictatorships of the 20th century, especially the notion of Eigensinn (which could be described as putting up with political power to the degree that one must, while pursuing one's own ends to the degree that one can).[42] Power, in their understanding, is a mutual connection between the oppressor and the oppressed, rather than a one-way relationship of dependence. An individual is not completely isolated from power, but rather actively tries to utilize the tools of power[43] to carve out their own autonomous space and realize their own ideas of living a fulfilled life.[44]

The mass protest model we have adopted for the purpose of this study utilizes both of the above perspectives, combining the social constructionist and functional approaches. It consistently distinguishes between objective functions and subjective motives, assigning both perspectives an equal historical significance. On a theoretical level, this approach has been inspired by contemporary sociological research and its notion of collective action, and especially the theory of new social movements (NSMs).[45]

PROTEST AS A PUBLIC PRESENTATION OF ALTERNATIVE AUTHORITY CAUSED BY MORAL SHOCK

Using NSM theories to interpret the protests of 1948–1953 has numerous advantages. First of all, they acknowledge that the various protest incidents (considerably spread out in time and space) were not isolated clashes with the ruling power but one of the many visible components making up the social movements of the time.[46] The importance of individual protests, such theories claim, lies in the fact that they highlight certain long-term, latent social conflicts. Rather than using the functional approach and interpreting such conflicts merely as acts of resistance against the political regime, social movement theories allow us to examine the protests' cultural and social constructionist aspects.[47]

Various branches of the social movement theory have differing perspectives on the mass mobilization process. Structuralists focus primarily on determining the structural prerequisites for a successful mobilization of the population. A very suitable tool for analyzing the Stalinist-era protests is the political opportunity theory, due to the restrictions and limitations imposed on public gatherings in the years 1948–1953.[48] Protesters took advantage of official state celebrations and turned legal gatherings into protests (commemoration of the anniversary of Pilsen's liberation in May 1948; the state funeral of President Edvard Beneš in September 1948). The structure of political opportunities also explains the fact that since 1949 most incidents of mass protest were workers' strikes; unlike other forms of protest, the Communist Party was forced to treat them with certain benevolence, considering its official ideology and fears of reduced economic performance.

The political opportunity perspective allows us to focus on favorable conditions for protests that emerged due to the weaknesses of the system itself. Analyzing the protests therefore offers the opportunity to explore the limits of the system's power (such as the strain that the party apparatus and security forces were put under during the currency reform of 1953).

Analyzing the influence of the social movements' organizational structure on the mobilization process is another productive avenue of research, since most mass protests were organized by groups of people with strong ties created by day-to-day interaction and a shared identity (workers, students, members of the Sokol organization). It was easier to coordinate people at work, in school, or within an association, and such protests were far easier to understand for the general public. Such informal social networks compensated for the lack of opportunities to create official organizational structures and the restrictions on the free sharing of information.[49]

Subjective motives of the participants, however, were the most important aspect of the mobilization process. A debate is still ongoing among social theorists as to the effects of rational thinking and emotion on mobilization.[50] Facing the possibility of repression, most protest participants likely did not react as calculating, rational thinkers, carefully weighing the pros and cons, as proposed by the rational choice theory.[51] We should not, on the other hand, assign too much importance to the effects of panic or crowd psychology, as formulated by Gustave Le Bon.[52] Even so, emotion played a significant role in the mobilization process, which becomes apparent once we look at the course of the protest events.

To analyze this problem, historians could utilize the concept of moral shock, coined by sociologists Jeff Goodwin and James Macdonald Jasper.[53] According to them, protests occur when outside circumstances challenge the potential participants' individual or collectively shared values and identities.[54] This incites a specific set of moral emotions, especially the sense of injustice, anger, fear, or outrage. Obviously, such emotions may not automatically spur people into action; they may simply end up in resignation. Sometimes, however, the raw emotions may create enough energy to spur people into action, resulting in a protest. Emotions also bolster a sense of unity and solidarity among the protesters. For some, the mere act of participation may be a strong, positive experience.

Unlike the political resistance model, the moral emotions model is capable of interpreting a wide range of motivations for a protest. To name but a few examples, such a moral outrage occurred in May 1948, after the local authorities in Pilsen tried to downplay the role of the American army in the city's liberation; in reaction to that, a part of the city's population organized their own memorial celebration. The protesters viewed the authorities' attitude as offensive to their own values. Moral outrage also arose among the workers during the 1950s whenever the dictatorship of the proletariat threatened their income or traditions, resulting in a distinct sense of injustice. In June 1953, moral outrage was apparent among the victims of political repression who had welcomed the opportunity to speak publicly about their prison experience. Ironically, many members of the Communist Party also expressed moral outrage in June 1953, complaining that the currency reform should have stripped the reactionaries of all their savings, instead of taking money away from the workers, and thus were reluctant to take action against the protesters.

The values that protest participants feel have been called into question may often be quite disparate and mutually incompatible, yet may still result in a single collective protest.[55] Apart from standard political resistance, the moral shock concept can also explain the instances of loyal resistance (i.e., the resistance of someone who still remains loyal to the regime as a whole).[56] Furthermore, it does not reduce the participants' motivation solely to political reasons. Protests are interpreted in a broader context, as the result of a conflict between an impersonal system based on instrumental rationality (i.e., the state socialist regime) and any values that stem from the participants' subjective experience, background, and personal history.[57]

From this perspective, the protest action itself should be seen as a specific type of communication[58] in which the participants use symbolic means to push through their values.[59] The communication is not merely bilateral, focusing on announcing the protesters' demands to the ruling power,[60] but multilateral, turning to numerous recipients. Protesters primarily attempt to get their message across to those who have chosen not to get involved, be they potential sympathizers or opponents. In 1948, for example, students in Pilsen decorated the monument to the American army and waited with bated breath for the reactions of workers leaving the factories at the end of their shift. Similarly, many of the protesters' activities in 1953 aimed at appealing to bystanders rather than overthrowing the establishment. In the context of the resistance concept, the protesters' vacillation may seem counter-productive; this, however, fails to grasp that one of the protesters' primary goals was to demonstrate their moral outrage to the general public. This was reflected in their choice of public spaces, which had a symbolic significance rather than being important military and strategic points; they were often busy areas where an ample audience was assured.[61]

The protests were also aimed at the local authorities (factory management, city officials) who acted as intermediaries between the individual and the system; very rarely did they address the nationwide state and party authorities (such as in June 1953).[62] The protest participants and participant groups were often both actors and audience. In general, one of the protesters' primary motives is the desire to be heard, as well as to reassure themselves that their fellow citizens share their moral outrage.

For a protest to successfully communicate its message, it has to take on a certain form and use symbols that its target audience can easily understand;[63] in other words, all parties involved must share a common cultural background. The form of protest is not chosen randomly; instead, it stems from a long-nurtured protest culture.[64] For this reason, the various protest events followed a very similar pattern, based on the protesters' previous experience and protest tradition. A considerable number of public protest gatherings in 1948 took advantage of events such as wreath-laying ceremonies (May 1948, September 1948, May 1949). Peaceful gatherings spontaneously transformed into protest marches. Similarly, workers' strikes followed a time-honored tradition, and usually started by the workers stopping the machines, gathering and debating in factory yards. Such forms of protests were universally intelligible, and therefore effective.

Protest events also spur the process of social learning. Both the participants and the power apparatus adjust their strategies based on the experience they acquire. Usually, the power apparatus does not merely intend to suppress the protests but prevent them from happening altogether, in order to gain control of the public space. In May 1948, protests had burst out as Pilsen was celebrating the end of the war; in September 1948, when a state funeral was held for former president Edvard Beneš, the security forces had anticipated the possibility of such incidents and imposed significant restrictions on public gatherings around the monuments in downtown Pilsen. On the next anniversary of Pilsen's liberation in May 1949, people deliberately opted to gather around less prominent monuments to downed American pilots on the city's outskirts.

This sort of multilateral communication of protest participants in a public space serves as a symbolic representation of the values and identities they feel to be threatened (slogan chanting, symbolic gestures, symbolic locations, and anniversaries). It is through these gestures that the hitherto latent social conflict is finally articulated.[65] All parties are now forced to define their attitude toward an issue that has previously not appeared as problematic, gradually determining the nature of the conflict and its sociocultural context (occupational, moral, or political).[66] This evaluation process then largely determines the choice of possible means of solving the conflict. Society is no longer the same as it was before the protest happened: each act of protest effectively transforms social reality and communication, albeit the various parties involved do not possess equal bargaining power. (Compared to the power apparatus, protest participants have less influence over the choice of the sociocultural context of the conflict, as well as the resulting social order.)

This dynamic transformation of social reality becomes apparent even during the protest incidents. The protests were usually initiated at a point where the conflict had not yet been clearly defined and articulated, and government officials had not yet taken a clear stand. In May 1948, for example, a number of regional Communist Party leaders in Pilsen considered holding the celebrations of the city's liberation even under the new regime, albeit provided with a suitable ideological framework. Celebrating American soldiers was not yet officially seen as inappropriate; in fact, the Communist Party's disapproval only began after the protests had escalated into what the party officials viewed as a political conflict. From then on, any attempts to honor the American army and its role in the city's liberation were considered unacceptable. A similar situation occurred in 1953, when the workers' strikes were first perceived by the Communist Party as a troublesome but legitimate reaction of the working classes to the currency reform. Only as the protests escalated did the party officials redefine the situation and brand the strikes as an attempted reactionary coup.

The above examples make it abundantly clear that the conflict had often transformed in the course of the protests and become a political issue, both on the part of the protest participants and the regime officials. The changed stance of the government officials also radically changed the protesters' situation: actions that could have been considered legitimate mere hours earlier abruptly lost their legitimacy.[67] Regardless of their subjective motivation, protest participants were retroactively branded as enemies of the state, or at least as having been led astray by such enemies. By defining the conflict, the regime actually created new enemies (albeit some of them might have been openly or secretly hostile even before that).[68] In effect, this reduced the possibility of continued or repeated protests, since joining up was no longer considered legitimate. Defining the conflict created a new social reality which made any subsequent attempts at a protest much more difficult.

In some cases, however, the regime found the protesters' demands acceptable, and the conflict no longer required a political solution. The protesters' moral outrage was often appeased by giving in to some of the protesters' demands, either immediately or subsequently. A number of the 1950s worker strikes, for example, resulted in changes in bonus payments, or in better provisioning of factory canteens. Similarly, after suppressing the demonstrations in June 1953, authorities punished the participants but also tried to handle the worst of the social issues caused by the currency reform as quickly as possible (by speeding up the money exchange process, so as to solve the acute insolvency of the population, and by additional payments of mistakenly withheld wage advances), effectively acknowledging some of the protesters' demands as legitimate.

The success of a protest cannot be measured solely by the degree to which it manages to achieve its demands; from a social constructivist perspective, every public protest is partially successful by virtue of having happened at all. Any act of public protest helps to maintain and develop a culture of protest which serves as an inspiration for the future.[69] Protests also introduce new values on the public stage. Protest is a process whereby its subjectively motivated participants become objective instigators of historical events, expanding the shared pool of cultural meanings by their own interpretations of current cultural models, shifting the contemporary thought frameworks and patterns of action.[70] The eventual suppression of a public protest limits its impact on the public but cannot eliminate it altogether, considering that it cannot erase it from the memory of those present.

Moreover, the values promoted by protest participants stem from moral authorities standing outside the dominant discourse (in this case, the communist ideology, as applied and construed at the time). Regardless of the participants' personal motivation, each protest utilizes these alternative authorities to objectively undermine the dominant discourse.[71] The pro-American demonstrations that broke out in Pilsen in May 1948 venerated American culture and the Western concept of plural democracy. The protests during president Beneš's state funeral in September 1948 invoked the ideals of the founders of the Czechoslovak state. The workers' strikes in the 1950s drew on the authority of the traditional labor movement. In June 1953, many disgruntled communists compared the actual government policies to the timeless authority of the communist ideology. Despite their differences, all of these authorities served as a public call for innovating the dominant discourse. From the functional perspective, each protest can therefore be construed as an act of cultural resistance[72]—and it was this particular function that was the reason the authorities often chose to politicize social conflicts.

The collective protest model, applied in this text to the Stalinist-era protests, combines the social constructivist and functional approach, distinguishing between an objective functional level and a subjective motivation level, and ascribing equal historical importance to both these aspects. On a theoretical level, it has drawn inspiration from analyzing the so-called NSMs. It ascribes the dominant role in a mobilization process to emotions, especially in the form of a moral shock that protest participants experience as a consequence of their values and identity being challenged. The subjective motive for a protest is construed using the social constructivist perspective as an attempt of the protest participant to utilize symbolic means for presenting the values they feel to be threatened in a public space—that is, as a distinctive form of social communication and interaction. On an objective, systemic level, however, such an attempt effectively challenges the dominant discourse by presenting an alternative authority to which the protester ascribes their values. The newly articulated social conflict then requires redefining the problem on both sides, marking out the sociocultural field where a solution to the conflict might be found. A protest can therefore be construed as a subjectively motivated type of social communication, but also as an objective factor which distorts the system's equilibrium—not necessarily on a political, but certainly on a discursive level.

Construed in this manner, a protest becomes a complex social phenomenon which only partially overlaps with the standard category of conscious anti-communist resistance; however, it allows the historian to retain both the perspective of a multidimensional subject (i.e., not reduced to the political level) and the perspective of a system challenged by the protest to innovate itself. This approach also provides the historian with sufficient theoretical tools to analyze some of the more complex events, simultaneously influenced not only by political but also social and cultural processes. The Pilsen revolt of June 1953 is a prime example of such a phenomenon spanning several sociocultural fields.

NOTES

1. Cf. Volker Koop, *Der 17. Juni 1953: Legende und Wirklichkeit* (Berlin: Siedler, 2003); Ostermann, Christian, ed., *Uprising in East Germany, 1953: The Cold War, the German Question and the First Major Upheaval Behind the Iron Curtain* (Budapest: Central European University Press, 2001); Regine Möbius, *Panzer gegen die Freiheit: Zeitzeugen des 17. Juni 1953 berichten* (Leipzig: Evangelische Verlagsanstalt, 2003); Richard Millington, *State, Society and Memories of the Uprising of 17 June 1953 in the GDR* (Basingstoke: Palgrave Macmillan, 2014).

2. Cf. Pawel Machcewicz, *Rebellious Satellite: Poland 1956* (Stanford: Stanford University Press, 2009), 87–124; Andrzej Paczkowski, *Půl století dějin Polska 1939–1989* (Prague: Academia, 2000), 177–186.

3. Cf. Paul Lendvai, *One Day That Shook the Communist World: The 1956 Hungarian Uprising and Its Legacy* (Princeton: Princeton University Press, 2008).

4. Matthew Stibbe, "The SED, German Communism and the June 1953 Uprising: New Trends and New Research," in *Revolution and Resistance in Eastern Europe: Challenges to Communist Rule*, ed. Kevin McDermott and Matthew Stibbe (Oxford: Berg, 2006), 37–55.

5. Cf. Christiane Brenner, *Mezi Východem a Západem: České politické rozpravy 1945–1948* (Prague: Argo, 2015).

6. Gareth Dale, *Popular Protest in East Germany, 1945–1989* (New York: Routledge, 2005), 9–56.

7. Machcewicz, *Rebellious Satellite*, 87–124.

8. The term "state socialism" is used here to describe a political and economic system that uses state power to create an egalitarian society through the

nationalization of large industrial enterprises, economic planning and social security for the population. Konrad Jarausch, "Care and Coercion: The GDR as Welfare Dictatorship," in *Dictatorship as Experience: Towards a Socio-Cultural History of the GDR*, ed. Konrad Jarausch (New York: Oxford University Press, 1999), 47–69.

9. The term "culture of protest" refers to a cultural representation based on shared understanding of different kinds of social practices, values and contexts of action, from which protesters derive a sense of identity as well as a sense of mutual solidarity. Radim Marada, *Kultura protestu a politizace každodennosti* (Brno: Centrum pro studium demokracie a kultury, 2003), 96.

10. Cf. Karl Wolfgang Deutsch, *Nervy vlády: modely politické komunikace a řízení* (Prague: Svoboda, 1971).

11. James Jasper, *The Art of Moral Protest: Culture, Biography and Creativity in Social Movements* (Chicago: Chicago University Press, 1997), 22.

12. A social movement is usually defined in sociology as a movement engaged in conflict with a clearly defined enemy, supported by a functioning social (solidarity) network and characterized by a shared identity. In the specific conditions of state socialist dictatorships, however, these features often could not be fully developed. Specialized organizational structures of the movement were therefore replaced by workers' crews, student classes, party organizations or other informal social networks with a shared identity. Cf. Mario Diani and Doug McAdam, eds., *Social Movements and Networks: Relations Aapproaches to Collective Action* (Oxford: Oxford University Press, 2003); James Scott, *Domination and the Arts of Resistance: Hidden Transcripts* (New Haven: Yale University Press, 1990).

13. Cf. Adam Skála, ed., *Dějiny města Plzně 3 (1918–1990)* (Pilsen: Statutární město Pilsen, 2018).

14. Vladimír Brichta, "Pokus o 'antiúnor' v Plzni roku 1953," *Minulostí západočeského kraje* 14, no. 1 (1978): 65–70.

15. Hana Konečná, "O pomníku a nejen o něm," *Pravda*, May 5, 1968; Věra Budilová, "Strhli pomník Plzeňští divadelníci?: Pravda o stržení Masarykova pomníku v Plzni," *Rudé právo*, June 9, 1968, 2.

16. Josef Brand, "Budeme rehabilitovat 1. June 1953?: Pokus o rekonstrukci událostí kolem měnové reformy v Plzni," *Pravda*, May 29, 1968, 3.

17. Otto Ulč, *The Judge in a Communist State: A View From Within* (Columbus: Ohio University Press, 1972).

18. Pavel Tigrid, *Dnešek je váš, zítřek je náš: Dělnické revolty v komunistických zemích* (Cologne: Index, 1982).

19. Zdeněk Štěpánek, *Utajené povstání 1953* (Prague: Michael, 1993).

20. Markéta Čekanová, "Před půl stoletím ztratili lidé iluze 1:50," *Radniční listy města Plzně*, June 1, 2003; Darina Zíbarová, "Cena 1. června," *Radniční listy města Plzně*, June 1, 2003.

21. Zdeněk Jirásek and Jaroslav Šůla, *Velká peněžní loupež v Československu 1953 aneb 50:1* (Prague: Svítání, 1992).

22. Dana Musilová, *Měnová reforma 1953 a její sociální důsledky* (Prague: ÚSD AV ČR, 1993).

23. Karel Kaplan, *Sociální souvislosti krizí komunistického režimu 1953–1957 a 1968–1975* (Prague: ÚSD AV ČR, 1993).
24. Jiří Bílek, "Československá armáda a měnová reforma v roce 1953," *Historie a vojenství* 44, no. 1 (1995): 66–91.
25. Jiří Pernes, "Neznámý dokument o peněžní reformě v Československu v roce 1953," in *Po stopách nedávné historie: Sborník k 75. narozeninám doc. Karla Kaplana*, ed. Jiří Pernes (Brno: Prius, 2003), 169–90.
26. Adam Skála, "Měnová reforma 1. června 1953 v Plzni v hlášení mocenských orgánů," *Minulostí západočeského kraje* 42, no. 2 (2007): 592–630.
27. Peter Heumos, *"Vyhrňme si rukávy, než se kola zastaví!": Dělníci a státní socialismus v Československu* (Prague: ÚSD AV ČR, 2006).
28. Smula, Johann, "The Party and the Proletariat: Škoda 1948–53," *Cold War History* 6, no. 2 (2006): 153–75.
29. Kevin McDermott, "Popular Resistance in Communist Czechoslovakia: The Pilsen Uprising, June 1953," *Contemporary European History* 19, no. 4 (2010): 287–307; Kevin McDermott, "Lidový odpor v komunistickém Československu: Plzeňské povstání v červnu 1953," *Minulostí západočeského kraje* 46, no. 1 (2011): 206–231.
30. Karel Bartošek and Karel Pichlík, *Hanebná role amerických okupantů v západních Čechách v roce 1945* (Prague: Svoboda, 1951); Karel Bartošek and Karel Pichlík, *Američané v západních Čechách v roce 1945* (Prague: Mladá fronta, 1953).
31. Jindřich Pecka, *Na demarkační čáře: Americká armáda v Čechách v roce 1945* (Prague: ÚSD AV ČR, 1995).
32. Tomáš Jílek, ed., *Národní odboj a politické, kulturní a vojenské aspekty osvobození Plzně a Západních Čech americkou armádou* (Pilsen: Západočeská univerzita v Plzni, 1996).
33. Jakub Šlouf, *Spřízněni měnou: Genealogie Plzeňské revolty 1. června 1953* (Prague: Univerzita Karlova v Praze, 2016).
34. Jasper, *The Art of Moral Protest*, 2.
35. František Svátek, "Koncept totalitarismu a historikova skepse: Poznámky o politické a historiografické diskusi," in *Stránkami soudobých dějin: Sborník statí k pětašedesátinám historika Karla Kaplana*, ed. Karel Jech (Prague: ÚSD AV ČR, 1993): 29–60; Miloš Havelka, "Srovnání nesrovnatelného aneb existovala v nejnovějších českých dějinách epocha totalitarismu?," *Soudobé Dějiny*, no. 4 (2009): 607–624.
36. Blanka Říchová, *Přehled moderních politologických teorií* (Prague: Portál, 2006), 61–82.
37. Deutsch, *Nervy vlády*, 166–169; Jan Keller, *Sociologie konfliktu* (Brno: Masarykova univerzita v Brně, 1990), 5–8.
38. Robert Merton, *Studie ze sociologické teorie* (Prague: Sociologické nakladatelství, 2000), 89–90, 116–131.
39. Peter Heumos, "K sociálněhistorickému výzkumu komunistických systémů," *Soudobé Dějiny*, no. 3 (2008): 686–702; Michal Pullmann, "Sociální dějiny a totalitněhistorické vyprávění," *Soudobé Dějiny*, no. 3 (2008): 703–717.
40. Jan Plamper, "Beyond Binaries: Popular Opinion in Stalinism," in *Popular Opinion in Totalitarian Regimes: Fascism, Nazism, Communism*, ed. Paul Corner

(Oxford: Oxford University Press, 2009), 64–80; Vítězslav Sommer, "Cesta ze slepé uličky 'třetího odboje': Koncepty rezistence a studium socialistické diktatury v Československu," *Soudobé Dějiny*, no. 1 (2012): 9–36.

41. Cf. Peter Berger and Thomas Luckmann, *Sociální konstrukce reality: Pojednání o sociologii vědění* (Brno: Centrum pro studium demokracie a kultury, 1999).

42. Thomas Lindenberger, ed., *Herrschaft und Eigen-Sinn in der Diktatur: Studien zur Gesellschaftsgeschichte der DDR* (Cologne: Böhlau, 1999), 13–45; Esther von Richthofen, *Bringing Culture to the Masses: Control, Compromise and Participation in the GDR* (New York: Berghahn, 2009).

43. Scott, *Domination and the Arts of Resistance*, 192; Sommer, "Cesta ze slepé uličky," 9–36; Stephen Kotkin, *Magnetic Mountain: Stalinism As a Civilization* (California: University of California Press, 1997), 1–24.

44. Ondřej Matějka, "'Jsou to berani, ale můžeme je využít': Čeští evangelíci a komunistický režim 1948–1956." *Soudobé dějiny* 14, no. 2 (2007): 305–340; Heumos, *Vyhrňme si rukávy*, 64.

45. Jasper, *The Art of Moral Protest,* 32.

46. Diani and McAdam, *Social Movements and Networks*, 1–18.

47. Alain Touraine, *Thinking Differently* (Cambridge: Polity Press, 2009), 148–167.

48. Scott, *Domination and the Arts of Resistance*, 192–197.

49. Ibid., 137–152.

50. Jeff Goodwin and James Jasper, "Emotions and Social Movements," in *Handbook of the Sociology of Emotions*, ed. Jan Stets and Jonathan Turner (New York: New York University, 2007), 611–635.

51. Martin Dlouhý and Petr Fiala, *Úvod do teorie her* (Prague: Oeconomica, 2009), 25; Keller, *Sociologie konfliktu*, 36–45.

52. Cf. Gustave Le Bon, *Psychologie davů* (Prague: Samcovo knihkupectví, 1946).

53. Goodwin and Jasper, "Emotions and Social Movements," 611–635.

54. Jasper, *The Art of Moral Protest*, 10.

55. Ibid., 10–13.

56. Sommer, "Cesta ze slepé uličky," 22.

57. Alberto Melucci, *Nomads of the Present: Social Movements and Individual Needs in Contemporary Society* (Philadelphia: Temple University Press, 1989), 11–14.

58. Plamper, "Beyond Binaries," 65–68.

59. Cf. Jürgen Habermas, *Strukturální přeměna veřejnosti: Zkoumání jedné kategorie občanské společnosti* (Prague: Filosofia, 2000).

60. Scott, *Domination and the Arts of Resistance*, 195; Deutsch, *Nervy vlády*, 166.

61. Zdeněk Hojda and Jiří Pokorný, *Pomníky a zapomníky* (Prague: Paseka, 1996), 18.

62. Marada, *Kultura protestu a politizace každodennosti*, 113.

63. NAKONEČNÝ, Milan, *Sociální psychologie* (Prague: Academia, 2009), 287–291.

64. Jasper, *The Art of Moral Protest*, s. 22.
65. Touraine, *Thinking Differently*, 148–167.
66. Marada, *Kultura protestu a politizace každodennosti*, 11–13.
67. Scott, *Domination and the Arts of Resistance*, s. 156–160.
68. Francoise Mayerová, "Vězení jako minulost, odboj jako paměť," *Soudobé dějiny*, no. 1 (2002): 42–64.
69. Scott, *Domination and the Arts of Resistance*, 184–192.
70. Touraine, *Thinking Differently*, 148–167; Plamper, "Beyond Binaries," 71–73.
71. Marada, *Kultura protestu a politizace každodennosti*, 111–112.
72. Scott, *Domination and the Arts of Resistance*, 184; Sommer, "Cesta ze slepé uličky," 9–36.

Chapter 1

Public Demonstrations in Pilsen in the Years 1948–1949

Public demonstrations are one of the primary forms of collective protest in any political system, and they occurred frequently throughout the entire era of Czechoslovak state socialism in the years 1948–1989. The largest of such incidents included the protests against the social impact of the currency reform in June 1953,[1] protests on the first anniversary of the occupation of Czechoslovakia by the Warsaw Pact armies in August 1969, and the series of public demonstrations preceding the Czechoslovak Velvet Revolution in 1989.[2]

A particular series of protests occurred during the first years of the Communist Party dictatorship in 1948–1949. The structure of the state socialist regime as we know it from the 1950s had only begun to take form, and the people were only gradually adjusting to the changed circumstances. It was in this interim period that a number of unwritten rules were defined (or negotiated) and new patterns of expected behavior were formed. People were slowly finding out, for example, what could and could not be said in public without risking punishment. Fear and self-censorship did not yet have such an impact on the people's behavior and preventive measures taken by the security forces were not yet as extreme as in the later years. Both protesters and members of the power structure were in the process of intensive social learning.

The regime had also begun to change its official policy. Shortly after the coup in February 1948, the new regime remained relatively benevolent, allowing former supporters of the defeated non-communist opposition to integrate into the new social order. This culminated with the presidential amnesty in June 1948 that pardoned a number of moderate political opponents of the Communist Party.[3] Influenced by the Yugoslav-Soviet split in early 1948, however, the Czechoslovak Communist Party leadership adopted the doctrine of blanket suppression of reactionaries. Besides the political and economic elites of the former regime, the communists now targeted the entire *petite bourgeoisie* as a social class (closing down small businesses, collectivization of agriculture, and purges in the bureaucratic machinery). Historians consider either the plenary session of the KSČ Central Committee (November 17–18, 1948) or the 9th party congress (May 25–29, 1949) to be symbolic turning points marking the end of the interim period.[4]

The gradual nature of social changes made it much easier for groups who rejected certain aspects of the socialist transformation to organize collective protests than in the later years. Protests usually occurred during official, government-organized demonstrations. A major wave of protests broke out in June 1948 in Prague, on the occasion of the 11th congress of the Sokol organization and during the state funeral of Edvard Beneš, the last non-communist president, in September 1948.[5] It was by no means a coincidence that protesters chose such ceremonial occasions: state celebrations and commemoration ceremonies were traditionally a means to articulate and visualize the official interpretation of major events and important historical figures. In 1948, the official interpretation generated by the Communist Party naturally clashed with other competing interpretations. Such cultural and social conflicts stemmed primarily from the growing discontinuity between the new state socialist regime and the preceding era of the Third Czechoslovak Republic (1945–1948), as well as the disproportionate increase of Czechoslovakia's international ties to Eastern powers, and the corresponding deterioration of its relationship with Western countries.

The state-organized demonstrations also provided the people with a unique opportunity to organize legal gatherings in city centers, and to maintain a possible double interpretation of their actions.[6] Protest activities could be seen as an illegitimate attempt to subvert the dominant discourse, but also as a perfectly legitimate participation in an official ceremony. This significantly reduced the likelihood of an early police intervention and possible subsequent repressions. The possibility to interpret the protesters' actions as legitimate participation considerably increased the number of people who were willing to take part; the agenda was broad enough to be acceptable for participants with a wide range of opinions. Under favorable circumstances, often after dark, peaceful demonstrations turned into loud protests with an openly illegitimate agenda.

These collective protests drew inspiration from the recent Nazi occupation (1939–1945): the anti-Nazi resistance frequently used allegorical forms of protest, such as ceremonial attire on important anniversaries, or gatherings at important symbolic locations. Even then, such activities could often become a precursor to open protests.[7]

The type of protest specific to the years 1948–1949, which could be characterized as creating protest alternatives to official public gatherings, virtually disappeared in the following years: the political and security apparatus learned to preempt any gatherings of disgruntled groups. Dual interpretation of the people's participation was no longer possible and this form of protest ceased to be an option. Protest events occurred even later: mass demonstrations broke out in 1951 in the streets of Brno;[8] a protest occurred in April 1953 in the town of Prostějov;[9] and a nationwide surge of protests broke out in June 1953 in reaction to the currency reform.[10] None of these events, however, emerged during state-organized ceremonies; instead, they were caused by outrage among a certain segment of society that was capable of organizing an unofficial gathering.

As for Pilsen, three collective public protests occurred in the city in the years 1948–1949; by comparing them, we gain a very detailed understanding of the pace of social development at the time. First in the series was the wave of pro-American riots in May 1948. For historians, they may serve as a typical example of protests that had evolved from an official demonstration into a protest, with a peaceful, symbolic ceremony gradually turning into loud processions and street brawls. The conflict was very sudden, and entirely unforeseen by members of the party apparatus and the security forces, as well as a substantial part of society. It was therefore through this conflict that people on the local level acquired the experience required to instigate such incidents, but also to predict and prevent them. The May incident laid the foundations for one of the primary forms of local protest culture.[11]

The second such incident was a student demonstration organized in September 1948 during the ceremonies connected with the state funeral of the former president Edvard Beneš. The security forces had been prepared for a possible disturbance and took a number of precautions to ensure that the event would remain peaceful. Thanks to their effort, the protests did not escalate into loud demonstrations; besides the official event, however, people organized unofficial acts of mourning that had great potential to escalate into protests. In Pilsen, they culminated in a silent student march that ended prematurely in a skirmish with workers outside the building of the Regional Secretariat of the Communist Party.[12]

The third such instance were the protest gatherings that occurred in Pilsen in May 1949 on the anniversary of the city's liberation by the American army. Unlike the previous year, the police did not permit even silent displays of pro-American symbols, such as wearing lapel pins with the U.S. flag that had still been common a year before. Because of that, the May 1949 protests never fully escalated, not even into the peaceful (legitimate) stage, as they did in September 1948. All of the above incidents, however, still shared certain common traits of protest culture: they generally occurred as a protest alternative during officially organized events; they were usually initiated through certain symbolic acts, usually the laying of flowers and wreaths, which led to spontaneous gatherings. In all of the above instances, the protests took place in public spaces that had a symbolic significance—by the foundation stone of the monument to American soldiers fallen during the city's liberation in May 1945, and by the National Liberation Monument commemorating the declaration of an independent Czechoslovakia in October 1918, with a statue of the first Czechoslovak president Tomáš Garrigue Masaryk. Last but not least, the protests usually involved similar social groups, especially students, former members of non-communist political parties, and small businessmen.

The form of public protests in Pilsen was significantly influenced by the fact that unlike the rest of Czechoslovakia, West Bohemia had been liberated by the American army in May 1945. The local people's gratitude was therefore aimed primarily at the Western Allied powers. The few months that American soldiers spent in the city, housed by the local families, had a profound impact on Pilsen's cultural climate. The American lifestyle was very popular among the young people, especially students.[13] Between 1945 and 1948, many boys and young men in West Bohemia went to see American movies, became pen friends with American girls, wore clothes inspired by American army uniforms, and learned English rather than Russian.[14] As international tension escalated in 1947 and the notion that Czechoslovakia could become a bridge between East and West collapsed, a social conflict emerged in Pilsen involving a substantial part of the local population, rather than a small group of political party members. People's disapproval of the fact that the state socialist regime after 1948 nurtured political and cultural ties with the East far more than the West became one of the primary motives for local protests.

One of the most active participants in the Pilsen protests of 1948–1949 were secondary school students, who had eagerly embraced Western culture and role models after the war. As early as November 1945, members of student governments in Pilsen for the portrait of American president Harry Truman to be placed in classrooms publicly denounced the installation of portraits of Soviet leader Joseph Stalin. To that end, they actively engaged in a press dispute with the regional communist newspaper, *Pravda*.[15] Many of Pilsen's students were dismayed by the one-sided praise of the Soviet Union and the effort of the Czechoslovak Union of Youth (ČSM) to exclusively follow Eastern models and examples. No longer wishing to be involved in the ČSM, they established their own independent Regional Secondary School Council in Pilsen.[16] In the years 1946–1947, the Council published its own magazine *Studentský hlasatel*, promoting Western culture and activities of alternative student organizations not affiliated with the ČSM.[17]

After the 1948 coup, a number of student government officials in Pilsen's secondary schools resisted ČSM's forced infiltration of their schools.[18] Some students actually created their own illegal organizations, combining politically motivated proto-resistance with a boyish sense of adventure.[19] It was this specific milieu that spurred the students' active involvement in public protests in West Bohemia.[20]

PRO-AMERICAN DEMONSTRATIONS, MAY 5–6, 1948

The wave of demonstrations that swept Pilsen on May 5–6, 1948, was one of the first mass protests against the newly established communist dictatorship in Czechoslovakia. Even more important than the large number of protesters was the symbolic issue that managed to incite unrest among a significant part of the Pilsen population: the protests erupted around the anniversary of Pilsen's liberation by the American army, provoked by the effort of local officials to suppress the people's memories of the Americans. In defiance of the city officials, the citizens of Pilsen organized their own celebration of the city's liberation. The peaceful tribute to the fallen American soldiers then gradually escalated into loud public protests.

To understand the outburst of protests, we should first briefly discuss the history of the so-called American problem in West Bohemia. On May 5, 1945, Pilsen revolted against the Nazi occupation. The Nazis were finally defeated when the American army entered the city on May 6.[21] Many people in Pilsen were proud of their city's liberation, and had mostly positive memories of the American soldiers, who had remained in the city for several months. Since 1945, the Communist Party in Pilsen faced a population that openly expressed its liking toward American culture. In 1945 and 1946, the communists chose to take part in the official celebrations of Pilsen's liberation alongside American officers. The regional communist press expressed a critical but not openly hostile attitude toward the American armed forces. The peculiar position of the Communist Party in Pilsen was demonstrated by a rather extraordinary example: Zdeněk Kejmar, organizational secretary of the KSČ District Committee in Pilsen, who helped set up most of the party's organizational structure in 1945, did so while wearing an American army uniform.[22] In the aftermath of the war, this did not seem as much of a contradiction, and was in line with the party's official policy, aimed at garnering widespread public support.

It was only in 1947, as international tension escalated, that the communist press began describing the United States as an imperialist power and an enemy of the Slavic peoples. After the 1948 coup, the Communist Party found itself in a quite precarious position in West Bohemia: it was no longer acceptable to express respect toward the American army, but neither was it possible to deny the U.S. contribution toward liberating the region. Instead of an outright ban on paying respects to American soldiers, party officials therefore skirted the responsibility by simply not mentioning them during the celebrations at all. They attempted to establish a new, ideologically acceptable narrative according to which Pilsen had actually liberated itself on May 5, 1945, before the Americans even arrived. In May 1948, on the first anniversary of the city's liberation celebrated under the socialist dictatorship, it was still possible to organize private tributes to the American army: it was this unofficial space and interpretation void that enabled the protests in Pilsen at the time.

The commemoration of Czechoslovakia's liberation was supposed to take place on May 9, the day that the Soviet Red Army arrived in Prague—at least according to the instructions issued on March 25, 1948, by the Permanent Inter-ministerial Committee, set up by the Ministry of Information to organize the celebrations.[23] However, the wording of the document allowed the towns and cities that had been liberated before that day to organize their own festivities "on the dates that the respective cities were really liberated."[24] Members of the former anti-Nazi resistance in Pilsen therefore pushed through the idea that the city should celebrate the anniversary of the anti-Nazi uprising that had taken place on May 5.[25]

Organization of the festivities fell upon the regional leadership of the National Revolution Union (SNR), an association of former members of the anti-Nazi resistance. The SNR engaged the assistance of the Public Awareness Council in Pilsen; on April 30, 1948, the Council issued an appeal to the principals of all secondary schools in the city to encourage their students to participate in the planned festivities.[26] The Council was well aware that Pilsen students did not hold the state socialist regime in particularly high regard;[27] the entire event was therefore meant to fulfill an educational purpose. "Due to inconsistent civic education, as well as inflammatory political and press campaigns, young students [in Pilsen] are particularly confused and most of them resent the current developments in our country; therefore, they need to be persuaded and indoctrinated at every opportunity."[28]

At 10 a.m. on May 5, 1948, official addresses were read at Náměstí Republiky, the largest public square in Pilsen. Student participation was very high. Unfortunately, the events began to unfold in a way that the organizers had not expected. The only officially displayed flags were those of the Slavic member states of the former Allied coalition, but on their own initiative, students came armed with paper American flags, or bought them right at the square. Former National Socialist and newsagent Josef Fencl[29] used the opportunity to peddle his stock of paper American flags that had largely become unsaleable after February 1948.[30] To the organizers' considerable displeasure, students waved these flags during the official addresses; yet no one had the courage to forbid them from doing it.[31]

The official part of the festivities ended at 11 a.m., and students returned in formations back to their schools, but were given the rest of the day off.[32] Many of them therefore began to gather at the busy intersection of Benešova and Stalinova streets, by the foundation stone of the monument to fallen American soldiers,[33] and stuck their flags into the grass surrounding the stone. In effect, this initiated a spontaneous, unplanned celebration that was out of the city officials' control, and which later escalated into a public protest. The flags around the monument inspired a great number of locals to start bringing flowers, banners and placards expressing their gratitude, and photos of the late American president F. D. Roosevelt and Czechoslovak foreign minister Jan Masaryk, known for his pro-Western attitudes, who had died in March 1948 under mysterious circumstances. The place was soon entirely covered in decorations.[34] Many people took photos of the banners and flower arrangements.[35] The flag-seller, Josef Fencl, moved from the square to the monument, and started selling a Czech/American flag combination for CZK 5, doing a brisk business until about 4.30 p.m. when he sold out of his entire stock of American flags, about 2,000 in total, and slightly more Czech flags, but hardly any Soviet ones "because nobody wanted them."[36] Some of the young people present bought dozens of American flags and gave them out to passers-by at no charge.

The authorities reacted to this development with considerable concern. However, the party leaders still maintained their evasive approach to the American problem, and decided to tolerate the still peaceful demonstrations. This is evidenced by the first telex that the State Security (StB) district office sent to the StB headquarters at 4.30 p.m.: "The events near the foundation stone of the American monument have gotten out of hand and escalated into a pro-American demonstration, organized most likely by secondary school students. In agreement with the Central National Committee security officer and the authorized officials, it was decided to leave the flowers and flags in place, and have the place monitored by the local authorities; anti-riot units have been charged with keeping order and making sure there is no traffic interference. Depending on the circumstances, the park & orchard department of the Central National Committee in Pilsen will ensure that all the flowers and flags are removed, either today or tomorrow."[37]

Around nightfall, the events around the foundation stone escalated into a full-blown protest. At 9 p.m., senior year students from the local secondary business school brought dozens of Chinese lanterns and placed them around the monument. The people gathered round welcomed them by singing the national anthem.[38] The Chinese lanterns were originally meant to illuminate the flower decorations but some of the bystanders warned the students that

Figure 1.1 Pilsen Residents Gathered on May 5–6, 1948, around the Decorated Cornerstone of the U.S. Army Monument at the Corner of What Was Then Stalinova and Benešova Avenue. Author unknown, probably the photos were taken by State Security. From the private archive of author of the book.

the wreaths and bouquets might catch fire from them. The students then tried to find an alternative use for the lanterns. Led by several students from the Pilsen medical school, the crowd moved over to the National Liberation Monument on the nearby Masarykovo Náměstí (Masaryk Square).[39] The monument had been used as a traditional gathering place for protesters, even during the Nazi occupation.[40] The students lined up in a formation and started marching.[41] According to a later SNB report, the procession started out with only about 500 participants, but more and more people joined up, and soon it became clear the whole thing had turned into a demonstration.[42]

The lantern procession set out from Masaryk Square, back toward the American monument foundation stone, and proceeded along Benešova street back to the main square, numbering several thousand people by that point. The crowd chanted slogans demanding a more respectable commemoration of Pilsen's liberation by the American army, but also a return to a more democratic system in Czechoslovakia, following the American example: "Following Beneš, now and forever! [. . .] Long live free America! [. . .] American flags in our squares! [. . .] Up with Masaryk's democracy! [. . .] Away with oppression! [. . .] Free speech, free press! [. . .] Ally with free America now! [. . .] Pilsen youth stands with America! [. . .] Stop defaming America! [. . .] Pilsen is with America!"[43] and, as the procession passed the building of the KSČ Regional Committee: "Shame on you!"[44]

Figure 1.2 The Pilsen demonstration in May 1948 took the form of a spontaneous thank-you ceremony for the liberation of the city by the American army at the end of World War II. Author unknown, probably the photos were taken by State Security. From the private archive of author of the book.

From the square, the procession set out back toward the American army monument. The students raised borrowed Czechoslovak and American flags, and the crowd honored the memory of the fallen soldiers by two minutes of silence. The whole event was entirely spontaneous and peaceful; there was no prepared program and no long-term agenda. Both the party officials and SNB officers were at a loss as how to deal with the whole thing, and so they let the procession pass, and even saluted to the flags carried at the front. They only managed to intervene once the procession marched back to the foundation stone, when they began asking the crowd to disperse.[45]

People were quite unwilling to leave, however; to stop the SNB units, they began singing the national anthem, whistling and jeering at the officers. Some had reluctantly yielded to authority, but others refused to leave the monument. This is evidenced by the records of the declarations and statements of those who had been apprehended by the SNB: "Shame on the SNB! [. . .] Bring back democracy! [. . .] What do you mean, you can't stand here? Well, I'll be damned. [. . .] Don't push me, I'm going, I'm going! [. . .] What do you mean, disperse? I'm the only one here!"[46] At one point, the crowd actually managed to break through the police cordon. Skirmishes broke out between the protesters and civilian bystanders who supported the police intervention. Randomly selected crowd members were asked to prove their identity or arrested. Some of the protesters who had been particularly active in organizing the march were arrested as alleged instigators of the whole event. The SNB continued arresting people gathered round the monument until the late hours, sometimes only by virtue of being present: they even arrested a troop of Boy Scouts who came to pay their respects and stand as guard of honor. StB investigators later described this peaceful initiative as "provocation by standing as guard of honor."[47]

Having learned their lesson on the preceding day, the Regional Office of the SNB sent reinforcements to the high-risk areas in the city center on May 6. The SNB also sent agents provocateurs to places where they expected people to start gathering. They were mostly civilians, either workers from the local factories or members of the workers' security guard units.[48] The agents provocateurs were to mingle with the protesters, follow those who were the most vocal and active, and turn them in to the police at the most opportune moment. This is clearly evidenced by statements made by the arrested persons and the agents provocateurs who testified against them. It was not a spontaneous act of politically concerned citizens but rather an organized security measure.[49]

On May 6, 1948, people had kept gathering round the American army monument since the morning hours. A rumor was going around the city about a possible visit from the U.S. ambassador to Czechoslovakia, Lawrence Steinhardt. Around 11 a.m., a crowd of about 2,000 had already gathered around the monument. Officials of the communist-run Revolutionary Union Movement (ROH) considered organizing a workers' counter-demonstration but did not receive the authorities' permission; the security forces wanted to calm the situation, not escalate it, and hoped that the anniversary of Pilsen's liberation would pass without any major incidents.

> Today's report, 9 a.m.: A crowd has again gathered near the foundation stone of the American army monument. The onlookers are mostly women. People are anticipating an unofficial visit of representatives from the American embassy who are supposed to lay a wreath by the monument; perhaps even Ambassador Steinhardt himself. The US embassy delegation was expected to arrive around 11 a.m. Benešova and Stalinova streets are currently lined by some 2,000 people. The gathering has caused irritation among the workers at Pilsen's factories, and union organizations are demanding to be allowed to organize their own march. The decision will be left to the relevant authorities. In light of last night's events, we may reasonably expect that a similar demonstration will occur again in the evening hours, but on an even larger scale. The regional SNB headquarters in Pilsen have been charged with deploying an anti-riot unit to deal with the situation.[50]

As dusk fell, the events unfolded much as they did the previous night. At around 9 p.m. the crowd that had gathered round the foundation stone, some 2,000–3,000 people, proceeded to the nearby National Liberation Monument on Masaryk Square and formed a procession. Apart from the most vocal and active protesters, however, many covert opponents of the demonstrations marched at the head of the procession. The crowd chanted much of the same slogans as they had done the previous night. Again, the procession marched along Benešova street toward the foundation stone of the monument to the American army. The core group of about 500 people walked in the middle of the road, flanked by the rest of the crowd on the sidewalks.[51] Before they had managed to reach the foundation stone, however, they were stopped by an SNB cordon which had swiftly emerged from a nearby office building.[52]

People at the head of the crowd tried to break through the cordon, walking five abreast and holding each other by the shoulder to strengthen the formation. To their considerable surprise, some of the protesters were seized by the agents provocateurs in their midst and handed over to the police.[53] Most of the protesters moved off the middle of the road to the sidewalks and started walking away from downtown. The crowd was only dispersing slowly, though; people were either unwilling to move or could not move for the crush on the sidewalks. The police were quite rough in their attempts to break up the mob, which predictably caused indignation among the people, resulting in a number of belligerent or sarcastic remarks toward the police—for which their authors were promptly arrested: "At 'em! [. . .] You call that freedom? [. . .] Police should stand with the people! [. . .] You better not start anything, or we'll beat the crap out of you! [. . .] You should be ashamed, treating your fellow Czechs this way!"[54] Surprisingly many people arrested during the May 6 protests were first seized by civilians and handed over to the police. Unlike the previous day, the crowd was infiltrated by observers and agents provocateurs sent by high-ranking Communist Party officials. "Thanks to a number of loyal, politically conscious workers, the main instigators were detained and the demonstration quickly dispersed. By 10 p.m., peace and order were fully restored."[55]

On the night of May 6, the police decided to remove the decorations surrounding the American army monument and left only a single official wreath. The anti-riot units were charged with preventing people from bringing more decorations and gathering in the area, which they managed to accomplish.[56] Similar precautions were used to secure this important symbolic location in subsequent years.[57]

We should also note that similar protests occurred on May 6, 1948, in other parts of West Bohemia as well. An StB report reveals tension escalating in the streets of Rokycany:

Figure 1.3 The lawn around the U.S. Army Monument in Pilsen was completely covered by American flags in May 1948. Author unknown, probably the photos were taken by State Security. From the private archive of author of the book.

> A quiet demonstration in a similar vein occurred in Rokycany today; flowers were laid by the commemorative plaque to the American army on the town hall, and a number of people promenaded outside the town hall in the evening hours, which would be very unusual on a regular day. No march had formed, however, and SNB reinforcements were sent from Pilsen.[58]

People arrested during the demonstrations were transported in police vans to the SNB headquarters in Pilsen, where interrogations were conducted by StB investigators. On May 5, the police performed spot document inspections on 43 people, of which 15 were immediately arrested and 28 charged and prosecuted without detention. On May 6, 35 people were inspected for documents, 19 of those being taken into custody.[59] The police investigated a total of 86 protesters: 23 students, 19 workers, 6 apprentices, 12 clerical workers, 19 traders and small business owners, 6 housewives, and 1 SNB officer.[60] StB interrogators relentlessly demanded to know the names of those who had organized the protests and seemed unwilling to accept that such mass protests could occur spontaneously. None of those who were interrogated, however, would confirm the theory that the event was a purposeful provocation set up by enemies of the regime.[61]

In fact, the demonstrations had not been organized by anyone. They had been born out of collective outrage when the Pilsen authorities refused to put up an American flag during the official festivities.[62] The collective mindset among certain segments of society (business and grammar school students, medical school students, Boy Scouts, former members of the National Socialist Party, and former private business owners) made it possible to pay respects to the fallen American soldiers in a coordinated manner. In the people's minds, honoring the fallen soldiers entailed an implicit criticism of the state socialist regime, especially its tendency to uncritically adopt Eastern cultural and political models. The protesters therefore mainly expressed their disapproval of the growing disparity in Czechoslovakia's foreign relations. They did not necessarily object to an alliance with the Soviet Union or against socialism in general, but disagreed with the regime abandoning the post-war concept of Czechoslovakia as a bridge between the East and the West. A number of bystanders who shared their opinion then joined in, as well as many random onlookers who were just carried away by the atmosphere. Some of them were even Communist Party members. For the most part, nothing explicitly illegal or illegitimate happened during the protest:[63] it was not officially forbidden to express gratitude toward the American army, and the local party officials had not publicly objected against such acts in the preceding years. The protesters were mostly young people who had been strongly influenced by their experience during the city's liberation in May 1945 and by the many months the American soldiers were stationed in the city.

We should also point out that the protests were by no means an attempt to overthrow the state socialist dictatorship, but rather a public expression of indignation over a perceived threat to people's alternative values. The protesters predominantly intended to address the rest of society in Czechoslovakia, as well as the general public in the Western countries. This was evidenced, for example, in uncensored anonymous letters sent from Pilsen to U.S. ambassador Lawrence Steinhardt: "To the esteemed American ambassador: The respects paid by the people of Pilsen to the USA deserve to be noted by the rest of the world. This spontaneous expression of love and gratitude comes at a time when any positive attitude toward the Western powers is considered to be high treason. I sincerely hope, Your Excellency, that you will make sure these acts are noted by the prominent figures in your great country."[64]

Numerous other social groups, however, such as some of the workers or members or factory security guards, loudly voiced their outrage over such provocations, and sometimes even resorted to physically assaulting the protesters. The so-called cult of America was, in their eyes, closely intertwined with anti-socialist and anti-patriotic (pro-German) values.[65] The protests were also made easier by the uncertainty of the police and party officials as to which acts honoring the American army were acceptable and to what degree, and which actions required swift intervention.

In May 1948, the Regional StB administration in Pilsen filed criminal charges against the people detained during the demonstrations for disturbing the peace and public order. Even though the investigators and party officials made a big production out of the entire thing, the protesters ended up receiving relatively mild punishments. Two factors played an important role in this: the politically enforced transformation of the judicial system after the 1948 coup went very slowly, and the authorities were under a lot of public pressure from the like-minded part of the West Bohemian population. Most of those who were arrested ended up serving a few days of jail time. Selected protest organizers were transported to the regional court prison but charges against them were eventually dismissed after the presidential amnesty of June 19, 1948.[66]

Apart from the justice system, the party apparatus was also involved in the attempts to find the instigators of the protests, using the National Front action committees, which were special authorities established after the 1948 coup in order to conduct political purges in public institutions. Thorough investigation was conducted into the activities of the National Revolutionary Union (SNR) which had organized the commemorative morning festivities on May 5, 1948.[67] However, it was the Pilsen secondary schools that became the focus of the authorities' investigation. Immediately after the demonstrations, the District Action Committee of the National Front in Pilsen began receiving resolutions from factory workers, demanding strict punishment of the protesters and subsequent cleansing in the local schools. The degree of hatred fomented in the Pilsen factories is apparent, for example, from the resolution sent by the local party organization in Pilsen-Lobzy:

> The riff-raff that took part in these demonstrations were the same sort of people who had collaborated with Hitler in 1933–1938 and who sent [Czechoslovak president] Emil Hácha to Berlin in 1939 and allowed him to offer up our people for extermination. The reactionaries' cries for new "protectors," albeit still quite timid, is a clear proof of that. [. . .] We have refrained from interfering up until now, relying on you to be watchful. Do not force us to go out in the streets and protect our national interests on our own. It is clear to everyone that these provocations were intentionally set up. Find those who instigated them and punish them as severely as they deserve! [. . .] Watching Czech citizens brandish American flags is just as painful as it was to watch flags bearing the hooked cross ten years ago.[68]

The action committees responded to these demands by suspending the secondary school leaving examinations and university exams for all detained students (at least 29 people in total)[69] until a thorough investigation of the demonstrations was completed. The investigation did not bring the expected results, however, and the regular exam dates were fast approaching. Entire secondary school classes submitted petitions defending their fellow students.[70] An important signal for the action committees in Pilsen was Klement Gottwald's presidential amnesty of June 19, 1948, which extended to offenses allegedly committed by the students, and was intended, to a certain degree, as a conciliatory gesture of the state socialist regime toward its moderate opponents.[71] On June 10, 1948, the District Action Committee therefore decided not to pursue strict punishment for the students, and opted for re-educational measures on the school level. It allowed the students to sit their exams on the regular date, on condition that their graduation certificates would be withheld until after the summer vacation, during which the students would have to demonstrate their loyalty to the regime by working as volunteers on youth construction projects or in coal mines.[72]

To that end, chairman of the District Action Committee Josef Vostradovský called a meeting with the affected students, their parents, and the school principals. At the meeting, it was announced that

> We do not want to punish; we want to educate. [. . .] The students are very young, no older than 19, which means that they were only about 7 to 10 years old [at the time of the collapse of the first independent Czechoslovak republic] in 1938. Their education [during the Nazi occupation] was twisted and corrupt; they were conditioned to oppose the Germans at every turn, which can be taken as a mitigating circumstance. However, they cannot be simply let off without a punishment. [. . .] I propose that the students join the young workers for a time, to gain a better understanding of what a working life is like. [. . .] I wish you all the best of luck in your exams. We shall withhold your graduation certificates for now, and the three students who committed the greatest transgressions will have their graduation exams postponed until the fall semester. We do not wish to cause anyone undue harm. Please accept that this is a necessary measure. I want us to remain friends and fellow Czechs.[73]

Most of the affected students managed to graduate in June 1948,[74] completed their summer jobs under the supervision of the labor protection office, and received their graduation certificates at the beginning of the next school year in September.[75]

The suppression of the May protests was a clear signal to the people of Pilsen that acts honoring the American army were going to be strictly regulated from now on, imposing new limits on freedom of expression. The local protests therefore became an important milestone for the whole of Czech society. However, suppressing the demonstrations did not solve the American problem in West Bohemia. Communist Party leaders could no longer tolerate vocal protests in the streets of Pilsen, but were still unsure how best to approach the newly emerged social conflict. After the May fiasco, caused by the authorities' decision to ignore the American problem, many of the regional party officials were of the opinion that it would be better to prevent public outrage by celebrating the American army's role in liberating Pilsen openly and officially.

The unexpected protest outburst caused shock and dismay among the regional party leadership. The Pilsen communists lost much of their confidence in the upcoming parliamentary election, scheduled for May 30, 1948. The official interpretation of the election as a nationwide endorsement of the state socialist regime seemed to have been challenged. Party officials became concerned that the pro-American protests would be perceived by the public as a rejection of the February coup's outcome, and that as a consequence, more people in the region would choose to submit blank ballots, which was the only possible alternative to the unified ballot led by the communists.[76] In the end, this prediction did not come true, and the Consolidated National Front received 88.21% of valid votes in the region.[77] Still, General Secretary of the Central Committee Rudolf Slánský tried to explain the poor results in the Pilsen region by an insufficiently aggressive campaign, interrupted by the pro-American demonstrations. "In places where the Party felt supremely confident, and where the comrades showed enthusiasm and induced mass psychosis, the reactionaries were afraid to turn in a blank ballot. But in places where they were lacking, [election] results were much poorer. Following the pro-American demonstrations on 5 May in Pilsen, the Party did not have enough confidence to rally."[78]

Under these circumstances, the party tried to find the culprits responsible for the protests among their own regional leaders. Opposition within KSČ used the plenary session of the regional committee to criticize the top regional party officials. Spokesmen for the opposition included especially two MPs, Karel Štekl and Jan Rych, and one of the leaders of the 1945 anti-Nazi uprising in Pilsen, physician Jaromír Hrbek. Oppositionists saw the protests as a consequence of the masses losing faith in the post-coup party officials, who often resorted to violent interventions.[79]

The oppositionists proposed moderate treatment of the protesters, claiming that it was the regional committee itself that gave people a pretext for protesting, by needlessly keeping hush about the American army's contribution toward liberating Pilsen, which motivated the locals to organize their own festivities. The debate about demonstrations escalated into a more general conflict about both party leadership and governance of the entire country. Some of the party officials showed willingness to carry on with the policies adopted in the years 1945–1948, when the party was still trying to garner widespread public support, and demanded that the government refrain from using open violence. It was no coincidence that such opinions were mostly voiced by the founding leaders from the years 1945–1946 who had, in actuality, already been shunted aside; it was this strategy, mindful of regional differences (such as the American problem) and public opinion, that had paid off before the parliamentary elections in 1946. Demonstrations had therefore caused a protracted crisis inside the West Bohemian Party organization, which slowly escalated into a power struggle between the elected bodies, who drew their authority from the local inter- and post-war communist movement traditions, and the leading party officials appointed to the regional secretariat in 1947 by the party headquarters.[80]

Karel Štekl, for example, believed it would be politically expedient for the KSČ to officially undertake the organization of the festivities commemorating Pilsen's liberation, introducing their own political agenda to the celebrations. He mentioned the experience of the previous party leaders who had actively participated in the festivities in the years 1945–1946 without being challenged by their opponents,

> not even during those first six months, when we were effectively occupied by the Americans. [. . .] We should not have denied the Americans' role; we should have put out an American flag on the town hall. The consequences would not have been nearly as serious as the fallout from the fact that it was not there. Many upstanding people noticed the absence, and they were told that the decorator had simply forgotten to put it out. That is not how things should be done. Pilsen had liberated itself but the Americans saved it from a bloodbath. There is no reason to keep this from the public; we can simply tell people that Americans came to defend democracy, that they had fought alongside the Soviets; at the same time, however, we should remind the public that the American army had only liberated a small part of the country, and that the Red Army liberated most of our territory. We should also state that we do not dishonor the memory of those who deserve our respect and the raising of flags by opposing the current American policies, which support the rise of fascism in America and continues to conspire against the people's democratic countries and against the Soviet Union. We have to sway the public opinion in our favor. [. . .] People had organized their own thing because not a word was said about the Americans' arrival. People with insufficient political acumen believe that the communists are not telling them the truth.[81]

Similar sentiments regarding the causes of the May protests were voiced by Jaromír Hrbek in a report sent to Marie Švermová, organizational secretary of the KSČ Central Committee:[82]

> The approach toward the celebrations of Pilsen's liberation on 5 May was utterly wrong and heavy-handed. Citizens were outraged by the pointless attempts to

> avoid and suppress any mentions of the American army. [. . .] And yet, nothing would have been easier than to use this opportunity to appreciate America's role in defeating Hitler's Germany, but at the same time, properly articulate our attitude toward the West, America's duplicitousness, etc. This kind of ostrich policy, as well as the mistakes that have been made, have become the grist to the reactionaries' mill, helping them persuade thousands of honest people that the communists are a nothing but a bunch of tactless, boorish ingrates who have no scruples about falsifying historical facts. This has even driven the citizens to organize demonstrations. [. . .] The embarrassing outcome of this poorly chosen strategy has been made even worse by the decision to deploy dozens of our comrades as agents provocateurs, armed with American flags, inciting the people to riot and then detaining them and handing them over to the SNB. These ill-chosen actions were rightly condemned by many upstanding citizens. None of the leading party officials chose to adopt the correct approach, either during the official addresses or during the gatherings of local citizens who placed flowers and flags near the American monument. Even after discussing the issue at a meeting of the regional [KSČ] committee, comrades from the regional [KSČ] secretariat, the [National Front] regional action committee and the [National Front] district action committee still insisted on their utterly unreasonable stance, suspending dozens of secondary school students who had carried American flags during the official address from sitting their exams and graduating. A number of innocent people have been persecuted, causing renewed outrage. Even though [Rudolf] Slánský announced no less than three times, in the presence of non-partisans, that the whole incident would be dealt with leniently, our regional [KSČ] secretariat and [National Front] regional action committee insisted on harsh punishments of the youngest participants, who had the least responsibility and were the most susceptible to persuasion, and often were completely innocent.[83]

As is evident from the above quotes, regional Communist Party leaders had only begun forming a definitive stance toward the celebrations of Pilsen's liberation by the American army after the demonstrations in May 1948. The issue of pro-American protests was one of the points of contention within a broader inside struggle within the party. By the end of 1948, party headquarters managed to quell any dissenting opinions among members of the regional committee, and debates over the American problem eventually died out within the party as a whole.[84]

Internal disputes among members of the Communist Party in West Bohemia had clearly shown that KSČ membership, which included many new communists who joined the party after the war,[85] had not yet fully accepted the principles of the so-called democratic centralism in 1948. The communists in Pilsen continued to show a tendency to demand a say in party leadership even on later occasions, especially during the show trials of 1951–1952 and after the currency reform announced at the beginning of June 1953. Despite that, they still remained generally loyal toward the central leadership.

A specific local protest culture emerged in West Bohemia during the pro-American protests, completely unheard-of on nationwide level in Czechoslovakia. By honoring the American liberators, it promoted closer ties with Western political and cultural models. It spread especially among students and was often utilized during similar incidents in later years. The local protest culture, as construed in this text, was based on a set of certain symbols and know-how that could be used to stage a protest on various occasions. It was not, however, a form of counterculture that would primarily and permanently oppose the official narrative. Its application had changed over time and was utilized during protest events that were widely different in character.

In reaction to the protests, the foundation stone for the American army monument in Pilsen was promptly removed in 1948. In the 1950s, the municipal committee of the Communist Party and the Regional National Committee requested that the amount of CZK 5,741,920, raised in a public collection before the February coup d'état, be spent on purchasing medical supplies to support North Korea during the Korean War.[86]

Even so, the area around the erstwhile foundation stone had become a symbolic focal point for pro-Western sympathizers, and a natural meeting place where people gathered for most protests and demonstrations in later years.[87] Thirty-two people were arrested there during the next year's celebrations on May 5, 1949. Most of the protesters were young industrial workers, due to the fact that factory workers around this time were often young people from the families of small businessmen and civil servants who had retained their admiration for the Western culture and lifestyle. A mere attempt to lay flowers near the monument or walk past with an American flag lapel pin could be a cause for arrest. Despite that, at least 500 people were present in the area shortly after 8 p.m., awaiting a charge to start a protest. At 9 p.m. the police blocked all access roads to the monument, effectively preventing the protests from escalating any further.[88] The intersection near the former monument was also an important strategic meeting point during the currency reform protests in June 1953.

The outcome of the social conflict that had arisen from the May 1948 protests determined the official interpretation of Pilsen's liberation by the American army up until the year 1968. The Americans' short presence was interpreted as an occupation, led by dishonorable intentions and with disastrous cultural consequences.[89] During the events of the so-called Prague Spring of 1968, certain groups in Pilsen began demanding that the monuments to the American soldiers be restored, and that the historical role of the Western allies in the war rehabilitated.[90] On May 6, 1968, an official celebration of the city's liberation by Americans was held in Pilsen for the first time since 1947. The authorities yielded to the pressure of university students and former members of the Pilsen branch of the Union of Friends of the USA; however, due to the unwillingness of the Communist Party to become involved, the festivities were held under the auspices of the National Front municipal committee and chiefly organized by the Czechoslovak Socialist Party—a minor political party tolerated by the regime which had been trying to set a new political course instead of following the official communist policy. The Pilsen events eventually became one of the symbols of the Prague Spring. About 10,000–15,000 people were estimated to participate—seven times more than under the restrictions in 1948.[91]

To conclude this chapter, we should note that the unique protest culture in Pilsen, based on the reverence of American soldiers and the ritual laying of flowers, was deeply ingrained in the local population. It was revived after the occupation of Czechoslovakia by Warsaw Pact armies in August 1968, albeit the traditional theme of disparity in the country's foreign relations acquired a brand-new meaning. On the evening of May 5, 1969, protests broke out in the vicinity of the former monument foundation stone, similar in character to those in the 1940s. Official celebrations in 1969 were held elsewhere, around the Monument to the Victims of Nazism on Náměstí Míru. By their own initiative, groups of people began gathering near the former foundation stone, with about 1,500 people being present at around 4 p.m. People began placing American flags on the lawn, as well as photos of President Tomáš Garrigue Masaryk and his son, Jan Masaryk. After the crowd repeatedly refused to disperse, officers of the Public Security (VB, regular uniformed police force) began dispersing it by force, albeit without using batons. Six protesters were arrested. The crowd began to gather again, however, and about 2,000 people were present at around 9 p.m., jeering at the police who were trying to clear the area, and even throwing small objects. The VB therefore had to resort to clearing the intersection using batons and two water cannons. Twenty-four people were brought in for questioning; three police officers were injured.[92]

The tradition of pro-American protests in West Bohemia was revived again during the turbulent year 1989. On the afternoon of May 6, a legally announced but subsequently banned demonstration took place in Pilsen. This time, people gathered at Náměstí Míru, a place officially used to celebrate the end of World War II. About 300–400 people participating in the protest were subjected to document inspection by the police.[93]

A new foundation stone for the monument to American soldiers in Pilsen was laid in its original place in 1990, shortly after the Velvet Revolution, in the presence of President Václav Havel.[94] The monument was successfully completed and officially unveiled on May 6, 1995.[95] The city of Pilsen also restored the tradition of official celebrations honoring the American army, which were extremely popular in the 1990s and became a formative element of the region's new, post-communist image.

STUDENT PROTESTS DURING THE STATE FUNERAL FOR PRESIDENT EDVARD BENEŠ ON SEPTEMBER 8, 1948

The death of former president Edvard Beneš on September 3, 1948, and the subsequent suppression of a nationwide wave of protests during the period of state mourning on September 3–10, 1948, was a significant milestone in the history of the Czechoslovak state socialist regime. For many critics of the post-1948 development, Beneš's death became a symbolic end to all hope of overturning the country's political situation. Moreover, after the protests died down, the Communist Party proceeded to take harsh measures against both real and perceived enemies of the system, leading to a deep politicization of both the private and professional sphere.[96]

In West Bohemia, protests during the September events following the state funeral continued in the same vein as the protests that had erupted in May 1948 during the anniversary celebrations of the end of World War II. Therefore, an alternative, unofficial commemorative gathering again occurred in downtown Pilsen near the monument to Czechoslovak independence of 1918, culminating in a silent student march on September 8, 1948.[97] However, the demonstrations did not turn into more advanced, open forms of protest because the police, having learned their lesson from the May celebrations, regulated the laying of flowers and wreaths around the monument, making it difficult to form a larger crowd.

Before we proceed to the actual analysis of the Pilsen protests, however, we need to put the entire event into nationwide context. In February 1948, under pressure from members of the Communist Party, President Beneš accepted their proposed solution to the government crisis, supplementing the cabinet with ministers nominated by the communist prime minister Klement Gottwald, thus allowing the party to take power in a seemingly democratic manner.[98] Leaders of the Communist Party were therefore not forced to drag President Beneš into a scandal; on the contrary, they purposely gave the public the impression that the solution was a result of a mutual understanding. Nevertheless, many citizens perceived Beneš as a guarantee for maintaining democratic principles of state management. Therefore, after the announcement of Beneš's abdication on June 7, a wave of demonstrations and minor protests erupted in support of Beneš. In the months that followed, major public gatherings occurred, particularly outside the President's villa in Sezimovo Ústí.[99] The protest actions reached mass proportions during the 11th national congress of the traditional Czechoslovak national physical education organization Sokol, held in Prague on June 20–27.[100]

Even after Beneš's death on September 3, the Communist Party leadership did not resort to public condemnation of the former president and resolved to emphasize those aspects of his legacy that the party could relate to.[101] The Prime Minister's office therefore immediately began preparations for an official state funeral. As news of Beneš's death spread, minor protest incidents and provocations began to emerge throughout the country. Major gatherings occurred in Sezimovo Ústí and Prague, where the president's coffin was lying-in-state from September 6. People formed a line several kilometers long in order to pay their respects, which led to numerous clashes with the police on the night of September 7–8.[102]

The official state funeral was held at 4 p.m. on the afternoon of September 8. Beneš's supporters poured into Prague from all parts of the country. Particularly active in this respect were the Sokol clubs, whose members originally expected to be asked to stand as honorary guard lining Wenceslas Square, Prague's main venue for public events. However, the Communist Party leadership received intelligence about the Sokols' alleged preparations for some kind of a demonstrative act during the funeral. Having assessed this as a State Security risk, they replaced the Sokols by members of the People's Militias, armed units of factory workers, Communist Party members, and supporters, who were supposed to cordon the area.[103] Unwanted provocations at Beneš's funeral were also prevented by some of the communist-leaning workers from Prague factories, who had been instructed in advance by the factory party organizations were warned about the reactionaries' intentions and were sent out in large numbers into the streets on the day of the funeral. Meticulous measures were also taken to prevent people from other parts of the country from going to Prague. No major incidents therefore occurred after the start of the ceremony and during the subsequent funeral procession. Rather, the onlookers paid peaceful tribute to the memory of their president.[104] Still, the nationwide wave of minor demonstrations on September 3–8, 1948 was the largest collective protest since February 1948.[105]

The situation in other regions was considerably different from that in Prague. The first incidents occurred in all regions as early as September 3, 1948, usually involving the distribution of illegal leaflets or painting anticommunist slogans.[106] In Pilsen, the population began to lay flowers at the monument to the National Liberation on Masaryk Square. The presidium of the Communist Party district committee in Pilsen-City reacted to this development as early as September 4, 1948, by putting the Party Secretariat on alert: "The death of our Mr. President is a pretext for the reactionaries to provoke incidents. We must prove to them that they are not doing this out of respect for Mr. Edvard Beneš, but that they are merely taking advantage of the situation to instigate various incidents. Selling flowers is a mere demonstration of their reactionary attitude. We will do our best to disperse the gatherings and try to make sure that the provocations have as little effect as possible. Should they wish to provoke some kind of action, we will be forced to resort to every measure necessary."[107]

All regional party secretariats received preliminary instructions from headquarters on the same day, outlining the course of official memorial services. It was announced that for the duration of national mourning, a ban on any public speeches would be imposed in addition to the ban on festivities and entertainment. To prevent any incidents, only a single commemorative event organized by the action committees was allowed in each town, which involved listening to a live radio broadcast from Prague. Party leadership intended for the unified local events to demonstrate national unity, but at the same time used them as a means to control the discourse. From the outset, regional secretariats were called upon to prevent an excessive influx of people into Prague: "We further urgently recommend that you prevent the dispatch of special buses and special trains to Beneš's funeral in Prague. Blame this on the shortage of gas, and coal, as well as the need to prevent Prague from getting overcrowded."[108]

Further instructions from the Secretariat of the KSČ Central Committee on September 7 ordered the regions to declare something akin to the state of emergency in larger cities the following day. The People's Militias, armed with rifles, were to patrol in the streets. Party organizations and factory workers were to be immediately put on high alert: "We recommend that you watch out for any signs that the reactionaries might instigate any provocations in your town during tomorrow's events. Pay special attention to the Sokols. Put the party action groups, party organizations and factory workers on alert. Send the factory militias, armed with rifles, to patrol at tomorrow's events, just as we are going to do in Prague."[109]

Reports sent to the party headquarters from regional party secretariats on the afternoon of September 7 emphasized the importance of measures that Prague found crucial: thorough monitoring of the main thoroughfares. Regions with the main railroad lines and roads conducted thorough raids on all means of transport; uniformed Sokol members were made to disembark from trains, and entire buses were made to turn around. Pilsen was no exception: "For the funeral of Dr. Beneš, arrangements were made to prevent the dispatch of special trains and buses. Cars will not be allowed to leave the city. All clubs and associations were advised to attend the memorial service in Pilsen and thus avoid sending delegations to Prague. Memorial service will be held in Pilsen's main square; there will be no speeches, and citizens will be able to listen to a live broadcast from Prague. The army will be present and will end the memorial service by reading the official orders issued on the day of the funeral. Furthermore, arrangements have been made within the party, the districts of Pilsen-City and Pilsen-Environs and the party organization in the Škoda Plants will mobilize all of its members to attend the memorial service. These security measures are made more difficult by the fact that a part of the police force has been redeployed to Prague and Sezimovo Ústí."[110] Nevertheless, reports from the Prague railroad stations on September 7 confirmed the arrival of a large number of people from Pilsen. The majority of them were allegedly former members of the Western army and Sokols in traditional folk costumes.

These measures largely determined the fate of the Pilsen demonstration on September 8, which is the main topic of this chapter. In the morning, workers in Pilsen factories were informed that a coup d'état was under way, and a certain pogrom-like sentiment arose among some of them, and they were on alert for any unusual behavior. Such sentiments occurred in factories across the country, as evidenced by a report from the KSČ regional secretariat in Pilsen on September 8: "Staff meetings were called in both large and small factories throughout the region, which went very well. Workers joined the meetings spontaneously, and the mood was decidedly against the reactionaries. The plants are on full alert. [. . .] Factory Militias are armed and ready and will fully participate in the afternoon memorial service."[111] The worker assemblies also passed resolutions demanding the severest possible punishment for any provocateurs who might choose to disrupt the upcoming commemorative events.[112] On September 8, the press issued appeals to workers to take part in subduing possible provocations.[113] In this way, communist propaganda attempted to construe social reality as an imminent attempt for a reactionary coup. Any form of protest, even those that were not politically motivated, could subsequently be interpreted in this way.

As in other regions, some disturbances occurred in Pilsen during the preparations for the state funeral. Illegal leaflets were spread containing information about the president's stance and actions during the February government crisis. Another type of leaflet intercepted was a statement of protest against the ongoing purge in the Sokol organization. The police arrested several groups distributing these printed materials. None of these people, however, could be truly seen as organizers of this unofficially distributed information. Interrogation reports of the State Security indicate that leaflet-spreading was a part of normal everyday communication between friends with a common political outlook. Most of the detainees were mere consumers of illegal printed materials, which they copied by hand or typed out in order to discuss the contents with their friends. The perpetrators who were caught knew that this was a dangerous activity, yet they did not engage in any sophisticated forms of conspiracy and, for example, discussed their views openly in the workplace. These circumstances suggest that the established mode of everyday interpersonal communication regarding political issues had not yet been fully distorted by fear in September 1948, and the Communist Party was far from fully controlling this sphere of private political expression. An example of the distribution of illegal printed materials in Pilsen was the group of Sokols, Antonín Novák, Václav Kovařík, and Ladislav Mudra;[114] and a group of Beneš's sympathizers, Josef Tolar, Slavomír Racek, Jaroslav Jäger, and Josef Houška; both of these illegal groups were entirely fabricated by the State Security.[115]

Another typical form of minor protest was a slogan "Communists have driven Dr. Beneš to death,"[116] written by an anonymous author in the morning hours of September 8 in the toilets of the Gambrinus brewery in Pilsen. Even such a minor incident was immediately investigated by the State Security authorities. The State Security also monitored other, more allegorical forms of public expression, such as the placing of crowns of thorns in shop windows by the image of the late president Beneš. For incidents of this sort, State Security took action against Božena Svobodová, head of the Orchidea company, and Jaroslav Jílek, owner of the Favorit shop. Arrests for various subversive statements, such as that of coachbuilder Václav Vlk, were no exception.[117]

These small, individual protests did not have the potential to appeal to a large number of people and could not therefore trigger any form of collective civil unrest. By prosecuting such acts, the establishment sought to redefine the rules and establish new precedents as to what constituted legal and safe conduct. Much more dangerous in the eyes of the Communist Party were the demonstrations that had taken place in Pilsen on May 5–6, 1948, on the anniversary of the city's liberation by the American army.[118] Similar attitudes, however, began to reemerge in Pilsen after Beneš's death on September 3. People once again brought flowers and wreaths to the National Liberation Monument, dominated by the statue of the first Czechoslovak president Tomáš Garrigue Masaryk, or stood in groups around it and watched as others laid flowers. A State Security report assessed this activity in the following manner: "Immediately after President Beneš's demise, some of the citizens began laying flowers at the monument to President-Liberator Tomáš Garrigue Masaryk. Someone later added a photo of Dr. Beneš. Rather than honoring the memory of the late president Beneš, their actions were an expression of their disapproval with our people's democratic regime; these individuals saw the late Dr. Beneš as someone sympathetic to their reactionary thinking, and undoubtedly wanted to express their views by laying flowers by his picture."[119]

To keep the peace in the streets on September 8, 1948, the Communist Party had to thwart this counter-memorial service and prevent people from gathering around the monument, so as not to have a repeat of the May events.

The police were therefore tasked with preventing the formation of a crowd at this important symbolic space. "One such measure was the decision to prevent people from gathering in front of the monument to President Tomáš Garrigue Masaryk in Pilsen. People could walk freely past the monument, but it was not allowed to stop and huddle in groups. In spite of this, small crowds formed at the monument to President Masaryk and were repeatedly dispersed by SNB officers."[120]

For security reasons, it was decided that the laying of flowers at the monument would only be tolerated until the end of the official commemoration on September 8, 1948, which took place on Náměstí Republiky. No such ban had been officially declared, however. The State Security considered the announcement of the official location of the commemoration ceremony as sufficient information as to which locations were acceptable for bringing flowers and wreaths.

> In agreement with the relevant officials, such actions would only be tolerated until the erection of the catafalque on Náměstí Republiky, in front of which a memorial service was to be held in honor of the deceased Dr. Beneš on 8 September 1948. After the erection of the catafalque and the end of the commemoration, no further laying of wreaths at the monument to the President Liberator was allowed, firstly because the public had been informed by the radio and press that the commemoration ceremony was to take place on Náměstí Republiky, but also due of justified fears that reactionary elements would attempt to form an illegal gathering in the vicinity of the monument to President Masaryk, possibly making illegal speeches, which would result in an incident similar to those which occurred on September 5–6, 1948. Such concerns were well-founded since small groups of people began to gather around the monument, apparently waiting for an opportunity to hold a similar demonstration.[121]

This ban and the absence of its public announcement, as we shall see, played a crucial role in the protests that broke out on September 8, 1948. Thanks to the aforementioned measures, the official Pilsen commemoration ceremony at 4 p.m. on Náměstí Republiky went entirely according to plan. Some 25,000 people came to listen to the radio broadcast, making the attendance at the Pilsen commemoration ceremony one of the largest in the country.[122]

After the official ceremony was over, the participants began to disperse. However, a large number of people headed from the ceremony toward the monument on Masarykovo Náměstí, with the intention of viewing the floral decorations, but also in anticipation that something would happen. Among them was, for example, Bedřich Marx, technical clerk from the Škoda Works.

Later he testified that when he arrived at Masarykovo Náměstí shortly after 5 p.m. with the rest of the crowd, he saw

> three little girls, each carrying about four white aster flowers; they wanted to place them with the other flowers in front of the monument, but the police patrols chased them away. This was noticed by other people who lingered in the square and started forming small groups. I remained standing with one such group. After a while, one of the SNB officers approached us and asked us to move on. We did not heed his instruction.[123]

At the same time, another police officer approached Marx from behind and asked him what he was waiting for. Marx, without realizing who he was talking to, spontaneously blurted out, "For more food rations."[124] Only then did he realize who he was talking to and tried to get lost in the crowd, which was later interpreted by investigators as assaulting the officer. Although he managed to escape, he was pursued by two civilian volunteers and handed over to the factory militias at the gates of the Škoda plant. What is particularly significant about Marx's testimony is the importance the laying of flowers had for spontaneous gatherings which could have resulted in protests. The commemoration ceremony, where it was legitimate for the public to gather, made it possible for a mob to form.

Another person arrested at the statue of Tomáš Garrigue Masaryk was young teacher Jan Topinka, who had taken a leave of absence the day before so he could go to the state funeral in Prague. On the morning of September 8, he tried unsuccessfully to leave Pilsen for Prague. "I was then stopped by the official authorities and sent back; they told me I could not go to Prague because I did not have the required permit."[125] He and his fiancée therefore decided to attend the commemorative ceremony on Náměstí Republiky. After the ceremony, they went to see the decorations around the statue of Tomáš Garrigue Masaryk on Masarykovo Náměstí. "Some minutes later, we were approached by an SNB officer who asked us to leave so as not to obstruct people from walking past. I said that we would step off the sidewalk, which we did, but we remained standing on the road. But the officer was not happy with this, asked us both to produce our IDs, and took us to the hallway of the nearby business school."[126] This was the mood in downtown Pilsen in the run-up to the student demonstration.

On September 8, 1948, classes were canceled for high school students all over the country, and students at the State Grammar School in Pilsen were made to listen to a live broadcast commemorating the late president.[127] The school PA system then urged all students to attend the aforementioned official commemoration ceremony, which was to take place at 4 p.m. on Náměstí Republiky. After the in-school mourning program, there was a free period, which the final year students used to discuss arrangements for the upcoming graduation party. Some students arranged to meet up in the afternoon before the ceremony, and all of them then went home.[128]

Otto Rösch, an eighth-year student who was later accused of organizing the entire subversive provocation, left school with two younger students to get ice cream. On their way, they passed the monument on Masarykovo Náměstí, and watched a group of students from another school bring a wreath to the monument. Several police officers were patrolling by the monument, but they did nothing to prevent the students from laying the wreath. Inspired by their example, Rösch decided that it would be a good idea for him and his classmates to lay their own wreath to commemorate the late president Beneš. As he later confessed, his decision was partly fueled by the desire to give himself some swag in front of his two girl companions.[129] Around noon, he and the girls went to a florist's shop, where he ordered a wreath worth CZK 600, with ribbons inscribed with the slogan "To President Edvard Beneš—To your democratic ideals we shall forever remain faithful."[130]

Shortly before 4 p.m., several students from the State Grammar School met up in the crowd gathered on Náměstí Republiky. They listened to the radio broadcast and agreed to go and lay Rösch's wreath together after the official wake was over. However, they were spotted and closely watched by worker Růžena Chlubná, who alerted others to their suspicious activity.[131] Just before 5 p.m., an unknown man telephoned the StB Regional Office in Pilsen to report the students' gathering. The StB promptly dispatched a police officer to the square, but the students had already left.

As mentioned above, after listening to the solemn army decree, the crowd began to disperse from the square. The grammar school students wove their way through the crowd to the flower shop where Rösch picked up the wreath. Two members of the group, Václav Herink and Josef Baudyš, both dressed in mourning, then took up the wreath, and all the students formed an orderly procession. The two students leading the procession were both politically active student officials. Herink was a school Communist Party secretary; Baudyš had served as the regional cultural officer of the Czech Youth Union in the previous school year, and on the morning of September 8, he was instructed by the school principal to invite students via the school PA system to attend the commemoration ceremony. The rest of the students could have arguably perceived the initial stage of the procession as an official school event.[132] At this point the mourning procession numbered approximately 25–30 people; female students wore black dresses adorned with white flowers, and male students wore black mourning ribbons with a tricolor attached on their lapels; some also had Scout badges. However, numerous workers patrolled the streets, keeping a close eye on any sign of unusual behavior. At least three persons were monitoring the students' procession and followed them along the way. After the first few steps, Václav Novák, a member of the Škoda Works' factory council, stopped the students and, by virtue of his position as regional Scout chief, confiscated Herink's Scout badge, claiming that this was not an official Scout event.[133] After this incident, Herink and Baudyš realized that the whole thing could be perceived as a provocation and were reluctant to carry the wreath any further.[134]

The task of carrying the wreath fell to Rösch, and the students went on in scattered groups, which was inevitable due to the large number of people proceeding in the same direction. The students did not attract much public attention and walked without any incident along Benešova Avenue to Masarykovo Náměstí. As they reached the National Liberation Monument, however, they were intercepted by a patrolling SNB officer. He strongly warned the students that their actions could be interpreted as provocation and that the official catafalque on Náměstí Republiky would be a more appropriate place to lay the wreath. It was only this intervention that aroused a greater response from the citizens passing by and standing around, and the SNB officer had to order the emerging crowd to disperse. The gymnasium students obeyed the order and returned along the same route along Benešova Avenue to the theater. The wreath was now carried by student Zdeněk Mraček, who later became Mayor of Pilsen in the years 1990–1994. Along the way, the students discussed

Figure 1.4 Photograph of the Commemorative Decoration of the National Liberation Monument in Pilsen in September 1948. Author unknown, probably the photo was taken by State Security. SOkA v Blovicích, f. OS Pilsen, zn. 2 T 3/1956.

the best way how to dispose of the wreath, and decided not to place it on Náměstí Republiky, as they had been advised, but inside the school, by the plaque commemorating the teachers and students martyred during the Nazi occupation. They therefore headed back down Benešova Avenue to Leninova Avenue toward the State Grammar School. It was not a demonstration in the true sense of the word; none of the people present chanted any slogans and the whole thing was not so much a procession as scattered pairs and trios of disillusioned students engaged in conversation, followed at a distance by curious onlookers.[135]

The fate of the student demonstration was largely determined by the fact that the route took them along Leninova Avenue, in close proximity to the building of the regional secretariat of the Communist Party. The fact that they even marched past this building was in itself perceived as a provocation by the communist-leaning bystanders. In the aftermath of Beneš's death, reports of provocations outside the party secretariats came from several regions, so the volunteers present were even more vigilant.[136] Moreover, the workers' antagonism toward possible provocateurs was reinforced nationwide that morning by the aforementioned briefing at the factories regarding the alleged preparations for a coup by the regime's enemies. Furthermore, the communists in Pilsen still vividly remembered of the wave of pro-American demonstrations of May 5–6 ,1948, also largely initiated by students.

Casual observers, whether sympathizers or opponents of the procession, could therefore quite rightly assume that the students, driven away from the monument to Tomáš Garrigue Masaryk, would protest by laying a wreath in protest outside the Communist Party regional headquarters.[137] This interpretation was later adopted by the final State Security report:

> We should note that demonstrations near the aforementioned monument to President Masaryk had taken place before, on 5 and 6 May 1948, and that perhaps this was the reason why the workers were so outraged on 8 September 1948, assuming quite rightly that the procession was not intended as an act of commemoration, but as yet another demonstration against the people's democratic regime. The workers were further enraged by the fact that the students returning with the wreath from Masaryk's monument, allegedly determined to lay it by the plaque inside the school building, could have taken a closer route along Tylova Avenue, but instead chose to walk past the Lenin Building, where workers were often present, and considered it as yet another provocation, which greatly contributed to the ensuing skirmishes.[138]

Witness accounts of what exactly occurred outside the Communist Party Secretariat building varied considerably. It is not clear from the surviving sources whether the students were actually walking peacefully past the secretariat toward the school and were attacked for no reason by the communist sympathizers standing around; whether one of the students actually provoked a skirmish by placing the wreath by the building wall, or whether the wreath was merely thrown against the wall after the clash erupted. However, the overwhelming majority of witness statements supported either the first or third option.[139]

All that is certain is that at the moment when the head of the procession with the wreath reached the entrance to the Communist Party headquarters, the students were attacked both by persons who had been secretly following them on the street for some time and by other people summoned from inside the Party Secretariat. The wreath-bearers were pushed into the passageway by the attackers and detained there.[140] In the ensuing confusion and scuffles (which occasionally escalated into a full-on brawl), most of the students took flight and were pursued. With them fled others who had not been a part of the core group of students, but took fright when punches began to be thrown willy-nilly.

Vladimír Ungerman, a Škoda Works official, found himself in such a situation: in an attempt to flee the scene, he collided with Jaroslav Kasl, a Škoda Works militiaman, and suffered a complicated fracture to his leg:[141]

> A group of civilians near the building surrounded the students who had laid the wreath, and chaos ensued; I saw people throwing punches, and both the students who had been directly involved as well as other young people who were only bystanders, started to flee in all directions, pursued by the civilians standing outside the Lenin House. I was afraid I would get a beating for no reason, since I had nothing to do with the whole incident, and so I started to run away, first across the street, but I was being pursued. A couple of civilians chased me on the sidewalk and started punching me; I tried to get away from them by running across Benešova Avenue toward the theater, [. . .] and as I darted across the road to the area outside the theater, I noticed a group of about five civilians standing there, two or three of whom started running to confront me when I tried to go past them. On the road I collided with an elderly man who meant to catch me, and though I tried to avoid him we collided, and both fell to the ground. [. . .] As I was lying on the ground, the man seized me by my collar and neck so I could not get up.[142]

The students were dispersed and detained exclusively by civilians (several of whom belonged to the Škoda Works factory militias) with no legal pretext whatsoever. The whole incident was therefore essentially a deliberate physical attack by a few indignant members of the working class, completely spontaneous and unprovoked. None of the detainees were actually handed over to the police; instead, they were all taken to the Party Secretariat building, where they were subjected to interrogation under the supervision of the communist functionaries. A total of 11 persons were detained on the spot, including four young women.[143] Only later were the detainees taken by car to the police headquarters in Pilsen, where they were interrogated by investigators from the Regional State Security Office in Pilsen.

While the civilian intervention outside Lenin House was probably largely motivated by an effort to prevent a provocation right outside the party headquarters, the State Security investigation was geared toward accusing the students of attempting to provoke a demonstration by laying a wreath at the statue of President Masaryk on Masarykovo Náměstí.[144] Most of the detainees were immediately punished by the police by a few days in jail.[145] Much harsher action was to be taken against the alleged instigators. In particular, the authorities sought to prosecute Otto Rösch, who had purchased the wreath, and his two helpers, Karel Voleník and Zdeněk Mraček.[146] In their defense, the accused stated that they did not intend to provoke any demonstrations, but only to honor the memory of the late president Beneš, and that they were unaware of the ban on placing wreaths at the monument to President Masaryk. They also stressed that they had immediately obeyed the SNB officer's warning and left Masarykovo Náměstí.[147] Proving their intention to provoke an incident would therefore be extremely difficult. Moreover, the regime's official favorable view of the late president Beneš made the whole case politically extremely sensitive. The accused's youth was also taken into consideration. After consulting the case with the Ministry of Justice, the Pilsen Public Prosecutor's Office finally decided that "the defendants' actions, as recorded in the file, do not qualify as an illegal gathering under Section 279 of the Criminal Code or under Section 283 of the Criminal Code."[148] The charges against the students were dropped.

The police punishment imposed on the students and other persons arrested on September 8 was relatively mild; however, it was a far cry from the last one. On September 24, the District Action Committee of the National Front in Pilsen-City decided on an out-of-court sentence for all the accused. On September 28, it ordered the State Grammar School in Pilsen to expel all the students who had been arrested and decreed that they be "put to work."[149] A similar letter was also sent to the Škoda Works factory council regarding employees Vladimír Ungerman, Bedřich Marx, and Jaroslav Voříšek, who were to be reassigned to manual labor.[150] Teacher Jan Topinka was to be dismissed from his job and sent to work in a factory.[151]

As soon as the students were released from custody, they sought voluntary work, hoping that this proof of reformation would persuade the authorities to mitigate their punishment by expulsion. The students' parents appealed the District Action Committee's decision.[152] The most successful in this respect were Dagmar Bystřická, Helena Linhartová, and Jindra Hrušková, students of the Faculty of Medicine of Charles University in Pilsen and former classmates of the grammar school students. In their appeal to the Regional Action Committee, they managed to prove that they were not active participants of the demonstration,[153] and their sentence was reduced to time served, plus a verbal reprimand from the Regional Action Committee.[154] Not everyone was so lucky. The Commission for the Purification of Public Life of the National Front Central Action Committee saw no reason for revising the decision to expel the other students.[155] The District Labor Protection Office in Pilsen was therefore able to report that five students from the State Grammar School had been assigned to unskilled labor jobs at the Prazdroj brewery as of September 29, 1948.[156] One of the detained students, Milan Jurčík from the State Industrial School in Pilsen, was assigned to work at the Drexler car repair shop in Pilsen on January 6, 1949.[157]

In this situation, however, public opinion showed its strength. Classmates of the affected students sent a letter of intercession to the Ministry of Education, Sciences and Arts, asking that their expelled classmates be allowed to continue their studies. In reaction to that, the Regional School Board therefore contacted the District Action Committee on January 13 to ask whether the expulsion of the students was permanent.[158] Pursuant to their inquiry, the board of the Action Committee decided on January 20 that "the students' punishment is to be only temporary, and if any of them prove, through effort and hard work, their positive attitude towards the people's democratic regime, they will eventually be allowed to continue their studies."[159] The local officials thus used the case of the allegedly misguided youth as an opportunity to demonstrate their leniency. The case also clearly shows that the definitions as to who qualified as an enemy of the regime was not yet quite fixed and clear-cut; they were being continuously redefined based on specific instances of social conflict.

Surprisingly, however, some segments of the working class expressed sympathy with the students. Not long after the January decision of the Action Committee, the factory council at the Pilsner Breweries—Prazdroj national enterprise sent a report regarding the students' conduct in their new jobs, stating that the students at the State Grammar School assigned to work in our plant were working "to the complete satisfaction of both their coworkers and the plant administration."[160] The Drexler factory employees' council also asked that apprentice Jurčík, who had been expelled from the industrial school the previous year, "be allowed to continue his studies, given that he has consistently shown exemplary conduct and a decidedly positive attitude towards the people's democratic regime."[161] Pursuant to these workers' resolutions, the District Action Committee decided on March 25, 1949, to allow the affected students to continue their studies, as it had become convinced that "said students will continue to maintain their positive attitude toward labor and the working class."[162] On April 13, 1949, both schools were asked to readmit the previously expelled students.[163] The expelled students at the State Grammar School all managed to graduate in 1949 and 1950 respectively, though most of them with poor grades.[164]

The response to the events in Prague and Pilsen during Edvard Beneš's state funeral was overwhelming. People were still accustomed to talking openly about their experiences in the workplace. They were aware of possible risks, since the official press labeled such conversations as rumor-mongering propaganda of the reactionaries, but self-censorship was not yet as firmly ingrained as it became in the 1950s. People had not yet fully grasped the danger of possible denunciation; ironically, this even included some of the informers who had failed to anticipate the consequences of reporting their coworkers to the authorities.

On the morning of September 9, for example, a lively debate occurred just before the start of shift among the workers in the maintenance office of the Škoda Works in Pilsen regarding the previous day's events. Anna Turiňská, a clerk who lived opposite the building of the Communist Party Secretariat, began to relate openly what she had seen with her own eyes the day before: how they "tried to catch the people who tried to carry the wreath to the monument. She said that they were carrying a beautiful wreath, but they were not allowed to put it there. [. . .] She also said that she had seen a young man being caught and that they took the poor boy somewhere. She said that she saw young people getting arrested by the monument and being taken away."[165] Everyone in the office agreed with her sentiments. The clerk Vladimír Sýkora, who had only been working in the office a week and did not know any of his coworkers all that well, joined in the conversation by offering a comment regarding Prime Minister Antonín Zápotocký's speech, broadcast live from Prague. He said: "Did you hear that thing on the radio yesterday? I mean when they announced that they'd come about a third of the way down on Wenceslas Square, did you hear the ruckus that broke out there? Something must have happened. And what a ruckus there was, after all, something had broken out there. And what did Zápotocký do? The cheek of that man, talking politics over a coffin. He should be ashamed. I was half expecting him to say something like 'Thank God you're dead, you filthy reactionary,' or something. He can sure pretend he's all moved and mournful."[166]

The whole discussion was overheard by another employee, Drahomíra Baumbruková, who diligently jotted everything down and reported it to the Škoda Works factory militias. Criminal charges were then filed against Sýkora on September 20 for insulting the prime minister, which allegedly constituted the crime of sedition under Section 300 of the Criminal Code and spreading false rumors under Section 18 of the Law for the Protection of the Republic. On trial before the Regional Court in Pilsen, Sýkora denied making any subversive statements. The remaining employees also testified that they had been too focused on their work and had no time for political debates. It was a testament to the employees' solidarity and friendliness that all of them not only deliberately covered for Sýkora, whom they barely knew considering he had only been working with them a week, but many of them made insinuations as to the work ethic of Ms. Baumbruková, who, they said, "spends most of her time with her nose in a book and [therefore] has the opportunity to follow [political] debates [unlike the rest of us]."[167] On December 9, the Regional Court therefore acquitted Sýkora of all charges.[168]

Open debates concerning the state funeral and the commemorative ceremony occurred not only among office employees but also among workers in factories. Josef Troch, shunter at the Škoda Works, was often in the habit of criticizing the political situation among his coworkers, even though most of them were communist sympathizers. Until September 8, the differences in opinion had no impact on his friendship with some of his colleagues. In the days following the state funeral, however, the smear campaign waged by the communists in factories against the alleged enemies of the regime bore its fruit, and Troch's behavior was reported to higher places as subversion of work morale. During the subsequent investigation, Troch's coworkers testified that on September 7, after reading the Communist Party's invitation to the official commemoration ceremony on Náměstí Republiky, Troch snidely remarked: "If the Communists have issued a decree, it must only be for the Communists, so I guess no one else will be allowed to go."[169] He went on to say that "he wouldn't go anyway, since it was just for the Communists, and he would rather go to Prague. [. . .] I'm not going to listen to any of that hogwash; I'd rather go home."[170] After being warned that he could be prosecuted for such talk, he replied, "It won't be long before all you Communists are locked up."[171] The following morning, he criticized the measures preventing people from going to Prague: "I have no idea why they won't let people go to Prague. Anyone should be able to go if they want to. If I wanted to go there, no one would stop me."[172] He also expressed the hope that some kind of a protest would break out in Prague: "They might just start brawling after the funeral. They could also beat the cops while they're at it. There will be people with guns in their pockets, I'm sure."[173]

The indictment filed by the State Prosecutor's Office in Pilsen on November 5 accused Troch of the crime of spreading false rumors under Section 18 of the Law for the Protection of the Republic. Particularly interesting about the whole case was the fact that Troch's coworkers apparently had no idea how much trouble they were going to get their comrade into, and probably regretted their actions later. Although they repeated their testimony before the Regional Court in Pilsen, most of them mentioned a number of mitigating circumstances that had not previously appeared in the police files. Most of the prosecution's witnesses, for example, expressed doubts as to whether Troch had intended to incite anyone at all with his statements. Many witnesses said that "they were more like friendly arguments rather than serious talk."[174] One witness even suggested that he might have misheard, and the defendant might have said something completely different. Despite that, Josef Troch was sentenced to eight weeks in prison on November 30, 1948.

Like the common people, the Communist Party leadership also responded to the events of September 3–8, 1948. General Secretary Rudolf Slánský summarized the events of the past few days at a meeting of the Presidium of the Central Committee on September 9. Besides the Prague protests, he also mentioned the Pilsen incident. He particularly praised the fact that the mobilization in factories had significantly changed the mood among the workers, who had recently begun to criticize shortages in supply and in many cases had been persuaded by the enemies' arguments: "We know from experience that once the regime itself is put in question, everything else falls to the wayside."[175] In his view, it was high time "to take decisive action against the reactionaries."[176] Following a preliminary agreement with Klement Gottwald, Slánský then proposed to use the defeat of the opponents of the regime to take even more vigorous action against them. The resolutions that were subsequently adopted marked a significant turning point in that they strengthened the repressive nature of the post-February regime in Czechoslovakia. The first stage was to be a campaign to expose the alleged nefarious plans of the enemies during the state funeral. The next measure was to speedily adopt a law regarding the establishment of forced labor camps, where the regime intended to send those opponents who had technically done nothing illegal for which they could be prosecuted. Members of the bourgeoisie were to be evicted from the centers of large cities, which was meant to prevent any further protests similar to those of September 3–8, and incidentally solve the current housing shortage.

In the regions, these instructions were almost immediately implemented by defining specific tasks. On September 13, the Presidium of the KSČ Regional Committee in Pilsen adopted a *Resolution on suppressing saboteurs and rumor-mongers*, which included the following instructions: "Continue a thorough purge within the Sokol organization. [. . .] Identify and take action against all rumor-mongers and alarmists."[177] At a meeting of the presidium of the KSČ Regional Committee on September 27, it was decided to evict 30 profiteers from Pilsen within a week, and to prepare "a labor camp for 200 profiteers."[178] It was characteristic of the legal practice in post-war Czechoslovakia that the law on forced labor camps had not yet been approved at this time and did not come into force until November

17, 1948. Nevertheless, the Council of the Central National Committee in Pilsen approved the initiative to establish a labor camp for alleged idlers and profiteers as early as October 1. A proposal was also approved for the Central National Committee to assess the size of apartments owned or rented by persons suspected of profiteering, based on unduly strict criteria. Those whose apartments were found to be oversized would either be evicted, or their apartments would be confiscated.[179] The aforementioned measures were accompanied by a massive press campaign against the so-called reactionaries, which began with the publication of factory resolutions demanding severe punishment for the alleged provocateurs at the state funeral.[180] These resolutions were used as a pretext for announcing the establishment of the Pilsen forced labor camp, claiming that the decision was adopted "by popular demand."[181]

The September 1948 protests in Pilsen clearly showed that the party and security apparatuses had successfully learned their lesson from the May events and were therefore able to effectively prevent the escalation of public protests into open demonstrations. In the following years, the police further improved their methods of preventing and dispersing protest gatherings on official occasions, and eventually managed to completely eliminate this type of unrest.

Although the protest in September 1948 failed to develop into an open demonstration, the people's behavior in the city center clearly indicated that the culture of protest formed in the pro-American riots of May 1948 was adopted and internalized by a relatively large number of citizens who then consciously attempted to build on it. One can therefore speak of a certain continuity within the protest movement. This time, some of the protesters were fueled by indignation, because as supporters of President Beneš, they felt that his legacy was being abused to legitimize the Communist Party's post-1948 policies. This was openly articulated in a number of illegal leaflets. The protesters attempted to promote alternative interpretations of the late president's legacy, which they symbolically expressed, for example, by ignoring the official catafalque intended for laying wreaths. However, the ranks of the protesters were also bolstered by a number of people who, confused by the two competing interpretations of Beneš's legacy, had no idea that they were engaging in activities that would soon be classified as illegitimate or even illegal. The social conflict as to the degree of continuity between the state socialist regime and the pre-1948 conditions was not yet clearly articulated, and participation in the protests could therefore seem fully acceptable even to people who were entirely loyal to the regime.

The police merely ordered students away from the forbidden areas, and the protest march was only dispersed due to a more vigorous and spontaneous intervention by a group of civilian workers supporting the Communist Party. This event clearly illustrates how deeply divided society was in September

1948. Some of the workers in Pilsen were triggered in their indignation by the party's intensive campaign warning against possible provocations during the commemoration ceremony. However, their irritation was by no means permanent and did not affect all workers, as evidenced by subsequent resolutions issued by workers in factories where the punished students had been sent to work, supporting their return to school. The deliberately hyped-up class antagonism, fueled by party propaganda and genuine workers' fears of losing what they had gained during the 1945 revolution, seemed to recede into the background, especially where members of the various social and professional groups interacted on a personal or professional level.

Finally, we should note that the initiative of some workers in intervening against the protesters in May and September 1948 was only seemingly in contradiction with the frequent workers' protests in 1949–1953, which will be discussed in chapter 2. The two types of protests were inherently different, utilized by different segments of society and motivated by different social conflicts. The majority of workers in September 1948 did not sympathize with the protesting students and even shared a certain antipathy toward the noisy actions of the non-working youth. A certain symbiosis between the strike and protest cultures therefore only emerged in Pilsen in June 1953, when the interests of different segments of society temporarily intersected.

The years 1948–1949 were a transitional period in the dynamic transformation of society which spurred a specific type of public collective action that tended to emerge during official, state-organized events, to which they offered a protest alternative. These incidents manifested the dissatisfaction of a certain segment of the population with the discontinuity of the state socialist regime established in February 1948 with the era of the Third Republic (1945–1948) in 1948–1949, as well as their disagreement with the country's nearly exclusive orientation on Eastern political models. In West Bohemia, this general social conflict manifested itself through the local people's veneration of the American army that liberated the Pilsen region at the end of World War II. Aside from a small group of supporters of the political opposition and members of the threatened private economic sector, the protesters also included those who merely sympathized with Western culture and lifestyle. Such tendencies were most pronounced among the youth, especially secondary school students, who were among the most active protesters. Cultural impulses from the United States seemed to appeal more to students (often coming from middle-class families) than to working-class youth.

The waves of protests on the anniversary of the city's liberation in May 1948 and during the state funeral of former president Edvard Beneš in September 1948 failed to have a major impact on either the official discourse or practical policies of the post-February regime. However, the protests generated universally understandable patterns of protest action, which were later used by the population in a revolt against the currency reform in June 1953. The public demonstrations of 1948–1949 became a major inspiration for the riots in the streets of Pilsen. In 1953, the population used improvised, alternative commemoration ceremonies to form public gatherings. As before, they gathered at important symbolic locations—the monument to the fallen American soldiers and the National Liberation Monument. Just as before, they decorated the sites and used similar slogans. Finally, the people's memories of the 1948 demonstrations and the way they were dispersed led the protesting crowd five years later to take a much more aggressive approach to undercover police and provocateurs attempting to infiltrate their gatherings.

NOTES

1. Cf. Zdeněk Štěpánek, *Utajené povstání 1953* (Prague: Michael, 1993).
2. Oldřich Tůma, "Protirežimní demonstrace v Praze," in *Opozice a odpor proti komunistickému režimu v Československu 1969–1989*, ed. Petr Blažek (Prague: Dokořán, 2005), 140–157.
3. Decree of the President of the Republic of 19 June 1948, No. 1178/1948 Ú.l.
4. Karel Kaplan, *Tábory nucené práce v Československu v letech 1948–1954* (Prague: ÚSD AV ČR, 1992), 79–81; Václav Průcha, ed., *Hospodářské a sociální dějiny Československa 1918–1992. II. díl* (Brno: Doplněk, 2009), 262–263; Jiří Knapík, *V zajetí moci: Kulturní politika, její systém a aktéři 1948–1956* (Prague: Libri, 2006), 29–39.
5. Cf. Karel Kaplan, *Poslední rok prezidenta: Edvard Beneš v roce 1948* (Prague: ÚSD AV ČR 1993).
6. Scott, *Domination and the Arts of Resistance*, 192.
7. Tomáš Pasák, "Demonstrace 28. října v Praze," *Pražský sborník historický* 14, no. 1 (1981): 120–147; Tomáš Pasák, "Pražská protifašistická demonstrace českého studentstva v listopadu 1939 a její důsledky," *Pražský sborník historický* 18, no. 1 (1985): 65–97.
8. ABS, f. A2/1, sv. 1861; Jiří Pernes, *Brno 1951: Příspěvek k dějinám protikomunistického odporu na Moravě* (Prague: ÚSD AV ČR, 1997).
9. ABS, f. 310, sv. 310–70–11; Miloš Trapl, *Prostějovský "Černý pátek" 10. dubna 1953* (Prostějov: Městský úřad Prostějov, 1998); Miloš Trapl, *Osudy sochy* (Prostějov: Městský úřad Prostějov, 1999).
10. Kevin McDermott, "Popular Resistance in Communist Czechoslovakia," 287–307.
11. Jakub Šlouf, "Proamerické demonstrace v Plzni 5.–6. Května 1948: 'Nesneseme v republice štvaní proti Americe!'," in *Třetí odboj: Kapitoly z dějin protikomunistické rezistence v Československu v padesátých letech 20. století*, ed. Václav Weber (Prague: ÚSTR, 2010), 83–103.
12. Ivan Martinovský, ed., *Dějiny Plzně v datech: Od prvních stop osídlení až po současnost* (Prague: Nakladatelství Lidové noviny, 2004), 439.

13. Bartošek and Pichlík, *Američané v západních Čechách*, 142–146, 177–183; Bartošek and Pichlík, *Hanebná role amerických okupantů*, 30–34; NA, f. ÚV KSČ – 1261/2/28, a. j. 75, Report on the activities of the Youth Commission of the KSČ Regional Committee in Pilsen, March 4, 1946; Ibid., a. j. 25, Minutes of the meeting of representatives of the Regional Youth Commissions of the Communist Party, December, 15, 1945

14. Jakub Šlouf, "'Nechceme svaz mládeže, když má rudé otěže!': Politický život pražských a Plzeňských středoškoláků v letech 1945–1948," *Soudobé dějiny*, no. 4 (2011): 627–668.

15. "Kdo je iniciátorem studentských demonstrací," *Pravda*, March 22, 1946, 3; "Jaký duch straší mezi Plzeňským studentstvem," *Pravda*, March 23, 1946, 3; "Ideová výchova pana profesora," *Svobodný směr*, March 26, 1946, 2.

16. Šlouf, "Nechceme svaz mládeže," 627–668.

17. Boris Mareš, "Studentský hlasatel: SČM: KSR," *Studentský hlasatel*, September 14, 1946, 5; Jakub Šlouf, "Obraz myšlení západočeských středoškoláků na stránkách nezávislého časopisu Studentský hlasatel (1946–1947)," in *Sborník k poctě Evy a Karla Waskových, západočeských archivářů*, ed. Marie Wasková (Pilsen: M. Wasková, 2011), 290–295.

18. ABS, f. KS MV Pilsen, sv. S–6257, Copy of the statement of Vlasta Bejčková taken down at the headquarters of the Rokycany SNB station March 19, 1948; SOA Pilsen, f. KAV NF Pilsen, kart. 15, inv. č. 25, Stanislav Martínek's case file.

19. SOkA v Blovicích, f. OS Pilsen, zn. T I 659/49; ABS, f. 305, sv. 305–46–7; NA, f. StS Praha, zn. Or. I 4/1948; Šlouf, ",Nechceme svaz mládeže," 627–668.

20. SOA Pilsen, f. KV ČSM Pilsen, kart. 1, inv. č. 3, Minutes of the meeting of the Regional Committee of the Czech Youth Union in Pilsen, November 11, 1948.

21. Cf. Pecka, *Na demarkační čáře*; Jílek, ed., *Národní odboj a politické, kulturní a vojenské aspekty*; Jan Boštík, ed., *Jak to bylo s osvobozením Plzně?: Protifašistický odboj v Plzni za druhé světové války a květnové povstání Pilsenanů v roce 1945* (Prague: Orego, 2012).

22. SOA Pilsen, f. KV KSČ Pilsen, Krajská disciplinární komise, kart. 570, č. 240; Ibid., kart. 639, č. 3467.

23. Ibid., kart. 534, č. 94, Circular of the Permanent Inter-Ministerial Committee for the 1948 celebrations of the Ministry of Information, March 25, 1948.

24. Ibid., Circular of the Provincial Public Awareness Council in Prague, April 2, 1948.

25. Ibid., investigation of the protests of May 5, 1948.

26. Ibid., Memo of the Pilsen Public Awareness Council, April 30, 1948.

27. In March 1946, a press shootout broke out between the Communist regional daily *Pravda* and the student councils of Pilsen's secondary schools over the removal of Stalin's portraits from classrooms. "Kdo je iniciátorem studentských demonstrací," *Pravda*, March 22, 1946, 3; "Jaký duch straší mezi Plzeňským studentstvem," *Pravda*, March 23, 1946, 3; "Ideová výchova pana profesora," *Svobodný směr*, March 26, 1946, 2.

28. SOA Pilsen, f. KV KSČ Pilsen, kart. 534, č. 94, Minutes of the meeting of the organizers of the May Revolution celebrations in Pilsen, April 29, 1948

29. Jakub Šlouf, "Byly Plzeňské demonstrace v červnu 1953 vyprovokovány spolupracovníkem StB?: Životní příběh kamelota Josef Fencla (1909–1979)," in *České, slovenské a československé dějiny 20. století VI*, ed. Sylva Sklenářová (Ústí nad Orlicí: Oftis, 2012), 85–96.

30. SOA Pilsen, f. KS Pilsen, kart. 250, zn. Tk X 879/1948, Josef Fencl's police statement, May 5, 1948.

31. ABS, f. 305, sv. 305–19–4, Telegram from the StB Regional Office in Pilsen to the StB Headquarters in Prague, May 5, 1948, 4.30 p.m.

32. SOA Pilsen, f. KS Pilsen, kart. 250, zn. Tk X 879/1948, Vladimír Drozda's police statement, May 6, 1948.

33. The ceremonial laying of the foundation stone of the U.S. Army Memorial in Pilsen took place on May 5, 1947, in the presence of U.S. Ambassador Lawrence Steinhardt.

34. For example, a large portrait of former U.S. president F. D. Roosevelt with the inscription "In grateful memory of the arrival of our liberators" was brought to the monument by the aforementioned Josef Fencl. SOA Pilsen, f. KS Pilsen, kart. 250, zn. Tk X 879/1948, Josef Fencl's police statement, May 6, 1948.

35. Ibid., Ladislav Langmajer's police statement, May 5, 1948.

36. Šlouf, "Byly Plzeňské demonstrace," 85–96.

37. ABS, f. 305, sv. 305–19–4, Telegram from the StB Regional Office in Pilsen to the StB Headquarters in Prague, May 5, 1948, 4.30 p.m.

38. SOA Pilsen, f. KS Pilsen, kart. 250, zn. Tk X 879/1948, Karel Urban's police statement, May 7, 1948.

39. Vladimír Havlic, *Památník národního osvobození v Plzni: Z materiálů archivu historie a obnovy památníku* (Pilsen: Karel Veselý, 1999), 108; Martinovský, ed., *Dějiny Plzně v datech*, 329.

40. Martinovský, ed., *Dějiny Plzně v datech*, 323–326.

41. SOA Pilsen, f. KS Pilsen, kart. 250, zn. Tk X 879/1948, Vlastimil Kraus's police statement, May 8, 1948.

42. Ibid., Summary report of the SNB Regional Office in Pilsen to the State Prosecutor's Office in Pilsen,.

43. Ibid., zn. Tk X 879/1948.

44. Ibid.

45. Ibid., Karel Urban's police statement, May 7, 1948.

46. Ibid., zn. Tk X 879/1948.

47. Ibid., Vladimír Drozda's police statement, May 6, 1948.

48. SOA Pilsen, f. KS Pilsen, kart. 250, zn. Tk X 876/48.

49. *NA*, f. ÚV KSČ – 1261/0/32, sv. 32, a. j. 217, Letter from Jaromír Hrbek to Marie Švermová, June 19, 1948.

50. ABS, f. 305, sv. 305–19–4, Telegram from the StB Regional Office in Pilsen to the StB Headquarters in Prague, May 6, 1948, 11:50 a.m.

51. Ibid., Telegram from the StB Regional Office in Pilsen to the StB Headquarters in Prague, May 7, 1948 12.30 a.m.

52. SOA Pilsen, f. KS Pilsen, kart. 250, zn. Tk X 876/48, Staff Sergeant's Rudolf Mařík's police statement, May 10, 1948.

53. Ibid., Václav Jelínek's police statement, May 11, 1948; Ibid., Josef Novák's police statement, May 8, 1948; Ibid., interrogation of witness Oldřich Mestek, May 5, 1948.
54. Ibid., kart. 250, zn. Tk X 876/48.
55. ABS, f. 305, sv. 305–19–4, Telegram from the StB Regional Office in Pilsen to the StB Headquarters in Prague, May 7, 1948, 12:30 a.m.
56. Ibid., Telegram No. 182 from the StB Regional Office in Pilsen to the StB Headquarters in Prague, May 7, 1948 11.55 p.m.
57. Ibid., f. KS MV Pilsen, sv. S 5873, Summary report, May 6, 1949.
58. Ibid., f. 305, sv. 305–19–4, Telegram from the StB Regional Office in Pilsen to the StB Headquarters in Prague, May 7, 1948, 12:30 a.m.
59. Ibid., Summary report of the SNB Regional Office in Pilsen to the State Prosecutor's Office in Pilsen, May 14, 1948.
60. Ibid., f. KS MV Pilsen, sv. S 5873, List of persons investigated for participating in the protests on May 5–6, 1948.
61. SOA Pilsen, f. KS Pilsen, kart. 250, zn. Tk X 879/1948; Ibid., zn. Tk X 870/1948; Ibid., zn. Tk X 920/1948.
62. Ibid., f. KV KSČ Pilsen, kart. 25, Minutes of the plenary session of the KSČ Regional Committee, May 10, 1948.
63. Ibid., f. KS Pilsen, kart. 250, zn. Tk X 879/1948; Ibid., zn. Tk X 870/1948; Ibid., zn. Tk X 920/1948.
64. ABS, f. KS MV Pilsen, sv. S 5873, Anonymous letter to the American ambassador, May 9, 1948.
65. SOA Pilsen, f. KAV NF Pilsen, kart. 15, Resolution of the local KSČ organization in Pilsen-Lobzy, sent to the National Front District Action Committee in Pilsen-City, May 24, 1948.
66. Ibid., f. KS Pilsen, kart. 250, zn. Tk X 879/1948; Ibid., zn. Tk X 870/1948; Ibid., zn. Tk X 920/1948.
67. Ibid., f. KAV NF Pilsen, kart. 1, Minutes of the meeting of the presidium of the National Front Regional Action Committee, May 8, 1948; Ibid., f. KV KSČ Pilsen, Krajská disciplinární komise, kart. 534, č. 94.
68. Ibid., f. KAV NF Pilsen, kart. 15, Resolution of the local KSČ organization in Pilsen-Lobzy, sent to the National Front District Action Committee in Pilsen-City, May 24, 1948.
69. Ibid., List of students ("Final Exams Deferral").
70. Ibid., Petition of classes VIII. A and VIII. B of the State Secondary Grammar School in Pilsen, sent to the National Front District Action Committee in Pilsen-City, June 5, 1948.
71. Decree of the President of the Republic of 19 June 1948, No. 1178/1948 Ú.l.
72. SOA Pilsen, f. KAV NF Pilsen, kart. 15, Report of the National Front District Action Committee in Pilsen-City to all schools concerned, June 10, 1948.
73. SOA Pilsen, f. KAV NF Pilsen, kart. 15, Meeting of students and their parents, June 15, 1948.
74. AMP, f. OA Plzeň, 4 c 219, final exam records, 1948.
75. SOA Pilsen, f. KAV NF Pilsen, kart. 15, purge in schools.

76. SOA Pilsen, f. KV KSČ Pilsen, kart. 25, Minutes of the plenary session of the KSČ Central Committee, May 10, 1948.

77. "Volby do Národního shromáždění v květnu 1948," Zprávy Státního úřadu statistického Republiky československé 29, no. 67 (1948): 505–515.

78. NA, f. ÚV KSČ - 1261/0/3, sv. č. 2, a. j. č. 125, Minutes of the meeting of the Central Committee presidium, June 4, 1948.

79. SOA Pilsen, f. KV KSČ Pilsen, kart. 25, Minutes of the plenary session of the KSČ Central Committee, May 10, 1948.

80. Jakub Šlouf, "Rivalita komunistické strany a sociální demokracie na Plzeňsku v letech 1945–1948: Poválečné dědictví prvorepublikových tradic," in *Bolševismus, komunismus a radikální socialismus v Československu VI*, ed. Zdeněk Kárník and Jiří Kocian (Prague: ÚSD AV ČR, 2012), 113–137; Jakub Šlouf, "Krajské vedení KSČ na Plzeňsku v letech 1945–1948," *Minulostí západočeského kraje* 44, no. 1 (2009): 261–352.

81. Ibid.

82. Marie Švermová, *Memories of* (Prague: Futura, 2008), 187–278.

83. NA, f. ÚV KSČ - 1261/2/5, sv. 32, a. j. 217, Letter from Jaromír Hrbek to Marie Švermová, June 19, 1948.

84. Šlouf, "Krajské vedení KSČ," 261–352.

85. Jakub Šlouf, "KSČ na Plzeňsku v letech 1945–1948: Početnost a struktura členské základny," *Minulostí západočeského kraje* 42, no. 1 (2007): 337–432.

86. "Milí hosté na Plzeňské slavnosti Město svorně s venkovem: Radostná přehlídka budovatelské práce," *Pravda*, July 8, 1952, 1.

87. Hojda and Pokorný, *Pomníky a zapomínky*, 18.

88. ABS, f. KS MV Pilsen, sv. S 5873, Summary report of May 6, 1949.

89. Bartošek and Pichlík, *Hanebná role amerických okupantů*; Bartošek and Pichlík, *Američané v západních Čechách*; Jan Fischer and Zdeněk Eis, *Americká okupace západních Čech v roce 1945* (Prague: Naše Vojsko, 1953).

90. Miroslav Tazler, "Je třeba rozlišovat," *Pravda*, May 29, 1968, 3.

91. SOA Pilsen, f. KV KSČ Pilsen, kart. 176, Minutes of the meeting of the presidium of KV KSČ, April 26, 1968, May 14, 1968 and May 21, 1968; Martinovský, ed., *Dějiny Plzně v datech*, s. 479.

92. ABS, f. A2/3, sv. 2401; SOA Pilsen, f. KV KSČ Pilsen, kart. 179, Minutes of the meeting of the presidium of KV KSČ, May 6, 1969. "Oslava památného výročí," *Pravda*, May 6, 1969, 1; "Západočeští poslanci se sdružují," *Pravda*, May 7, 1969, 1; "Informace správy Veřejné bezpečnosti: K událostem 5. května v Plzni," *Pravda*, May 7, 1969, 2.

93. Martinovský, ed., *Dějiny Plzně v datech*, 515.

94. Hojda and Pokorný, *Pomníky a zapomníky*, 236.

95. Helena Baťková, "*Plzeňské povstání 1953 a jeho důsledky*" (PhD diss., Univerzita Karlova v Praze, 2002), 86.

96. Cf. Kaplan, *Poslední rok prezidenta*; Kaplan, *Tábory nucené práce*.

97. Martinovský, ed., *Dějiny Plzně v datech*, 439.

98. Václav Veber, *Osudové únorové dny 1948* (Prague: Nakladatelství Lidové noviny, 2008), 326–344.

99. Pavel Hrabic and Zdeněk Hrabic, *Vila pana prezidenta: Historie rodinného sídla Edvarda Beneše v letech 1929–2001* (Prague: Nakladatelství Erika, 2005), 102–108.

100. Kaplan, *Poslední rok prezidenta*, 67–72.

101. NA, f. ÚV KSČ – 1261/0/3, sv. 3, a. j. 132, Minutes of the meeting of the presidium of ÚV KSČ, September 9, 1948.

102. Ibid., f. MV NA, kart. 44, inv. č. 26, č. 2262, Situational report on the death of Edvard Beneš, 1948; Ibid., f. ÚV KSČ – 1261/0/32, sv. 25, a. j. 178, Daily News, September 1948.

103. Ibid., sv. 214, a. j. 1343, Minutes of the preparatory meeting of the Prime Minister's Office prior to Edvard Beneš's state funeral, September 20, 1948; Ibid., f. ÚV KSČ – 1261/0/3, sv. 3, a. j. 132, Minutes of the meeting of the presidium of ÚV KSČ, September 9, 1948.

104. Ibid., f. ÚV KSČ – 1261/0/32, sv. 25, a. j. 178, Daily news, September 8, 1948.

105. Kaplan, *Poslední rok prezidenta*, 72–83; Věra Olivová and Alena Šubrtová, *Tryzna za Edvarda Beneše 1998* (Prague: Společnost Edvarda Beneše, 1998), 47.

106. NA, f. ÚV KSČ – 1261/0/32, sv. 25, a. j. 178, Daily news, September 7, 1948.

107. AMP, f. MV KSČ Pilsen, kart. 37, Minutes of the meeting of the presidium of OV KSČ Pilsen-City, September 4, 1948.

108. NA, f. ÚV KSČ – 1261/0/32, sv. 25, a. j. 178, Instruction No. 1 ze September 4, 1948.

109. Ibid., Instruction No. 7 of September 7, 1948.

110. Ibid., *Daily News*, September 8, 1948.

111. Ibid.

112. Ibid., *Daily News*, September 9, 1948; PA Škoda, f. Pilsen, kart. 159, Resolution of the ROH factory committee of September 8, 1948.

113. "Jednotní vzdáme poslední čest," *Pravda*, September 8, 1948, 1.

114. SOA Pilsen, f. KS Pilsen, kart. 760, Tk VII 1434/1948.

115. AMP, f. ÚNV Pilsen, kart. 205, Report of the Regional Office of the StB in Pilsen to the Security Department of the Central Committee of the Statutory City of Pilsen, January 10, 1948.

116. SOA Pilsen, f. KS Pilsen, kart. 760, Tk VII 1420/1948.

117. SOA Pilsen, f. KAV NF Pilsen, kart. 23, Report of the Regional Office of the StB in Pilsen to the OAV NF Pilsen-City "Provocations during the national mourning," October 13, 1948.

118. Jakub Šlouf, *Podvedená strana: Zrod masového komunistického hnutí na Plzeňsku, jeho disciplinace, centralizace a byrokratizace (1945–1948)* (Pilsen: Západočeská univerzita v Plzni, 2016), 302.

119. AMP, f. ÚNV Pilsen, kart. 205, Report of the StB Regional Office in Pilsen to the StB Headquarters in Prague, September 13, 1948.

120. SOA Pilsen, f. KS Pilsen, kart. 760, Tk VIII 1582/1948.

121. AMP, f. ÚNV Pilsen, kart. 205, Report of the StB Regional Office in Pilsen to the StB Headquarters in Prague, September 13, 1948.

122. NA, f. ÚV KSČ – 1261/0/32, sv. 25, a. j. 178, Daily news, September 9, 1948.

123. SOA Pilsen, f. KS Pilsen, kart. 760 (i), Tk VIII 1582/1948.
124. Ibid.
125. SOA Pilsen, f. KAV NF Pilsen, kart. 23, SNB report on the interrogation of Jan Topinka, September 8, 1948.
126. Ibid.
127. "Smuteční slavnosti v obcích a ve školách," *Pravda*, September 7, 1948, 1.
128. SOA Pilsen, f. KS Pilsen, kart. 760, Tk VII 1406/1948, report of the StB Regional Office in Pilsen on the interrogation of Josef Baudyš, September 8, 1948.
129. Ibid., report of the StB Regional Office in Pilsen on the interrogation of Otto Rösch, September 8, 1948.
130. AMP, f. ÚNV Pilsen, kart. 205, Report of the StB Regional Office in Pilsen to the StB Headquarters in Prague, September 13, 1948.
131. SOA Pilsen, f. KS Pilsen, kart. 760, Tk VII 1406/1948, report of the StB Regional Office in Pilsen on the interrogation of Růžena Chlubná, September 8, 1948.
132. Ibid., report of the StB Regional Office in Pilsen on the interrogation of Josef Baudyš, September 8, 1948.
133. Ibid., f. KAV NF Pilsen, kart. 23, Václav Novák' statement for KAV NF Pilsen, September 1948.
134. Ibid., f. KS Pilsen, kart. 760, Tk VII 1406/1948, report of the StB Regional Office in Pilsen on the interrogation of Josef Baudyš, September 8, 1948.
135. Ibid., report of the StB Regional Office in Pilsen on the interrogation of Otto Rösch, September 8, 1948; Ibid., report of the StB Regional Office in Pilsen on the interrogation of Pavel Naxera, September 8, 1948; Ibid., report of the StB Regional Office in Pilsen on the interrogation of Zdeněk Mraček, September 8, 1948.
136. NA, f. ÚV KSČ – 1261/0/32, sv. 25, a. j. 178, Daily news, September 7, 1948.
137. SOA Pilsen, f. KS Pilsen, kart. 760, Tk VII 1406/1948, report of the StB Regional Office in Pilsen on the interrogation of Vladimír Ungerman, September 9, 1948.
138. AMP, f. ÚNV Pilsen, kart. 205, copy of the report of the StB Regional Office in Pilsen to the StB Headquarters in Prague, September 13, 1948.
139. SOA Pilsen, f. KS Pilsen, kart. 760, Tk VII 1406/1948, report of the StB Regional Office in Pilsen on the interrogation of Vladimír Ungerman, September 9, 1948; Ibid., f. KAV NF Pilsen, kart. 23, testimony of Václav Klail, member of the People's Militias in the Škoda Works, 1948.
140. Ibid., f. KS Pilsen, kart. 760, Tk VII 1406/1948, report of the StB Regional Office in Pilsen on the interrogation of Otto Rösch, September 8, 1948; Ibid., report of the StB Regional Office in Pilsen on the interrogation of Karel Voleník, September 8, 1948.
141. AMP, f. ÚNV Pilsen, kart. 205, copy of the report of the StB Regional Office in Pilsen to the StB Headquarters in Prague, September 13, 1948.
142. SOA Pilsen, f. KS Pilsen, kart. 760, Tk VII 1406/1948, report of the StB Regional Office in Pilsen on the interrogation of Vladimír Ungerman, September 9, 1948.
143. Ibid., f. KAV NF Pilsen, kart. 23, Václav Novák' statement for KAV NF Pilsen, September 1948.

144. Ibid., f. PŘ Pilsen, všeobecná registratura, kart. 1279, zn. U-1707, criminal complaint against Vladimír Ungerman, September 9, 1948.

145. ABS, f. KS MV Pilsen, sv. S-5919 Pilsen, List of persons arrested as participants in the demonstration with a wreath in Pilsen, September 1948; *AMP*, f. ÚNV Pilsen, kart. 205, copy of the report of the StB Regional Office in Pilsen to the StB Headquarters in Prague, September 13, 1948; *ABS*, f. 304, sv. 304–254–7, Telegram from the StB Regional Office in Pilsen to the StB Headquarters in Prague, September 9, 1948.

146. SOA Pilsen, f. KS Pilsen, kart. 760, Tk VII 1406/1948, report of the SNB Regional Office in Pilsen to the State Prosecutor's Office in Pilsen, September 10, 1948; AMP, f. ÚNV Pilsen, kart. 205, copy of the report of the StB Regional Office in Pilsen to the StB Headquarters in Prague, September 13, 1948.

147. SOA Pilsen, f. KS Pilsen, kart. 760, Tk VII 1406/1948, report of the StB Regional Office in Pilsen on the interrogation of Pavel Naxera, September 8, 1948.

148. Ibid., f. SZ Pilsen, kart. 247, St 2730/1948, report of the State Prosecutor's Office in Pilsen to the Ministry of Justice, October 27, 1948.

149. Ibid., f. KAV NF Pilsen, kart. 23, Memorandum of the OAV NF Pilsen-City to the State Secondary Grammar School in Pilsen, September 28, 1948.

150. Ibid., Memorandum of the OAV NF Pilsen-City to the Škoda Works Factory Council, September 28, 1948.

151. Ibid., Memorandum of the OAV NF Pilsen-City to the District School Committee in Stříbro, September 28, 1948.

152. Ibid., letter from Pavel Naxera to OAV NF Pilsen-City, October 11, 1948; Ibid., letter from Otto Rösch to OAV NF Pilsen-City, October 11. 1948.

153. Ibid., f. KAV NF Pilsen, kart. 23, Dagmar Bystřická's appeal against the decision of OAV NF Pilsen-City of September 27, 1948; Ibid., Heleny Linertová's appeal against the decision of OAV NF Pilsen-City of September 27, 1948.

154. Ibid., Memorandum of the KAV NF Pilsen to OAV NF Pilsen-City, November 15, 1948.

155. Ibid., report from ÚAV NF Prague to OAV NF Pilsen-City, December 11, 1948.

156. Ibid., report from the District Labor Protection Office in Pilsen to OAV NF Pilsen-City, November 4, 1948.

157. Ibid., report from the District Labor Protection Office in Pilsen to OAV NF 18. 1. 49.

158. Ibid., report from the Provincial School Board in Prague to OAV NF Pilsen-City, January 13, 1949.

159. Ibid., report from the OAV NF Pilsen-City to the Provincial School Board in Prague, January 21, 1949.

160. Ibid., letters from the Pilsen Breweries Factory Council to OAV NF Pilsen-City, February 17 and March 15, 1949.

161. Ibid., letter from the Dresler Employees' Council to OAV NF Pilsen-City, April 7, 1949.

162. Ibid., notice from the OAV NF Pilsen-City to the director of the State Secondary Grammar School in Pilsen, April 13, 1949.

163. Ibid., notice from the OAV NF Pilsen-City to the director of the College of Industrial Engineering in Pilsen, April 13, 1949.

164. AMP, f. SG Pilsen, inv. č. 59, 15 e 26, Final Exam Records, 1948–1950.

165. SOA Pilsen, f. KS Pilsen, kart. 760, Tk VII 1463/1948, report of the StB Regional Office in Pilsen on the interrogation of Drahomíra Baumbruková, September 18, 1948.

166. PA Škoda, f. Pilsen, kart. 36, report of the Škoda Works Factory Guard on the interrogation of Drahomíra Baumbruková, September 16, 1948.

167. SOA Pilsen, f. KS Pilsen, kart. 760, Tk VII 1463/1948, report of the StB Regional Office in Pilsen on the interrogation of Jaroslav Jaroš, September 18, 1948.

168. Ibid., Tk VII 1463/1948.

169. PA Škoda, f. Pilsen, kart. 153, disciplinary file against Josef Trocha, September 8, 1948.

170. Ibid.

171. Ibid.

172. Ibid.

173. Ibid.

174. SOA Pilsen, f. KS Pilsen, kart. 760, Tk VII 1401/1948.

175. NA, f. ÚV KSČ – 1261/0/3, sv. 3, a. j. 132, Minutes of the meeting of the presidium of ÚV KSČ September 9, 1948.

176. Ibid.

177. SOA Pilsen, f. KV KSČ Pilsen, kar. 87, Minutes of the meeting of the presidium of KV KSČ, September 13, 1948.

178. Ibid., Minutes of the meeting of the presidium of KV KSČ, September 27, 1948.

179. AMP, f. NV Pilsen, 29 d 6, Minutes of the meeting of the Central National Committee of the Statutory City of Pilsen, October 1, 1948.

180. "Reakci je každá příležitost dobrá," *Pravda*, September 9, 1948, 2; "Dobrý návrh soudruhů horníků: Pracující lid žádá potrestání provokatérů," *Pravda*, September 10, 1948, 2.

181. "Zřízení pracovních táborů pro flákače," *Pravda*, September 25, 1948, 1; "Krajský akční výbor zakročuje: Šmelináři a flákači do pracovních táborů," *Pravda*, September 26, 1948, 1; "Šmelináři ven z bytů, rozvratníci do pracovních táborů," *Pravda*, October 1, 1948, 1.

Chapter 2

Worker Strikes at the Škoda Works in 1949–1953

Strikes of industrial workers were the most widespread form of public collective protest in Czechoslovakia in the years 1948–1953.[1] They were usually isolated incidents that took place inside the factory premises, and only rarely did they turn into open protests in the streets. Such exceptions were, for example, the November 1951 protests against the reduced Christmas bonuses in Brno,[2] or the nationwide wave of resistance against the currency reform in June 1953.[3] Most strikes or work stoppages did not last long and were usually resolved quietly and internally, without involving the State Security or higher party authorities. A substantial part of these conflicts was therefore never extensively documented in writing. Similar incidents occurred in other industrialized countries of the Eastern Bloc at the time.[4]

Immediate causes of the strikes included social issues and supply problems, wage disputes, and unsatisfactory working conditions. For these reasons, the phenomenon of strikes largely escaped the attention of Czechoslovak historians after 1989, who focused mainly on political history; it was a German author, Peter Heumos, who first began researching the issue in more depth.[5] For the first time in Czech historiography, he was able to consistently separate the ideological image of the working class created by the Communist Party from the real lives of the workers, and to view industrial workers as a distinct social group with its own traditions, values, and interests.

Heumos's perspective offered a plausible explanation for the apparent incongruity in the frequency with which worker strikes occurred in the years 1948–1953. Workers were given preferential treatment by the state socialist regime, both on an ideological and material level, which meant that they had seemingly no reason or cause to protest. A deeper analysis of industrial workers as a social group, however, offered a new possible interpretation of worker strikes, seeing them as a consequence of their social privilege.

Workers protested more than other social groups simply because they could dare to do so; and they protested precisely when they were stripped of some of those social privileges, when social changes disrupted their daily routine, or when long-established traditions in their workplace were violated or abandoned.

In the history of West Bohemia, worker strikes of the Stalinist era carry a special significance, since it was out of this culture of workers' protests that spurred the stormy reaction of local workers to the announcement of the currency reform in 1953. We cannot therefore reliably determine the causes of the Pilsen revolt without a deeper understanding of the gradual development of the situation in Pilsen industrial plants. For the above reasons, this chapters focuses primarily on the connection between the workers' strike movement of the early 1950s and the Pilsen events of June 1953. We will focus on the largest of Pilsen's industrial enterprises, the Škoda Works, where the revolt originated and where most of its protagonists were employed.

WORKERS' ATTITUDE TOWARD THE COMMUNIST PARTY IN 1945–1948

From the interwar period onward, social and political conditions in Pilsen were strongly influenced by the fact that the city was home to the core plants of Škoda Pilsen, a world-renowned engineering concern which employed tens of thousands of workers and whose influence transcended not only the borders of the region but also the entire country. Even then, the Škoda Works were sort of a world unto their own, a distinctive entity that was largely beyond the reach of local political authorities but had a tremendous impact on social development within its sphere of influence.[6] In April 1945, this symbiotic coexistence of the city and the company was temporarily disrupted by an Allied air raid which severely damaged the main Škoda plant.[7] In the post-war period, however, the rebuilt factory quickly regained its international presence and importance. In the meantime, the political situation had changed, and the company's ownership and organizational structures had been entirely transformed: in October 1945, key industrial enterprises in Czechoslovakia were nationalized.[8]

After the nationalization of the key industries, the privileged position of the Škoda plants within the country's economic structure created an unprecedented degree of self-confidence in the workers themselves. Their privileged social status, already supported by the current ideology, social and political factors, was further bolstered by the fact that they were virtually indispensable for the successful rebuilding of the bombed-out factory. The need to rebuild the factory was in fact the most decisive argument for its nationalization.[9]

The fact that it was not entirely clear why the Škoda plants had even been targeted by bombing greatly supported the anti-American propaganda in the region after 1946.[10]

After the war, decision-making power in the Pilsen Škoda plants was seized by the factory council, a revolutionary body established in May 1945 and later legalized as a representative body of the employees.[11] A number of projects were implemented during the post-war crisis under the auspices of the council that provided the workers with basic necessities outside the scope of the standard supply system (food, clothing). The council also set up several social funds from which workers were paid substantial sums. Being an employee of the Škoda Works thus provided the workers with disproportionately greater social security than those working for smaller enterprises.

In 1945, the employees' demands for greater involvement in the company's management and in activities of the factory council were in line with the Communist Party's policies. Members of the factory council were mostly communists, which meant that as early as May 1945, they began building a systematic structure of party organizations within the factory.[12] All former trade union organizations established by various political parties were disbanded during the Second Republic, and a unified Revolutionary Trade Union Movement (ROH) was created after the war, which essentially eliminated direct political competition in the factory. This made it relatively easy to eliminate the strong influence that social democracy traditionally had within the enterprise.[13] Communist recruitment at the Škoda Works proceeded with astonishing speed. By mid-September 1945, 9,297 out of a total of 12,000 employees joined the party.[14] The factory organization became so powerful that it was actually granted the status of a separate district within the party structure.[15] Unfortunately, data regarding membership in other political parties within the factory for the years 1945–1948 is lacking, since other political parties were mainly organized on a local basis, rather than within factories.

The Communist Party's dominant position within the factory palpably affected the political development of the entire region in 1945–1948. Its large membership within the factory meant that the party had an easily mobilizable force at hand right in the center of the region. The communists often used it as a ready pool of volunteer workers (e.g., during the post-war rebuilding of the town and factory, during coal shortages and harvests, or to aid in the implementation of the two-year economic plan). They then capitalized on these actions, using them as an alleged proof that it was their party that deserved the greatest credit for the economic reconstruction of the city and country. Škoda workers also actively participated in the demonstrations organized in the city streets by the Communist Party in June 1946 and February 1948.[16] Some of them even later helped pacify protests by other groups in May and September 1948.

This kind of collaboration between workers employed in the Škoda Works and the Communist Party was, however, contingent on the fact that it benefited both sides for the time being, and never evolved into a stronger alliance. In some cases, the factory workers did not hesitate to strike for their social demands without consulting the political officials. In October 1945, for example, some of the Škoda workers went on a spontaneous strike, demanding additional ration coupons for hard workers.[17]

Moreover, the workers at the Škoda works were by no means universally sympathetic toward the Communist Party; only a part of the plant's workforce openly supported the communists. This was clearly demonstrated during the first regular elections to the factory council in the spring of 1947. According to the relevant legislation, only a single ballot nominated by the factory committee of the ROH was allowed and needed 80% of the votes to be elected.[18] Voting for the ballot was presented by the trade union as a moral obligation for every employee who supports the country's economic recovery.[19] The ballot included 14 communists, 6 Social Democrats, and 5 National Socialists.[20] Before the elections, however, Social Democrats and National Socialists criticized the way factory councils operated, and successfully organized a boycott of the proposed ticket.[21] The first round of elections on March 28, 1947, was therefore unsuccessful. Out of a total of 21,172 eligible voters, 18,780 came to vote. Only 59.95% (11, 258) voted for the ticket, while a full 38.92% (7,310) of the workers opposed it.[22] The ballot was slightly modified, but the second round of elections, which took place on May 23, 1947, still ended in a stalemate.[23] Approximately 70% of the employees voted the straight ticket this time.[24]

The high number of employees voting against the factory council's ballot indicated that the stratification of political sympathies in the factory was not at all clear in 1947 (as opposed to 1945). Another available indicator that may support this hypothesis is the data on the development of the Communist Party's membership. In the course of 1948, it had undergone two consecutive radical reversals. The post-February purge at the factory was limited to a few exemplary cases. Thirty-five workers were dismissed, and five members of the factory council were removed.[25] Rather than by repression, the Communist Party tried to consolidate its position within the Škoda Works in the first months following the coup by assimilating their political rivals. It therefore launched an intensive (sometimes even coercive) recruitment, especially among factory clerks and members of former non-communist parties. This process culminated in an involuntary merger with the Social Democratic Party in June 1948, officially interpreted as a unification of the working class. Party membership in the factory thus rose from 9,904 to 14,304 between February and December 1948.[26] The average number of factory employees in that year was 26,993 (of whom 21,157 were workers and 5,836 were clerks).[27] As a result of the above measures, approximately 56% of the factory's employees became party members.[28]

At the same time, however, almost a third of the party members were newcomers with varied personal histories on whom the party could not fully rely. At the end of 1948, the party conducted a thorough vetting of its members, and the number of communists in the factory was again reduced to its original level.[29] The membership base in the factory did not substantially increase in the following years, and recruitment was limited exclusively to shock workers (*udarniks*).[30]

This statistical overview shows that the actual number of communists in the factory in 1948 did not exceed the 10,000 from the pre-February days. Moreover, a vast majority of them were recruited in the period of euphoria immediately following May 1945, not during the period of growing social conflict in the years 1946–1948.

We should point out that the atmosphere at the Škoda Works had a strong impact on the situation in the entire city of Pilsen. The mass of nearly 30,000 employees who came from all over West Bohemia was by no means a negligible factor, given that based on the March 1950 census, the city of Pilsen itself had a recorded population of 123,875, of which only 51,110 were gainfully employed.[31]

CONSEQUENCES OF THE IMPLEMENTATION OF THE FIRST FIVE-YEAR PLAN

The coup d'état in February 1948 allowed the Communist Party to take complete control of the state. In the following years, therefore, the lines began to blur between the state and party bodies as to the scope of power and authority. This gradual process also trickled down to the operation of the Škoda Works. In addition to the relevant ministries, day-to-day operation of the factories from the year 1948 onward was managed by the District Committee of the Communist Party of Czechoslovakia (OV KSČ) for the Škoda Works, which was eventually transformed into the KSČ Factory Committee of the Vladimir Ilyich Lenin Factories in Pilsen in December 1951.[32] Factory director František Brabec was also a member of the presidium of these party committees, which ensured a personal connection between factory management and the party.[33] Over the entire period discussed here, the party therefore exerted a major influence on the factory's management.

Conversely, the importance of the once powerful factory council was rapidly declining; its existence was now perceived as unnecessary, as its activities could be taken over by the unified Revolutionary Trade Union Movement (ROH). As early as 1949–1950, therefore, meetings of the factory council and the ROH factory committee were held jointly. The de facto merger of the two bodies, which had begun with the election of the factory council in 1947, when the trade unions had drawn up the ballot for the new factory council, was gradually deepening. From 1949 onward, it was only a matter of time before the formal existence of the factory council came to an end.[34] It was the KSČ District Committee that appointed its candidates to leading positions on the factory council and the ROH factory committee, often against explicit objections of the trade unionists themselves. The party secretariats therefore had the final say in all essential matters of the factory operation.[35]

In addition to the KSČ District Committee, some of the higher party authorities also tried to exert their influence in the factory. Hanuš Lomský, regional secretary of the Communist Party in the years 1949–1950, often presented his demands directly to the factory director.[36] The factory management itself took a non-systemic approach to solving many production problems (e.g., lack of raw materials), trying to use the influence of high party officials in Pilsen with connections outside the region (MPs, head secretary of the KSČ Regional Committee).[37] Such complicated management mechanisms naturally gave rise to various clientelist networks linked to influential people. In the years 1948–1949, an exceptional degree of decision-making power fell into the hands of Josef Dvořák, chairman of the ROH factory organization, and subsequently Miloslav Mudra, chairman of the KSČ factory organization, in 1950–1951. Factory director František Brabec also maintained a fair share of power for the period under scrutiny, that is, 1948–1953. These three usually had the last word in negotiations between key party authorities and in backstage conflicts.

The process of the intermingling of party, trade union, and state bodies had a number of incidental consequences. The Communist Party became an indirect, de facto employer of the staff in the nationalized enterprises. From February 1948 onward, the workers' attitude toward the Communist Party was therefore influenced not only by the promised prospect of social security but also by the new relationship of employee (worker)–employer (Communist Party). As the holder of state power, however, the party was forced to begin implementing certain unpopular measures. However, the principle of the so-called democratic centralism actually eliminated true democratic principles within the party, which means that workers had little influence on the workings of central and local party authorities. They were far from being the masters in the newly nationalized enterprises. In certain conflicts and critical situations, part of Škoda's workforce was just as mistrustful and defensive toward local party representatives as they had previously been toward the management of a private company. The manifestations of the workers' discontent in 1948–1953 could by no means be construed as permanent and universal, yet their frequent outbreaks pointed to a latent incongruity of expectations between the workers and Communist Party representatives.

After February 1948, industrial workers enjoyed a highly privileged position in society. From 1945 onward, for example, workers' wages increased steadily, unlike those of administrative staff.[38] In 1950 workers at the Škoda Works earned more on average (CZK 22.53 per hour) than administrative staff (CZK 20.00–22.40). Workers paid on a piece rate basis earned even more (CZK 25.01), while those with hourly wages earned slightly less (CZK 18.99). Of the factory employees, the only ones who earned slightly more than the piece rate workers were the foremen (CZK 26.50–29.70) and technical clerks (CZK 26.60–29.80).[39] This evening out in wages was actually demanded by the workers themselves, who still considered it insufficient at the time.[40]

Hard manual laborers also received additional economic benefits in the form of various allowances and increased food rations under the still existing wartime coupon system. In 1951, for example, a total of 14,000 employees at the Škoda Works received additional ration coupons for extremely hard labor, and 8,000 for hard labor.[41] The official cult of manual labor gave factory workers unprecedented social prestige. Workers loyal to the party were also given preferential treatment in career advancement. In the years 1949–1950 alone, for example, 1,064 workers were promoted to clerical positions at the Škoda Works. Many workers were also recruited into the National Security Corps, the army, and various positions in the civil service.[42]

However, bolstering the workers' self-confidence had a darker side. The Communist Party found it difficult to find ways to motivate workers to increased productivity. Even so, the pressure exerted on industrial plant workers gradually increased after February 1948. This process was fueled by the economic policy in post-war Czechoslovakia. After the successful completion of the two-year economic plan (1947–1948), the Communist Party proceeded to implement the first five-year economic plan (1949–1953), during which the output of heavy industry was to increase significantly. The bill of October 27, 1948, No. 241/1948 Sb., on the first five-year plan stipulated that by the end of 1953, the national volume of industrial production should increase by 57% compared to 1948, and engineering production by as much as 93%.[43]

The Czechoslovak economy was further reinforced in its focus on developing heavy industry by the deteriorating international political situation that was brought on by the emerging Cold War, which divided the world into two distinct political and economic systems. As a result, the volume of Czechoslovak foreign trade with the developed Western world fell from 80% to 20% between 1947 and 1953.[44] In this situation, Czechoslovakia had to find new markets for its products. With the most advanced industry of the Eastern

Bloc countries and a high number of skilled workers, it seemed a natural solution to make Czechoslovakia the industrial powerhouse of the Council for Mutual Economic Assistance (Comecon, founded on January 5, 1949).

The demand for heavy industrial products was further bolstered by the general arms race.[45] The growing demands on arms production and the fulfillment of Czechoslovakia's commitments in aiding the industrialization of the Eastern Bloc states were seen at the time as a preventative measure against the imminent invasion of Western armies and were therefore given the highest political priority. For these reasons, the production growth plan increased considerably in 1950 and 1951. The existing plan was fundamentally revised by a resolution of the Central Committee of the Communist Party in February 1951. According to the resolution, total industrial production was to increase by 98% by the end of 1953 instead of the original 57%.[46] As investments in armaments increased in 1951, the living standard of a majority of the population began to stagnate.[47]

The situation at the Škoda Works was all the more complicated because of its status as the largest heavy engineering plant in the country, which was reflected in the volume of commitments assigned to it. During the first five-year plan, the newly nationalized enterprise was to generate 25% of the country's heavy engineering production, 10% of precision engineering production, 28% of electrical engineering production, and 38% of steelworks production.[48] However, Škoda's obligations went beyond the fulfillment of the prescribed production volume. The company had to supply machinery to equip newly built and renovated factories, which was absolutely essential for the successful implementation of the nationwide plan. Škoda Works participated in the production of equipment for mines and steelworks, as well as the construction of new industrial complexes in other parts of the country. It was therefore imperative to meet the individual production goals within the prescribed deadlines. These tasks were often seen as a national or international priority, especially because one of the company's most politically sensitive tasks was to manufacture products and equipment for other democratic states, including the USSR. Products for the USSR were therefore given priority and were marked in the workshops with special labels; initially, it was "For express delivery to the Soviet Union,"[49] but for security reasons (fear of sabotage) this was later changed to a simple "urgent" or "essential."[50]

Implementation of the five-year plan was made even more difficult by the ongoing restructuring of the company's production program. The original industrial concern was split up, and on January 1, 1950, the Pilsen plant became an independent national enterprise, Škoda Works Pilsen, which specialized mainly in heavy engineering, iron and steel production.[51] On the anniversary of the birth of Joseph Vissarionovich Stalin in December 1951, the company changed its name to the Vladimir Ilyich Lenin Factories in Pilsen (ZVIL).[52] The wide range of products made by the former concern was gradually reduced, with light engineering generally being replaced by heavy engineering. From 1951 onward, the production program of entire departments was changed (Automatic Machinery, Vehicles and Engineering I), and the plant handed over a number of its established operations to other national enterprises.[53] The change in production required the construction of new production facilities, such as the Gigant shop floor in the Elektrotrakce Doudlevce subsidiary plant, designated for building large electrical machinery, or the TS shop floor in the main plant for heavy engineering production. As the pressure on productivity increased, the factory had to reassign a large number of personnel and faced other technical complications. In 1951 alone, 9,628 personnel transfers were made within the plant.[54] During 1951 and 1952, the plant was to increase its production volume by 40–45%.[55]

Moreover, the factory had to achieve the required results without the possibility of a significant increase in personnel. Between 1950 and 1953, the number of employees in the Pilsen plant rose from 27,272 to only 30,029, which was not nearly enough for the required growth in production volume.[56] Even though several thousand new employees joined the plant every year, a significant number of people quit.[57] The high staff turnover was caused mainly by the lack of available housing and poor working conditions for newcomers. A large number of workers left after the coup d'état in February 1948 to join the National Security Corps or the army, to become members of party secretariats and obtain public (especially economic) posts in the civil service. The factory therefore functioned as a ready source of working-class cadres.[58] The factory also lost a number of skilled workers who were deployed to help build new industrial plants in the Ostrava region and in Slovakia. Many workers retired.[59] Between 1948 and 1950, the factory lost approximately 3,600 skilled workers and continued to experience high attrition in the following years.[60] New employees were mainly women, former farmers, tradesmen, or clerks who had to be retrained for their new professions. The factory therefore admitted a high number of untrained workers while trained employees kept leaving, and the loss of qualified personnel could not be replenished by training apprentices.[61]

The greatest shortage of trained workers was in machine operation. On the other hand, there was a relative surplus of skilled manual piece work workers, who preferred their current assignment to serial machine production. Factory management tried to solve this problem throughout the entire five-year plan, albeit without much success. Rather than forcefully reassigning existing employees, the management attempted to solve the issue by continually increasing the formal requirements for new employees.[62]

Work morale also improved very slowly. During the Nazi occupation, slow work was seen as a means of national resistance, and the attitude still persisted.[63] The workers did not see the nationalized factory as their property.[64] Late arrivals and clocking out early were common. Some workers racked up dozens of unexcused absences in a single year. Drunkenness[65] and disorderly conduct[66] in the workplace were a common occurrence. Employees often went to the pub during working hours or slept on night shifts.[67] Theft of tools and materials from the plant was rampant. Several work crews actually used the plant premises and tools to make washing machines for their own use.[68] Obviously, the surviving records of disciplinary action only represent a fraction of the total number of employees, but they still indicate the multitude of issues the factory faced, which was not conducive to the smooth implementation of the plan.

As new supervision mechanisms were developed and improved, however, work morale showed a decisively upward trend.[69] In 1948, for example, the average weekly number of late arrivals was 2,736; by 1949, this number had dropped to 1,721.[70] Punishment for misconduct was governed by a disciplinary code that allowed the disciplinary commission to impose a warning, a reprimand, or a fine (up to the amount of average daily earnings), and finally, termination of employment. As additional punishment, the names of offenders were published in the factory magazine or on a blackboard in the workshops.[71] In reality, minor punishments prevailed. For a missed shift, a double of that time was deducted from the employee's holiday time, and offenders lost their ration coupons.[72] In extreme cases, workers were threatened with being sent to a labor camp. This punishment was also widely used as a conditional warning (in the case of chronic absenteeism, for example).[73]

For all the aforementioned reasons, fulfilling the tasks imposed by the plan was almost beyond the plant's capabilities. At the end of 1949, the factory was already behind schedule in the delivery of some products.[74] In 1950, the plant was assigned additional tasks in the form of several key contracts.[75] Machine Shop I was a particularly overburdened department and factory management repeatedly discussed its excessive plan in 1950.[76] Due to changes in production programs, production in the department collapsed completely in the following year.[77] In 1951, the factory only managed to meet the overall plan at the cost of a massive reassignment of administrative workers to the production facilities.[78] In 1952, Locomotive Works became another problematic department that was unable to meet the plan, largely because other factories had failed to deliver the sheet metal required for its production.[79]

The political need to meet the plan at any cost led to the considerable disorganization of the production process. The situation can best be illustrated by the measures adopted to save the plan in 1951. On August 20, 1951, factory director František Brabec evaluated the factory's dismal performance at a meeting of the presidium of the KSČ District Committee and asked the committee's permission to implement drastic remedial action. At that time, the factory was short of 3,756 employees. As part of a nationwide program of reassigning administrative workers to production facilities, the factory planned to transfer 900 people (in the end, only 700 of them were actually transferred).[80] A further addition of approximately 1,500 clerks from other enterprises was planned; unfortunately, the new employees were mostly untrained and would therefore not have made a major contribution to fulfilling the plan in 1951. The factory director therefore decided to assign the newcomers to lighter auxiliary jobs and to recruit workers from among the current skilled employees to work the machines. All design work was suspended for the remaining four months of 1951, and 720 technical clerks were sent to work on the lathes. They were joined by hundreds of other trained employees from the ranks of machine fitters. In total, 2,000–2,500 people were temporarily reassigned to work the machines. Such massive transfers obviously did nothing to help the smooth running of production. The technical clerks were chosen based on their previous experience with machine work, which meant that they were mostly former workers who had been promoted to clerical positions for their political loyalty. In this case, therefore, short-term goals of fulfilling the plan outweighed not only long-term efficiency, but also long-term political plans.[81]

WORKERS' RESPONSE TO INCREASED PRODUCTIVITY DEMANDS

The drastic increase in production volume required a much more intensive use of the existing human and material resources. From 1949 onward, the so-called new work methods therefore began to be gradually introduced at the Škoda works (and nationwide). These included, in particular, transition to multi-shift operation, socialist competition, shock worker movement, and stricter performance standards. Introduction of the new methods was initiated by the KSČ District Committee in November 1948,[82] as a response to the critical remarks made by Soviet generals who, on visiting the factory, expressed their surprise that socialist competition was not being implemented on a mass scale.[83]

The new measures provoked resistance from workers at the Pilsen plant and other industrial enterprises in the country.[84] In the following paragraphs, therefore, we will discuss the ways in which the new methods interfered with the daily running of the factory as well as the workers' private lives.

The change to three-shift operation at the end of 1950 was meant to enable the Škoda Works to increase its production volume without having to invest in additional machinery. The existing machines were to be used all day, not just for a single shift. At the same time, the factory planned to reduce power consumption at peak times. In the short term, the factory's production was increased in order to meet the plan; from the long-term perspective, however, continuous operation put more wear and tear on the machinery.

The new measures encountered a number of unexpected obstacles. The introduction of second and third shifts disrupted the employees' personal and family schedules and was obviously not very popular. In addition, approximately half of the employees commuted to Pilsen from further afield and found it difficult to get home at night. In the first days of January 1951, the factory guards had to chase away crowds of workers who came to the morning shift from the gates and tell them to come in the afternoon or in the evening.[85] The factory did not have enough foremen to fully staff all shifts.[86] Productivity during night shifts was therefore generally much lower and many workers (especially young people) actually slept through them.[87] At the beginning of 1951, party reports described the night shifts at the Elektrotrakce Doudlevce subsidiary plant, stating that though the entire shop floor was lit up, only a few people were actually working.[88] As late as December 1951, only 25% of the plant's employees were working second and third shifts,[89] and the situation did not much improve in the following years.[90]

The new work methods were also aimed at a more efficient use of the existing workforce. The previous projects of volunteer brigades evolved in 1949 into an institutionalized form of the so-called socialist competition of both individuals and entire work teams. The competition was intended to spur the workers to achieve the highest possible labor productivity. It was first introduced at those plants where fulfillment of the plan was threatened. At the beginning of January 1949, competition was therefore introduced in the engine production department at the Elektrotrakce Doudlevce subsidiary plant and in the casting production department at the gray cast iron foundry.[91] It was not until the summer of 1949 that the competition movement gained general momentum. Competition was linked to politics through such things as work commitments adopted on various festive occasions, such as Communist Party congresses or various statesmen's jubilees. An employee who crossed the 125% performance threshold was considered an *udarnik* (shock worker).[92]

Many workers, however, understood quite clearly that socialist competition was simply a means of increasing work performance, and were therefore initially reluctant to participate in such schemes. They frequently argued that unlike mass production, piece manufacturing did not allow objective competition. Such objections were raised by workers in Machine Shop II, the Joiner Shop, Pattern Shop, and Machine Tool Shop. Frequent fluctuations in the supply of raw materials and semi-finished products were also considered an obstacle. Last but not least, socialist competition clashed with the general collective spirit in the workshops, because the workers resented the idea of preferential treatment for a select few individuals.[93] Nevertheless, socialist competition was at least formally introduced in all workshops, and even technical clerks and administrative workers were made to participate. By April 1950, a total of 19,587 workers had joined the competition movement at the factory.[94]

Following the example of the Brno region, a movement of special shock worker shifts, inspired by older Soviet practice, began spreading around the country from autumn 1949 onward.[95] The first *udarnik* week at the Škoda Works was declared for October 17–23, 1949.[96] Workers publicly competed in work performance and their achievements were popularized by radio and the press. They routinely exceeded established performance targets by hundreds or even thousands of percent.[97] However, this was often a one-off occurrence that was impossible to sustain day after day, since it required extensive preparation during the previous shift, and often could not be accomplished without the help of other shop employees.

Successful *udarniks* received numerous awards and were presented as role models to other workers. They also earned some material benefits, such as additional food rations. Apart from genuine work enthusiasm, workers were therefore frequently motivated by material reasons to participate in the shock worker movement.[98] Jan Liška commented on this at the presidium of the Party District Committee: "I have a feeling that once we stop giving the *udarniks* benefits, people will lose interest in participating altogether."[99]

The overwhelming majority of shock workers were party members.[100] Initially, the shock work movement was taken up predominantly by young people, and only gradually did some of the more experienced, older workers become involved. It was the age structure that gave rise to frequent conflicts. Many of the older workers were uncomfortable with having someone younger and less qualified as a role model. Photos of the *udarniks* displayed in the workshops were therefore sometimes torn down or spattered with mud[101]

Closely related to these conflicts was the problem of the quality of the shock work.[102] The emphasis on quantitative performance, which found its ultimate expression in the *udarnik* shifts, impaired workers' attention to quality and led to a higher number of rejects. In some cases, employees whose actual work results were questionable were promoted and rewarded as exemplary workers. This in turn provoked resentment among the rest of the workers, who either had no desire to participate in this farce, or whose job content simply did not allow for such outbursts in productivity. Some even resorted to physical altercations. On July 25, 1951, Vojtěch Čermák, who had been declared an exemplary worker, drilled a hole in a boiler in the wrong place. His coworker Karel Kroc snarled at him, "Watch what you're doing, mister perfect worker!"[103] For this taunt, Čermák punched him. However, the disciplinary committee considered Kroc's criticism of Čermák's work an intentional mockery of socialist competition and reprimanded both workers with a warning.

Some party officials were aware of the reasons the *udarniks* were so unpopular and pleaded at party forums for a greater emphasis on product quality. They would say:

> What does the *udarnik* movement actually mean? For some it means wage cuts, for others it's workers collapsing with fatigue at their machines. [. . .] We cannot focus only on shock work; all of us need to act as good stewards in the workplace. Being a shock worker does not mean destroying the machines; the machines are national assets and should be treated with care. *Udarniks* need to save power just like any worker. [. . .] Unfortunately, this is not always true. Let's be honest. Sometimes even well-meaning workers sneer at the word *udarnik*.[104]

For the above reasons, there were only 515 *udarnik* certificate holders in the factory at the beginning of January 1950. Due to pressure from party authorities, the need to report as many shock workers as possible meant that the criteria for an *udarnik* award were considerably reduced, and by January 1951 the factory had 5,722 shock workers.[105] In March 1951, however, the issue of *udarnik* certificates was suspended nationwide, as the honorary award had turned into an easy way of obtaining social benefits.[106] Most of such official labor initiatives and socialist forms of work gradually declined after 1953.[107]

In the post-war period, plan implementation was initially achieved mainly by increasing the amount of overtime work rather than by boosting productivity during regular working hours. This suited the workers just fine: paid overtime was a handy opportunity to increase their earnings.[108] Some workers (or even entire work crews) even deliberately put aside work so they could complete it in overtime.[109] This made production prohibitively expensive and the growth in labor productivity did not match the growth in wages. Factory management therefore tried to gradually reduce the number of overtime hours. From 1945 onward, it began increasing the number of employees who were paid piece work wages that were far easier to monitor; by 1947, 58% of workers were piece work wage earners.[110] From 1947 onward, artificial wage growth was regulated by tightening the performance targets for employees whose monthly wages increased by more than 25%. This set a de facto wage ceiling.[111]

A similar approach was subsequently used to stimulate labor productivity during the first five-year plan. The company implemented a factory-wide process known as the tightening of targets which reduced the prescribed production times for individual products. Workers whose targets had been tightened were forced to produce more in the same amount of time. This also reduced the wage part of the production costs. Socialist competition was another reason for the comprehensive reform of labor standards: workers were unhappy with the fact that soft performance targets allowed some of their colleagues to considerably exceed the set targets without much effort.[112]

The tightening of targets was first introduced at the factory in 1949, initially in the form of voluntary commitments undertaken by employees in some workshops (e.g., the metal foundry).[113] This was later followed by factory-wide target reviews, which resulted in the signing of contracts between the employees, represented by the factory council, and the factory management.[114] The first such blanket performance review took place in 1950, reportedly resulting in the reduction of production times by more than 2 million hours. Many work teams used various pretexts to boycott the reviews.[115] Factory management therefore had to launch a campaign promising the workers that compliance with the tightened performance targets would be facilitated by a more flexible production organization (material supply) and better working conditions. Unfortunately, the factory did not manage to implement the necessary technical improvements or ensure a smoother supply of raw materials, which meant that the workers had to meet the increased targets under the existing conditions.[116] Moreover, performance reviews had to be repeated in 1951 due to adjustments to the five-year plan,[117] resulting in the transfer of surplus administrative workers to production.[118] Performance reviews continued even in the following years.[119] Selected production times in all departments were reduced by tens of percent each year, without improving the workers' ability to meet the targets in any other way than occasional crash shifts, because the supply of materials was slow and unreliable.

Despite assurances from officials that the tightening of targets combined with better work organization would not result in lower earnings, many workers believed otherwise.[120] Some therefore refused to tighten their targets unless their coworkers with higher wages did so.[121] Entire departments sometimes decided to boycott the performance reviews.[122] The workers' less-than-enthusiastic approach to tightening targets is also evidenced by a number of disciplinary cases. In 1951, for example, employee Alfréd Měsíček complained to a party official that "all you want is to run people ragged with your targets, you just want to destroy us and take away our earnings."[123] In April 1953, blacksmith Josef Bican declared that "It's the ministers and officials who should tighten their targets, not the workers,"[124] for which he was dismissed from the factory in the interest of maintaining peace in the department.

Part of the workers' resentment for target tightening rubbed off on the shock worker movement. Many shop managers adopted a passive attitude, and factory management used shock workers as a means to uncover hidden reserves in the workplaces,[125] who then set a high bar for other workers in the department. This did not earn the *udarniks* much popularity. After her first week as an *udarnik*, a Ms. Hrabáková was rudely reproached by one of her coworkers, a Mr. Sojka, for working too much;

> he told her she would only manage a year at this rate, while others would have to keep working there. [. . .] He further said that at the pace she was working, she would spoil everything for our children who would have to work that much harder. Ms. Hrabáková complains that she has nothing to work on for two hours every day.[126]

In some cases, entire workshops stood up against the new udarniks. In 1952, two exemplary workers from another plant, Comrades Hnátová and Ryplová, were transferred to a problem department at the Elektrotrakce Doudlevce subsidiary plant to aid in the tightening of targets. "However, after the transfer of these comrades to the copper works, the entire staff threatened not to work with them. The shop management capitulated and removed the comrades from the workplace."[127]

For the aforementioned reasons, some foremen tried to prevent shock workers from setting too fast a pace. They had other justified reasons for doing so, such as the need to coordinate production pace across the entire factory. In fact, short-term *storming* (frantic attempts to meet the planned targets at the end of the month) led to higher scrap rates and an uneven supply of parts to other production sites.[128] Periods of frantic effort thus alternated with unproductive periods of waiting for materials and parts supplied by other departments. The deliberate slowing down of the shock workers' pace was often motivated both by the economic benefit to other employees and the desire to prevent unreasonable fluctuations in the work pace. Criticism was even voiced at party meetings in this connection, warning that "we run people ragged half the time, and half the time we have nothing for them to do."[129] Miloslav Mudra, head secretary of the KSČ District Committee of the, commented on the causes of this problem:

> If we give [the workers] everything they need, can make 25% to 30%. If we give them steady work, they won't have to pace themselves just to have something to do. [. . .] I think that the comrades would be willing if they always had work to do and could fulfill their tasks smoothly, instead of storming to meet the targets at the end of the month.[130]

It is therefore obvious that although the Communist Party managed to mobilize a large number of workers to get on board with fulfilling the five-year economic plan in 1949–1953, its success depended on the extent it was able to provide the employees of industrial enterprises with economic incentives. If some measures disrupted the workers' existing habits or put too much pressure on performance, some of the workers would come up with various ways of circumventing or boycotting them. Through such resistance, a large enough team of workers was often able to impede or even completely stop changes they did not agree with. The workers' discontent grew even further from 1949 onward, as pressure on labor productivity increased in the effort to fulfill the five-year plan, and work organization in the overloaded factory began to collapse. In the following years, the negative sentiments that the workers had to suppress at work found an outlet in a number of phenomena we will discuss in the following paragraphs.

CRISIS IN THE FUNCTIONING OF LOWER PARTY AUTHORITIES AT THE FACTORY

The absolute priority given to the implementation of the plan had another serious consequence. Communist Party authorities devoted almost all their attention to ensuring the required rate of production and promoting the measures needed to do so. Ideological education of the workers took a back seat and was often seen as merely another step in ensuring the implementation of the plan. Moreover, workers who were too busy with work lost interest in party meetings. Some could not attend due to the three-shift system,[131] others were part-time subsistence farmers and preferred to work at home in the afternoon, some preferred paid overtime,[132] and many lost interest in party activities when they found they had no say in anything.[133] They said, "What's the use in going to all these meetings and criticizing anything? It gets written down, but nothing ever gets done about it."[134] Attendance at party meetings in Machine Shop I, for example, dropped to 25% in 1951.[135] The seriousness of this phenomenon was openly discussed among the officers: "Meetings are poorly attended, and many comrades only see them as a necessary evil."[136] "Work in Party organizations depends entirely on a handful people who are overloaded with tasks, and the rest are nothing but dead weight."[137] Moreover, KSČ department committees often failed to encourage active participation, taking virtually no action and only calling meetings when an official from a superior party authority was scheduled to speak.[138]

The employees' political apathy can be well illustrated by an incident that took place in June 1949. A crowd of workers gathered at Gate 4 of the Škoda Works, demanding to be allowed to leave at the end of their shift, even though the Secretary of the Central Committee of the Communist Party, Rudolf Slánský, was holding a speech inside the factory at the time. The gate was closed to ensure maximum attendance at the official event. Nevertheless, the crowd forced their exit from the factory by attempting to break down the gate.[139]

The workers also demonstrated an alarming lack of interest in lower-ranking, unpaid party posts. While some workers did take up these positions in an attempt to promote their careers, most preferred gainful employment to unpaid party tasks. Miloslav Mudra, secretary of the KSČ District Committee, commented on this: “They would all gladly work 20 hours a day if they got paid for it, but when it comes to unpaid positions, they run away as fast as they can.”[140] Comrade Jan Pelnář made a similar point: “We have a shock worker in the gearwheel department who will happily do 20 hours of overtime, but when the Party gives him a task, he only cares what he will get from the Party in return.”[141]

However, the causes of the workers’ disinterest in political work ran much deeper. The problem was that the activities of the lower-level officials, who were the only direct link between party leadership and ordinary members, comprised thankless tasks. Lower-ranking officials were required to push through measures in their workshops that they did not fully believe in, and subsequently had to face their coworkers’ discontent. Their superiors also held them personally responsible for any failures. For example, the following opinions were voiced at meetings of the KSČ District Committee: “Being a Party official is difficult. Whenever you make a mistake, you will get a dressing down from the bigwigs, but nothing will ever happen to *them*. People hoarding Party offices are nothing but politicos and careerists.”[142] “When it came to electing factory Party officials at the annual meeting in Doudlevce, Franta nominated Tonda, and everyone just raised their hands and voted him in. Obviously, Franta did it just so he wouldn’t get elected himself.”[143] In some workplaces, shock workers repeatedly refused the offer to join the party for fear they would be immediately given an office. “They are not trying to say that they don’t agree with what the Party is doing, but they panic for fear of being given a post.”[144]

Some lower-ranking party officials even made no secret of their views to the employees, introducing any unpopular changes to the workers as a directive from above, which they disagree with but can personally do nothing about. When stripping away additional rationing coupons from hard workers, some party officials would say, “I know that the coupons should be yours by rights, and I would love to give them to you, but I can’t. I have to do what they tell me.”[145] Communist Party leadership called such natural behavior “popularity contests” and mistakenly regarded it as a relic of the earlier “social-democratic mentality.”[146]

According to party reports, the situation in factory organizations was the worst in those departments which had problems meeting the planned targets (Machine Shop I) or which experienced major conflicts between workers and factory management (Elektrotrakce Doudlevce subsidiary plant). The phenomenon might have been much more widespread, however, since party leadership only scrutinized the activities of its organizations in those workplaces where it was necessary to determine the causes of production and political failures. At the same time, economic failures were commonly interpreted at party forums as the result of insufficient ideological and organizational effort.

The District Committee was fully aware how passive the base party organizations were but until 1953was unable to rectify the situation. During the national screening of all party members in 1950–1951, only 11,754 of the original 12,770 members and candidates were successfully vetted (957 persons were struck off and 59 excluded), which did nothing to help the situation.[147] Historian Johann Smula has even spoken in this context of a "chronic dysfunction" of the party apparatus in the factory.[148]

The trade unions were also losing their authority among the workers and, due to their role in ensuring labor productivity, they came to be perceived by the workers as part of the management. Milling machine operator Emil Opočenský, for example, blamed both the shop manager and the shop council for having to work on a malfunctioning machine, making no distinction between the factory management, the trade unions, and members of the Communist Party, declaring that "we should just grab sticks and give them all a solid thrashing, from top to bottom."[149] The workers did not show much interest in the functioning of the trade union organization. A survey conducted at Machine Shop I in 1951 found that many workers had no idea who was acting as chairman of the shop council at their workplace. When asked whether they knew the chairman of the factory council, they replied that they had "never met him at all."[150] The results of the survey were all the more surprising because the photographs of these officials had been displayed all over the factory during the recent factory council elections.

The situation among young people was not much better. There were approximately 6,500 persons of eligible age for membership in the Czechoslovak Union of Youth working at the V. I. Lenin Factories in 1953. However, only 21.95% of them were organized in the Union and, only half of the members attended meetings regularly.[151] As in the Communist Party and the trade unions, the Youth Union suffered from its members' total lack of interest in political work, and a consequent shortage of people willing to accept political office. Here, too, the acceptance of an office alienated the holder from their peers. Records speak of an incident in which Josef Kočí, chairman of the regional committee of the Youth Union, lost his temper and beat up a fellow employee who accused him of being a careerist. Ideological education among the youth was sadly lacking; no suitable entertainment was organized for the young people staying in worker dormitories, who were thus left to their own devices and engaged in all sorts of undesirable activities.[152]

These findings are particularly significant since it was the young workers and apprentices who formed the core of the June 1953 protests. This group of workers had not been given due attention for years, however. Neither the work nor the ideological activities in the factory and in the dormitories offered young workers any prospects which would reflect their actual interests and their own ideas of a fulfilled life.

CONSEQUENCES OF THE TRIAL OF HANUŠ LOMSKÝ, REGIONAL SECRETARY OF THE COMMUNIST PARTY

Party officials who had been recruited from the ranks of former workers quickly became alienated from their peers and were often seen by the factory staff as careerists who did not have the interests of ordinary people in mind.[153] In this respect, the relationship of the workers to factory management and the factory party organization was not much different from their relationship toward the former private owners. For example, Miloslav Mudra, head secretary of the KSČ District Committee, was feared by most of his subordinates and coworkers as a dictatorial, vindictive person.[154] A number of other local officials were rumored among the employees to be enriching themselves in various ways at the expense of the company. Frequently mentioned in this context was director František Brabec, the chairman of the ROH factory committee Josef Dvořák, secretary of the regional trade union council Milada Netušilová, head of the regional StB office Matěj Bálek, and head secretary of the regional Communist Party committee Hanuš Lomský.

In 1951–1952, a nationwide wave of show trials against leading party officials broke out in Czechoslovakia after the arrest of Brno official Otto Šling, with the most prominent of the accused being Rudolf Slánský, former general secretary of the Central Committee of the Communist Party. In Pilsen, head secretary of the KSČ Regional Committee Hanuš Lomský fell victim to this purge.[155] The trials were accompanied by a massive campaign that blamed economic failures on the nefarious activities of alleged traitors within the party. In the first half of 1951, party leaders in all regions engaged in introspection and self-criticism, examining their work for erroneous management methods adopted from the alleged traitors. At the same time, party members were encouraged to criticize the higher authorities, and suppression of criticism from below was identified as one of the main sources of problems that had been plaguing the party.

At the local level, these imposed rituals had the side effect of temporarily relaxing freedom of speech in party forums. During the national search for traitors, it was therefore suddenly possible to voice some well-founded suspicions of corruption and despotism that the employees had long been whispering about.[156] For many lower-ranking party officials the 1951–1952 purges actually heralded a certain degree of democratization within the party structures.[157] Ironically, the official campaign against the victims of show trials in Pilsen was indirectly linked to the earlier discussions regarding the need to improve communication processes within the party that had occurred among leading party officials in May 1948. In the years that followed, many communists complained that "Lomský is gone and yet the chaos goes on."[158] It was generally expected that many more officials would be removed from their posts.[159] In particular, the arrest of Rudolf Slánský in the autumn of 1951 sparked rumors among workers at the Škoda Works as to which members of the factory management would be imprisoned. Engaging in such debates was understandably very dangerous for the local party leaders and did not contribute to their popularity among the workers.[160]

Criticism of existing policies during the show trial period also extended to production issues. The ubiquitous formal implementation of the plan for the sake of mere appearance, for example, was suddenly publicly branded as a form of industrial sabotage. The activities of the *udarnik* movement, which had previously taken root in Pilsen following the model set up by Otto Šling in the Brno region, also came under scrutiny. This meant that some of the fundamental pillars of the company's operation after 1948 were now publicly questioned. In the search for the culprits, however, most of the failures and wrongdoings were mistakenly attributed to the remaining few senior factory officials whose expertise allowed them to hold on to their positions even under the new regime, such as Vladimír Bárta, director of the Elektrotrakce Doudlevce subsidiary plant, or head of the Machine Shop II department Bohuslav Jičínský. Their work was now being described as traitorous, and they were accused of using the so-called false expertise method.[161]

For many workers, however, the show trials and the associated campaign undermined their trust in the leading factory officials. This was most evident in the cases of suspected corruption. From 1951 onward, for example, there was open talk of the lack of transparency in the management of the so-called Foreigners' House, a facility operated by the Škoda Works which served as a luxury hotel for foreign delegations visiting the factory. In January 1948, Miroslav Hříbek was appointed manager of the building. After February 1948, discrepancies began to appear in the handling of food and alcohol supplies at the Foreigners' House. Luxury furniture from the building was being sold off cheaply to senior factory officials, including company director František Brabec. Hanuš Lomský, head secretary of the regional party committee, and Matěj Bálek, head of the regional StB office, often went there to eat free lunch with their families.[162] Wild drinking parties were organized for the foreign dignitaries, which did not escape the attention of the factory guards patrolling round the building.

Jan Zítek, member of the factory council and chief of the factory guard, began to investigate the goings-on at the Foreigners' House and demanded that Hříbek be removed from his post. However, he met with resistance from the leadership of the KSČ Regional Committee and the StB Regional Office, who told him that Hříbek had been appointed by the Ministry of the Interior and the Central Committee of the Communist Party and was gathering intelligence at the Foreigners' House on behalf of the StB.[163] During the vetting process in May 1949, Hříbek was vetted secretly, which was a direct violation of party regulations, and all charges against him were dropped. Matěj Bálek, head of the StB Regional Office, defended Hříbek by claiming that he [Hříbek] was allowed certain behavior that did not conform to the communist principles, so as to avoid the enemies' suspicion when gathering intelligence.[164] However, Bálek's efforts to cover for Hříbek were not entirely altruistic, and his arguments were false. In fact, the StB Regional Office in Pilsen kept no records of Hříbek's activities, and Hříbek signed a promise of cooperation only later in 1951 at Bálek's urging.[165]

At a district party convention in 1951, the wave of official demand for criticism and self-criticism after the arrest of regional head secretary Hanuš Lomský enabled Jan Zítek to speak openly about the events at the Foreigners' House. He also voiced the suspicion that Hanuš Lomský was consorting with French spies there.[166] The hitherto secret case thus became a public matter and in July 1951, under the pressure of public opinion, the KSČ District Committee had to look for a replacement for Hříbek.[167] Ironically, Jan Zítek also faced disciplinary action for publishing secret information about the StB's work.[168] He was only saved from punishment by the fact that the Communist Party was promoting greater openness to criticism at the time.[169] Moreover, Hříbek's and Bálek's punishment did not fall within the authority of the District Committee, which meant that despite demands from the factory staff, no formal charges were brought against the guilty parties, even in a flagrant case like this.[170]

A number of similar affairs emerged after 1948.[171] However, they usually remained uninvestigated because they involved high-ranking party officials. For example, the Prime Minister's Office repeatedly received anonymous letters from the employees of the V. I. Lenin Factories, demanding that the situation in Pilsen be remedied.[172] Their authors complained about the alleged embezzlement of fabrics at the Economic Cooperative of Škoda Works Employees. However, the people who were actually punished by the disciplinary commission of the Pilsen Central National Committee in March 1949 for discrepancies in the cooperative's accounts were mere scapegoats: vice-chairman of the cooperative Josef Kutzendorfer and shop manager Karel Bezděk.[173] The suspected fabric buyers, among whom were company director František Brabec, chairman of the ROH factory committee Josef Dvořák,[174]

MPs Milada Netušilová[175] and Jaroslava Krafková,[176] and head of the Škoda Works social and political department Bohuslav Brůha, as well as some members of the factory council, all went unpunished.[177] Chairman of the cooperative Josef Hora, who was also chairman of the Škoda Works factory council at the time, also managed to avoid punishment.

The affair caused considerable resentment among the employees because the stolen goods were purchased using their ration coupons entrusted to the cooperative. Workers actually began gathering in the workshops. The employees trusted the rumors of a cover-up involving the highest regional officials, because they originated in the Machine Shop I plant, where Josef Kutzendorfer had been transferred as a punishment.[178] In a subsequent dispute, the party's base organization stood up for Josef Kutzendorfer, rejected pressure from MP Karel Poláček demanding Kutzendorfer's expulsion from the party, and sent a protest resolution to the Central Committee of the Communist Party.[179]

The affair at the economic cooperative created a rather explosive atmosphere at the factory that threatened to affect elections to the factory council, which were to take place on April 14, 1949. The situation was addressed at a meeting of chairmen of the trade union groups on April 8, 1949, and at an emergency meeting of the chairmen of the party base organizations four days later. At the meetings, top factory officials were subjected to severe criticism from the lower-ranking officials from the factory's workshops, demanding that chairman of the ROH factory organization Josef Dvořák renounce his candidacy for the factory council. Both Josef Dvořák and factory director František Brabec were forced to express public self-criticism for their involvement in the shady fabric purchases made by their wives.[180] However, this did nothing to calm down the general indignation, since Josef Kutzendorfer was not invited to the meetings at all and could not defend himself against the accusations. The whole incident therefore had a considerable negative impact on the general mood in the factory, which persisted even during the subsequent elections to the factory council and its immediate aftermath.[181] Some workers publicly declared that they did not vote for the unified ballot because it included officials implicated in the fabric affair. The popularity of ROH factory organization chairman Josef Dvořák took a major hit and he was even booed out of some meetings.[182]

The case then dragged on for years, greatly reducing the enthusiasm of workers from all the directly affected plants. For example, only 70 of the 1,500 trade union members at Machine Shop I attended union meetings.[183] Workers huddled in groups on the shop floors, saying that "they would not mind stealing if nothing would happen to them anyway, just like the others," and that "people are stealing right, left and center, while we are made to cut down our [production] times."[184] A new investigation was launched within the party after the arrest of Hanuš Lomský, head secretary of the Communist Party's Regional Committee, for alleged traitorous activities within the party. In his complaints sent to the Central Committee and to the President, Kutzendorfer claimed that he had been removed from his posts at Lomský's behest, without having been given the chance to defend himself. In addition, most of the suspects Kutzendorfer pointed at were Lomský's close associates.[185] As a criminal case, however, the whole affair remained unsolved even after 1951, although the ongoing show trials would have made it politically feasible.

The Prime Minister's Office ordered the authorities of the Ministry of the Interior to investigate the contents of the anonymous letters sent from Pilsen. After six months, it received a reply that the information contained in the denunciations was probably true, but for political reasons it was not possible to continue the investigation. The officer dealing with the case was transferred to another post, and subsequently told the Prime Minister: "Since the persons involved in the various machinations and discrepancies included several Party officials, the directives I received at the beginning of the investigation made it impossible to continue."[186] The uninvestigated corruption scandals tarnished the reputation of the Communist Party as a whole, and left room for speculation about possible wrongdoings on a much larger scale. They were denounced both by non-partisan workers and by low-ranking communists and minor party officials. The former may have gradually come to see instances of individual misconduct as a more general systemic error, while the latter found an explanation for the shortcomings in the dubious personal history of some of the culprits (such as former affiliation with the Social Democratic Party), which was fully consistent with the overall ethos guiding political processes within the party.[187]

The workers' mistrust of the local Communist Party leadership was further fueled by the fact that instead of being punished, officials accused of shady dealings were often bundled off to the central party authorities in Prague. At the Škoda Works, such an approach was chosen in the case of Jan Piller, head secretary of the KSČ District Committee, head of the Škoda Works social and political department Bohuslav Brůha, and Josef Reitmajer, political secretary of the KSČ factory organization at the Elektrotrakce Doudlevce subsidiary plant.[188] The most flagrant case of this kind, however, was the career advancement of chief secretary Miloslav Mudra, whom the workers nicknamed the Red Baron.[189] He was well known for his dictatorial tendencies and his insidious methods of getting rid of his rivals.[190] Despite the fact that Mudra was clearly unsuitable for positions with higher responsibility, he was recommended in December 1951for the post of chief secretary of the newly formed KSČ Municipal Committee in Pilsen, and later for the post of deputy minister of heavy engineering. Opposition of low-ranking party members to his person later became one of the impulses for the protests following the currency reform in 1953.

Apart from the personal failings of some local functionaries, the party's credibility in the eyes of the workers was further weakened by the fact that it often failed to provide them with truthful information in a timely manner. In some cases, non-partisan workers were informed of important events earlier (e.g., via foreign radio broadcast) than lower-ranking party officials on the shop floor. Out of political caution, the latter often refuted claims that were subsequently proved to be true. Such situations understandably undermined their influence and persuasive potential.

This became fully apparent especially before the currency reform of 1953 (the campaign against panic buying), but certain tendencies were evident on a number of earlier occasions. On the day of the death of President Klement Gottwald on March 14, 1953, news of his death began to circulate among the factory staff as early as around 12 p.m. However, the leading party officials did not know where the news came from and considered it to be enemy propaganda. Before 2 p.m., an all-workers' meeting was convened where the chairman of the party organization denied the reports of Gottwald's death. A few minutes later the radio broadcast the news that Gottwald had died at 11 a.m.[191]

POLITICAL CONFLICTS IN THE FACTORY

The political atmosphere in the factory was significantly influenced by the fact that, in 1948–1953, the factory hired a number of people who had previously worked in other non-worker professions. This was caused both by the general pressure to increase employment in industry and by the transformation of the social structure after February 1948. This included, for example, gradual elimination of private farmers, tradesmen, and merchants; the transfer of clerical workers to production; and the removal of politically unreliable people from their previous positions.[192]

Thus in 1953, the V. I. Lenin Factories employed 2,703 former distribution and private sector employees; 903 former clerical workers transferred to production during a nationwide campaign in 1951; 633 former civil servants; 564 former private farmers; 242 former self-employed tradesmen and merchants; and 116 former police officers and soldiers. A total of 19.65 % of the employees (5,161 persons) therefore came from other professions and were often transferred against their will. As these people brought their personal experiences and attitudes to the workplace, the mood in the factory began to change.[193]

Moreover, new employees were often seen as intruders, and no consistent effort was made to integrate them into the existing work teams. They were assigned to the worst jobs and often lacked the necessary qualifications, which is why they initially earned significantly less than other workers. In most cases, they were much worse off than in their previous occupations, and had difficulty adjusting their family spending accordingly.[194] For these reasons, they were increasingly involved in the various social conflicts that began to break out in the factory.

Actual political incidents in the factory between 1948 and 1953 were kept to a minimum. Most of them involved subversive statements made by individual workers, usually after excessive alcohol consumption. The company's disciplinary mechanism was relatively lenient toward such excesses, especially if the perpetrators had not been previously punished and were otherwise exemplary workers. The punishments imposed for such offenses by the factory disciplinary committee were considerably less severe than if the perpetrators had been previously investigated by law enforcement authorities for offenses committed elsewhere. Recommendation for reassignment to a forced labor camp was only used as a punishment in the most egregious cases.

Let us give a few typical examples. In February 1950, worker Ludvík Brejcha grumbled in the locker room that "the Communists are worse than the Gestapo; [that] they caused the death of former President Edvard Beneš and that they will all hang, including President Klement Gottwald, as soon the whole thing goes under."[195] He was only punished for drunkenness (not for his subversive statements), by a deduction of a half-day's wages and a two-year probation. In April 1951, worker Karel Trnka spent most of his shift in a pub. When he was not allowed inside the factory by the factory guard afterward, he shouted, "Those Communist bastards kicked me out of the Party, but I'll show them. I have this device, I only need to set the timer and I can blow up the entire factory. I'm a foreign soldier and guerilla fighter, but I love America."[196] He was given a two-year probation. In November 1951, locksmith Miloslav Jarolímek told the apprentices under his supervision that his uncle Bohuslav Stanislav Jarolímek, abbot of the Strahov Premonstratensian Monastery, had been tortured to death in prison by the communists. He was merely transferred to a different workplace, where he could no longer manipulate impressionable young people.[197] In August 1951, locksmith František Šašek argued with his fellow employees: "Why are we supposed to learn from Soviet engineers, when we use far more advanced technology?"[198] After he was admonished by a coworker to focus on his work, Šašek punched the man several times in the face. The disciplinary committee referred him to the National Committee for reassignment to a labor camp.

Of the offenses referred to regular law enforcement authorities, the most prominent group consisted of defamatory statements made during the commemoration ceremonies for Joseph Vissarionovich Stalin and Klement Gottwald in March 1953. On March 14, 1953, design engineers Robert Trčka (former member of the opposition Czechoslovak National Socialist Party) and Otakar Andrée (former worker, member of the Communist Party) made derogatory comments regarding President Gottwald's demise. Trčka said: "Another one down. We liked Gottwald, but if God likes him better, He is welcome to him. I bet he's going to start nationalizing in Heaven."—"In hell, more like," Andrée replied. "Possibly, considering what a devil he was,"[199] Trčka added. Criminal charges against both men were dropped following the presidential amnesty of May 1953. On the same day, metal founder Václav Šimek declared: "They're dropping like flies, aren't they? One had a stroke, Klement Gottwald is dead, and Wilhelm Pieck, Mátyás Rákosi and Mao Zedong are all ill."[200] Looking at a photograph of the newly elected President Antonín Zápotocký, he commented on his obesity by saying that "he has already built socialism."[201] He was sentenced to six months in prison.

It is clear that individual political protests did occur in the factory during the relevant period, but they were not particularly frequent. Moreover, factory management tolerated them as long as they did not cross a certain line (such as resorting to violence or disrupting an official ceremony). Factory management often chose to interpret them as a non-political offense (drinking in the workplace). In this respect, the position of factory workers inside the factory was quite different from the social reality outside the factory gates. Frequent workers' strikes, motivated by social issues, were not directly related to the individual workers' occasional political excesses.

STRIKES

In some cases, disgruntled employees at the Škoda factory did not stop at a silent boycott, but vented their dissatisfaction openly through strikes or short-term work stoppages. Responsible officials were aware of how politically sensitive workers' protests were, and often tried to resolve them inside the factory, without informing higher authorities or the police.[202] Most of these collective conflicts were therefore never properly investigated, nor was there any in-depth analysis of their course and causes. This has had an unfortunate effect on the amount of surviving sources, but it is still possible to make a rough outline of the various types of strikes, based on documents produced by the various party and trade union bodies inside the factory.

One of the first causes of conflict was the corruption among factory management, which, considering the ever-increasing pressure on workers' productivity, was a fairly explosive issue. Temporary work stoppages occurred in some workshops as early as the spring of 1949, around the time of the aforementioned fabric incident.[203] This was the first known attempt by local workers since February 1948 to achieve their demands by stopping work.

The second reason for collective protests was the chaotic restructuring of production programs in the first phase of implementation of the five-year plan. Entire plants were being closed down, and employees were naturally concerned about their future, which was made even worse by the fact that the management often failed to inform them of the planned measures in time. On February 14, 1950, for example, workers in the Metalworking Department went on strike to protest against the transfer of the rolling mill for railroad wheel flanges to another factory. The strike was only quelled by the intervention of company director František Brabec and chairman of the ROH factory organization Josef Dvořák. A tense atmosphere also prevailed in the Vehicles Department since the production of tractors was reassigned to another enterprise. Workers in both departments declared that the Regional KSČ Committee and the Škoda District KSČ Committee were worthless, and were considering sending a deputation to the government. In both departments, a few workers canceled their party membership in protest.[204]

At the beginning of 1951, the Automatic Machinery II department was next in line to be shut down; the machines were to be taken away and employees reassigned to other production departments. The state-of-the-art plant was to become a warehouse. The management promised the employees that by February 1951 they would be told where they would be reassigned. However, the machines were being gradually removed, and still nobody was able to tell the workers where they would go. The final decision as to the fate of the plant was constantly postponed, which incited a rather rebellious mood in the department. The workers insisted that no machines should be moved until a final decision had been made regarding the entire department. Workers claimed that the management wanted to "destroy their workshop."[205] In March 1951, clerk Bedřich Poul even put up a satirical obituary which claimed that "the workshop that survived American bombing did not survive the impact of our planning."[206] He was subsequently investigated by the disciplinary commission. The workers finally decided to resolve their precarious situation by sending a delegation to the Central Committee of the Communist Party.[207]

The third frequent cause of strikes was work overload and unsuitable working conditions. On December 2, 1950, workers in the sheet metal pressing department at the Elektrotrakce Doudlevce Subsidiary Plant left their workshop because it was freezing and the heating was broken. Their demonstrative action was provoked by the response of the steam distribution department to their demand that they repair the heating system: "Fix it yourselves."[208]

On Sunday, June 3, 1951, some of the employees from the Steelworks department went home after the night shift, even though they were instructed to work the entire morning shift as well: the factory went into non-stop operation mode in order to meet the steel production plan. The employees claimed exhaustion to justify their action. Nevertheless, the disciplinary committee fined them 100 Kč each for a collective breach of discipline. In addition, the works council reported the case to the national committees in their places of residence. The names of the offenders were announced via the municipal PA systems and to children in local schools.[209]

The fourth group of protests was related to the poor supply situation. Work stoppages in such cases were usually provoked by the shortage of food in factory canteens. In June 1951, employees in the Engineering II department went on strike because bread rolls were not available.[210] Similar actions by workers at the V. I. Lenin Factories occurred during the panic buying in May 1953, shortly before the currency reform. This type of strike was always caused by a general crisis in supply, not just within the factory itself. The factory canteens served as a symbol of the general shortages outside the factory and were used to vent the latent outside conflicts within the safe bounds of the factory. Moreover, factory canteens in large enterprises were often stocked with goods on a priority basis in times of shortage, which allowed workers to purchase foodstuffs that were otherwise in short supply. Canteen shortages eliminated this social benefit, much to the chagrin of the workers.

Dissatisfaction with irregular supply, food prices, and the too-slow growth in the living standard was widespread among workers from 1950 at least. This was reflected in surveys of workers' attitudes, carried out by the factory guard on behalf of the State Security in all departments of the factory. The results were so alarming that company director František Brabec tried to censor them before passing them on to the higher authorities.[211]

The most frequent cause of strikes were the negative changes in employees' financial evaluation. The largest strike in the Škoda Works took place in July 1950 at the Elektrotrakce Doudlevce Subsidiary Plant, provoked by the management's decision to order extra working shifts during the public holidays in July. The workers were given the order without the party or trade union authorities having been informed, and the announcement was therefore made without any prior publicity. This went against the usual methods of persuasion adopted by the management. The workers spontaneously discussed the announcement on the shop floor and, according to information from the trade union authorities, three-quarters of the workers were against the shifts.[212]

What made the whole incident extraordinary was the fact that extra shifts on holidays and Sundays were quite common at the time. The problem was therefore not the workers' reluctance to work, but that no one had formally discussed the decision with them. Many workers, for example, described the actions of the director Brabec as dictatorial and wondered why their representative bodies (factory council, trade unions) allowed the director to bypass their authority.[213] One of the reasons for the workers' resistance was therefore the desire to maintain at least a formal position of co-owner in the national enterprise, and to continue to be not just a human resource, but a respected partner for the factory management. Although the workers were often dissatisfied with the actions of the factory council, they understood that the council symbolized, at least on a theoretical level, their claims to co-management of the nationalized industry. For this reason, party officials hesitated until the last moment to implement the holiday shifts against the will of most of workers. In the end, the KSČ District Committee retroactively approved their decision.[214]

The case of the extra shifts in July made it clear how crucial for enforcing any measures at the factory it was to shroud them in the proper propaganda. Through the network of party and union authorities, workers were given a clear indication regarding the officially supported opinions. Propaganda also offered the right arguments to those workers who were willing to actively advocate such a conformist position. This effectively prevented any unregulated discussions among workers, because it set clear boundaries for possible solutions. Whenever the management decided to implement unpopular changes without a prior propaganda campaign and without managing to mobilize its mechanisms apparatus in advance, serious complications were almost inevitable. This was fully manifested during the currency reform in 1953.

The extra July shifts thus became a pretext for a worker strike at the Elektrotrakce Doudlevce Subsidiary Plant on July 21–22, 1950. On their own initiative, some department managers promised the workers bonuses if they worked the required holiday shifts.[215] They had forgotten, however, that the company's bonus regulations only allowed bonuses to be awarded to salaried clerical workers, but not to workers on piece work wages. The conflict then erupted with renewed force when the workers received their July advances; they were surprised to discover that unlike the clerical workers, they had not received any bonuses.[216] Moreover, employees from the accounting office leaked to the workshops that subsidiary plant director Vladimír Bárta had been paid CZK 21,000 in bonuses and Josef Reitmajer, political secretary of the factory organization of the Communist Party at Elektrotrakce Doudlevce, had received CZK 24,000.[217] Such provocation obviously caused extreme indignation among the previously misinformed employees.[218]

On Friday July 21, the employees stopped working, gathered in the factory courtyard, and sent a delegation (binder Josef Fajfrlík and crane operator Antonín Stainbach) to the subsidiary plant management. They demanded an immediate investigation into the system of bonuses and threatened to call a strike for the following day. Unfortunately, they met with evasion from the local officials, who were themselves responsible for the unfair distribution of bonuses. Reitmajer, chief secretary of the factory organization of the

Communist Party at Elektrotrakce Doudlevce, was absent that day, and director Bárta refused to discuss the matter with the workers altogether, offering a dubious argument that the strike was a purely political matter, and was therefore exclusively within the purview of the party authorities. None of the responsible officials thus took any steps at all to prevent or avoid the strike.[219]

On Saturday July 22, workers on the morning shift did not start working at all, and most of them gathered in the factory courtyard around 8 a.m.[220] (Přesnější údaje o počtu stávkujících bohužel podobně jako u ostatních stávek nejsou dostupné.) (Unfortunately, as with other strikes from that time, more precise figures regarding the number of strikers are not available.) The crowd demanded that a protest resolution be sent to the government. Participants included mainly poorly paid auxiliary workers (such as crane operators, binders, and cart operators); some of them had been reassigned to their current jobs from other non-worker positions. Most of the active protesters were young people (about 60%).[221] Foremen and lower-level union officials adopted a passive attitude and did not attempt to intervene against the strike: they had received bonuses themselves, and would therefore have difficulty persuading the workers to calm down. Some of the lower-ranking party officials even supported the strike because they believed the bonuses had been distributed unfairly.[222]

Josef Reitmajer, chief secretary of the party organization, tried to calm the heightened emotions, but considering he was one of the officials who had received a high bonus, the workers booed him out.[223] MP Milada Netušilová was another who tried to pacify the crowd, but the workers did not listen to her either. Company director František Brabec arrived specially to deal with the situation, but the workers jeered at him for having arrived in a Tatraplan and made fun of him for driving such a high-end vehicle. "But it's your car, too,"[224] he tried to reason with them. "It may be our car, Comrade, but it's you who's driving it,"[225] they replied. "We can only look at it."[226] Officials from the KSČ District Committee, Jan Piller and Miloslav Mudra, also tried—and failed—to negotiate with the strikers.[227] The People's Militias, which had not intervened up until then, were therefore called in around noon to assist in dealing with the situation.[228] Using the Militias as a deterrent, the strike was gradually subdued without any major violence. It is likely that none of the protesters were actually prosecuted. Tension was further eased by adopting a measure which partially complied with the worker's demands by increasing wage advances.[229]

The strike at the Elektrotrakce Doudlevce Subsidiary Plant met with a strong reaction in the main plant, where employees in some departments (especially the Locomotive Works workshop) demanded that the bonus regulations be changed and that bonus amounts be made public in future.[230] Despite the newly enforced wage transparency, however, bonuses continued to provoke heated discussions in the following years.[231] Complaints were particularly vociferous in those departments (e.g., Engineering III) that did not meet the planned targets and whose employees were therefore not entitled to bonuses no matter how hard they worked, even though the failure to meet the targets was often caused by external factors unrelated to the departments' performance. Other departments (such as Engineering I) demanded that bonuses should not be paid at the discretion of factory officials, but that every employee in the department should receive an equal share.[232] That kind of collective spirit and egalitarianism was actually an authentic part of the workers' mindset in those days.

News about the strike also leaked outside the factory gates and reportedly elicited considerable interest among the townspeople.[233] This seemingly trivial fact was actually of vital importance. A certain segment of society outside the factory was apparently beginning to realize during the 1950s that the propaganda image of a harmonious relationship between the regime's representatives and the working class was largely illusory, and was beginning to understand the potential significance of the workers' protests.[234] This became apparent on June 1, 1953, when the message "Škoda workers are heading for the town square!"[235] began spreading like an avalanche throughout the city, providing a decisive impetus for other social groups to join in the revolt.

The strike in July 1950 was a foreshadowing of the events of June 1, 1953, in the way the local party officials reacted to it. The top-ranking officials from the factory did not learn their lesson from the incident and did not realize how important it was for them to communicate with the workers regarding social and wage issues. Instead, they blamed the whole incident on alleged political opponents within the factory. They ascribed undue importance to the fact that the strikers included many former members of non-communist political parties and persons who had formerly held non-worker occupations.[236] The leadership of the KSČ District Committee even wrongly inferred from this fact that the strike had been provoked by the former right-wing Social Democrats and former private tradesmen, and that real workers had been led astray by them.[237]

The fact was that the former Social Democratic Party officials were generally experienced, skilled pre-war workers, often promoted to foremen before 1950,[238] and had little in common with the new unskilled workers recruited from the ranks of former tradesmen. Yet neither of these politically determined groups of alleged instigators were significantly represented in the most active core of the strikers. In an internal analysis of the events, party officials explained the discrepancy between ideological justification and reality by the fact that reactionary elements were allegedly stirring up the workers from behind the scenes, without having the courage to act openly. "Certain elements who have recently come to ET[D] are just waiting for something like this to happen; but they are happy to stay in the background and egg the others on. All of the hecklers hung well back; you could constantly hear someone making seditious comments."[239] As early as 1950, an official interpretation of the workers' protests began to emerge at the Škoda plants, identifying the instigators of strikes and protests outside the ranks of the working class and labeling the strikers as mere victims of manipulation by an abstractly defined enemy. In June 1953, this particular school of thought was universally accepted.

The strike was therefore the first incident which forced the KSČ District Committee leadership to focus on the dynamic change in the structure of the company's workforce and the problem that the reassigned employees may pose. Measures were immediately taken to tighten the supervision over the party organizations at the Elektrotrakce Doudlevce Plant in order to eliminate alleged social democratic tendencies within the local party organization. It was also decided to draw up lists of employees who had joined the factory after January 1, 1950. Each of them was assigned a patron from among more experienced and politically reliable colleagues. The patrons were not only to help the newcomers adjust to their new jobs, but also to work out their political views.[240]

In their need to point to a culprit behind the July strike, party officials found a handy scapegoat in Vladimír Bárta, director of the subsidiary plant, who was dismissed from his post and later branded a saboteur who had tried to disrupt the smooth operation of the factory by his so-called false professionalism. The main reason he had been singled out, however, was the fact that he had held high management positions in the factory since 1928, that is, under the previous political regimes.[241]

Incidents of collective resistance by the workers were a frequent occurrence in the following years whenever the employees were stripped of some economic or social benefits. For example, some workers expressed considerable indignation following the cutbacks of ration coupons for hard workers in the summer of 1951.[242] This provoked another attempt to call a strike at the Elektrotrakce Doudlevce plant[243] as well as the factory power station, where "the comrades threatened to halt operation and put a part of the factory out of commission."[244]

Another wave of protests, this time nationwide, broke out after the announcement of a reduction in Christmas bonuses in November 1951.[245] In fact, the government measure was announced in such a blundering manner that the workers learned of it before local party officials could launch a proper publicity campaign. In the city of Brno, large-scale worker protests broke out in the streets as a result.[246] The situation in Pilsen was a bit calmer, but the mood among the workers was so rebellious that the People's Militias had to be called in again. This was the second time authorities used the Militias as a deterrent against the workers in Pilsen. Just as in July 1950 and June 1953, the Communist Party could not rely on its lower-ranking officials, who wavered between supporting the government resolution or their disgruntled colleagues.[247] There were heated debates at union meetings and several party officials were booed out.[248] The Iron Foundry union organization even demanded that a protest resolution be sent to the government.[249] The Pilsen communists openly admitted that "had we not sent in the Militias, things would have turned out the same way they did in Brno."[250]

The last big strike in Pilsen, which took place at the Iron Foundry on January 15, 1953, was motivated by similar causes. This time the cause of discontent was the withdrawal of recruitment bonuses for metallurgical workers.[251] The protests were again triggered by the fact that the Communist Party had not had time to organize a publicity campaign to explain the decision.[252] The disgruntled workers sent a protest deputation to Prime Minister Antonín Zápotocký.[253] A number of party members joined in the protests,[254] as well as a few members of the People's Militias.[255] Workers also attempted to call a strike at other metallurgical plants of the V. I. Lenin Factories (the Steel Foundry and the Metal Foundry).[256] Some workers commented: "We were doing fine until February [1948, when the Communist Party seized power]. Now we're much worse off. They're just taking away more and more."[257]

The strike was eventually suppressed thanks to ad hoc party assemblies which denounced the attempts of lower-ranking officials to defend the protesting workers. They managed to break up the unity of the resistance, by first persuading the party officials and ordinary members to stand down, then use their help in calming down the non-partisan protesters. In this respect, the additional party activities made up for the lack of a preliminary propaganda campaign. Similar methods of pacifying factory unrest were used after the currency reform in June 1953. The strikers in January 1953 received no punishment beyond making up for their absence from work.[258]

Finally, we should note that the above typology of strikes is, to a certain extent, an over-simplification of the much more colorful reality of factory life. In fact, the various categories of strikers' motives often combined and overlapped. Apart from the immediate impulses, there were undoubtedly some longer-term factors at work that had a negative impact on the general mood among the workers: lack of communication between senior officials and employees, as well as growing chaos in the production process, which the government sought to compensate for by putting pressure on workers to increase productivity.

The relationship between the Communist Party and the workers at the Škoda Works underwent a dynamic development between 1945 and 1953. In the early months of the Third Republic, the vast majority of the factory workers were actually impressed by the Communist Party which secured their cooperation when it came to nationalization of industry, social policy, and administration of the newly nationalized enterprises. At the time of escalating social and political conflicts of 1946–1948, however, workers' support for the Communist Party was no longer as unequivocal as before. This was strongly manifested in the failed election of the factory council in 1947 and was evident in the development of the party's membership base within the factory, which was essentially stagnant from the autumn of 1945 until June 1953, even though the number of workers increased significantly.

More serious cracks in the apparent symbiosis between the majority of workers and the Communist Party began to appear after February 1948, especially when it came to the implementation of the first five-year economic plan in 1949–1953. During this period, the pressure to increase factory output led to a considerable disorganization of the production process, which caused much discontent among the employees. Workers were also gradually losing interest in political involvement, which led to an ongoing crisis within the party, the trade union, and youth organizations in the factory. Workers were also able to effectively boycott some of the unpopular measures, and often did not hesitate to resort to work stoppages or large-scale strikes. The causes of these collective public protests generally fall into several categories: corruption of the senior officials in the factory; poor organization of the production process; inadequate working conditions; disruptions in supply; lack of communication from the factory management; wage issues; and the withdrawal of existing social benefits.

The high level of employee protest activity was made possible by the fact that industrial enterprises in general (and the Pilsen plant in particular) were, to a considerable extent, independent subsystems separated from the outside world, with different norms of behavior and practices. Industrial workers constituted one of the most important ideological pillars of the regime: they received social privileges and were the party's human resource pool for filling public positions. Their demands were therefore always seen as legitimate, at least on a theoretical level. Local party officials therefore preferred to resolve social and political conflicts at the factories quietly and internally, and tried to avoid employing excessive sanctions and punishments against the workers. Whenever a more forceful intervention was necessary, instead of blaming the workers for instigating protests, the propaganda machine sought to create an abstract construct of a hidden enemy that allegedly manipulated workers into protesting and exploited their legitimate demands for their own illegitimate ends.

The situation at the Škoda Works was unique in that the company was the cornerstone of the first five-year plan, even on a nationwide scale, and all the processes outlined above therefore took place more intensively and visibly than in other, smaller plants. The enormous pressure on meeting the planned targets in an effort to fulfill international orders destabilized the production process in Pilsen, demanded increased employee productivity, and caused widespread dissatisfaction among the factory's workforce. The factory's exceptional prestige was reflected in the self-confidence of its workers, which was the essential prerequisite for staging public protests. The Škoda Works employees also commanded natural respect from workers at other factories in the region, who traditionally saw the protests of the Škoda workers as a signal to declare a solidarity strike. Such a scenario was common in the interwar period and was repeated again in June 1953. The influence of the Škoda Works on the social situation in West Bohemia was made even more prominent by the fact that there was no other comparably massive industrial complex in the region. Last but not least, the supra-regional scope and importance of the company meant that it created its own, closed environment that was not subject to the control mechanisms of the outside world.[259] This meant that the outside party and law enforcement authorities were largely uninformed of what was really going on inside the factory, which in turn meant that the ever-increasing problems within the company were long overlooked. This factor also played a major role in June 1953.

Even though the strikes were triggered by different causes, broke out in different departments, and reflected different conflicts, they all led to a collective development of a specific protest culture, which was based on the interwar labor movement traditions and only became more widespread and relevant again in the years 1949–1953. The factory workforce therefore viewed the various forms of boycott described above, as well as the threats of work stoppages, as perfectly normal and legitimate tools for negotiating working and social conditions. The same well-established principles came into play on the critical day of June 1, 1953, which will be discussed in the following chapter.

NOTES

1. Heumos, *Vyhrňme si rukávy*, 64.
2. Cf. ABS, f. A2/1, sv. 1861; Pernes, *Brno 1951.*
3. McDermott, "Popular Resistance," 287–307.
4. Cf. Koop, *Der 17. Juni 1953.*
5. Cf. Heumos, *Vyhrňme si rukávy.*
6. Cf. František Janáček, ed., *Největší zbrojovka monarchie: Škodovka v dějinách, dějiny ve Škodovce 1859–1918* (Prague: Novinář, 1990); Vladimír Karlický, ed., *Svět okřídleného šípu: Koncern Škoda Pilsen 1918–1945* (Pilsen: Paseka, 1999).
7. Eduard Jukl, "Z kroniky bojů Plzeňských leninovců za obnovu svého závodu a za upevnění lidově demokratického zřízení," in *K dějinám závodů V. I. Lenina Pilsen*, ed. Eduard Jukl (Pilsen: Krajské nakladatelství v Plzni, 1962), 24; Miroslav

Eisenhammer, "Škody způsobené městu Plzni nálety v době druhé světové války," *Západočeský sborník historický* 5, no. 1 (1999): 319.

8. Cf. Bauerová, Marie, *Škodovy závody v letech 1945–1949* (PhD diss., Universita Karlova v Praze, 1974).

9. Eduard Jukl, "Plzeňští leninovci v boji za splnění úkolů první pětiletky a rozvinutí výstavby socialismu v Československu (1949–1953)," in *K dějinám závodů V. I. Lenina Pilsen*, ed. Eduard Jukl (Pilsen: Krajské nakladatelství v Plzni, 1964), 7–104; Lenka Kalinová, *Společenské proměny v čase socialistického experimentu: K sociálním dějinám v letech 1945–1969* (Prague: Academia, 2007), 84.

10. Cf. Bartošek and Pichlík, *Hanebná role amerických okupantů*; Bartošek and Pichlík, *Američané v západních Čechách*; Fischer and Eis, *Americká okupace západních Čech.*

11. Decree of the President of the Republic on factory and company councils, No. 104/1945 Sb., of October 24, 1945.

12. NA, f. ÚV KSČ – 1261/2/5, sv. č. 35, a. j. č. 230, press report on the activities of the Communist party in the Pilsen region between the first and second post-war regional conference, March 1946; Bauerová, "Vznik revolučních orgánů dělnické třídy," 13–33.

13. Šlouf, "Rivalita komunistické strany a sociální demokracie," 113–137.

14. NA, f. ÚV KSČ – odborová komise, sv. č. 1, a. j. č. 18, report of the KSČ Škoda Works factory organization regarding the state of its membership, 1945.

15. Šlouf, "KSČ na Plzeňsku v letech 1945–1948," 337–432.

16. AMP, f. NV Pilsen, č. kart. 833, report of the founding meeting of the reconstituted Municipal National Committee of the Statutory City of Pilsen, June 27, 1946; VOA, f. ÚRO – ORG, č. kart. 25, č. inv. 106, report of the Škoda Works Factory Guard to ÚRO in Prague, July 4, 1946; Marie Olšanová, *Únor 1948 na Plzeňsku: Dokumenty ke 20. výročí Února* (Pilsen: KV KSČ v Plzni, 1968).

17. SOA Pilsen, f. KV KSČ v Plzni, kart. 87, inv. č. 411, Minutes of the meeting of the presidium of KV KSČ, October 5, 1945; Jukl, "Z kroniky bojů Plzeňských leninovců," 40.

18. VOA, ÚRO – ORG, č. kart. 8, č. inv. 58, Explication of the Central Council of Unions (ÚRO) regarding the rules of elections to factory councils, November 21, 1946; PA Škoda, f. Pilsen, TS 1475, election committee ordinance, March 21, 1947.

19. Ibid., PL 159 6, propaganda leaflet for factory council elections, March 1947.

20. Jukl, "Z kroniky bojů Plzeňských leninovců," 64–65.

21. Kalinová, *Společenské proměny v čase socialistického experimentu*, 108–109.

22. PA Škoda, f. Pilsen, TS 1475, election committee ordinance, March 21, 1947.

23. Ibid., f. Pilsen, TS 1475, election committee ordinance, May 12, 1947.

24. Jukl, "Z kroniky bojů Plzeňských leninovců," 66.

25. Jukl, "Z kroniky bojů Plzeňských leninovců," 80.

26. SOA Pilsen, f. PV KSČ Škoda, kart. 1, inv. č. 1, PV KSČ Škoda conference, April 1949; Ibid., f. KV KSČ Pilsen, kart. 1, Regional conference, May 7–8, 1949.

27. Ibid., f. PV KSČ Škoda Pilsen, kart. 21, inv. č. 8, critical remarks of the director of Škoda Works on the state of the heavy engineering industry, April 28, 1949; Vladislav Krásný, "Vývoj, složení, kvalifikace, pohyb pracovníků a rozvoj podniku,"

in *K dějinám závodů V. I. Lenina Pilsen*, ed. Eduard Jukl (Pilsen: Krajské nakladatelství v Plzni, 1965), 98.

28. SOA Pilsen, f. PV KSČ Škoda, kart. 17, inv. č. 4, minutes of the meeting of PV KSČ Škoda, October 19, 1948.

29. Ibid., kart. 1, inv. č. 1, PV KSČ Škoda conference, April 1949.

30. NA, ÚV KSČ – 1261/2/31, a. j. 376, kart. 66, monthly report of OV KSČ Škoda, 1949–1952.

31. *Census taken in the Czechoslovak Republic as of March 1, 1950, part 2: Population age and occupational structure* (Prague: State Statistical Office, 1958), 280; *Census and Inventory of Houses and Apartments in the Czechoslovak Republic as of March 1, 1950, Part 1: Most Significant Results of the Census and Inventory of Houses and Apartments in the Regions, District and Cities* (Prague: State Statistical Office, 1957), 85.

32. SOA Pilsen, f. PV KSČ Škoda, kart. 1, inv. č. 2, PV KSČ Škoda conference, March 15–16, 1952; AMP, f. MV KSČ Pilsen, kart. 42, Minutes of the meeting of the presidium of MV KSČ in Pilsen, June 11, 1953.

33. PA Škoda, f. Personální spisy zaměstnanců, č. 11855–A, František Brabec.

34. Ibid., f. Pilsen, Pilsen 159 15, Minutes of the meeting of the factory council, January 28, 1949; Ibid., minutes of the meetings of the factory council and the Škoda Works ROH factory organization committee, February 15, 1949 and March 8, 1949.

35. Ibid., f. ROH, ROH 13 669, Minutes of the meeting of the factory council, April 1950; Ibid., f. ZVIL, ZVIL 1494 PV 554, Minutes of the meeting of the factory council and chairmen of the workshop councils, May 2, 1950.

36. SOA Pilsen, f. PV KSČ Škoda, kart. 4, inv. č. 3, Minutes of the meeting of the plenary session of PV KSČ Škoda, March 2, 1951; Ibid., kart. 1, inv. č. 2, PV KSČ Škoda conference, March 31–April 1, 1951.

37. Ibid., kart. 4, inv. č. 3, Minutes of the meeting of the plenary session of PV KSČ Škoda, March 2, 1951.

38. Cf. Kalinová, *Společenské proměny v čase socialistického experimentu*, 149–167; Jan Hron, *Změny v oblasti mezd v období 1945–1953* (Prague: Ekonomický ústav ČSAV, 1968).

39. PA Škoda, f. ROH, ROH 12 ZR 130, report on the activities of the factory council for the year 1951.

40. SOA Pilsen, f. PŘ Pilsen, unsorted files, StB situational report on the fulfillment of the Five-Year Plan in the Škoda Works in Pilsen, June 6, 1950.

41. PA Škoda, f. ROH, ROH 13 669, Minutes of the meeting of the factory council, June 22, 1951.

42. SOA Pilsen, f. PV KSČ Škoda, kart. 1, inv. č. 2, PV KSČ Škoda conference, March 31–April 1, 1951; František Janáček, *Čtení o Škodovce* (Pilsen: Škoda Pilsen, 1978), 84.

43. Act of October 27, 1948, No. 241/1948 Sb., on the First Five-Year Economic Plan for the Development of the Czechoslovak Republic.

44. Průcha, ed., *Hospodářské a sociální dějiny Československa*, 265.

45. Průcha, ed., *Hospodářské a sociální dějiny Československa*, 251–261.

46. Jukl, "Plzeňští leninovci v boji za splnění úkolů," 40–41; Průcha, ed., *Hospodářské a sociální dějiny Československa*, 249–278.
47. Kaplan, *Sociální souvislosti krizí*, 11–13.
48. Janáček, *Čtení o Škodovce*, 84; Jukl, "Plzeňští leninovci v boji za splnění úkolů," 8–9.
49. SOA Pilsen, f. PV KSČ Škoda, kart. 1, inv. č. 2, PV KSČ Škoda conference, March 29, 1953.
50. PA Škoda, f. ZVIL, ZVIL 1515 PV 1286, Minutes of the meeting of the presidium of ZR ZVIL, December 17, 1953.
51. Jukl, "Plzeňští leninovci v boji za splnění úkolů," 25.
52. SOA Pilsen, f. PV KSČ Škoda, kart. 1, inv. č. 2, PV KSČ Škoda conference, March 15–16, 1952; "Závody V. I. Lenina – pevná a nerozborná hráz míru," *Pravda*, December 28, 1951, 1–2.
53. SOA Pilsen, PV KSČ Škoda, kart. 4, inv. č. 3, minutes of the plenary session of PV KSČ Škoda, December 8, 1950.
54. Jukl, "Plzeňští leninovci v boji za splnění úkolů," 40–41.
55. SOA Pilsen, f. PV KSČ Škoda, kart. 4, inv. č. 3, minutes of the plenary session of PV KSČ Škoda, December 8, 1950.
56. Krásný, Vladislav, "Vývoj, složení, kvalifikace," 87–156.
57. SOA Pilsen, f. PV KSČ Škoda, kart. 1, inv. č. 2, PV KSČ Škoda conference, March 15–16, 1952.
58. Ibid., PV KSČ Škoda conference, March 31–April 1, 1951; Smula, "The Party and the Proletariat," 159.
59. SOA Pilsen, f. PV KSČ Škoda, kart. 18, inv. č. 4, Minutes of the meeting of the presidium of PV KSČ Škoda, June 23, 1950.
60. Ibid., Minutes of the meeting of the presidium of PV KSČ Škoda, August 1, 1950; Jukl, "Plzeňští leninovci v boji za splnění úkolů," 53.
61. Ibid., f. PV KSČ Škoda, kart. 18, inv. č. 4, Minutes of the meeting of the presidium of PV KSČ Škoda, August 1, 1950.
62. PA Škoda, f. ZVIL, ZVIL 1494 PV 722, Minutes of the meeting of the presidium of ZR, December 5, 1952.
63. Kalinová, *Společenské proměny v čase socialistického experimentu*, 80.
64. SOA Pilsen, f. PV KSČ Škoda, kart. 4, inv. č. 3, minutes of the plenary session of PV KSČ Škoda , August 8, 1950; Smula, "The Party and the Proletariat," 160.
65. PA Škoda, f. ZVIL, ZVIL 181 Osob 983, ZVIL disciplinary committee files on Václav Lohr and Jaroslav Hobl, August 27, 1953.
66. Ibid., ZVIL 181 Osob 996, ZVIL disciplinary committee file on Bohumil Kreuzer, June 19, 1952.
67. Ibid., ZVIL 180 Osob 995, ZVIL disciplinary committee file on Josef Kouřil, September 14, 1951.
68. Ibid., ZVIL disciplinary committee file on Jaroslav Němeček, May 31, 1951.
69. Dalibor Státník, *Sankční pracovní právo v padesátých letech* (Prague: ÚSD AV ČR, 1994), 63–96.
70. SOA Pilsen, f. PV KSČ Škoda, kart. 1, inv. č. 2, PV KSČ Škoda conference, April 15–16, 1950.

71. PA Škoda, f. ZVIL, ZVIL 1 PŘ 2052, disciplinary code, undated.

72. Ibid., ZVIL 181 Osob 996, ZVIL disciplinary committee file on Barnabáš Hank, June 19, 1952; Státník, *Sankční pracovní právo*, 24.

73. PA Škoda, f. ZVIL, ZVIL 181 Osob 983, ZVIL disciplinary committee file on Josef Polan, May 22, 1953.

74. SOA Pilsen, f. PV KSČ Škoda, kart. 1, inv. č. 2, PV KSČ Škoda conference, April 15–16, 1950.

75. Jukl, "Plzeňští leninovci v boji za splnění úkolů," 29.

76. SOA Pilsen, f. PV KSČ Škoda, kart. 18, inv. č. 4, Minutes of the meetings of the presidium of PV KSČ Škoda, December 12 and 14, 1950.

77. Ibid., Minutes of the meeting of the presidium of PV KSČ Škoda, February 28, 1951.

78. Ibid., kart. 1, inv. č. 2, PV KSČ Škoda conference, March 15–16, 1952.

79. Ibid., kart. 19, inv. č. 4, Minutes of the meetings of the presidium of PV KSČ Škoda, November 18, 1952; Ibid., kart. 1, inv. č. 2, PV KSČ Škoda conference, March 29, 1953.

80. Ibid., kart. 4, inv. č. 3, minutes of the plenary session of PV KSČ Škoda, June 8, 1951; Ibid., kart. 19, inv. č. 4, Minutes of the meetings of the presidium of PV KSČ Škoda, December 14, 1951; *AMP*, f. MV KSČ Pilsen, kart. 14, minutes of the meeting of MV KSČ in Pilsen, August 31, 1953.

81. SOA Pilsen, f. PV KSČ Škoda, kart. 4, inv. č. 3, minutes of the plenary session of PV KSČ Škoda, August 20, 1951.

82. Ibid., kart. 1, inv. č. 1, PV KSČ Škoda conference, April 1949.

83. Ibid., kart. 17, inv. č. 4, minutes of the meeting of PV KSČ Škoda, November 12,. 1948.

84. Heumos, *Vyhrňme si rukávy*, 22.

85. SOA Pilsen, f. KV ČSM Pilsen, inv. č. 44, kart. 46, situation in the Škoda Works in Pilsen, 1951.

86. Ibid., f. PV KSČ Škoda, kart. 18, inv. č. 4, Minutes of the meetings of the presidium of PV KSČ Škoda, July 27, 1950.

87. Ibid., f. KV ČSM Pilsen, inv. č. 44, kart. 46, situation in the Škoda Works in Pilsen, 1951.

88. Ibid., f. PV KSČ Škoda, kart. 18, inv. č. 4, Minutes of the meetings of the presidium of PV KSČ Škoda, January 2, 1951.

89. Ibid., kart. 19, inv. č. 4, Minutes of the meetings of the presidium of PV KSČ Škoda, December 14, 1951.

90. Heumos, *Vyhrňme si rukávy*, 29.

91. SOA Pilsen, f. PV KSČ Škoda, kart. 1, inv. č. 1, PV KSČ Škoda conference, March 1949.

92. PA Škoda, f. Pilsen, Pilsen 159 15, minutes of the meetings of the factory council and the Škoda Works ROH factory organization committee, March 8, 1949.

93. SOA Pilsen, f. PV KSČ Škoda Pilsen, kart. 21, inv. č. 8, critical remarks of the director of Škoda Works on the state of the heavy engineering industry, April 28, 1949; Ibid., survey of the situation in the Škoda Works, August 7, 1950.

94. PA Škoda, f. ZVIL, ZVIL 1452 ZR 352, state of socialist competition in the ZVIL, April 30, 1950.

95. Heumos, *Vyhrňme si rukávy*, s. 44–48.

96. PA Škoda, f. Pilsen, Pilsen 159 15, Minutes of the meetings of ZR, November 2., 1949.

97. Jukl, "Plzeňští leninovci v boji za splnění úkolů," 23.

98. PA Škoda, f. ZVIL, ZVIL 1452 ZR 352, report on socialist competition, May 8, 1950.

99. SOA Pilsen, f. PV KSČ Škoda, kart. 18, inv. č. 4, Minutes of the meetings of the presidium of PV KSČ Škoda, December 3, 1950.

100. Ibid., kart. 1, inv. č. 2, PV KSČ Škoda conference, March 15–16, 1950.

101. Ibid., kart. 18, inv. č. 4, Minutes of the meetings of the presidium of PV KSČ Škoda, November 8, 1950.

102. Heumos, *Vyhrňme si rukávy*, 35.

103. PA Škoda, f. ZVIL, ZVIL 179 Osob 994, ZVIL disciplinary committee file on Vojtěch Čermák, November 29, 1951; Ibid., ZVIL 1459 ZR 138A, Minutes of the meetings of the presidium of ZR, August 3, 1951.

104. SOA Pilsen, f. PV KSČ Škoda, kart. 1, inv. č. 2, PV KSČ Škoda conference, April 15–16, 1950.

105. Ibid., PV KSČ Škoda conference, March 31–April 1, 1951; Ibid., kart. 18, inv. č. 4, Minutes of the meetings of the presidium of PV KSČ Škoda, December 12, 1950.

106. Heumos, *Vyhrňme si rukávy*, 45–48.

107. Ibid., 58.

108. NA, f. ÚV KSČ – 1481, sv. 15, a. j. 110, Minutes of the nationwide meeting of chief secretaries of KV KSČ, heads of the departments of ÚV KSČ and chief officials of mass organizations, held on June 11, 1953; speech by Antonín Zápotocký.

109. PA Škoda, f. ZVIL, ZVIL 179 Osob 994, ZVIL disciplinary committee file on Antonín Jelínek, June 7, 1951.

110. Jukl, "Z kroniky bojů Plzeňských leninovců," 56–57; Kalinová, *Společenské proměny v čase socialistického experimentu*, 86–87.

111. Heumos, *Vyhrňme si rukávy*, 44.

112. SOA Pilsen, f. PV KSČ Škoda, kart. 4, inv. č. 3, minutes of the plenary session of PV KSČ Škoda, March 3, 1950; Ibid., kart. 1, inv. č. 1, PV KSČ Škoda conference, April 1949.

113. PA Škoda, f. ZVIL, ZVIL 1452 ZR 352, report on socialist competition, May 8, 1950.

114. Ibid., ZVIL 1452 ZR 353, factory contract on guaranteeing targets for the year 1951 by employees of the Škoda Works main plant in Pilsen, December 22, 1950.

115. SOA Pilsen, f. PV KSČ Škoda, kart. 1, inv. č. 2, PV KSČ Škoda conference, March 31–April 1, 1951.

116. Ibid., kart. 19, inv. č. 4, Minutes of the meeting of the presidium of PV KSČ Škoda, July 2, 1951; Ibid., kart. 4, inv. č. 3, minutes of the plenary session of PV KSČ Škoda, July 13, 1951.

117. Ibid., kart. 19, inv. č. 4, Minutes of the meeting of the presidium of PV KSČ Škoda, July 2, 1951; Ibid., kart. 1, inv. č. 2, PV KSČ Škoda conference, March 15–16, 1952.

118. PA Škoda, f. ZVIL, ZVIL 1452 ZR 146, documentation on targets review in 1951.

119. Ibid., ZVIL 1452 ZR 382, documentation on targets review in 1953.

120. Ibid., f. ROH, ROH 13 669, Minutes of the meeting of the ZR, June 22, 1951.

121. SOA Pilsen, f. PV KSČ Škoda, kart. 4, inv. č. 3, minutes of the plenary session of PV KSČ Škoda, October 27, 1950; Ibid., minutes of the plenary session of PV KSČ Škoda, July 13, 1951.

122. PA Škoda, f. ZVIL, ZVIL 1452 ZR 382, documentation on targets review in 1953.

123. Ibid., ZVIL 181 Osob 983, ZVIL disciplinary committee file on Alfred Měsíček, November 28, 1951.

124. Ibid., ZVIL disciplinary committee file on Josef Bican, August 28, 1953.

125. SOA Pilsen, f. PV KSČ Škoda, kart. 4, inv. č. 3, minutes of the plenary session of PV KSČ Škoda, March 21, 1950.

126. PA Škoda, f. ZVIL, ZVIL 178 Osob 987, ZVIL disciplinary committee file on Marie Hrabáková, March 25, 1950.

127. SOA Pilsen, f. PV KSČ Škoda Pilsen, kart. 21, inv. č. 8, Minutes of the meeting of the KSČ workshop committee, ETD Gigant, October 15, 1952; Smula, "The Party and the Proletariat," 161.

128. SOA Pilsen, f. KV KSČ Pilsen, kart. 29, inv. č. 101, minutes of the plenary session of KV KSČ, July 5, 1953.

129. Ibid., f. PV KSČ Škoda, kart. 19, inv. č. 4, Minutes of the meeting of the presidium of PV KSČ Škoda , November 18, 1952.

130. SOA Pilsen, f. PV KSČ Škoda, kart. 18, inv. č. 4, Minutes of the meeting of the presidium of PV KSČ Škoda, May 15, 1951.

131. Ibid., kart. 19, inv. č. 4, Minutes of the meeting of the presidium of PV KSČ Škoda, December 14, 1951.

132. *NA*, f. ÚV KSČ – 1261/2/1, sv. 361, a. j. 2190, report on political volunteering in the Pilsen region, February 24–March 7, 1953.

133. SOA Pilsen, f. PV KSČ Škoda, kart. 4, inv. č. 3, minutes of the plenary session of PV KSČ Škoda, August 8, 1950.

134. Ibid., kart. 199, inv. č. 4, Minutes of the meeting of the presidium of PV KSČ Škoda, December 14, 1951.

135. Ibid., kart. 1, inv. č. 2, PV KSČ Škoda conference, March 31–April 1, 1951.

136. Ibid., kart. 21, inv. č. 8, report on the political situation in the Steeelworks department, 1951.

137. NA, ÚV KSČ – 1261/2/1, sv. 361, a. j. 2190, report on political volunteering in the Pilsen region, February 24–March 7, 1953.

138. SOA Pilsen, f. PV KSČ Škoda, kart. 199, inv. č. 4, Minutes of the meeting of the presidium of PV KSČ Škoda, December 14, 1951.

139. Ibid., f. PŘ Pilsen, unsorted files, StB report on the situation in the Škoda Works, June 7, 1949.

140. Ibid., f. PV KSČ Škoda, kart. 4, inv. č. 3, minutes of the plenary session of PV KSČ Škoda, June 8, 1951.
141. Ibid., minutes of the plenary session of PV KSČ Škoda, July 21, 1950.
142. Ibid., minutes of the plenary session of PV KSČ Škoda , September 22, 1951.
143. Ibid.
144. Ibid., kart. 18, inv. č. 4, Minutes of the meeting of the presidium of PV KSČ Škoda, December 3,. 1950.
145. Ibid., kart. 1, inv. č. 2, PV KSČ Škoda conference, March 15–16, 1952.
146. Ibid., kart. 21, inv. č. 8, report on the political situation in the Steeelworks department, 1951.
147. Ibid., kart. 18, inv. č. 4, Minutes of the meeting of the presidium of PV KSČ Škoda, January 16, 1951; Ibid., kart. 1, inv. č. 2, PV KSČ Škoda conference, March 31–April 1,1951; *NA*, f. ÚV KSČ – 1261/2/31, a. j. 376, kart. 66, monthly reports of OV KSČ Škoda, 1951–1952.
148. Smula, "The Party and the Proletariat," 155.
149. PA Škoda, f. ZVIL, ZVIL 178 Osob 987, ZVIL disciplinary committee file on Emil Opočenský, December 3, 1949.
150. Ibid., f. ROH, ROH 13 669, Minutes of the meeting of the ZR, October 22, 1951.
151. AMP, f. MV KSČ Pilsen, kart. 14, Minutes of the meeting of MV KSČ in Pilsen, December 7, 1953.
152. Ibid.
153. SOA Pilsen, f. KV KSČ Pilsen, kart. 452, inv. č. 3603, Minutes of the meeting of the officials of CZV KSČ in ZVIL in Pilsen, September 10, 1953.
154. Ibid., f. PV KSČ Škoda, kart. 19, inv. č. 4, Minutes of the meeting of the presidium of PV KSČ Škoda 24. 7. 1951; Ibid., f. KV KSČ Pilsen, krajská revizní komise, kart. 629, č. 3059, report for the presidium of KV KSČ on the investigation of the dispute between Miloslav Mudra and Václav Telín, May 31, 1951.
155. Šlouf, "Krajské vedení KSČ," 261–352.
156. SOA Pilsen, f. PV KSČ Škoda, kart. 1, inv. č. 2, PV KSČ Škoda conference, March 31–April 1, 1951.
157. Knapík, *Vzajetí moci*, 195–196.
158. SOA Pilsen, f. KV KSČ Pilsen, kart. 452, inv. č. 3603, Minutes of the meeting of the officials of CZV KSČ in ZVIL in Pilsen, September 10, 1953.
159. Ibid., Minutes of the meeting of the ROH ZVIL factory organization committee in Pilsen, September 11, 1953.
160. Ibid., f. PV KSČ Škoda, kart. 19, inv. č. 4, Minutes of the meeting of the presidium of PV KSČ Škoda, December 7, 1951.
161. Ibid., kart. 18, inv. č. 4, Minutes of the meeting of the presidium of PV KSČ Škoda, December 12, 1950.
162. ABS, f. 319, sv. 319–5–1, investigation of complaints against Matěj Bálek in 1954.
163. PA Škoda, f. PV KSČ 1 271, Minutes of the meeting of the OV KSČ Škoda special commission regarding the case of Jan Zítek, Jan Danda and Jan Piller, May

10, 1951; *ABS*, f. A8/1, sv. 41, report on the results of investigation of Matěj Bálek's case, May 22, 1954.

164. SOA Pilsen, f. PV KSČ Škoda, kart. 1, inv. č. 2, PV KSČ Škoda conference, March 31–April 1, 1951; PA Škoda, f. PV KSČ 1 271, report on Miroslav Hříbek's vetting, May 20, 1949.

165. ABS, f. A8/1, sv. 41, report on the results of investigation of Matěj Bálek's case, May 22, 1954.

166. SOA Pilsen, f. PV KSČ Škoda, kart. 4, inv. č. 3, minutes of the plenary session of PV KSČ Škoda 2. 3. 1951.

167. Ibid., kart. 19, inv. č. 4, Minutes of the meeting of the presidium of PV KSČ Škoda 24. 7. 1951.

168. PA Škoda, f. PV KSČ 1 271, Minutes of the meeting of the OV KSČ Škoda special commission regarding the case of Jan Zítek, Jan Danda and Jan Piller, May 10, 1951.

169. SOA Pilsen, f. KV KSČ Pilsen, kart. 452, inv. č. 3603, Minutes of the meeting of the officials of CZV KSČ in ZVIL in Pilsen, September 10, 1953.

170. Ibid., f. PV KSČ Škoda, kart. 4, inv. č. 3, minutes of the plenary sessions of PV KSČ Škoda 1. 4. 1951 a June 8, 1951.

171. PA Škoda, f. Pilsen, Pilsen 159 15, Minutes of the meetings of ZR 28. 1. 1949 a 8. 3. 1949.

172. NA, f. ÚPV-T, sig. 52–2–20, č.j. 1835/1949, anonymous letter of a Škoda Works employee to the Prime Minister, May 23, 1949.

173. SOA Pilsen, f. KV KSČ Pilsen, krajská revizní komise, kart. 579, spis. č. 589, criminal ruling of the ÚNV in the statutory city of Pilsen, March 24, 1949; *NA*, f. ÚPV-T, sig. 52–2–20, č.j. 1835/1949, anonymous letter of a Škoda Works employee to the Prime Minister, May 23, 1949; SOA Pilsen, f. KV KSČ Pilsen, krajská revizní komise, kart. 579, spis. č. 589, Minutes of the meetings of the committees of local KSČ organizations in Nová Hospoda I and II, April 10–13, 1951; PA Škoda, f. Pilsen, Pilsen 159 15, Minutes of the meeting of ZR, March 30, 1949.

174. SOA Pilsen, f. KV KSČ Pilsen, krajská revizní komise, kart. 570, spis. č. 241, statement of Josef Kutzendorfer regarding the economic cooperative, undated.

175. Ibid., kart. 602, č. 1821, report on the results of investigation of Milada Netušilová, undated; Ibid., kart. 579, spis. č. 589, statement of Milada Netušilová, undated.

176. Ibid., kart. 634, spis. č. 3253.

177. NA, f. ÚPV-T, sig. 52–2–20, č.j. 1835/1949, anonymous letter of Škoda Works employees to the Prime Minister, February 9, 1951.

178. Ibid., letter of the Minister of Interior to the Prime Minister's Office, March 18, 1950.

179. SOA Pilsen, f. KV KSČ Pilsen, krajská revizní komise, kart. 579, spis. č. 589, Minutes of the meetings of the committees of local KSČ organizations in Nová Hospoda I and II, April 10–13, 1951.

180. Ibid., f. PŘ Pilsen, unsorted files, StB report on the discontent among Škoda Works workers in Pilsen, April 4, 1949.

181. PA Škoda, f. Pilsen, Pilsen 159 15, Minutes of the meeting of the ZR, 19. 4. 1949.

182. SOA Pilsen, f. KV KSČ Pilsen, krajská revizní komise, kart. 579, spis. č. 589, Minutes of the meeting of the ZR regarding the case of Josef Kutzendorfer, July 21, 1949.

183. Ibid.

184. Ibid.

185. Ibid., Minutes of the meetings of the committees of local KSČ organizations in Nová Hospoda I and II, April 10–13, 1951.

186. NA, f. ÚPV-T, sig. 52–2–20, č.j. 1835/1949, letter from Lt. Col. Vacek to the Prime Minister's Office, February 21, 1950.

187. SOA Pilsen, f. PŘ Pilsen, unsorted files, StB report on the situation in the Škoda Works in Pilsen, June 7, 1949.

188. Ibid., f. KV KSČ Pilsen, kart. 452, inv. č. 3603, Minutes of the meeting of the officials of CZV KSČ in ZVIL in Pilsen, September 10, 1953.

189. Ibid., kart. 109, inv. č. 813, Minutes of the meeting of the KV KSČ executive committee, August 7, 1953.

190. Ibid., f. PV KSČ Škoda, kart. 19, inv. č. 4, Minutes of the meeting of the presidium of PV KSČ Škoda 24. 7. 1951; Ibid., f. KV KSČ Pilsen, krajská revizní komise, kart. 629, č. 3059, report for the presidium of KV KSČ on the investigation of the dispute between Miloslav Mudra and Václav Telín, May 31, 1951.

191. Ibid., f. PV KSČ Škoda Pilsen, kart. 21, inv. č. 8, complaint of the KSČ factory organization regarding the Large Rotating Machinery department, May 25, 1953; Ibid., report to the ÚV KSČ of July 9, 1953; Ibid., f. KV KSČ Pilsen, kart. 449, inv. č. 3603, report to the 2nd dpt. of the KV KSČ secretariat in Pilsen, 1953; Smula, "The Party and the Proletariat," 168.

192. Cf. Pavel Marek, *České živnostnictvo 1945–1960: Likvidace živnostníků, řemeslníků a obchodníků v českých zemích* (Brno: Doplněk, 2006); Karel Jech, *Soumrak selského stavu 1945–1960* (Prague: ÚSD AV ČR, 2001).

193. SOA Pilsen, f. KV KSČ Pilsen, kart. 450, inv. č. 3603, ZVIL employee structure, 1953.

194. Ibid., f. PV KSČ Škoda, kart. 1, inv. č. 2, PV KSČ Škoda conference, March 15–16, 1952.

195. PA Škoda, f. ZVIL, ZVIL 178 Osob 987, ZVIL disciplinary committee file on Ludvík Brejcha, February 28, 1950.

196. Ibid., ZVIL 180 Osob 995, ZVIL disciplinary committee file on Karel Trnka, April 23, 1951.

197. Ibid., ZVIL 179 Osob 994, ZVIL disciplinary committee file on Miloslav Jarolímek, November 29, 1951.

198. Ibid., ZVIL 180 Osob 995, ZVIL disciplinary committee file on František Šašek, August 17, 1951.

199. SOkA v Blovicích, f. OS Pilsen, zn. 3T 77/1953.

200. SOkA v Blovicích, f. OS Pilsen, zn. 3T 95/1953.

201. Ibid.

202. SOA Pilsen, f. KV KSČ Pilsen, kart. 451, inv. č. 3603, minutes of the extraordinary meeting of the KV KSČ executive committee, September 10, 1953.

203. NA, f. ÚPV-T, sig. 52–2–20, č.j. 1835/1949, letter of the Minister of Interior to the Prime Minister's Office, March 18, 1950; *SOA Pilsen*, f. KV KSČ Pilsen, krajská revizní komise, kart. 579, spis. č. 589, Minutes of the meetings of the committees of local KSČ organizations in Nová Hospoda I and II, April 10–13, 1951.

204. Ibid., f. PŘ Pilsen, unsorted files, StB report on the situation in the Škoda Works in Pilsen, February 16, 1950.

205. PA Škoda, f. ROH, ROH 13 669, Minutes of the meeting of the ZR, May 28, 1951.

206. Ibid., f. ZVIL, ZVIL 180 Osob 995, ZVIL disciplinary committee file on Bedřich Poul, April 25, 1951.

207. SOA Pilsen, f. PV KSČ Škoda, kart. 18, inv. č. 4, Minutes of the meeting of the presidium of PV KSČ Škoda, March 23, 1951; Ibid., kart. 1, inv. č. 2, PV KSČ Škoda conference, March 31–April 1, 1951.

208. PA Škoda, f. ZVIL, ZVIL 179 Osob 994, ZVIL disciplinary committee file, January 21, 1951.

209. Ibid., ZVIL disciplinary committee file regarding the breach of work discipline in Kolíkárna, September 6, 1951.

210. SOA Pilsen, f. PV KSČ Škoda, kart. 4, inv. č. 3, minutes of the plenary session of PV KSČ Škoda, June 29, 1951.

211. Ibid., f. PŘ Pilsen, unsorted files, StB report on the fulfillment of targets in the Škoda Works in Pilsen, June 6, 1950; AMP, f. MV KSČ Pilsen, kart. 14, Minutes of the meeting of the MV KSČ v Plzni, February 3, 1953.

212. SOA Pilsen, f. PV KSČ Škoda, kart. 18, inv. č. 4, Minutes of the meeting of the presidium of PV KSČ Škoda, June 21, 1950; PA Škoda, f. ZVIL, ZVIL 178 Osob 987, ZVIL disciplinary committee file on Miroslav Vokoun, August 23, 1950.

213. SOA Pilsen, f. PŘ Pilsen, unsorted files, StB report on the situation and mood in the workshops, undated.

214. Ibid., f. PV KSČ Škoda, kart. 18, inv. č. 4, Minutes of the meeting of the presidium of PV KSČ Škoda, June 23, 1950.

215. Ibid., minutes of the extraordinary meeting of the presidium of PV KSČ Škoda, August 3, 1950.

216. Ibid., kart. 1, inv. č. 2, PV KSČ Škoda conference, March 31–April 1, 1951; Ibid., f. KV KSČ Pilsen, kart. 451, inv. č. 3603, minutes of the extraordinary meeting of the KV KSČ executive committee, September 10, 1953.

217. Ibid., f. PV KSČ Škoda, kart. 18, inv. č. 4, Minutes of the meeting of the presidium of PV KSČ Škoda, July 27, 1950.

218. Ibid., minutes of the extraordinary meeting of the presidium of PV KSČ Škoda, August 3,1950.

219. Ibid., kart. 21, inv. č. 8, report on a strike in ETD, July 24, 1950.

220. Ibid., kart. 18, inv. č. 4, minutes of the extraordinary meeting of the presidium of PV KSČ Škoda, August 3, 1950.

221. Ibid., kart. 21, inv. č. 8, report on a strike in ETD, July 24, 1950.
222. Ibid., kart. 18, inv. č. 4, minutes of the extraordinary meeting of the presidium of PV KSČ Škoda August 3, 1950.
223. Ibid., kart. 21, inv. č. 8, report on a strike in ETD, July 24, 1950.
224. NA, f. ÚPV-T, sig. 52–2–20, č.j. 1835/1949, anonymous letter of the Škoda works employees (allegedly from the Vehicles and Machine Tools departments) to the Prime Minister, February 9, 1951.
225. Ibid.
226. Ibid.
227. SOA Pilsen, f. PV KSČ Škoda, kart. 18, inv. č. 4, Minutes of the meeting of the presidium of PV KSČ Škoda, July 27, 1950.
228. Ibid., kart. 21, inv. č. 8, report on a strike in ETD, July 24, 1950.
229. NA, f. ÚPV-T, sig. 52–2–20, č.j. 1835/1949, anonymous letter of the Škoda works employees to the Prime Minister, February 9, 1951.
230. SOA Pilsen, f. PV KSČ Škoda Pilsen, kart. 21, inv. č. 8, survey of the situation in the Škoda Works, August 7, 1950.
231. PA Škoda, f. ZVIL, ZVIL 1494 PV 722, Minutes of the meeting of the presidium of ZR, October 6, 1952.
232. Ibid., Minutes of the meeting of the presidium of ZR, August 30, 1952.
233. SOA Pilsen, f. PV KSČ Škoda, kart. 18, inv. č. 4, Minutes of the meeting of the presidium of PV KSČ Škoda, August 1, 1950.
234. ABS, f. A 8, sv. 1191, recorded statement of Dobroslav Souček for the Ministry of Interior inspectorate, May 11, 1965.
235. SOkA v Blovicích, f. OS Pilsen, zn. 1T 136/1953, court file of the main hearing at the People's Court in Pilsen, July 13, 1953.
236. SOA Pilsen, f. PV KSČ Škoda Pilsen, kart. 21, inv. č. 8, report on a strike in ETD, July 24, 1950.
237. Ibid., kart. 18, inv. č. 4, minutes of the extraordinary meeting of the presidium of PV KSČ Škoda, August 3, 1950; Ibid., kart. 1, inv. č. 2, PV KSČ Škoda conference, March 31–April 1, 1951.
238. Ibid., kart. 21, inv. č. 8, report on the political situation in the Steelworks department, 1951.
239. Ibid., kart. 18, inv. č. 4, minutes of the extraordinary meeting of the presidium of PV KSČ Škoda, August 3, 1950.
240. Ibid., Minutes of the meeting of the presidium of PV KSČ Škoda, August 1, 1950.
241. Ibid., Minutes of the meetings of the presidium of PV KSČ Škoda, July 27, 1950 and August 3, 1950.
242. Ibid., kart. 4, inv. č. 3, minutes of the plenary session of PV KSČ Škoda, June 29, 1951.
243. Ibid., kart. 1, inv. č. 2, PV KSČ Škoda conference, March 15–16, 1952; Ibid., f. KV KSČ Pilsen, kart. 109, inv. č. 813, Minutes of the meetings of the KV KSČ executive committee 7. 8. 1953; Ibid., kart. 451, inv. č. 3603, minutes of the extraordinary meeting of KV KSČ executive committee, September 10, 1953.

244. Ibid., f. PV KSČ Škoda, kart. 1, inv. č. 2, PV KSČ Škoda conference, March 15–16, 1952; Ibid., f. KV KSČ Pilsen, kart. 109, inv. č. 813, Minutes of the meeting of the KV KSČ executive committee, August 7, 1953.

245. PA Škoda, f. ZVIL, ZVIL 524 PŘ 203, instruction on the payment of Christmas bonuses, issued by the accounting department of the ZVIL in Pilsen, November 28, 1951.

246. Cf. Pernes, *Brno 1951*.

247. SOA Pilsen, f. PV KSČ Škoda, kart. 4, inv. č. 3, minutes of the plenary session of PV KSČ Škoda, November 23, 1951.

248. NA, f. ÚV KSČ – 1261/2/1, sv. 361, a. j. 2188, report from Jan Zika sent to the ÚV KSČ, December 26, 1951.

249. Ibid., report from Jan Zika sent to the ÚV KSČ, November 23, 1951.

250. SOA Pilsen, f. PV KSČ Škoda, kart. 4, inv. č. 3, minutes of the plenary session of PV KSČ Škoda November 23, 1951.

251. PA Škoda, f. ZVIL, ZVIL 544 729A, report of Comrade Haas to the Ministry of State Control, 1953; Ibid., f. ROH, ROH 14 PV 61, Minutes of the meeting of the presidium of ZR ZVIL in Pilsen, January 14, 1953.

252. Ibid., f. ZVIL, ZVIL 544 729A, report of director František Brabec to the Ministry of State Control, March 26, 1953; SOA Pilsen, f. PV KSČ Škoda, kart. 1, inv. č. 2, PV KSČ Škoda conference, March 29, 1953; NA, f. ÚV KSČ – 1261/0/2 sv. 11, a. j. 145, information bulletin No.. 7/II, February 23, 1953.

253. PA Škoda, f. ROH, ROH 14 PV 61, Minutes of the meeting of the presidium of ZR ZVIL in Pilsen, January 15, 1953.

254. NA, f. ÚV KSČ – 1261/2/1, sv. 361, a. j. 2190, report on political volunteering in the Pilsen region, February 24–March 7, 1953.

255. SOA Pilsen, f. PV KSČ Škoda, kart. 1, inv. č. 2, PV KSČ Škoda conference, March 29, 1953.

256. PA Škoda, f. ZVIL, ZVIL 544 729A, report of director František Brabec to the Ministry of State Control, March 26, 1953.

257. Ibid., f. ROH, ROH 16 PV 989, report from the ROH members' meeting in the ZVIL Large Forging Plant department, February 26, 1953; Skála, "Měnová reforma," 607.

258. PA Škoda, f. ZVIL, ZVIL 544 729A, report of director František Brabec to the Ministry of State Control, March 26, 1953.

259. Lindenberger, *Herrschaft und Eigen-Sinn*, 13–45.

Chapter 3

Pilsen Strikes and Protests on June 1, 1953

From June 1 to 6, 1953, a nationwide wave of resistance against the currency reform broke out in Czechoslovakia. The key protagonists of the protests were industrial workers, who went on strike in 129 factories throughout the country.[1] In a number of places, workers even tried to move the protests out of the factories and take to the streets: this included such enterprises as ČKD Stalingrad in Prague,[2]Aero Vysočany in Prague,[3] Gustav Kliment's Ironworks in Bohumín,[4] the mines in Orlová,[5] the Czech Armaments Factory in Strakonice,[6] and the industrial enterprises in Vimperk.[7]

By far the most turbulent protests were those staged by the workers of the V. I. Lenin Factories in Pilsen, who were joined in the streets by a significant part of the city's population. This resulted in a peculiar amalgamation of the two types of protest analyzed earlier (workers' strikes of 1949–1953 and the public protests of 1948–1949). That way, the officially recognized legitimacy of the workers' protests was also transferred to anyone who joined them. This fusion of different protest cultures was further enhanced by a widespread sense of existential threat that brought an unprecedented level of emotion to the protests, as well as previously unprecedented forms of violence, such as attempts to lynch some local public officials. On a regional scale, the party and law enforcement authorities temporarily failed to function during the implementation of the reform and the ensuing protests, and the situation had to be handled by an intervention from the central authorities and deployment of law enforcement forces from outside Pilsen.

Before proceeding to the actual analysis of the West Bohemian protests, a brief outline of the currency reform and the events that immediately preceded its announcement is required.

THE CURRENCY REFORM

Despite the aforementioned increase in industrial production during the first five-year plan, the wartime rationing system of supplying the population was still in operation in Czechoslovakia in 1948–1953. Although the government had long considered abolishing it, the state of the economy made such a move very risky. There was a serious danger that the removal of the restricted market would result in panic buying and stockpiling, which would lead to disruptions in the availability of basic necessities. This situation was mainly caused by the fact that between 1945 and 1953, people's incomes grew considerably, but the possibilities of purchasing consumer goods and foodstuffs remained very limited.[8] Household savings thus reached such a level that they could cause a supply crisis if they were suddenly utilized on a free market.[9]

The significant disproportion between the amount of currency in circulation and the volume of production was nothing new in the 1950s. Governments of the Third Republic (1945–1948) had already faced a similar problem. In the autumn of 1945, currency reform was implemented to integrate the war-fragmented system of currencies used in the country and, at the same time, to restrict the excess purchasing power of the population created by wartime inflation. At that time, only 500 Kč per person could be exchanged (at a ratio of 1:1), and the remaining funds were tied up in bank accounts. These tied-up deposits were only to be released in emergency circumstances, such as impoverishment. Nevertheless, the people could still theoretically hope to be able to use these savings in the future.[10]

Gradual steps toward the abolition of the restricted market were eventually initiated in January 1949, when some products were transferred to the free market. This created a dual pricing mechanism: the socially acceptable prices within the restricted coupon system were in a stark contrast with the exorbitant prices on the free market. The wide gap between the two price systems enabled the state socialist regime to give preferential treatment to selected segments of society by allowing them higher rations on the restricted market (hard-working workers and members of the armed forces) or conversely, to materially weaken other groups by depriving them of the right to participate in the coupon system (self-employed small farmers and tradesmen).[11]

Nevertheless, the currency reform of autumn 1945 did not provide a long-term resolution of the market disproportions. Inconsistent supervision of the release of tied-up deposits (in 1945–1948); overly dynamic wage growth that was not proportionate to labor productivity (in 1945–1953); and the excessive focus of the national economy on expanding heavy industry (in 1948–1953) made it impossible to eliminate the deficit in the supply of consumer goods in relation to demand. From 1951 onward, the gradual easing of restrictions on the sale of goods began to fail and basic foodstuffs (especially flour and meat products) were frequently unavailable or in short supply. It thus became clear that the abolition of the restricted market could only be achieved by a sharp increase in prices to compensate for the chronic imbalance between supply and demand. Another possible solution was a currency reform which would drain the population's surplus savings and allow the government to abolish the restricted market without drastic price increases.[12] Along with the planned end of the regulated supply system, the government started secretly preparing a currency reform in 1952,[13] which was originally intended as an auxiliary measure to facilitate the abolition of the ration system, and only later did it become an important tool of political propaganda, when it was introduced as a way to eliminate the former wealthy elite.[14]

After several months of secret preparations, the Central Committee of the Communist Party of Czechoslovakia and the government approved the implementation of both measures on May 30, 1953.[15] On the same day, the National Assembly adopted the Currency Reform Act,[16] the specific implementation of which was outlined in a directive of the Minister of Finance on the method of implementing currency reform. On June 1, 1953, the restricted market was abolished, and a new wage scale and price tariff were introduced.[17] Nominal wage levels rose slightly after the conversion to the new currency, while price levels dropped relative to the former free market, but nearly doubled compared to the former restricted market.[18] Physical currency exchange was introduced at the same time, resulting in a significant reduction in people's savings. The tied-up deposits of 1945 were canceled completely. Cash was exchanged at a ratio of 5:1 for amounts of up to CZK 300 per person, and then at a ratio of 50:1 for any amounts over that limit. Current deposits in financial institutions were converted in several stages at ratios from 5:1 (amounts up to CZK 5,000) up to 30:1 (amounts over CZK 50,000).[19]

In the long run, the reform helped consolidate the national economy and created conditions for more stable growth in production and consumption in the following years. At the same time, however, this happened at the expense of the citizens and at the cost of a temporary sharp decline in consumption.[20] The currency reform posed a significant existential threat to such groups as pensioners with low incomes (by reducing their savings) and families with children, especially those with only one working parent (by eliminating the benefits of the restricted market). In the following months, therefore, pensioners and housewives began to increasingly search for employment.[21] In general, the drain on savings deepened the people's dependence on the state.[22]

An often unjustly overlooked outcome of the reform was the abolition of the ration system, which had been one of the pillars of social privilege for selected population groups, including a significant part of the industrial workforce.[23]

Besides the long-term social impact of the currency reform, it was the tense social situation around that time that was a crucial factor for the emergence of public protests. Despite the best efforts of its authors, preparations for the reform did not remain completely secret.[24] People found out about it both from foreign radio broadcasts and from the suspicious behavior of the state administration. A particularly important factor in this respect was the sudden introduction of wage advances, which caused a nationwide panic in mid-May 1953, resulting in a complete collapse of the supply system before the currency reform had even begun.[25]

The aforementioned government resolution of May 5, 1953, ordered national enterprises to pay employees' wages in two installments. Advances were to be paid in the middle of the month (May 15–20, 1953) and the rest of the wages at the beginning of the following month. The purpose of this change was to provide people with sufficient funds to be able to stock up on food before the currency reform and get through the most difficult period. Officially, the change was justified by the requirements for corporate accounting and the need to ensure continuous supply to shops.[26]

Deprived of any credible sources of information, however, the population reacted to this signal with considerable panic. Rumors immediately began to spread in Pilsen that "the currency was to be devalued and that new money was to be put into circulation at a ratio of 1:10."[27] There was also talk among the people that it would only be possible to trade in Soviet rubles from now on. Some alarmist reports even spoke of an impending war. This wide range of explanations, spread by word-of-mouth, shows that the population's assumptions about the forthcoming measures were rather inaccurate, and the resulting panic reached even greater proportions than the reform actually warranted.

The people had already experienced shortages of various kinds and had tried to stock up in such situations, just in case.[28] On Monday May 18, 1953, panic buying broke out in Pilsen, during which people bought food, clothing, or any goods which could serve as an immediate investment. In the following days, the mass run on the stores swayed even those who did not initially succumb to panic. In Pilsen, people bought salami by the kilo, purchased shoes without trying them on, and women's fur coats were sold out of season. On May 18, department stores were routinely meeting their sales targets by more than 700%.[29] By May 19, 1953, stores selling everyday goods, which were understocked even in normal conditions, were almost sold out.[30] Even products which had been in stock for many years without attracting much customer interest had disappeared.[31] In the days that followed, people therefore went on to buy industrial and luxury goods, the high price being considered more of an advantage. Bicycles, sewing machines, radios, motorcycles, and furniture in particular dominated this phase, with the stores concerned once again breaking daily sales records.[32]

A similar situation occurred nationwide, which forced the Ministry of Internal Trade to close all stores selling unrestricted goods on May 25, 1953.[33] Unfortunately, store closures forced by the panic buying caused even more panic in turn. Many people began to believe that once the stores reopened they would be selling at even higher prices. They were thus forced to continue spending their money in stores selling rationed goods (mainly textiles and foodstuffs). Those who no longer had food stamps began to eat in pubs. In large factories with their own canteens, employees tried to stock up on food through the company.[34] People began depositing surplus money back into savings bank accounts.[35]

Paradoxically, this meant that the panic buying caused panic to break out even before the currency reform was officially announced, and people had thus only aggravated the situation, causing a general shortage of goods in the stores and a fortnight of stress. This amplified the overall sense of threat even more. Empty shop windows and closed stores seemed to portend impending famine. Some people actually did go hungry, because the closed stores had forced them to cut down on food for days.[36]

These factors had a marked impact on the events at the V. I. Lenin Factories. As early as May 25, 1953, a wave of small strikes broke out in the factory. After the payment of wage advances, workers began to increasingly demand factory-provided snacks so they could stock up on food even though the stores had been sold out and closed. However, the company failed to provide sufficient quantities of food (especially salami) and cigarettes. Consequently, clusters of indignant workers began forming in some workshops (Engineering I and Finishing II), debating the sense of closing the stores. Workers with physically demanding occupations refused to start work and defended themselves by claiming they "had nothing to eat."[37] Factory management tried to explain things and calm the workers down, but things only improved after it managed to secure an additional delivery of food through the Regional National Committee. The workers thus forced the establishment of a free food market in the plant and work was gradually resumed.[38] However, none of the officials called to the factory were able to refute the criticism of the government voiced by the workers.[39]

Even though historians have not given these events much attention to date, they were a clear precursor to the events of June 1, 1953, indicating the atmosphere of suspicion prevailing in the factory and the very limited willingness of its workers to make concessions in response to poorly explained government measures. The workers had long felt that the government was acting without the necessary knowledge of how ordinary people live. Even the Party members in the factory criticized the closing down of stores and expressed the view that the country was "hurtling down the road to the unknown."[40]

For the party and law enforcement authorities, the currency reform presented an extremely difficult task. At the political level, an extensive campaign of persuasion had to be launched to make the people accept the official justification of the highly unpopular government measures. At the administrative level, it was necessary to ensure a rapid exchange of money, take inventory in all stores, organize the transition to sales at the new prices, and to prevent supply outages. Law enforcement focused on protecting the exchange centers and on eliminating the expected protest incidents during currency exchange. It was a complex undertaking which in itself would have required extensive effort from the administration in any regime.

The situation was further aggravated by the fact that the currency reform was being prepared in secret, and the lower-level party organizations and law enforcement units did not have time to prepare for it; they had to implement it on the fly, practically overnight. It was this circumstance that was crucial to the course of the Pilsen protests. The power apparatus was so overrun with political, security, and administrative tasks that it was virtually unable to perform its basic duties, let alone mount an adequate response to an outbreak of public unrest.

The Pilsen regional officials (like officials from other regions) had only learned of the upcoming reform through official channels an hour before its announcement and less than two days (!) before it was to begin. This happened at a meeting of the extended KSČ Regional Committee held on Saturday May 30, 1953, at 5 p.m.,[41] where secretaries of the district party committees and members of the Regional National Committee council were briefed by chief secretary Jan Hlína.[42] At 6 p.m., the radio announced the currency reform to the public. The party apparatus therefore had very limited time to employ the usual mechanisms of political persuasion.

The persuasion process usually started by explaining the government's measures to the individual levels of the party's organizational structure, from the top down, followed by personal campaigning carried out by the lowest-ranking party organizations, aimed at the non-partisan part of the population. The regional committee meetings were therefore followed on Saturday evening by meetings of the extended district party committees.[43] Officials from the KSČ Central Committee were deployed throughout the region to help the local officials implement government measures.[44] On Sunday May 31, meetings of the local party organizations took place,[45] followed at last by meetings of the factory organizations on the Monday morning.[46]

For several reasons, however, this campaign of meetings of the district, local, and factory party organizations did not fulfill its intended purpose. First of all, a number of officials did not attend the weekend meetings of the district and local organizations. Some of them were involved in the administrative preparation of the reform,[47] others preferred to save the family budget.[48] Moreover, those communists who were present felt caught off guard by the sudden announcement of the reform and were unable to maintain the required party discipline and look past their personal financial losses.[49] "It was evident that those comrades who had some considerable savings could not reconcile themselves to the idea of exchanging money at an unfavorable rate."[50] Some party members (especially pensioners) even expressed fears that they would have nothing to live on. The reform also affected many workers in heavy industry, which paid higher wages and had allowed them to amass considerable savings over the past years through temporary assignments and overtime, often in the hundreds of thousands. These funds, acquired through ideologically promoted effort, were to be taken away from them, even though they hardly classified as the bourgeoisie against whom the reform was officially directed.[51] Moreover, the reform was based on a number of outrageously unfair technical parameters. Among the most contentious were the unfavorable exchange rates of freshly awarded newlywed loans and unclaimed overtime bonuses.[52] However, it was not only the reduction in the population's savings that was the subject of heated debate, but also the very way in which the reform was communicated to the party's membership base. Many communists criticized the fact that they had only heard about the reform on the radio, just like the rest of the population, without having been at least formally consulted beforehand.[53]

The previous campaign, through which the Communist Party had tried to counter the rumors about the upcoming currency reform, and the ensuing panic buying over the past two weeks, had also played a significant role. Those communists who had previously believed the party's campaign against the panic buying were now entering the reform at a great disadvantage because they had not had time to spend even a part of their savings. This made them feel that they were actually being unfairly punished for their loyalty to the party, and that the party's measures had, in fact, justified the actions of those who had been mistrustful toward the communists and could now rightly ridicule them.[54] Moreover, they were now required by the party to explain to an irritated population the usefulness of the currency reform, even though up until recently, they had followed the party line and spoken of it as a fabrication of imperialist propaganda. They feared, quite realistically, that they would now be seen as liars.[55]

The recent show trials against top communist officials had also had a significant impact on the mindset of the party's membership base, spreading an atmosphere of distrust toward local and national party leaders. As a result, some communists assumed from the recent panic buying that "someone at the Central Committee had information" and that "there must be enemies of the state in the highest places."[56] They based their assumption on the fact that opponents of communism were informed of the upcoming reform before party members. Some debaters noted the fact that many high-ranking party officials actively participated in the run on stores.[57] They often mentioned Miloslav Mudra, former secretary of the KSČ Municipal Committee in Pilsen, whose mother-in-law was seen making large purchases (she bought a carpet for CZK 21,000).[58] In the eyes of the people in Pilsen, it was the universally unpopular Mudra who became an embodiment of an arrogant local politician who had completely alienated himself from his working-class origins.[59] This alienation of leading officials was felt intensely, especially among the workers of the V. I. Lenin Factories. Rumors circulated in the factory about the leading officials' corruption and impropriety, and in situations of escalated tension, such as the currency reform, this growing distrust escalated into a full-blown conflict.[60]

Another source of the workers' outrage was the ill timing of May wage advances. Contrary to government instructions, factory management did not pay the advances in the middle of the month but three weeks into the month.[61] When the employees finally received the money, they were no longer able to spend it, because stores were sold out due to the panic buying.[62] As a result, employees lost a substantial part of their monthly earnings during the currency reform, as they were forced to exchange the cash advances at a 50:1 ratio.[63] This enraged the factory employees almost as much as the currency reform itself.[64] The method of paying advances was therefore publicly labeled as sabotage by many party members at meetings, and eventually became one of the strong impulses for launching strikes and demonstrations.[65]

Finally, fears were voiced at meetings of local party organizations that the abolition of the existing ration system of supply would mean that the stores would get sold out again and the supply crisis caused by the panic buying would continue.[66] Such fears were quite widespread in the early days of the reform, and they were fully justified. Even leading party officials were not sure whether they could handle the supply situation after the restricted market had been abolished. Indeed, there were temporary shortages of basic foodstuffs in some areas after the stores reopened.[67]

Resistance to the currency reform therefore came from a wide variety of positions within the Communist Party and did not correspond with what historians today describe as anti-communist resistance. Apart from the above reservations, various voices at party meetings demanded that "severe action be taken against those who have been hoarding food and the like in these past few days [of the panic buying]."[68] In the same category of criticism was the frequent question as to why capitalists were being granted a 50:1 ratio for the exchange of savings, rather than simply having all their money taken away.[69] Many debaters complained that workers would have almost no money left of their hard-earned savings after the exchange, whereas the speculators who exchanged hundreds of thousands would still have considerable capital after the reform.[70] Anger had therefore turned against senior party officials as well as against former private tradesmen with relatively larger assets. From this point of view, the 1953 reform failed to facilitate any sort of unification of the divided society.

There were also many voices at the meetings that saw the reform as a necessary measure and a positive step forward. While these voices were not predominant (and informants may have deliberately exaggerated their frequency), they could not be completely ignored. A significant part of the membership base was probably willing to acknowledge the officially promoted positive consequences in the upcoming currency reform.[71] These included the abolition of the restricted market, which theoretically promised the population the possibility of unlimited purchases and could be seen as a means to prevent illegal speculation on the black market.[72] In this respect, acceptance of the currency reform was entirely dependent on the people's subjective trust—or lack thereof—in the future positive development of the national economy. Such a development could compensate those who were most affected by the reform for their personal losses—but it was by no means a certainty.

Although the participants in party meetings were eventually persuaded (with a few exceptions) to formally withdraw their reservations,[73] at least some of them no doubt still harbored certain feelings of uncertainty, which made them reluctant to assist in resolving the ensuing conflict.[74] Heated discussions took up so much time that the party boards had no time to discuss the best ways to promote the reform, or to impart basic facts about the practical implications of the reform. The communists, who were soon to explain the reform to the population, therefore remained indecisive and uninformed.[75] This failure of the party apparatus to serve its primary purpose culminated, as we will describe below, in the morning meetings of factory organizations on June1, 1953. By botching the announcement of the reform, party leadership had lost one of its most effective tools, thus opening the way for the emergence of unrest.

Preparations of the security forces did not go smoothly in Pilsen either. The first instructions to secure the implementation of the reform were only received by the top Pilsen police officials on May 28, 1953, at a meeting of the chiefs of the regional State Security administrations and the Public Security regional administrations.[76] Two days later, the People's Militias were put on alert. Three squads of rapid detachment units of the People's Militias were placed at the disposal of the chief party secretary in the regional capitals, and in each district another 20–60 militiamen were assigned to the local chiefs of police.[77] The army allocated 15 trucks to assist in Pilsen and 4 more for each district. From Sunday onward, the new money was distributed from warehouses to the State Bank branches, and from there it was further transported to the exchange centers.[78]

On Saturday May 30, a special regional security implementation team was set up in the regional party secretariat building to implement the reform. The team included Matěj Bálek, chief of the Regional State Security administration, who was in charge of the entire operation; Antonín Vintr, chief of the Regional Public Security Administration; and Václav Drozd, regional commander of the People's Militias.[79] The team focused mainly on ensuring the protection of the exchange centers. A total of 346 exchange centers were set up in the region, of which 305 were civilian, 35 military, 3 for SNB officers, and 3 for members of the Border Guard.[80] There were 85 civilian centers in the district covered by the Consolidated National Committee in Pilsen. Exchange centers were also set up by the State Bank of Czechoslovakia at its branches, post offices, national committees, and in large industrial enterprises.[81]

Each exchange center was to be guarded by two members of the National Security Corps.[82] In addition to Public Security and State Security officers, 492 members of the People's Militias (160 of whom were stationed directly in Pilsen) were assigned to guard the exchange centers in the region.[83] In addition, the Minister of National Security issued an instruction that the security of the centers could be reinforced in exceptional cases by members of the Czechoslovak Army (ČSA).[84] The Pilsen regional headquarters therefore decided to ask the army to lend 900 soldiers to provide additional security and sent a delegate to Prague to negotiate this. Although the army's deployment had the support of Deputy Minister of National Security Antonín Prchal, representatives of the Ministry of National Defense disagreed and promised only to discuss the matter further. On Sunday May 31, 1953, the regional headquarters, following a local agreement with the district military commanders, received a reinforcement of 30–45 soldiers for each district, who were immediately sent to the exchange centers.

In the evening of the same day, however, the General Staff of the Ministry of National Defense, in the spirit of its previous reservations, rejected the deployment of the army.[85] On the night of Monday June 1, 1953, the soldiers were therefore hastily withdrawn from the centers. This measure caused considerable difficulties, as the centers had to be re-staffed with members of the People's Militias and reserve officers from the National Security Corps.[86] Thus, the number of People's Militias members deployed in the region rose to 917 (290 in Pilsen alone), almost double the originally anticipated number.[87] The troops placed at the last minute at the exchange centers were then desperately needed in Pilsen during the attempts to suppress the Monday protests.

PROTESTS ON JUNE 1, 1953

After feverish preparations, the currency reform was finally launched on Monday June 1, 1953. The money exchange centers, where people were to receive the new currency, began to operate. The stores gradually switched to selling at the newly set prices. Unfortunately, the timing of these measures added to the panic among the population. Not only did people lose most of their savings but they had no idea what their living expenses would now be, because they did not yet have the new money and new prices had not yet been displayed in shop windows in many places.

Confidence in the newly introduced price system was further undermined by the fact that until a person exchanged their money, they had to shop using the old currency and pay at the unfavorable exchange rate of 50:1.[88] A worker who had received a wage advance of CZK 2,500 the week before would often spend 700 Kč in the old currency, just to buy a snack.[89] Train fares to work had also become considerably more expensive. If an employee did not have a weekly season ticket, they paid fifty times the new price in old money. For a tram ticket that would have cost 50 hellers in the new currency, workers had to pay CZK 25 in the old currency.[90] Obviously, such experiences became the proverbial last straw, triggering feelings of despair and resentment.

Social tension was exacerbated by the fact that people had no idea what their new wages would be, which provoked feelings of uncertainty and anxiety about the future. The population was thus temporarily deprived of a wide range of basic life securities during the money exchange period of June 1–4—from the loss of financial reserves, to fears of wage and price instability, to the risk of a continued supply crisis that had already lasted two weeks. On Monday morning June 1, 1953, all of these factors converged and triggered the subsequent protests.

Apart from the actual launch of the reform, Monday morning was particularly significant for another reason. For the first time since the government resolutions had been announced, people had the opportunity to legally assemble in their workplaces and discuss the implications of the reform with their coworkers. The future course of events depended entirely on whether the party apparatus would ensure a peaceful entry of workers into the workplace after the weekend, and how it would deal with their questions and objections.

Instead of a properly organized political and promotional campaign, however, chaos ensued at the large industrial enterprises. The party leadership underestimated the situation and called meetings of their factory organizations as late as the start of the Monday morning shifts.[91] This delay had two major consequences. First, party members at the factories were persuaded to support the currency reform at a point when they themselves were needed to start actively reassuring their non-partisan colleagues. The party membership base was not at all ready to fulfill their duty and indeed failed to fulfill it in the hours to come. Second, the party meetings, which took place behind closed doors, led to the complete absence of party members from the workplaces. Desperate, indignant non-partisan workers were given no answers to their pressing questions, and no one actually paid them any attention. Moreover, having been left completely unsupervised in the workshops allowed them to freely share their indignation.[92]

The situation at the V. I. Lenin Factories was particularly symptomatic in this respect. An additional reinforcement of 70 officials from the Central, Regional, and Municipal Party Committees was sent to the factory at 6 a.m. (the start of the morning shift).[93] They had, however, arrived late for the meetings they were supposed to conduct; they were delayed because they had to be granted permission to enter first.[94] Once the meetings finally started, they dragged on because many party members were greatly upset by the currency reform. In addition, the designated speakers themselves had not had enough time and information to study the implications of the reform in detail and were therefore unable to provide adequate answers to some of the debaters' questions. In response to the frequent questions such as "How much are we going to get paid now?"[95] they replied that they had not yet received any guidelines regarding the new wages. Nevertheless, most party members were gradually persuaded to express at least a passive support for the reform; only in the Locomotive Works department did all persuasion fail and the workers refused to retract their open reservations.[96]

The heated, protracted party meetings also meant that all communists were absent from their workplaces for several hours. During the meetings, which often lasted eight hours or more, a rather rebellious mood grew in some workshops, and no amount of persuasion or threats could dispel it. Such a model situation developed especially in the Engineering III department. The meeting there was chaired by propaganda secretary of the Regional Committee Čestmír Císař, who later became Minister of Education.[97] Despite warnings from his colleagues, Císař completely ignored the outbreak of a strike called by non-partisan workers and continued the agenda of the meeting uninterrupted. A number of workers from his department actually formed the most radical core of the protesting employees.[98]

The workers' protests of June 1, 1953, exhibited the same characteristics as all previous strikes. The workers gradually stopped the machines and got into heated debates in the workshops. Eventually they began to demand explanations of various aspects of the reform from the local party officials (especially regarding the new wages and the incorrectly paid wage advances). However, since no party representatives were currently present inside the workshops, some of these groups demanded access to party meetings at their own plants. Those who were not granted access started gathering in the factory courtyard.

Employees from the various departments formed large groups and addressed their demands to the factory management. Once the workers left the workshops, they opened the way to a factory-wide protest. In the last phase of the protest, the workers took to the streets—an extreme solution which had never before been used in Pilsen and which transformed the strike into a public protest and moved the conflict beyond the safe space of the factory.

The employees of the Engineering I, Engineering III, and Locomotive Works departments played a significant role in the unfolding of events:[99] not only did they stop production but they went out into the courtyard to demand an explanation of the changes to the wage system. The most prevalent slogan at this rally was "Come with us to the director's [office]; you don't know how much you work for."[100] According to various sources, a crowd of about 1,000–4,000 people formed in the factory courtyard around 9 a.m.[101]

However, the strike did not progress in the same way in all departments and did not reach the same phase and intensity in all parts of the factory. In some workshops (especially the steelworks) the officials reacted more flexibly to the morning situation. They skipped the required party meetings, either in whole or in part, and informed both party members and non-partisan workers alike. In some cases, they even contacted the company's headquarters to find out about the new wage guidelines on the workers' behalf. The situation was generally much more favorable for the party in those workshops where the party members stayed put. In many workshops, the mere threat that a strike would be considered an act of sedition was enough to keep the workers out of the courtyard. The communists also tried to provide an example and return to their machines, which did not help the strikers' cause.[102] Wherever the officials managed to handle the situation in this way, they tried to close all entrances to isolate their workshop from the surrounding chaos.[103]

The radical part of the strikers who had gathered in the courtyards, on the other hand, started going through the more passive workshops and demanded that they stop work. They appealed to traditional workers' solidarity and egged the workers on by shouting things like "Come with us, you'll get a snack for 500 crowns!"[104] At first, strikers came to some of the departments peacefully and individually. In others, they entered by force in larger groups of several hundred people. However, they were usually pushed out by the communists, and most crews refused to join them. Sources document such incidents especially in the metallurgical workshops, where about 250–300 workers from Machine Shop III tried unsuccessfully to provoke a riot around 9 a.m.[105] Strikers from Engineering I, on the other hand, successfully managed to rally workers from Engineering III,[106] and they in turn roused the workers in the Locomotive Works department.[107] The strikers threw stones at the windows of the workshops whose workers did not show solidarity and threatened to return in greater numbers.[108]

When the crowd in the courtyard of the main plant had grown sufficiently large, it headed for the company headquarters building. Some of the participants expected Director Brabec to explain the contentious wage issues to them,[109] while others were already planning to leave the factory through the main gate at this point. However, the gate was closed and guarded by the People's Militias.[110] The procession therefore turned back, crossed the footbridge connecting the two parts of the factory, stopped at several other departments along the way, and headed for Gate 5.[111]

At this juncture, officials from the KSČ factory committee tried to prevent the workers from going into the city and sent all their propaganda staff to the gates to try to dissuade the strikers. They did not, however, deploy any organized force against the protesters, be it the People's Militias or a large contingent of low-ranking party members. The committee had trouble establishing communication with the various departments and was therefore unable to coordinate any systematic response. Moreover, the communists in many workshops adopted a passive attitude toward the protesters and could not be expected to exert any spontaneous effort to pacify them.[112] Moreover, the situation in those departments which had not joined in the strike was still unpredictable, and the factory committee could consider it a great success that it managed to restrict the protests inside the factory only to certain departments. Larger troops of the People's Militias, sufficient to close all exits from the factory, were not available.

The top officials present at the factory addressed the protesters gathered at the factory gates over the factory PA system. However, the speeches of Central Committee representative Ladislav Kopřiva, Regional Committee secretary Václav Kolena, chief secretary of the Municipal Committee Josef Žák, factory committee chairman Bedřich Perlík, and company director František Brabec failed to reverse the course of events.[113] None of them found the courage to talk to the waiting workers face to face.[114] Moreover, the speech of the unpopular factory director František Brabec actually bolstered the workers' indignation, because he had failed to address their issues altogether.[115]

In some cases, verbal reprimands from lower officials sent to the factory gates were successful; however, some strikers started physically attacking the unfortunate propagandists. Some workers who had previously been transferred to manual labor from other occupations engaged in acrimonious debates, quantifying the financial impact of the reform on the workers and providing them with arguments for resistance. The officials were not sufficiently prepared to be able to refute their calculations and workers like former high school professor Václav Vrzal repeatedly received applause from the onlookers.[116] Unlike the party officials, the foremen distanced themselves completely from the attempts to suppress the strike, even though they were formally responsible for the smooth running of production.[117] They justified their passive attitude by saying things like, "This is all because of the advances. The men wanted out, and so I let them. I'm not gonna have my head bashed in because of this."[118] Many low-ranking party members were hesitant to remain neutral because they themselves felt affected by the currency reform and were therefore in no mood to discourage anyone from expressing their indignation. When the strikers did not receive an adequate response from the company's headquarters, they forced a walkout shortly after 9 a.m.[119]

A similar situation developed at the Elektrotrakce Doudlevce subsidiary plant, which had been one of the centers of unrest in previous years (see the strikes of 1950 and 1951).[120] Workers' protests in the subsidiary plant were triggered especially by the problematic payment of May wage advances.[121] Similarly to the main factory, a strike broke out in Doudlevce during the morning party meetings. "It has been found that provocateurs came to the site and said: the Communists are having meetings, let's have one too, and then they all went out into the courtyard."[122] Local officials failed to persuade the workers to calm down and some of the strikers, about 250–600 people,[123] eventually left the plant. This happened without any resistance from the factory guards.[124]

The workers of Elektrotrakce Doudlevce formed a procession and, shouting slogans against the implementation of the reform, marched down Doudlevecká Street and Prokopova Avenue toward Náměstí Republiky square. The procession was allegedly led by the same persons who had organized the previous strike in 1951.[125] Some workers had phoned the main factory to see what was going on, and began acting as messengers on bicycles, informing the strikers from both factories about the joint action.[126] This echoed the traditional forms of protest coordination among factory workers, in which the smaller factories always respected what was decided at the largest industrial enterprise in Pilsen. Along the way, the Doudlevce workers also stopped at the nearby gasworks, but most of the local workers chose not to join them.[127]

At the same time, approximately 2,000 people left the main plant in several smaller processions.[128] The largest procession made it out through Gate 5 and passed by the factory along Korandova Street.[129] At the corner of Korandova Street it split into two groups, one heading down Tylova Street to Náměstí Republiky, and the other heading down Tylova Street in the opposite direction to the main factory gate and the building of the experimental institute of the V. I. Lenin Factories.[130] At the main gate, some members of the factory council spoke to the protesters but failed to dissuade them.[131] After receiving news that the workers from Doudlevce had already arrived at Náměstí Republiky, the second group also headed downtown.[132] Along the way, the protesters tried to win the support of workers from some of the smaller enterprises, with varying results. Workers also stopped trams on 1. Máje Avenue and tried to persuade passengers and passers-by to join them.[133] Some of the protesters outside the main gate were not convinced that marching downtown was the right thing to do and tried to get back inside the factory instead. By this time, minor confrontations had begun to break out at Gate 4, and by the afternoon, they had grown into one of the most violent conflicts of the Pilsen protests.

The actions of some of the more prudent protesters were symbolic of the ambiguous results of Monday morning's events. Despite the apparent success of the protesting workers, long-term results of the morning strike were highly questionable. While a more radical section of the strikers left the plant (approximately 2,000 people), they constituted only a fraction of the entire workforce and only about half of those who went out into the factory courtyard in the morning (approximately 4,000 people). The vast majority of workers remained inside the factory and were soon persuaded to at least formally resume work.[134] Returning to the factory to obtain further workers subsequently proved impossible. The party had therefore managed to maintain control over the V. I. Lenin Factories on June1, 1953, and a large part of the employees remained completely passive toward the protests. The sources do not provide a clear answer as to what extent this was due to disagreement with the protesters, the belief that nothing could be achieved by protesting, or fear of reprisal.[135] Moreover, the protesters left their civilian clothes at the workplaces and were not able to clock out at the end of their shift, which made it easier to identify them later. The departure of the core of the strikers from the factory was, from this point of view, more of a Pyrrhic victory.

At other large industrial plants in Pilsen, such as the Czechoslovak State Railroad Works (ČSD) or the Pilsen Breweries, party officials gradually managed to placate the workers, persuade the protesting crowds to start work, and prevent the mass exodus of workers into the city streets.[136] At ČSD, the situation was most heated in those workshops where the workers' indignation was fueled by the inappropriate response of party officials. "In some workshops, workers were outraged by the report read by a representative of the Municipal Committee [of the Communist Party] in Pilsen who, instead of justifying the resolution, enumerated the purchases made in the past few days by the bourgeois elements in Pilsen, which provoked discontent among those who had been persuaded [by the Party] not to get involved in the panic buying and keep their money at home."[137] Before 11 a.m., however, work in the ČSD workshops was back to normal.[138] At the Pilsner Breweries, the workers' discontent was effectively mitigated after the management allowed employees to buy snacks on credit and avoid paying in the old currency at the

50:1 exchange rate.[139] Apart from the V. I. Lenin Factories, only a few smaller industrial plants experienced mass walkouts.[140]

The processions of employees of the main plant and the Doudlevce subsidiary plant met and merged on 1. Máje Avenue at around 10 a.m., marched together down Prešovská and Riegrova Streets to Náměstí Republiky, and gathered in front of the City Hall (headquarters of the Consolidated National Committee in Pilsen).[141] Having had their demands rejected by the company management, the workers turned to the city administration as another traditional authority of Pilsen's public life.[142] Náměstí Republiky square itself had been a traditional venue for all past large protest rallies, including demonstrations against the adoption of the Munich Agreement in September 1938,[143] the anti-Nazi uprising in May 1945,[144] and the communist demonstrations during the coup d'état in February 1948.[145]

The initial conflict, which had only focused on specific wage issues, gradually turned toward more general issues outside the factory walls and transformed into a complex critique of the social impact of the currency reform. The crowd demonstrated its loss of trust in the government and chanted the slogan "We want to hear the truth."[146] Workers also expressed their panic by chanting "We are hungry!"[147] and showed their indignation over the loss of savings by chanting such slogans as "We want our money back,"[148] "We will not be robbed,"[149] or "Everyone can see what swindlers the government are."[150] People symbolically tore up banknotes devalued by the reform.[151] There were sarcastic cries of "Long live the hard currency."[152] Some participants even commented on the social impact of the reform by making cynical jokes.[153]

Meanwhile, the racket in the square attracted a lot of attention from people who happened to live or work downtown. Word of mouth spread lightning-fast, claiming that "Škoda workers are going to the square."[154] The people, regardless of their political convictions, left their workplaces and homes and came to find out what was going on. The first clusters that gathered outside the town hall included only about 700 workers in working clothes, of which about 200–300 could be classified as the more radical of the protesters.[155] However, the city center was full of people nervously waiting to exchange money or for the stores to open.[156] The demonstrating workers were gradually joined by members of other discontented groups, especially young people, but also housewives and former tradesmen. The radical core of the protesters approximately doubled in number.[157]

The character of the protest was also changing, taking on increasingly clear political overtones. The protesters picked up themes similar to those of 1948–1949, chanting such slogans as, for example, "We want a new government,"[158] "Down with the government, the government has betrayed us,"[159] "Down with the Communists,"[160] "We want free elections,"[161] "Long live free

Pilsen,"[162] or "Long live free Europe."[163] Sources report rare instances when the crowd chanted "Death to the Communists."[164] However, the slogan "We want a workers' government"[165] reminded everyone that workers were the driving force of the protest, legitimizing it by their presence.

Numerous onlookers and debaters clustered round the actual core of protesters, forming a wider backdrop of the demonstration. This made for a rather motley crowd (approximately 1,000–5,000 people)[166] whose participants had diverse motives for being there. However, the mere passive presence of bystanders gave considerable moral support to the protesters, as it visually increased their numbers and their silence actually gave the appearance of approval. Some people even explicitly showed their support by clapping, shouting slogans, or singing the national anthem, without otherwise actively participating in the protest. However, not all actions of the more radical group of protesters met with universal approval (especially not the acts of violence).[167] Last but not least, the people gathered in the square included a fairly large number of party officials, militiamen, secret police officers, and low-ranking communists, who trickled down to the square in an attempt to dissuade the protesters and save the situation (approximately 300–600 people);[168] however, as will be discussed in more detail below, they utterly failed to do so.

In reaction to the protesters' arrival at the square, Josef Mainzer, chairman of the Consolidated National Committee in Pilsen, went outside the City Hall, climbed onto the front hood of a parked truck and attempted to address the gathering. His words, however, were completely drowned out by the disgruntled crowd, and Mainzer returned to the City Hall building and addressed the protesters via the city's PA system. In response to this, however, a group of about 150 of the most active young protesters broke through the doors and windows of the unprotected City Hall building and occupied the radio room, located on the ground floor near the entrance.[169] Mainzer was pushed away from the microphone and the broadcast was taken over by the protesters themselves, who began shouting their slogans into the PA system.[170] The shouts from the radio room, transmitted through loudspeakers into the streets, alerted even more people to the situation in the city center, who immediately headed for the square. A few minutes later, the staff of the Civil Defense Headquarters (CO) of the Consolidated National Committee in Pilsen managed to switch the power off in the entire building, putting the PA system out of service.[171]

Some 250 protesters then made their way up the stairs to the first floor of the City Hall, where they met with almost no resistance: police officers and city officials were out helping to take inventory in the stores, and very few were actually present.[172] By the stairs on the ground floor, a few members of the State Security Service and six Public Security officers tried unsuccessfully

Figure 3.1 Crowd Demonstrating Outside the Pilsen City Hall on the Morning of June 1, 1953. Author unknown, probably the photo was taken by State Security. SOkA v Blovicích, f. OS Pilsen, zn. 1 T 149/1953.

to prevent more people from storming the upper levels.[173] Groups of debaters clustered in the hallways. Several party officials present debated with the protesters and urged them to calm down. In doing so, they realized that the young people were so frightened by the reform that they believed rumors about the totally unrealistic future prices of basic foodstuffs.[174] Approximately half of these young people belonged to working-class professions. Yet they "would not be called comrades; they claimed they were simply workers."[175] After some discussion, some of them were willing to admit that they were committing a crime by storming the National Committee building, and chose to leave.

A few skirmishes occurred, however, as some of the protesters took out their indignation on the city officials present.[176] The mob assaulted Matěj Bálek, head of the regional StB administration.[177] Some protesters began chasing chairman of the Consolidated National Committee Josef Mainzer and labor resources officer František Mudra, wanting to beat them up for having recommended one of the protesters for reassignment to a forced labor camp.[178] They actually dragged some of the officials outside the City Hall and beat them up.[179]

Another group of protesters, led by worker Ilja Nazarkevyč, forced themselves into the offices of the city's Civil Defense headquarters on the second floor. One of the State Security officers they had been chasing was hiding there,[180] and the protesters demanded that the staff hand him over. The Civil Defense officers present in the office succumbed to the pressure and allowed Nazarkevyč, together with workers Václav Dobízl and Karel Doležal, into the headquarters so they could make sure that the person in question was not there.[181] Meanwhile, the pursued officer left through the back entrance.[182] Many uninformed bystanders among the protesters assumed that the workers were looking for their detained colleagues, which led to the rumor that the attack on the City Hall was in fact an attempt to free the arrested protesters.[183] Czechoslovak historians after 1989 actually adopted this assumption, claiming that the break-in at the City Hall was triggered by the arrest of a delegation of protesters. However, the sources available to the author of this text lack any evidence for such a claim.[184]

Other groups of protesters went through the offices and vandalized the furnishings.[185] A significant number of protesters entered the City Hall merely out of curiosity. They went through the offices and observed the havoc wreaked by other protesters.[186] Many people were quietly smoking in the corridors and watching with interest what was happening around them.[187]

Most importantly, a group of protesters began tearing down the ideological decorations in the offices and throwing them out of the windows of the City Hall.[188] This action had both symbolic and practical significance. The defenestration of pictures and busts of communist leaders (Klement Gottwald, Joseph Vissarionovich Stalin) was a clear insult to the communist supporters in society. It was a transparent, aggressive rejection of the ruling ideology, or at least of its representatives. It was actually carried out in a very theatrical manner, with the discarded object first being shown out the window to the crowd below and then spectacularly smashed on the stone sidewalk, amid a great uproar from the crowd. This entertained the protesters for some time and represented a sort of a unifying ritual. A demonstration needs continuous stimuli to rouse its participants to action in order to keep going. Without such seemingly pointless activities, the crowd would soon disperse, as the wider circle of participants would have nothing to observe. The protests of June 1 were more about venting accumulated frustration than a rational action directed toward longer-term goals.

Slogans were also shouted from the windows of the City Hall, repeated by the assembly outside the building.[189] A picture of the last non-communist president Edvard Beneš[190] was displayed in the window of the office of the National Committee chairman.[191] It was probably found in the City Hall during the looting, forgotten behind other pictures of statesmen.[192] After the portrait was displayed, the crowd in the square chanted the slogans "Black Pilsen is loyal to Beneš"[193] (the "black Pilsen" reference was an allusion to the industrial identity of the region) and "We miss you, Beneš."[194] The protesters also seized two Czechoslovak flags at the City Hall, one of which they hoisted on a flagpole outside the City Hall and honored it by singing the national anthem.[195] The second flag was later used when organizing the next procession.

The protesters' attack on the City Hall marked another major turning point in the development of the Pilsen protests. Events were now completely out of control, not only on the part of the party apparatus, but also of a substantial part of the original workers' assembly, and were inevitably heading toward an open confrontation that few had expected and no one had deliberately planned. The fact that the form of the protest had shifted so many times (strike—walkout—public protest with political overtones—attacks on public officials) makes it extremely difficult to examine the subjective motives and intentions of the protesters. It is hard to establish a clear motivation, not only due to the official nature of most of the surviving documents, but especially due to the dynamic gradation of the protests, driven by unusually heated emotion. In fact, the crowd effect drove individuals to acts they would not normally have committed. At the same time, people's actions greatly depended on the phase of the protests they participated in, and the group they belonged to at that particular moment.

Social motives prevailed during the early stages of the protest. A significant part of the workers who left the factory gates in the morning believed that the procession would only go to the factory headquarters to discuss the issue of wage advances.[196] Even as they moved to the square, many of them expected a protest resolution to be sent to the government.[197] Some groups of protesters who joined up outside the City Hall hoped that the protests would lead to the withdrawal of the currency reform as a whole.[198] Many people were also motivated to participate by panic and fear of an uncertain future.[199] However, their collective actions opened up the space for protests that soon took overtly political and then violent forms.

Some of the protesters also saw the protests as an opportunity to avenge past wrongs. During the demonstrations at the City Hall, former farm manager Bartoloměj Chudoba, sought out the chairman of the Consolidated National Committee, with whom he wanted to settle accounts for the National Committee previously prosecuting him for failure to meet the targets in agricultural supplies.[200] For others, the protests were a rare platform where they could speak publicly about their experiences in communist prisons.[201] For example, Margarita Kuráňová, imprisoned for aiding illegal border crossings, cried and showed the bystanders her scars.[202] Gaggles of local protesters lent these people a sympathetic ear; some even chanted the slogan "Open the concentration camps!"[203]

In such an atmosphere, some protesters began to believe that the protests would bring down the government. They hugged strangers in the streets and shouted "The ice is cracking, things are in motion!"[204] Libuše Dlouhá, for example, recalled under questioning: "I thought people were fighting for their rights."[205] Some of the protesters therefore consciously began to clamor for a return to the political situation before 1948 and were even willing to admit their motives during the subsequent trials.[206] Some former tradesmen saw the protests as an opportunity to reestablish freedom of enterprise.[207] Most likely, such demands were not entirely compatible with the strikers' actual interests, but no one minded at the time. The joint protest did not grow out of mutual discussion but of shared emotion.

It would be a mistake to assume, however, that all the protesters had serious reasons to get involved. Many of those who were watching the events or even entered the City Hall did so out of mere curiosity.[208] For some people, the protests were a welcome diversion from tedious work.[209] Many young men and women actually used the protests as an opportunity to meet and arrange dates.[210] People therefore saw the protests as simply an unusual form of entertainment—which could also explain some cases of looting and beating of public officials. Indeed, events where state property is vandalized and blows are struck invariably attract a certain amount of people who have a propensity for such actions in everyday life.

In addition to the above motives (and their combinations), the presence of certain individuals in particular places was motivated by fairly prosaic reasons. For example, the protests outside the City Hall were interrupted for several minutes in the morning by torrential rain, from which the protesters took shelter in the surrounding passageways or in the City Hall building.[211] Some people therefore entered the City Hall in an attempt to hide from the rain.[212] This may have led some individuals to participate more actively in the protest than they had originally intended.

Between 10:30 and 11:00 a.m., one of the active groups of protesters headed from the square toward the nearby seat of the Regional Court and the Regional Prosecutor's office, followed by a crowd of approximately 800–1,200 people.[213] Another reason for heading to the Palace of Justice was that one of the State Security officers, whom the crowd had chased from the square in an attempt to lynch him, was hiding there.[214] Others later headed to the Palace of Justice because they heard the news of arrested protesters being held there.[215] This was probably a misunderstanding, however, as the mass arrests did not occur until much later.[216]

The protesters managed to break down the front gate of the Regional Court with a battering ram, and around 11 a.m. approximately 100–120 persons entered the building.[217] As in the City Hall, they engaged in the ritual destruction of ideological decorations. Images of statesmen were thrown out of the windows and the symbol of the five-pointed star was torn off the façade.[218] Again, most of the protesters watched the turbulent events out in the street.

Officials present in the building did not attempt to resist and tried to hide from the irritated protesters. Several employees from the state notary's office disguised themselves as cooks in the local canteen, and public prosecutor JUDr. Josef Herger waited out the demonstrations locked in the ladies' restroom.[219] In a bout of panic, JUDr. Miroslav Tlapák, Chief Justice of the People's Court in Pilsen, and Judge Jaromír Fikrle barricaded themselves in an office and shot at the protesters through the door. The protesters therefore blocked the door with furniture to prevent injuries.[220]

One of the chief goals of the protesting mob in the Palace of Justice was to burn court files, which was taken as an expression of their opposition to the post-1948 justice system. The protesters searched for criminal files in the building, threw any documents they could find out the windows, and burned them in large piles in the street.[221] In the ensuing confusion, however, the protesters had made a mistake and the documents burned included mostly civil agenda.[222] Reportedly, a total of 400 kg of files was damaged or destroyed.[223]

One of the groups also tried to break into the Regional Court jailhouse,[224] believing that some of the protesters were imprisoned there, and demanded their release. However, the entrance was guarded by armed guards with machine guns. Some protesters therefore unbuttoned their shirts, faced the machine gun barrels with their chests exposed, and shouted, "You'll be shooting at workers."[225] No violent clash occurred, however, neither side having any interest in a bloody solution. The protesters eventually sent a three-person delegation to the prison authorities and offered to stop the destruction of the building in exchange for the prisoners.[226] Members of the delegation had their identity checked, and were assured that there were no detained protesters in the building.[227]

Outside the courthouse, protesters continued to harass both real and presumed State Security officers. One of them was beaten up by the mob who then took him hostage and later tried unsuccessfully to exchange him for the detained protesters.[228] Another officer was about to be drowned by the mob in the nearby Mže River.[229] Fortunately, this plan was not carried out, because passers-by identified the beaten man as a worker at the V. I. Lenin Factories.[230] Similar mistakes were nothing unusual in Pilsen that day. The crowd was willing to physically assault completely unknown persons simply because one of the protesters had pointed a finger at them, without knowing the details of the case.[231]

After some of the protesters left Náměstí Republiky for the Palace of Justice, the rest chose a different course of action.[232] Between 11 and 12 a.m., the crowd, numbering approximately 800–1200 persons, was distracted by a group of persons who seized a police car[233] and a vehicle belonging to the Consolidated National Committee.[234] They began to drive around the city center in the hijacked vehicles, calling on passers-by to join in the protest.[235]

The protesters decorated the police car with a national flag and a portrait of Edvard Beneš,[236] and put it at the head of the procession as a trophy.[237] They proceeded to march down Stalinova Avenue and 1. Máje Avenue, to the site of the former foundation stone of the American Army Monument (removed in 1948), and on to Dukelské (formerly Masarykovo) Náměstí square to the National Liberation Monument.[238] Along the way, the procession stopped cars traveling in the opposite direction and encouraged onlookers to join in the demonstration.[239]

The sites of the two monuments had already functioned as a natural meeting place for protest marches during the demonstrations in May and September 1948. Not only did it lend the protests the symbolic significance of the memory of the American liberators and the first Czechoslovak president, Tomáš Garrigue Masaryk, but also offered a convenient strategic position with busy traffic and a high number of onlookers. Unlike the Náměstí Republiky square, 1. Máje Avenue, which connected the two sites, was the real traffic artery of the city. In June 1953 the protesters thus took up the proven tactics and culture of protest from 1948–1949.

It would seem that this kind of theatrically staged entertainment was merely wasting precious time until the law enforcement authorities recovered from the moment of surprise. The protesters did not think of it this way, however.[240] They had not yet met with any organized resistance and were enjoying the feeling of crowd euphoria. The demonstrations were a spontaneous protest, not a premeditated attempt at a coup d'état, and the forms and means of protest corresponded with this fact, seeking to attract the public's interest and promote alternative authorities. At the intersection of 1. Máje Avenue and Stalinova Avenue, the parade stopped briefly at the site where the foundation stone of the monument to fallen American soldiers used to stand. By this time the lawn was decorated with a flower bed in the shape of a red five-pointed star.[241] The crowd pulled up the flowers and placed them reverentially around the site of the former monument.[242] After four years, the American theme, which resonated so much with the people of West Bohemia, reappeared as an underlying theme of the protests. The slogan "Long Live America"[243] could be heard at times in the procession, and several protesters were trying to procure an American flag.[244]

However, this was far from a minor local eccentricity. Western cultural influences in the region had much deeper roots. Many young people still proudly wore pieces of U.S. military uniforms and kept various souvenirs at home commemorating the city's liberation by the former Western allies. Apart from keeping these private reminders of the past, many young people tried to emulate the Western lifestyle, reflected in such things as fashion, dance, movies, and the reading of dime novels.[245] This cultural orientation was widespread not only among the high school students in Pilsen who had taken part in the 1948 protests but also among young workers, some of whom came from the families of civil servants and former tradesmen in 1953.[246] Some protesters in June 1953 even hoped that, as a result of their pro-American sympathies, the U.S. military might come to the city's aid a second time.[247] They did not hesitate to openly declare their positive relationship toward the United States to the police officers present at the scene.[248] There are also documented cases of protesters threatening the intervening police officers with the impending arrival of the American army.[249] The notion of the exceptional bond between the people of Pilsen and their powerful Western ally therefore bolstered some protesters' confidence.

Only a small crowd of about 150–200 people remained on Náměstí Republiky between 12 and 1 p.m.[250] The protests here did not go on continuously all day; the morning rain had temporarily driven the people away, and the crowd had almost dispersed shortly after midday. Jaroslava Valentová, who went to see what was going on downtown around that time, could only say, "I only saw a few people and workers sweeping the square."[251] After the police intervention outside the courthouse shortly after 12 p.m., and the protesters' march back to Náměstí Republiky between 1 and 2 p.m., this part of the city became almost empty; and most people left for lunch without much resistance, or gradually headed to the 1. Máje Avenue and Dukelské náměstí square to the monument to Tomáš Garrigue Masaryk, where they merged with the previous procession led by the hijacked police car.[252] A gathering of about 3,000 people then became the epicenter of the afternoon riots.[253]

Protesters on Dukelské náměstí stormed the building of the Klement Gottwald Higher School of Economics and tried to persuade the students to join them. This move was also reminiscent of the 1948 riots, as secondary school students were very active in the protests then, especially students at this particular school.[254] Once inside, the protesters repeated the tried and tested ritual of throwing ideological decorations out of the windows. However, the students did not join the protesters. In the case of the previous protests in 1948, they had taken to the streets outside of school hours. Leaving school during school hours, on the other hand, would have posed a much greater risk. Most students opted to stay in their classrooms, and some of them later joined the evening protests. However, references in the sources mentioning that the students forcibly pushed the protesters out of the building were probably an afterthought, added to protect the school from a more thorough investigation.[255] None of the protesters recalled such a conflict when questioned. The protesters left the building voluntarily once they realized that most students would not join them.

Meanwhile, the crowd gathered at the National Liberation Monument launched an impromptu protest and commemoration ceremony. A young

Figure 3.2 A Gathering of Protesting Citizens on Dukelské Náměstí Square in Pilsen on the Afternoon of June 1, 1953. Author unknown, probably the photo was taken by State Security. Ibid.

man with a national flag and a girl with a picture of the last non-communist president Edvard Beneš were hoisted up on the statue of first Czechoslovak president Tomáš Garrigue Masaryk.[256] Various sympathizers started bringing other portraits of Beneš, for which they received enthusiastic applause from the audience. The crowd sang the national anthem as each portrait was put up.[257] People shouted slogans and the most courageous protesters attempted spontaneous speeches. Sources document some of the protesters describing the currency reform as government's betrayal of the workers. Protesters also smashed and overturned a large banner promoting Czechoslovak-Soviet friendship, which provocatively obscured the statue of Tomáš Garrigue Masaryk from view.[258]

Several times during the day, the idea was floated among the protesters that the crowd should occupy the Pilsen radio building, located on Náměstí Míru square in the southern outskirts of the city, and use it to spread information about the ongoing unrest beyond the city limits.[259] The suggestion was inspired by the protesters' use of the PA system in the City Hall earlier that morning. Even though transmission was interrupted after a few minutes by a power cut, it encouraged the protesters to attempt it on a larger scale.[260] Radio was, after all, one of the most important information media of the time, and the predecessor of the Pilsen studio had previously been one of the first targets during the anti-Nazi uprising in May 1945.[261] The protesters therefore had sufficient experience to build on. In 1953, the public was unaware that the technical equipment of the Pilsen studio did not allow wide-range broadcast because the transmitter was not located in the city.[262]

Throughout the day, the protesters' intentions changed dynamically, depending on which of the more active groups had managed to attract the attention of bystanders, which determined where the crowd would head next. The morning protest rallies involved spontaneous actions all over the city, and there was no rush to get to the radio building. The idea of marching to the radio station had only materialized only during the afternoon demonstration at Dukelské náměstí square.

Around 1 p.m., a part of the protesters set off from Dukelské náměstí along 1. Máje Avenue toward the railroad bridge, with the intention of proceeding to the radio building on Náměstí Míru.[263] However, after the attack on the City Hall and the Palace of Justice, the police focused all their efforts on defending strategically important locations, which included the radio building. Part of the law enforcement troops were therefore charged with preventing any possible movement of protesters in that direction.[264] As a result, the bridge on 1. Máje Avenue was blocked off,[265] and the procession of protesters was forced to turn into the adjacent Hálkova Street.[266]

At the corner of Hálkova Street and 1. Máje Avenue, however, the protesters encountered the first organized resistance from a fairly large troop of the People's Militias, who were called to the scene from the V. I. Lenin Factories and began to disperse the protesters. Chaos ensued; some protesters fled, others engaged in minor skirmishes with the militiamen, resulting in numerous injuries on both sides. Most of the protesters from Dukelské Náměstí and Hálkova Street eventually retreated to Gate 4 of the V. I. Lenin Factories.[267] After 1 p.m., the first army troops arrived at Dukelské Náměstí; the soldiers weaved their way through the remaining groups of protesters, trying to persuade them to leave and pushing them gradually onto the sidewalks in surrounding streets. In the process, they singled out the most active protesters and handed them over to the State Security officers who took them away in their cars.[268] The protesters' numbers had thus begun dwindling considerably.

The protesters' retreat route to Gate 4 of the V. I. Lenin Factories had several advantages.[269] Some of the protesters intended to get reinforcements from inside the plant to counter the changed situation in the city center. There was another very compelling motive for their decision: the workers from the V. I. Lenin Factories, who formed the bulk of the most active protesters, had left all their personal belongings (civilian clothes and IDs) at work in the morning, and now had to return for them.[270] In addition, they needed to clock out at the end of their shift at 2 p.m. so their absence from work could not be used as evidence of their participation in the protest,[271] and they needed to get inside the factory by the same covert route they had used to get out.

Still during the morning demonstrations, some protesters therefore headed back to the plant, once they realized this was not a regular strike and that their absence was likely to result in punishment. Some managed to sneak back into the factory undetected,[272] while others were registered as protesters on arrival.[273] Half an hour before noon, however, the factory management issued a complete ban on protesters attempting to get back inside.[274] The rest of the workers remained stuck outside the gates, waiting for a suitable opportunity to get in, or went home in their working clothes (blue overalls).[275] As a result, clusters of workers began gathering near Gate 4 still during mid-morning.[276] Most workers, however, relied on collective strength and stayed with their protesting colleagues until the procession decided to return to the factory.[277] This must have occurred still before the end of the shift at 2 p.m., quite independently of the incident in Hálkova Street described above.

The gate was guarded by a detachment of the People's Militias, which the protesters tried to persuade to join their side. They said such things as "We are the people, there are more of us, you are supposed to defend us. We don't want this kind of socialism."[278] However, their effort was futile. After arriving from Dukelské Náměstí at around 1 p.m., the protesters started throwing stones at the militiamen,[279] causing the defenders numerous injuries.[280] They used a meat factory car, which had been stolen earlier by its drivers on Dukelské Náměstí, to break down the closed gate.[281] The sheer mass of people eventually managed to break through the cordon of militiamen, and some 300 protesters managed to enter the factory and advance several dozen meters inside.[282] Some of the protesters had achieved their goal and went back to their workplaces.[283] Others began shouting by the broken-down gates: "Come out, Škoda workers!"[284] The protesters smashed the windows of the gatehouse and, like before, destroyed the ideological decorations adorning the gates.[285] Several employees (especially those from the Engineering IV department) actually left their workplaces and watched the events outside the gate from a distance. Some of them actually joined the protesters,[286] but they only numbered a couple dozen people.[287]

The KSČ Factory Committee responded to the dangerous situation by sending reinforcements from the ranks of the People's Militias, and hastily called volunteers to the broken-down gate. However, the defenders only succeeded when the People's Militias was backed up by a unit of the Ministry of National Security's Internal Guard, permanently assigned to protect the factory. Shortly before 2 p.m., the workers were finally pushed out of the factory, and the People's Militias gradually cordoned off the surrounding streets and arrested the more riotous protesters.[288]

In the Gate 4 incident, security forces used warning fire in the air for the first time during demonstrations.[289] No serious injuries are believed to have occurred. This was the only case of the use of firearms in the suppression of the June protests in Pilsen (not counting the shots fired by the civilian staff in the courthouse mentioned above). Eyewitnesses claimed that only one shot had been fired,[290] or a few at most.[291] Official sources avoided a detailed description of this politically sensitive event. However, at a closed meeting of the Party Regional Committee, chief secretary Jan Hlína later confessed to having been responsible for the order to use weapons against the workers.[292] The order was personally issued by chairman of the KSČ Factory Committee Bedřich Perlík, who was in charge of the factory's defense on that day. He justified his decision by having been concerned for the well-being of the militiamen, pushed back into a vulnerable position by the crowd which had broken through the gate.[293] A report sent by the Pilsen communists to the headquarters repeated this interpretation of events: "Only when they [the People's Militias unit] were pushed into a desperate position did they use their weapons as a warning. With the help of the Internal Guard, they managed to fight the attack off."[294]

Word-of-mouth rumors about the use of firearms immediately grew into a rumor about a mass shooting of workers, or even a bloodbath (a girl was allegedly shot). This was quite understandable from a psychological perspective, since even a few warning shots must have elicited considerable respect among the protesters. Other protesters who did not witness the conflict firsthand spread a far more adventurous interpretation of the events.[295] A by-product of such rumors was the growing anti-government sentiment among the local population and radicalization of the protests.[296] Between 1 and 2 p.m., the security forces managed to break up all the large protest gatherings (on Náměstí Republiky, at the Palace of Justice, on Dukelské Náměstí, and outside Gate 4 of the V.I. Lenin Factories) and were seemingly well on the way to suppressing the unrest entirely. However, there were still many rebellious people milling around, huddling in groups and waiting for the next opportunity to express their discontent.[297]

The apparent calm did not last long. At 2 p.m., after the end of the morning shift at the V. I. Lenin Factories, some workers who had not previously taken part in the protests outside the factory joined the protesters downtown. Around this time, workers heading for the afternoon shift were passing through the streets, having learned of the previous conflicts along the way.[298] The crowd in the streets grew considerably, and many people joined the ranks of the protesters for the moment. Between 2.30 and 3 p.m., the crowds waiting on Náměstí Republiky and Dukelské Náměstí began to swell rapidly and mobilize all over again.[299] The national anthem sounded again by the National Liberation Monument.[300] The protesters turned their attention to the large propaganda boards celebrating Czechoslovak-Soviet friendship standing near the statue of President Masaryk.[301] During the earlier protests, the crowd had tried unsuccessfully to knock the wooden boards over. Now, a group of about 25 people tried a different way of destroying them, pouring gasoline on the banners and setting them on fire. The protesters also tried to prevent the fire brigade from extinguishing the fire.[302]

Around 3 p.m., a crowd of some 1,000 people on Dukelské Náměstí square got moving and headed back along 1. Máje Avenue to Náměstí Republiky.[303] The protesters carried a national flag at the head of the procession. The procession stopped again at the site of the former foundation stone of the monument to fallen American soldiers and sang the national anthem.[304]

The main Pilsen meeting place, Náměstí Republiky square, was seemingly cleared out before 2 p.m., but there were not enough troops stationed in the access streets to completely cordon off the area. As a result, protesters began to gather in the square again after 2 p.m. They were also reinforced by the crowd heading from Dukelské Náměstí, which easily broke through the cordon of soldiers. The soldiers did not make much effort to stop the protesters, and some of them even apologized "that it was not their fault, and that they were ordered to be there."[305]

In the square, this procession merged with the crowd who had gathered there earlier. Some 3,000–7,000 people eventually gathered outside the City Hall, which was the site of the culmination of the Pilsen protests on June 1, 1953.[306] Some sources report 10,000 to 12,000 participants,[307] but this figure is based on the sum of all the protest rallies in different spots in Pilsen over the course of the day. It therefore does not correspond to the number of people gathered in the square at one time, nor to the total number of protesters throughout the day, since many people joined more than one protest meeting and were therefore included in the total several times.[308] After 1989, Czechoslovak historians have often claimed that the police and party authorities tended to underestimate the number of protesters in order to mitigate the extent of their failure, and that the demonstrations were much larger than official documents claim. This assumption is, however, unfounded, because the authorities were equally keen to exaggerate the number of protesters in internal documents to give themselves more credit for saving the situation (in the case of the national authorities) or, in the case of the local Pilsen authorities, to justify their failure to suppress the demonstrations on their own. The reporting of figures and data regarding police intervention was an integral part of the struggle for taking credit and denying responsibility that broke out between the various ministries and institutions following the suppression of the protests.

The peak number of protesters therefore amounted to approximately 2.27% to 5.3% of the city's population of 132,000.[309] This calculation leaves aside the fact that some 27,000 people from the surrounding districts commuted to Pilsen to work, and that the actual number of people present in the city on that day was therefore much higher.[310] This means that, as in other regions, only a fraction of the population actively participated in the Pilsen riots.[311]

The mood of the protesters became more combative in the evening than it had been in the morning. The protesters attempted to storm the City Hall again.[312] The assembled crowd demanded the release of several detainees held at the headquarters of the Consolidated National Committee.[313] To that end, they even sent a delegation to the City Hall.[314] People chanted slogans like "We want new elections! [. . .] Down with the government! [and also] Release the prisoners from the City Hall!"[315] Police officers and members of the People's Militias were standing guard outside the National Committee building, but the unexpected onslaught of protesters forced them to retreat to the lobby of the building. During the retreat, a number of skirmishes broke out between the defenders and the attackers. The crowd tore off the police officers' hats and threw them into the air. Some members of the People's Militias were pulled from the retreating formation of defenders, beaten and trampled.[316] Some were stripped of their rifles by the mob, which were then destroyed by the protesters and thrown at the building's security guards.[317] The crowd threw stones and small coins of the old currency at the windows of the City Hall.[318] Some of the protesters had already armed themselves with makeshift weapons in the morning, such as sticks or tools.[319] One protester even brought a handgun and grenades to the city center but did not use them.[320] Weapons seized from the police during the protests were generally not used by the protesters and were mostly thrown away. Neither the security forces nor the protesters wished for shooting to occur in the streets.

A number of officers defending the City Hall building were injured, and a makeshift infirmary was therefore set up inside the building. The only way for the City Hall crew to stop the advancing mob was to close the iron gates behind them. The fire brigade was called to the rescue after 3.30 p.m. and began to spray the protesters with water, pushing them back toward the wall of the church on the other side of the square.[321] Some of the protesters got into scuffles not only with the police but also with the fire brigade, slashing their fire hoses. The fire truck had to be called away as unusable.[322]

As the day progressed, the protests, which had begun with a peaceful strike in the morning, had become so violent that by the evening they resembled a peculiar form of street warfare in which any means of combat except firearms was allowed. This type of demonstration had essentially lost the last vestiges of its former legitimacy within the political system of the time, and the regime's representatives had no choice but to suppress it by brute force. As local party officials prepared to disperse the protests, they adopted a new definition of the conflict and, for the first time, publicly labeled the protests an attempt to overthrow the government. This was a symbolic climax of the protest's development, which had shifted from political demonstrations combined with occasional riots to an outright act of subversion.

At approximately 4.30 p.m., Josef Mainzer, chairman of the Consolidated National Committee in Pilsen, tried again to address the protesters via the city's PA system. He called on the crowd to disperse and attempted to convince the protesters that they had been misled into participating in an anti-state demonstration. He mentioned the names of some of the alleged organizers and used them as proof that this was not a workers' protest against currency reform, but rather a provocation organized by the class enemies in Pilsen.[323] His speech, however, did not convince the protesting crowd to retreat. Shortly after 5 p.m., the authorities proceeded to clear the square by brute force.

CAUSES OF THE GRADUAL ESCALATION OF PROTESTS

Throughout the morning, the protesters did not encounter any armed or at least organized resistance, neither from the regional political authorities nor from law enforcement. They did not, however, represent any unified force, nor were there enough of genuinely determined activists among them to pose, under normal circumstances, a serious threat to the security forces. Nevertheless, the protesters managed to take control of some key public spaces in the city center, and to occupy two important administrative buildings. At this point, we should therefore try to find out how such a thing was possible in the first place.

The main reason for the unusually smooth escalation of the demonstrations was the moment of surprise caused by the fact that the responsible regional officials had not been regularly informed about the situation in large industrial enterprises. Although special staff had been set up in Pilsen over the weekend to oversee security matters during the implementation of the currency reform, they had not at all considered the possibility that riots might break out in industrial plants, whose employees were considered by party officials to be the most loyal segment of society. In the preceding years, the party apparatus had focused on industrial plants only as tools required to meet economic targets; no one supervised the political agenda in factories, and party leadership was unaware that the indoctrination of the workers, aimed at turning them into the pillar of the future socialist society, was not going as well as the party had imagined.[324] This autonomy suited the officials of the V. I. Lenin Factories for a long time. They tried to solve their problems independently, without interference from law enforcement and higher party echelons. Moreover, meeting important production targets gave both the local party leaders and ordinary workers a degree of self-confidence that mentally distinguished them from other, smaller enterprises.[325] The factory had become a world of its own, secluded from outside society.[326]

The State Security authorities suffered from a similar lack of information. The Heavy Engineering Department of the StB Regional Administration, for example, was not in contact with the Personnel Department of the V. I. Lenin Factories at all and did not register any potential enemies in the factory. It did recruit 27 employees of the plant as collaborators, but they were not selected according to criteria that would allow them to provide information on potential subversive sentiments among the employees.[327] The long-standing rivalry between some factory officials and the State Security personnel (see the Foreigners' House affair above) also had a negative impact on this situation.[328]

Thus, one of the factors for the outbreak of the Pilsen protests was the party officials' and State Security officers' general ignorance of the working-class environment. For the last five years they had overlooked important signals, such as previous strikes, the apathy of the workers toward party meetings, and their distrust of the party leaders at the factory. On June 1, 1953, all local authorities were therefore extremely surprised by the development of the protests at the V. I. Lenin Factories. After the protests outside the factory became overtly political and eventually violent, the initial surprise turned into panic and genuine fear for personal safety. These feelings were particularly palpable among those officials who came face to face with the enraged crowd (such as Josef Mainzer, chairman of the National Committee, on Náměstí Republiky square). It soon became clear to the more astute officials that their future careers were at stake. Few therefore showed their own initiative, and all sought to confirm instructions from their superiors.

Another reason for the dynamic escalation of the protests was the general overload of the security and administrative apparatuses caused by the rapid implementation of the currency reform. According to instructions, the regional headquarters allocated most of the members of the National Security Corps and the People's Militias to protect the exchange centers. Moreover, the deployment was extremely chaotic, because the requested help of the army was denied at the last minute on Sunday night. The troops sent to the exchange centers could not be withdrawn by the regional headquarters during the protests, as this would have put the centers at the mercy of the protesters. Therefore, the troops guarding the centers were scattered throughout the city and did not take action against the protesters, even though in some cases the protests took place in the immediate vicinity of the exchange centers. The protesters also intuitively respected the security measures taken at the centers and did not attack any of them, suspecting they would most likely encounter armed resistance. State Security personnel were also deployed at the centers. The regional headquarters lost not only the forces that could normally be deployed to pacify the protests on June 1 but also the network of informants which should have warned it of the risk of protests in time, since there was no one to manage it.[329]

The regional headquarters was only left with a small contingent of reserves for dealing with sudden events. They consisted of less than 50 members of the National Security Corps and three rapid response teams of the People's Militias.[330] Moreover, this handful of people, which was the only immediately available defense force in the city, consisted mainly of older men and women, since the physically fittest and most ideologically conscious men were assigned to protect the exchange centers.[331] Most of the reserves were therefore not really capable of armed combat. In addition, most of the detachments of the People's Militias were tied to their workplaces because of the unstable situation in the factories and did not intervene in the morning events on the streets of Pilsen. Under these circumstances, the protesters had almost unlimited leeway in the city and had free access to important official buildings that had been left almost completely unprotected. The main reason the demonstrations became more radical and widespread was because there was virtually nothing to stand in their way.

A third major reason for the unhindered advance of the protesters was the uncertainty of the leading regional officials as to whether it was acceptable at all for them to intervene by force against the protesting workers, considering they were seen as representatives of the official ruling class. Until the afternoon hours, the party and law enforcement authorities considered the demonstrations to be a legitimate workers' protest. Later, internal party assessments of the action spoke very critically of the fact that "the leading comrades of the Regional Committee, charged with managing the party's actions during the implementation of the currency reform, failed to identify the class enemy among the masses in time, and wrongly interpreted the reactionaries' actions as a manifestation of the peoples' discontent."[332] The reaction of law enforcement units was in line with this definition of the conflict.

In the early hours of the morning, the regional party secretariat and the StB Regional Administration of State Security consulted on the situation with the central authorities and based on their recommendations, chose to try to pacify the protests through verbal persuasion. The protesters gathered on Náměstí Republiky square were addressed by the city PA system as comrades and not as participants in a subversive demonstration.[333] At the same time, all party authorities sent out their officials and volunteers in small groups to campaign for the currency reform among the protesters. For example, dozens of employees of the Regional National Committee and the Regional Committee of the Communist Party were present in the square, having been systematically directed there.[334] Members of some of the base party organizations reported for duty on their own initiative and were also used in this manner.[335]

However, their task was completely unfeasible. The mob often physically attacked the groups of communists, tore off their party badges and Pioneer scarves, and in some cases even beat them up. The communists thus reached out to the square individually, in a disorganized manner, and were subjected to demoralizing humiliation and chased away.[336] Some walked away, others covered up their party badges so as not to be conspicuous. An employee of the Regional National Committee was verbally attacked by the protesters: "Make short work of him! Kill him! The bastards have ruined the entire nation, and now they're trying to lecture us?"[337] One of the representatives of the Central Committee who was present actually ordered his comrades to hide their party badges for safety reasons.[338]

Although the communists flocked to Náměstí Republiky square in fairly large numbers that could perhaps have rivaled the most active core of protesters, they did not manage to create a centrally directed formation, which under the circumstances was the only possible way to change the course of events. Unlike in 1948, the situation in the factories did not allow the deployment of organized processions of workers in the streets. The party leaders were rightly concerned that many of them might join the protesters. Due to these misgivings, a large communist procession did not form until the evening hours.

A large part of the People's Militias reserves suffered a similar fate to the volunteer party officials and members. At the onset of the protests, they were also sent out, unarmed and in small groups, to try to persuade the protesters to disband. The militiamen were spread out among the crowd in the square, and were often physically attacked, resulting in a number of injuries. Eventually, law enforcement authorities realized that this form of intervention was pointless; however, there was no time to recall these troops, arm them and send them back into action with different instructions.[339] The demoralizing effect of such unrealistic orders was later apparent from the indignant complaints sent from the ranks of the Pilsen militiamen to the Central Committee of the Communist Party: "We feel justified in this criticism, considering that the protesters spat in our faces, threw small change at us, called us names, insulted us and humiliated us. We did not want weapons so we could actually use them, but only as a deterrent, which would have definitely helped."[340]

A substantial number of State Security officers found themselves in the same situation as the militiamen: they were also ordered to mingle in the crowd without the use of weapons and try to persuade them to calm down while also observing the most active of the protesters.[341] Many StB officers sustained injuries; some of those who had been exposed as secret police by the protesters in the morning hours were literally chased through the streets by the angry mob.[342] Most of the State Security personnel therefore hid in various public buildings during the day and were completely cut off from the action at the headquarters of the Regional StB Administration on the Charkovské Nábřeží waterfront. In all of the above cases, the initial decision to persuade the protesters by personal campaigning without weapons made any later forceful action difficult.

Members of the Public Security Corps (the police) were the only law enforcement units who were not attacked as frequently by the protesters as the other security forces in the morning. Most of them adopted a passive attitude toward the protests, generally standing in designated positions without any unrealistic attempts to stop the processions, intervening only when an attacked person explicitly demanded protection. In such cases, the crowd respected police authority and left the affected person alone, at least for the time they remained near the police patrol.[343]

In some cases, however, police officers stood idly by and did not intervene in the attacks on party officials, militiamen, or undercover officers, unless they expressly had to. The militiamen who had suffered attacks and beatings viewed their actions as disloyal, which later resulted in numerous disputes and accusations. In their complaints, the People's Militias members stated bitterly: "It was right not to give the order to shoot, but the attitude of some (most) SNB officers was completely unacceptable: they stood idly by as women and party officials were being insulted, they let young rapscallions and whores hug them, they put up with such heckling as 'Come with us, the SNB should join the people!', and one of the officers patrolling by the theater in the morning actually said he would join the protesters if he could."[344] There were even numerous suspicions that district police chief Josef Herian himself had merely stood by and watched as the communists and militiamen were attacked.[345]

Extensive documentation has been preserved regarding the actions of chief constable Václav Huncl: he and another officer were given the task of closing off the corner of Dominikánská and Solní Street, to prevent more people from coming to Náměstí Republiky. However, when part of the crowd headed from the square to the Palace of Justice, Huncl did not try to stop them. He remained in his post, and successfully defended several communists who had been attacked by the mob. Nevertheless, some members of the People's Militias and State Security were beaten up near him, but Huncl did nothing to help them.[346]

From these findings, it is evident that the actions of the various security forces on Náměstí Republiky were highly inconsistent, resulting from their (un)willingness to take initiative. Their unwillingness to cooperate led to ineffective or non-existent coordination in situations where there was no time to wait for commands from above.[347]

The fourth reason for the unhindered escalation of the protests was the collapse of the management mechanisms of the regional security apparatuses. The regional security staff, established specifically for this purpose, was completely incapable of coordinating and directing operations. The cause of this failure lay primarily in the fact that the officials received inaccurate, delayed information about the protesters' behavior and movements, meaning they could offer nothing but a belated response throughout the morning.[348] Moreover, the leading security officers did not anticipate the protests and were often absent as they broke out. For example, Chief of Staff Matěj Bálek, head of the Regional StB Administration, began his day by inspecting the exchange centers. Through interventions with the Pilsen branch of the State Bank, he made it his priority to open the centers at the V. I. Lenin Factories, because he rightly suspected that if they were not up and running as soon as possible, it might contribute to the workers' discontent. However, when he arrived at the plant, the workers were already on their way to the square. Bálek then headed for the City Hall building, where the protesters had already gathered. He then got stuck in the besieged City Hall building until the afternoon and was therefore unable to fully direct the staff's actions.[349]

A similar situation occurred at the regional headquarters of the People's Militias. In the morning, regional commander Drozda, who had just returned from a few days' business trip, went home to shave, and only returned to his post after the protests had already broken out. Instead of coordinating action, his political deputy František Petrucha personally guarded the entrance to the regional party secretariat with a machine gun. Operations officer František Čala was celebrating his 40th birthday on that day and was moving around the headquarters in casual clothes without a uniform. All of these instances of misconduct naturally caused even greater confusion and made the smooth cooperation between the various security forces impossible.[350]

The security apparatus was thus thrown into the midst of the protests under alarming circumstances: it had no information about the gravity of the situation at the V. I. Lenin Factories; it was swamped with work required for a hasty implementation of the currency reform; it had been given unrealistic political orders; and it had received virtually no support from the regional governing bodies. The result could hardly have been anything other than a total collapse of all local security structures.

ACTIONS OF LAW ENFORCEMENT

The regional headquarters of the People's Militias was the first to be informed of the morning strike at the V. I. Lenin Factories by the heads of the security forces. Unfortunately, it had clearly underestimated the situation and chose to act after it received a report that the workers had left the workshops, gathered in the factory courtyard, and were preparing to go out in the streets. The headquarters then contacted Jan Hlína, chief secretary of the KSČ Regional Committee, who issued an order to stop the protesters. However, the workers had already passed through the factory gates. On the orders of Jan Hlína, the regional headquarters therefore sent one squad of 25 unarmed militiamen against them, with an order to persuade the protesters to return peacefully. Unfortunately, this was a decision that Hlína shortly came to regret; at the time, he had no idea how few reserves the headquarters had in Pilsen.[351] Hlína also telephoned the Secretariat of the KSČ Central Committee and informed them about the workers' unrest in the V. I. Lenin Factories. However, he mistakenly declared that he had the situation under control, which changed completely in the next few minutes.[352]

The deployed squad of the People's Militias attempted to confront the procession of about 700 workers, stop them, and persuade them to return. The protesters simply ignored them. The unit was therefore called back to the headquarters of the regional party secretariat. Afterward, the militiamen vividly described the utter chaos that then prevailed within the region's governing body:

> We were surprised by the chaos and complete unpreparedness of the regional headquarters, which was totally incapable of giving us any sensible orders or taking any measures. We were put in one room, and after about a quarter of an hour, Comrade [Jan] Hlína came in with Comrade [Václav] Drozda, regional commander of the People's Militias, who told us, in a very confused manner: "Go to the square, Comrades; the protesters are trying to get into the City Hall. Move among them, try to persuade them, break them up into small groups and clear the square." It is clear that Comrade Hlína had no clear idea of how large the protests really were.[353]

The regional headquarters of the People's Militias, led by Václav Drozda, took the same position as the chief secretary of the Regional Party Committee Jan Hlína and shortly after 10 a.m., Drozda informed the commander-in-chief of the People's Militias in Prague that he was sending out his troops to confront the protesters "wearing blue overalls, carrying no weapons."[354] The squad of militiamen mentioned in the previous paragraph therefore split up into small groups and headed for Náměstí Republiky square in an attempt to carry out their orders. This rendered the only unit of the People's Militias deployed in the first phase of the demonstrations completely ineffective.[355] Its members were either beaten up or abandoned their attempts to persuade the protesters in time and resorted to trying to position themselves in the surrounding streets to prevent people from going into the square.[356]

The Regional Public Security administration (the police) only received reports of a strike at the V. I. Lenin Factories at around 9 a.m. At the same time, they were also informed of the situation at the Elektrotrakce Doudlevce subsidiary plant. They immediately reported the facts to chief secretary of the Regional Party Committee Jan Hlína and to the Regional administration of the State Security Service, where the report was received by Captain Josef Jindřich, on behalf of the absent Matěj Bálek. Jan Hlína assured the Regional Public Security Administration that he had sent political officers to both plants to explain the reform to the workers. For the time being, he considered this measure fully sufficient.[357] At 9.45 a.m., representatives of the Regional Public Security Administration contacted the commanding officer of the StB Regional Administration, Josef Jindřich, who told them that he had just discussed the whole thing with the authorities in Prague and had received instructions that no intervention should be made against the protesters, and that party officials would try to persuade the protesters verbally. Intervention was to be made only if the exchange center was attacked.[358] Having learned about the problems at the V. I. Lenin Factories, regional State Security commander Matěj Bálek discussed the situation with Jan Hlína, and agreed with his decision not to send police officers against the striking workers.[359] The Regional Public Security Administration asked the Main Public Security administration in Prague to confirm this order.[360]

Non-violent, unarmed resolution of the conflict was therefore supported by all the decision makers present in the city during the initial stage of the protests, as well as by at least four higher national authorities (the Secretariat of the Central Committee of the Communist Party, the Main Administration of State Security, the Main Administration of Public Security, and the staff of the Commander-in-Chief of the People's Militias). Thus, the later disputes among Pilsen officials as to who had pushed for more vigorous action against the protesters on June 1 were just belated acts of self-preservation, fueled by the desire to shift as much responsibility for the failure as possible onto someone else.

Around 10 a.m., the situation in the city center changed dramatically as protesters forced their way into the City Hall building. It was only this attack on the administrative backbone of the city that forced officials to reassess the security risks the protests posed, and to gradually adjust the security forces' strategy. However, the riot police were still hampered by the political orders to intervene in a non-violent manner, as well as the shortage of troops. The first step in the new course of action was taken by the head of the Regional Public Security Administration, who decided to liberate the headquarters of the Consolidated National Committee. To this end, he deployed 29 members of the National Security Corps, supported by another 20 members of the People's Militias. About half an hour later, the City Hall building was secured. However, this success was only made possible by the fact that the most militant core of protesters had already moved on toward the Palace of Justice. Even though the protesters had in effect voluntarily surrendered their positions, the troops deployed did not even manage to clear the area outside the City Hall.[361] Even after the police liberated the City Hall, they actually left the picture of former president Edvard Beneš hanging on the façade so as not to irritate the protesters unnecessarily.[362]

Following the events at the City Hall, the remaining reserves were sent to guard strategically important buildings, such as the State Radio building, the main post office, the Regional National Committee, and the Regional Party Secretariat, based on an agreement between the Regional State Security administration and the Regional Public Security administration.[363] When these reserves were exhausted, Regional Public Security Administration was left with only 25 available officers.[364] Therefore, the administration asked the chief secretary of the KSČ Regional Committee for assistance from the People's Militias.[365] They pressed the Committee to send the reinforcements especially after receiving information that the Palace of Justice had been invaded by protesters.

However, the expected reinforcements did not arrive. In fact, the Regional Headquarters of the People's Militias only issued an order to mobilize all units until around 10 a.m., in response to the occupation of the City Hall by the protesters. Moreover, the People's Militias members gathered rather slowly, showing signs of wavering in conviction, and some of them did not even join the action at all.[366] Moreover, the People's Militias headquarters itself was hesitant to deploy its men to the streets because there was a fair chance that the troops would still have to be used to stabilize the situation inside the industrial enterprises.[367] Most of the active units of the People's Militias were therefore deployed to the V. I. Lenin Factories for the day, and other large contingents also remained in their respective enterprises and were not deployed against the protesters in the morning at all.[368]

Commanders of the Pilsen security forces had to call for extraordinary reinforcements to deal with the overall failure of the riot forces in the city. Around 11 a.m., chief of the StB Regional Administration Matěj Bálek asked for help from the Internal Guard of the Ministry of National Security and the Czechoslovak Army.[369] Army units stationed in Pilsen and units of the Internal Guard, which were normally responsible for defending the V. I. Lenin Factories in the city center and the Košutka radio transmitter in the suburbs, were deployed to deal with the situation.[370] At 12 p.m., chief secretary of the Regional Party Committee Jan Hlína telephoned Secretary of the Central Committee Antonín Novotný to request the dispatch of the People's Militias from Prague, which meant that the Pilsen conflict had now gained nationwide importance. A total of 328 militiamen left the capital after 1.30 p.m. and arrived in Pilsen in the evening.[371]

The first of the reinforcements only managed to intervene in the streets of Pilsen at around 12 p.m. A 30-strong detachment of the Internal Guard arrived at the besieged courthouse, cleared the building, and for the first time that day, arrested a large number of protesters who were trapped on the upper floors of the building.[372] Meanwhile, a detachment of the People's Militias numbering some 40–50 men also arrived in the area. However, a large crowd was still present outside the Palace of Justice, which the security forces were unable to control for the time being.[373]

The riot forces had only managed to gain significant ground after the arrival of army units of some 200 men[374] on Náměstí Republiky square between 12 p.m. and 1 p.m.[375] The army units first took up positions in the streets adjacent to the square, and advanced toward the nearby regional courthouse. However, people were jumping in front of their vehicles and prevented them from moving.[376] In some cases, they even unscrewed the tire valves of the army vehicles.[377] After the arrival of the army, members of the National Security Corps and the People's Militias still patrolling around the square could be recalled to the City Hall building, whose garrison had thus been considerably reinforced.[378] Another platoon of the Internal Guard was also sent to the City Hall at 12.30 p.m.[379] The area outside the Palace of Justice was gradually cleared with the help of the Internal Guard, the People's Militias, and the Czechoslovak Army. Between 1 and 2 p.m., the protesters were gradually pushed out of the nearest part of Náměstí Republiky (the western section of the square and the adjacent Sedláčkova Street). These operations were personally overseen by chief of the Regional StB Administration Matěj Bálek, along with the army commanders.[380] However, the main reason for the successful stabilization of the security forces' positions in this part of the city was that most of the protesters began moving of their own accord along 1. Máje Avenue and Dukelské Náměstí toward the National Liberation Monument, where a new epicenter of the protests formed between 12 p.m. and 1 p.m.

After the procession arrived at Dukelské Náměstí, units of the People's Militias from the V. I. Lenin Factories were promptly dispatched to this location with the task of preventing the protesters from moving toward the State Radio building. The militiamen then clashed with the protesters in a series of minor skirmishes in Hálkova Street and by the bridge over the railroad tracks on 1. Máje Avenue.[381] Around 1 p.m., army units also intervened on Dukelské Náměstí,[382] managing to push the people onto the sidewalks and into the surrounding streets.[383] This was not a particularly difficult feat, however, considering that a substantial part of the protesters had already left for Gate 4 of the V. I. Lenin Factories.

The gate was initially defended against the protesters by a six-man patrol of the People's Militias.[384] The defensive actions were directed by the KSČ Factory Committee. Final decision belonged to Committee chairman Bedřich Perlík, who had only been in office since April 1953 and was not yet sufficiently familiar with the inner workings of the factory.[385] He reacted to the protesters' efforts to break into the factory by trying to rally enough politically reliable employees from the workshops to reinforce the building's security. People only volunteered reluctantly, however, and not many could be persuaded to come, as the party members did not want to intervene against their fellow workers and "were not really convinced that this was a counter-revolutionary coup."[386] In the end, only about 150 volunteers aided in the factory's defense.[387]

Armed reinforcements sent by the regional headquarters of the People's Militias, which provided first 70 and then a total of 170 members, also arrived late.[388] The militiamen's determination had its limits, however, and the first of the deployed detachments arrived at the gate with about half the numbers, as "some comrades had fallen behind on the way."[389] The attack was finally repulsed with the help of a mere 60 men from the Internal Guard of the Ministry of National Security.[390] The People's Militias then managed to cordon off the streets around Gate 4.[391] Before the end of the morning shift at 2 p.m., the Factory Committee reinforced the security at all the gates, posting 20–30 loyal workers at each gate to carry out thorough checks of everyone going in and out, so as to prevent individual protesters from breaking in. There were no further incidents at the factory entrances after these measures were implemented.[392]

At 3 p.m., the main focus of the riot operations moved back to Náměstí Republiky, along with the protesting crowd. Joined by the defenders of the City Hall, the People's Militias was relatively more willing to use force to intervene against the protesters. Some police officers, on the other hand, were trying to hold their positions without engaging in violent skirmishes with the protesters. They tried to explain to the people that maintaining order was their official duty and that they could not let them inside the City Hall.[393] Later in the day, three police officers were relieved from duty for their reluctance, and five others were later charged by the military prosecutor.[394] Some of the soldiers were visibly taken aback by the protesters' negative attitude toward the military's presence in the city and were unwilling to do anything beyond their clearly stated orders. Some women spat at the soldiers or called them names, "You bastard, this is how your mother raised you? To go against the workers?"[395] Other protesters tried to grab the soldiers' guns and disable their cars by ripping out the ignition cables.[396] Other protesters tried to persuade the soldiers to join the protests or at least not to intervene,[397] shouting, "This is the people's army, it should side with the people!"[398] The

Deputy Minister of National Security later commented: "I was right there, and I saw people pulling soldiers out of their cars, and the soldiers actually joined them."[399]

The low morale of the anti-riot forces was the main reason why additional reinforcements were needed to suppress the protests. A 90-man detachment from the Border Guard NCO School of the Ministry of National Security in Poběžovice,[400] sent personally by the Deputy Minister of National Security, Colonel Jindřich Kotal, arrived at Náměstí Republiky shortly before 6 p.m.[401] Around that time, the 12th Emergency Storm Troop of the Internal Guard of the Ministry of National Security from Karlovy Vary entered the City Hall by the rear entrance.[402] Units of the Internal Guard, the Czechoslovak Army and the State Security, which had previously cleared the streets around the regional courthouse, also moved to Náměstí Republiky. They were joined by the People's Militias units that had previously intervened in the streets around Gate 4 of the V.I. Lenin Factories.[403] These units then made the first attempt to secure the immediate vicinity of the City Hall between 4 and 4.30 p.m. using water cannons.[404]

Overall coordination of all the assembled security forces was still very poor, however. They managed to form a cordon that partially blocked the access routes to the square, but a large crowd of protesters still remained there. Many troops were also stationed quite far from the epicenter of the conflict and could therefore not effectively contribute to stabilizing the situation.[405] A joint intervention of all the forces present was necessary to finally clear out the square. Unfortunately, the various security forces each answered to different ministries and had long lacked a unified command whose authority would extend beyond regional level.[406]

This lack of an adequate command was only rectified at 2.30 p.m., when the Deputy Minister of National Security, Colonel Jindřich Kotal, arrived in Pilsen and took control over the entire operation from Matěj Bálek in the building of the Regional StB Administration.[407] Subsequently, he put Brigadier General Miroslav Kuchař in charge of the combined forces.[408] The combined security forces then surrounded the square, formed a cordon, and between 4.30 and 5 p.m. they began pushing the crowd into the side streets.[409] By 5.15 p.m. the entire area of Náměstí Republiky square had been cleared out.[410] The People's Militias units from Prague, which arrived in Pilsen after 4 p.m., also joined in the action.[411] Shortly before 6 p.m., a motorized Internal Guard battalion from Prague arrived on the square. Between 6 and 7 p.m., the riot police pushed the remaining groups of protesters out of the surrounding streets.[412] The failure of the Pilsen security forces was therefore resolved not only by calling in emergency reinforcements from other parts of the country, but also by the national authorities taking control of the intervention. Only then did the situation stabilize.

Some sources provide different time frames for the afternoon operations of the riot forces. According to them, the out-of-town units had supposedly arrived in the city earlier and protests had been dispersed around 4 p.m. There seems to be two reasons for these discrepancies. Due to inflexible command, there were often considerable time delays between the arrival of the reinforcements in Pilsen and their actual deployment.[413] In addition, the various security forces later tried to exaggerate their merits in suppressing the protests by using different time figures in their reports. The greatest discrepancies occurred between the reports of the Ministry of National Defense and the Ministry of National Security.[414]

Disputes over credit for the successful execution of the Pilsen operation remained a hot topic for the leading officials for many years to come. In 1957, for example, departmental rivalry between Interior Minister Rudolf Barák and Minister of National Defense Alexej Čepička led to an extensive investigation into the Pilsen events, which both sides hoped to use as evidence of their importance at a session of the Political Bureau of the Communist Party Central Committee.[415] Even back then, however, attempts to provide an accurate reconstruction of events were unsuccessful due to the conflicting reports from different authorities—in spite of the fact that unlike today's historians, the persons in charge were provided with all available sources, including personal testimonies of the decision makers.[416]

Testimonies of the detained protesters also fail to provide an exact time frame of the events, since the protesters did not form one large procession but moved around in smaller groups. For these reasons, the above description of the actions of both the protesters and the security forces is necessarily a simplified version of events, and the time figures should be seen as approximate, sometimes deviating by as much as an hour.[417]

During the evening intervention on Náměstí Republiky, the police continuously arrested randomly protesters, loaded them into cars and took them either to the prison located in the building of the Regional StB administration, or to the Bory Prison.[418] The grounds for arrest were often wet clothes (from the water cannons), visible injuries (scuffles with security forces), or even the person's mere presence somewhere near the square.[419] People were often unable to produce their IDs because they had given them to family members in order to exchange money. Many people were also detained for attempting to prevent the arrest of other protesters.[420] Some were arrested for making derogatory remarks about the intervening riot forces. Locksmith Josef Honzík, for example, ironically commented on the handgun carried by a member of the People's Militias: "So this is the new currency."[421]

During the initial phase of the protests it was mostly the more active protesters who were detained; in the afternoon, however, the security forces resorted to mass arrests in an effort to clear the square, which resulted in a number of mistakes, with some of the party persuaders being wrongfully arrested.[422] Denunciations then led to another wave of arrests during the night and in the following days. Some 250 people were arrested on Monday June 1, 1953,[423] and the number of detainees reached at least 351 in the following weeks.[424]

Taking control of the square was by no means the end of the security forces' operations in Pilsen. Units of the Internal Guard, the Border Guard, the Czechoslovak Army, the People's Militias, and the Public Security secured some 30 strategically important buildings and areas in Pilsen before nightfall[425] and participated in patrolling the streets of the city.[426] A curfew from midnight to 4 a.m. was announced over the PA system.[427] These measures were subsequently approved by Minister of National Security Karol Bacílek, who personally arrived in Pilsen around 9 p.m. and remained there until midnight.[428] The tanks of the First Motorized Regiment of the Internal Guard, which took up position by the Bory Prison, evoked the atmosphere of a state of emergency.[429] The emergency measures were kept for another week. The last of the emergency reinforcements left the city in the morning hours of June 8, 1953. The People's Militias and State Security units were called off on the same day.[430]

Units of the Czechoslovak Army numbering 1,140 men, units of the Internal Guard and Border Guard of the Ministry of National Security numbering 592 men, and units of the People's Militias numbering 460 men participated in the suppression of the Pilsen riots. In total, 2,192 members of the security forces were deployed in Pilsen.[431] Other sources mention as many as 1,279 soldiers and a total of 2,329 anti-riot forces.[432] However, a significant amount of these men probably did not confront the protesters directly and acted as reserves and patrols, or provided additional security in the city. The above-mentioned figures regarding the deployed soldiers (1,140 and 1,279, respectively) were estimates given the Army command after the fact, while the Regional StB Administration in Pilsen registered only 500 army personnel who were directly involved in the suppression of the protests.[433] On the other hand, the local Public Security and State Security officers were not included in the above-mentioned head counts.

With the exception of the warning shots at Gate 4 of the V. I. Lenin Factories, no shots were fired during the suppression of the protests. At least 32 members of the People's Militias, 19 State Security officers, 5 Public Security officers, and 1 member of the fire brigade were injured during the protests. No data is available regarding the number of injuries among the protesters, but in all likelihood there were no casualties.[434]

ACTIONS OF THE PARTY APPARATUS AND THE COMMUNIST PARTY'S EVENING RALLY

The morning protests paralyzed both the local security forces and the party apparatus. The local party leaders chose to adopt a non-violent strategy against the protesters, sending out all available volunteers in small groups to Náměstí Republiky.[435] Unfortunately, they soon realized that verbal persuasion was completely ineffective. The communists returned from the square demoralized and badly beaten, criticizing the chosen approach and demanding more systematic, forceful action.[436] Some therefore floated the idea to organize a counter-procession of communists to prevent the protesters from dominating the streets.[437]

However, setting up such a counter-demonstration was not a simple matter under the circumstances. The situation in the industrial enterprises did not allow the sending of large processions of communist workers into the streets, since their presence in their workplaces was necessary to neutralize the rebellious sentiments of non-partisan workers. Some party leaders feared that the workers might actually join the protesters.[438] The party leadership kept vacillating, rejecting offers from subordinate organizations and continuing to send volunteers to the square. Party authorities in the city, including Central Committee representative Ladislav Kopřiva, secretary of the Regional Committee Václav Kolena and chief secretary of the Regional Committee Jan Hlína, maintained this approach even after the attack on the City Hall.[439]

It was not until around 3 p.m. that preparations for the communist procession finally began.[440] Its core was a small group of officials from the V. I. Lenin Factories, reinforced later by employees of the KSČ Municipal Committee, the KSČ Regional Committee, and the Regional National Committee.[441] Organizing the procession proved very difficult, however, because the low-ranking communists were unwilling to get involved in suppressing the riots. The Municipal Committee officials made countless phone calls and personally visited the chairmen of street organizations but were met with almost no enthusiasm.[442] From organizations numbering some 200 members, often no more than 15 people showed up for the march.[443] Mobilization of the factory organizations was announced too late. While some workers actually went to support the protesters in the streets after the end of their morning shift, party officials were reluctant to mount a major counter-action and allowed a large part of their sympathizers to leave the factories and go home. Chief secretary of the Municipal Committee Josef Žák later summed up the futile effort to recruit supporters: "It was our fault that we did not give clear instructions to all the factories that all Communists should stay put in case they were needed. Instead, they simply clocked off at 2 p.m., grabbed their bags and went home to relax. We even know of one person—actually he was an employee of the

Consolidated National Committee, perhaps even a higher official – the comrades came to get him in the afternoon, but he was lying on the couch and reading the newspaper. They told him, 'Come with us, comrade,' but he said, 'Whoever made this mess should clean it up.'"[444]

Nevertheless, the assembled communists trickled down in small groups toward Palackého Náměstí square, an area strategically located near the city center and the V. I. Lenin Factories, but at a sufficient distance from the epicenter of the protests. A small procession of ZVIL employees was the first to arrive at 4:30 p.m.[445] Organized groups of communists also arrived from the Regional National Committee and the Czechoslovak State Railroad Works.[446] They still waited for more reinforcements, however, so that the procession would not seem pathetic. The crowd did not take to the streets until shortly before 6 p.m., numbering about 800 people. By that time, Náměstí Republiky had already been cleared, so the party members present were in no danger of physical confrontation with the protesting crowd.[447] The procession marched along 1. Máje Avenue toward Náměstí Republiky, singing revolutionary songs[448] and carrying Czechoslovak and Soviet national flags, as well as portraits of President Antonín Zápotocký, and Chairman of the USSR Council of Ministers Georgy Malenkov.

More people joined the procession as it went along. Eventually, the number of participants allegedly grew to some 1,000–5,000 people. This figure included both the marching communists and numerous bystanders.[449] However, even this inflated number was considered insufficient by the organizers,[450] as the registered party membership base in Pilsen was much higher with a total of 28,292.[451] From this point of view, the evening rally could not really be considered a success.[452]

Most of the participants were senior party officials, for whom it was practically an official duty. Among those who walked in the front rows, for example, was Deputy of the party Central Committee and writer Marie Majerová.[453] Most of the political staff of the Party Central Committee joined in, as did members of the Party Regional Committee, the Party Municipal Committee, and the Regional National Committee. During later purges in the party, they used their participation as evidence of their allegedly firm ideological convictions.[454] Many of the officials present had been campaigning for the currency reform in the local factories since that morning and were very tired.[455] However, their party duties were far from over: after the evening demonstration many of them went on to patrol in the streets and often stayed up all night.[456] This clearly shows how small the group of the most loyal and dedicated party members was that day.

Passers-by who showed their disapproval of the party rally were arrested on the spot.[457] Some supporters of the previous protests shouted at the procession from the windows, "How much are they paying you for this?"[458] However, some of those who had participated in the recently suppressed protests actually joined the communist rally.[459] A number of bystanders watch the communist procession; some of them were actually opponents of the rally's program.[460] Shortly after 6 p.m., the procession entered Náměstí Republiky, where the communists chanted such slogans as "Long live the Communist Party of Czechoslovakia! [. . .] Long live our army! [. . .] Long live the government and the Soviet Union! [. . .] Long live Comrade Zápotocký! [and] We will make short work of the loafers!"[461] The idea arose to destroy the National Liberation Monument on Dukelské Náměstí square. The monument was dominated by a statue of first Czechoslovak President Tomáš Garrigue Masaryk who had been decidedly pro-Western in his thinking. The crowd shouted such slogans as "Down with Masaryk"[462] or "Masaryk to the scrap heap."[463]

The plan to tear down the statue of Tomáš Garrigue Masaryk was nothing new; it stemmed from a nationwide anti-Masaryk campaign that the Communist Party leadership had been stepping up since 1950.[464] The first concrete plans of the Presidium of the Regional Committee of the Communist Party to remove the Pilsen sculpture dated back to 1952.[465] In April 1953, the Regional Committee resolved to instruct its subordinate organizations to hold public meetings and to send resolutions demanding the destruction of the Pilsen monument.[466] However, the participants in the discussions were not enthusiastic about this plan. The meetings in the Bolevec and Karlov districts even had to be disbanded with police assistance.[467] Public resistance therefore led to the temporary postponement of the plan.

The plan to tear down the statue of Masaryk in Pilsen came up again during the evening party procession on June 1, 1953. This was not a spontaneous demand of the people, as the official state propaganda later claimed. In fact, the tearing down of the statue was instigated by top party officials present in the crowd, who had discussed it in advance with leaders of the Regional Committee and representatives of the Central Committee present in the city.[468] The act was motivated by longer-term strategic considerations, combined at that moment with the communists' unusually strong emotional reaction to the previous protests.[469] The statue of Tomáš Garrigue Masaryk had been a traditional marshalling point for protest marches during the 1948 and 1953 demonstrations. By removing it, the communists hoped to prevent a repetition of similar incidents. At the time, however, it was also a symbolic retaliation for the smashed busts of communist statesmen and a convenient way to vent the accumulated frustration.[470] The communists, who had been repeatedly humiliated and physically assaulted earlier that day, were so outraged that they destroyed the monument in a highly theatrical manner, without considering the possible political consequences. Many people in Pilsen saw the removal of the statue as a sign of disrespect for the country's founding father, and as evidence of the local party leaders' cultural barbarism. Even the Central Committee of the Communist Party later criticized the indiscriminate manner in which the monument was torn down.

The actual destruction occurred extremely quickly. The communists assembled on Náměstí Republiky sent a delegation to the City Hall, demanding the immediate removal of the sculpture.[471] This pre-arranged step was formally approved at 7 p.m. by an extraordinary meeting of the Consolidated National Committee council.[472] The crowd then proceeded to Dukelské Náměstí square, where an estimated 6,000–7,000 spectators gathered.[473] The assembly sang *The Internationale* and between 7 and 8 p.m., the statue was toppled over.[474]

The communists originally assumed they would be able to remove the statue by themselves. The communist officials borrowed a rope, fastened it around Masaryk's neck and, with the assistance of some of the young people, began pulling the statue down.[475] Eventually, however, heavy equipment had to be called in and the statue was removed by a crane provided by the V. I. Lenin Factories fire brigade.[476] Some popular actors from the Pilsen theater were actively involved in this spectacle, especially Josef Větrovec, who was said to have attached the noose to the neck of the Masaryk statue as part of

Figure 3.3 Evening Rally of the Communist Party in Pilsen on June 1, 1953. Author unknown, probably the photo was taken by State Security. AMP, f. OF Josef Brand.

his dramatic performance[477] Josef Větrovec's involvement in the tearing down of the monument later became a media-worthy topic in 1968 and 1989, as a symbol of the uncultured behavior of Communist Party supporters.[478] However, Větrovec himself had consistently claimed since the 1960s that though he had actively supported the removal of the statue, the whole thing with the noose was the work of another Pilsen actor.[479] The written sources found so far do not provide sufficient evidence to objectively assess this dispute. Also, a substantial part of the witnesses' testimonies written down after November 1989 does not clarify the course of events, because they were clearly influenced by the previous discussions from 1968 and contained a suspiciously high amount of contradictory information.[480]

The torn-down statue was transported by crane to the smelters of the V. I. Lenin Factories, where it was melted down in the night.[481] In place of the statue, the communists placed portraits of Antonín Zápotocký and Georgy Malenkov.[482] The crowd then proceeded to the building of the Secretariat of the KSČ Regional Committee, where it listened to speeches by chief secretary Jan Hlína, representative of the Central Committee Ladislav Kopřiva. The rally ended at 10 p.m.[483]

Official reports also claimed that the communist youth danced joyfully in Pilsen's squares through the night.[484] This information tends to be disputed by post-1989 historians as a mere fabrication of official propaganda. However, the merrymaking on the square was also mentioned in the personal reports of some officials of the Czechoslovak Youth Union. These were internal documents written for the purpose of personal vetting, so it would be highly risky to include any explicit untruths.[485] Summary reports on the activities of the Pilsen youth also stated that groups of apprentices, accompanied by a band, were sent to the square from the local vocational schools.[486] It is therefore likely that attempts to create an atmosphere of joy at the defeat of the regime's alleged enemies did indeed occur in Pilsen. In fact, the witnesses' memories regarding the behavior of the Pilsen actors described the destruction of the monument as a theatrical romp. Both the Pilsen protesters and the local party apparatus had therefore succumbed to heightened emotion on June 1, 1953, and vented their feelings of threat and frustration through ostentatious, excessive gestures.

THE COMPLETION OF THE CURRENCY EXCHANGE AND THE DECREASE OF TENSION IN SOCIETY

The period of June 1–4, 1953, designated for the currency exchange, subjected the people to unprecedented pressure. They had lost a substantial part of their savings; they distrusted the new price system; they were not sufficiently informed about future wage levels; they feared a continuation of the supply crisis; and on the whole they faced a totally unpredictable future. In order to overcome this difficult social situation, it was necessary to complete the exchange of cash as quickly as possible, in order to provide the public with funds and enable them to make purchases at the new prices.

However, the exchange process in the Pilsen region was going anything but smoothly, and instead of easing tensions, it significantly contributed to the people's indignation. The exchange centers were set up in a hurry, and neither adequate staffing nor a continuous supply of currency were properly ensured. As a result, many of them started operating with considerable delays, that is, not at the scheduled 7 a.m. but often as late as the afternoon.[487] Problems occurred, at the exchange center at the V. I. Lenin Factories, which was only opened at 12 p.m. after several urgent requests.[488] People waited in lines for hours, which made the transition to the new currency even more difficult. In addition, people from rural areas tried to avoid exchanging larger sums at their place of residence and headed to Pilsen in the hope of maintaining greater anonymity; this, however, extended the waiting times even more. This led to numerous expressions of discontent among the waiting people.[489]

The working-class district of Petrohrad suffered the greatest strain in Pilsen: the three exchange centers opened there had to handle around 14,000 clients. Lines started forming as early as 3 a.m.[490] The State Bank was forced to deal with the excess rush by reinforcing its staff and significantly increasing the number of centers. Instead of the planned 168 centers, 242 started operating in the region on June 2, and this number was increased to 346 in the following days.[491] Nevertheless, waiting times were still very long on June 2, 1953, with people routinely standing in line for more than 10 hours.[492] The situation gradually improved in the following days. By Thursday June 4, all the centers had managed to successfully complete the exchange, and by the afternoon there were no longer any lines.[493] However, on the day of the protests on Monday June 1, the new currency was completely unavailable to the vast majority of society, and people could only start buying at the new prices on Tuesday June 2. As the exchange process went along, social tensions gradually eased as people learned the value of the new currency and began to accept the new prices.

The completion of the cash exchange process also eliminated the people's fears of a continuing supply crisis, which were another cause for protest. The panic buying in May caused disruptions in the supply of goods in the early days of the reform. In some places, the reform resulted in temporary shortages of basic foodstuffs (especially sugar, butter, and oil), which increased the people's panic.[494] After the completion of the exchange on June 4, 1953, however, people stopped buying out any available goods with the old currency and began to spend the new money, albeit only on necessities. As a result, continuous supply was gradually restored.[495]

Changes in the payment of wage advances, introduced by the Ministry of Finance and confirmed by the Secretariat of the Central Committee of the Communist Party, also contributed to easing the people's discontent. Although the measure did not compensate the workers for their financial losses caused by the reform, it did correct some of the mistakes that had previously incited the strikes at the V. I. Lenin Factories. On Wednesday June 3, 1953, workers were paid advances in the amount of 20% of their May wages; they were paid in the new currency, at a ratio of 5:1.[496] On June 10, factory management announced the remittance of the rest of May's wages, with the money earned in the first half of the month being issued at a ratio of 50:1 and the money for the second half of the month at a ratio of 5:1. Employees who had been erroneously paid a portion of their wages for the second half of May in the old currency, subsequently exchanged at a 50:1 ratio, were to be compensated up to the amount of the 5:1 exchange ratio.[497] Dividing the earnings for the two halves of the month eliminated the differences created by the belated payment of the previous advances at the end of May.[498] Advances for June wages were paid on June 20.[499] On that occasion, employees were informed of their new wage levels for the first time. The wages were basically only recalculated at a ratio of 5:1 and slightly raised in some cases.[500] However, their real value had fallen as a result of the abolition of the restricted market.

The payment of wage advances on June 3 and 10 at least partially stabilized the critical financial situation in many households, caused by the loss of savings during the currency reform.[501] After June 4, 1953, every household was provided with at least a minimum amount of funds in the new currency, obtained through the exchange or wage advances, and could start making purchases at the new prices. The chronic shortage of goods in the stores, which had lasted for several weeks, was finally resolved. The most difficult stage of the reform was over, and society could begin to adapt to the new, more stable reality. As a result of this process, the population's resistance to the currency reform was gradually diminishing. In this respect, it is not at all coincidental that the nationwide wave of protest incidents triggered by the reform subsided on Thursday June 4, 1953.[502] In addition to the vigorous repressive measures, the above-mentioned psychological and social factors also contributed to the calming of the strikes and demonstrations. The number of people willing to protest was considerably reduced, particularly because fear of the future was a much stronger motivation for action than devaluation of savings or disapproval of the political situation.

The official propaganda was fully aware of this aspect of the unrest. From June 2 onward, therefore, the press tried to dampen social tensions by publishing statements by people who had lost their savings in the reform yet accepted it with the confidence that it would pay off in the future. The press even published personal recollections of people who had experienced the Great Depression of the 1930s, as a point of comparison. The establishment also took care to publish thorough information about the new wage and price levels.[503]

Although the main wave of panic subsided after June 4, some causes for popular outrage still persisted. These included the fact that the reform caused substantial financial losses among the population. A review of the currency exchanges in the region was carried out between June 7, 1953, and March 13, 1954, by the Regional Commission for the closing of the exchange centers in Pilsen.[504] According to its findings, the centers in the region accepted a total of 1,949,388,000 Kč in the old currency and paid out 69,208,000 Kč in the new currency. They handled a total of 193,572 clients who exchanged money on behalf of a total of 533,684 people.[505] The average resident therefore exchanged 3,653 Kč in the old currency and received only 130 Kč in the new currency.[506] Unfortunately, the documents found so far do not provide accurate information regarding the average amount of cash exchanged at the centers at the V. I. Lenin Factories. Such data would be particularly important for a more accurate assessment of the extent of the workers' financial losses.[507] However, fragmentary references in other sources suggest that the reduction in their savings was considerably higher than the average losses among the general population.[508]

On June 6, 1953, all deposits and current accounts in savings banks were also converted into the new currency.[509] In the Pilsen region, 2,060,306,000 Kč were deposited in savings banks in the old currency, that is, approximately half of the population's financial reserves. These deposits were then converted into 233,832,000 Kč of the new currency.[510] The exchange of these savings thus resulted in considerably lesser losses than the cash exchange. The reform therefore hit hardest those households that kept their savings outside financial institutions.

However, even the above-mentioned reduction in people's savings after June 4, 1953 did not become a reason for further socially motivated protests in the longer term. Communist Party leaders learned a valuable lesson from the violent protests: that the stability of the regime largely depended on the people's living standard. In the future, they used this experience to avoid the escalation of social conflicts with industrial workers.[511] In the following years, the government repeatedly reduced retail prices and liberally used these measures for propaganda purposes.[512] The policy of the so-called New Direction, inspired by its development in the Soviet Union in the summer of 1953, gradually changed the strategy of governance in Czechoslovakia from repressive Stalinism to a rudimentary form of a (still repressive) socialist consumerism.[513] The death of Joseph Vissarionovich Stalin in March 1953 helped ease international tension, and the July armistice in Korea ended the heated phase of the Cold War.[514] The Communist Party leadership reacted to Moscow's policy developments by adopting the so-called August Principles, which opened the way for the first tentative revision of the existing economic policy.[515] From September 1953 onward, Czechoslovakia underwent serious adjustments in social policy and the structure of production (reduced investments in armaments), and the years 1954–1955 brought a significant increase in personal consumption.[516] According to some authors, this implicit social contract, in which the material needs of the public were satisfied in exchange for political loyalty, even led to the fact that unlike neighboring countries (Hungary, Poland), Czechoslovakia did not experience any significant social unrest in the turbulent year 1956.[517] The relative economic stability, hard-earned as it had been in June 1953 by the currency reform and the ensuing protests, remained one of the fundamental pillars of the political system in the following years.[518]

THE CONTINUATION OF STRIKES ON JUNE 2–4, 1953

Apart from the repressions and the decline in social panic, another factor that influenced the relatively rapid stabilization in the region was the dissension among the discontented population. The party meetings of May 31 to June 1 had shown that despite the almost universal indignation over the currency reform, critique of the reform came from widely differing positions among the various social groups.[519] Opposition to the currency reform was by no means homogeneous. The protest participants resorted to very different solutions. The strike at the V. I. Lenin Factories, for example, was launched on June 1, 1953, by only a small number of workers, and only about half of those actually took to the streets.[520] The majority of the workers (including lower-ranking party officials and ordinary communists) adopted a position of passive resistance and while they did not explicitly support the protests, they had enabled them by their inaction. At the same time, the number of actively protesting residents was relatively small, and their actions were only made possible by the passive resistance of other segments of society who chose not to get actively involved.

In the course of the day, the demonstrations transformed from the original workers' protest into violent anti-government riots. This, however, presented the wider group of protest participants with a dilemma as to what solution to the initial social conflict was still acceptable and what crossed the line.[521] For many workers, the political protests were not a natural culmination of the strike, but rather an unintended by-product of the actual workers' protests inside the factory, and a result of the spontaneous development in the streets.[522] Moreover, the Communist Party leadership branded the evening protests as an attempted counter-revolutionary coup, putting pressure on the loyalist section of the protesters to distance themselves from the unrest. It was therefore uncertain how the dissenting workers would behave in the new situation.

The consequences of these actions were particularly evident in the V. I. Lenin Factories. On the night of June 1, some workers tried to return to the original form of protest and renewed their strikes. Work was stopped by the night shift staff in the Vehicles, Locomotive Works, Tool Works I, and Tool Works II departments.[523] However, the possibility for continuing the strikes was already very limited. The fact that the demonstrations had been officially labeled as a subversive act did not allow the disgruntled workers to continue the strike without risking an open conflict with the Communist Party. The initial legitimacy of the workers' strikes was considerably shaken by the protests; the workers could not continue protesting and remain loyal to the party. Moreover, the communist rally in the evening sent a clear signal as to how the still undecided low-ranking party members should behave. On Tuesday morning party officials in the workshops could already rely on a small section of the workers who assisted them to calm the unrest; they demanded the punishment of the participants in Monday's demonstrations, reported yesterday's absentees and handed them over to the People's Militias.[524]

In addition to the threat of reprisals, another significant factor influenced the course of events. The official interpretation of the riots as an alleged conspiracy of the former bourgeoisie gave the striking workers a viable way out. They could distance themselves from the protests in the streets, express their approval of the currency reform, and declare themselves victims misguided by the regime's enemies. Many strike participants and sympathizers took advantage of this offer; they began claiming they had been deceived in their support for the riots, expressed their approval of the reform, and made work commitments to compensate for the idle time.[525]

These retreat strategies were also adopted on a collective scale. Entire shop crews managed to avoid harsher penalties by passing the required resolutions celebrating the currency reform. Such a declaration was approved in the Machine Shop III department, one of the former epicenters of the unrest.[526] Following the official party line regarding the workers' seduction by the bourgeoisie, the resolutions placed the responsibility for inciting the protests on a convenient scapegoat, which was only referred to by the abstract phrase Pilsen reactionaries, which meant that the employees of the V. I. Lenin Factories, who had in fact initiated the protests, could declare themselves blameless. The resolutions even demanded the eviction of the bourgeoisie from their flats in the city center and giving these premises to the factory workers. In line with Pilsen's established tradition, the resolutions also urged for a thorough purge of the schools, even though they had been only marginally involved in the 1953 demonstrations.[527] The workers therefore distanced themselves from the protests rather quickly. Under pressure, they accepted the currency reform and shifted political responsibility for the largely unintended course of the protests to other social groups with whom they felt no affinity.

Under such circumstances, attempts to continue the protests by a minority of workers could hardly have been successful. During the morning shift of June 2, 1953, 2,000 workers from the Machine Tools I department and the Elektrotrakce Doudlevce subsidiary plant went on strike, but resumed work after several hours of persuasion.[528] By a well-chosen tactic, the party leaders therefore managed to gradually stabilize the situation at the V. I. Lenin Factories.[529] On Wednesday June 3, there were no more attempts to instigate strikes at the plant. Moreover, most of the workers had already exchanged their money that day. They could start making purchases using the new currency and familiarize themselves with the new prices. The expected supply crisis did not come, and the people's indignation and panic lost its initial edge.[530] Meetings of the basic organizations of the Communist Party expelled the protagonists and sympathizers of the protests, which further helped to pacify the discontented workers.[531] Any further workers' strikes would thus lack the support previously provided by some of the lower-level factory officials and rank-and-file party members. After that, protest actions in Pilsen remained limited to individual, private expressions of resistance. From June 4 to 7, for example, leaflets were distributed around the city with the slogan "Down with the criminal Communist government! We demand free elections!"[532]

Although the wave of collective protests in Pilsen died down, rumors of the demonstrations quickly spread throughout West Bohemia, despite the police checks of vehicles on the roads out of the city[533] and the ban on long-distance telephone calls ordered by the Secretariat of the Central Committee.[534] A significant number of employees of the Pilsen industrial enterprises (26,597 people in total) commuted to work from the surrounding districts.[535] A great commotion therefore occurred in these places in the afternoon of June 1, as the workers returned home from Pilsen. In the neighboring towns of Blovice and Stod, crowds even began gathering in the streets to discuss the events in Pilsen, and had to be dispersed by the police.[536]

The oral accounts of the protests were not entirely accurate. It was commonly reported that the shooting of the Škoda workers ended in mass bloodshed.[537] Rumors about shooting protesters spread far and wide;[538] in Prague, for example, a rumor circulated that eight workers and a woman with a child had been killed in Pilsen.[539] Inaccurate information about the Pilsen protests also reached Western countries through Czech émigrés.[540] Spreading news about the events in Pilsen was prosecuted as the crime of disseminating alarmist news, regardless of its truthfulness.[541]

Information about the situation in the regional city of Pilsen sparked a series of solidarity strikes inspired by the V. I. Lenin Factories in smaller industrial plants throughout West Bohemia.[542]

TRIALS OF PROTESTERS

As the events on the streets on June 1, 1953, became increasingly radicalized, the initial dilemma of the Pilsen officials as to whether or not treat the demonstrations as a legitimate workers' protest against the social effects of the currency reform gradually disappeared. By late afternoon, they had embraced the official interpretation that the currency reform had merely been exploited by former members of the bourgeoisie to stage subversive provocations.[543] The party officials claimed that the protesting workers had been misguided and noted that there were many persons of formerly non-worker professions among the employees of the V. I. Lenin Factories. The excessive emphasis on the professional background of some of the protesters had slowly transformed in official rhetoric into the claim that the protesters were not in fact genuine workers but reactionaries "disguised as such."[544] The legend gradually lost all vestiges of truth and gained a life of its own.

The investigation of the Pilsen protests followed a similar course. Authorities tried to find the alleged organizers of the seditious actions among the arrested protesters. The investigators' ideologically determined thinking did not permit describing the demonstrations as a spontaneous, unguided act. Uncovering the alleged instigators of the riots was necessary to provide a politically acceptable explanation for the protests. The authorities therefore picked the alleged instigators from the ranks of the arrested protesters, based more on their social class than on their actual role in the protests. Prominent roles in the upcoming trial were assigned to two former tradesmen, Jan Holeček and Rudolf Krüger, and Anežka Krinesová, a rich farmer's daughter.[545]

The Ministry of National Security, which was responsible for preparing the trial, proceeded with considerable haste. The trial was to be public and was to take place as soon as possible, in order to support the official interpretation of the riots. Even though a thorough interrogation of hundreds of detainees took time, the Ministry planned to hold the trial of the 40 main organizers within the next few weeks.[546] The Main Administration of State Security took charge of the investigation, and operatives from Prague were immediately dispatched to Pilsen.[547] From June 3, their activities in Pilsen were personally directed by Milan Moučka, head of the Main Investigation administration. The whole operation was conducted under the sole direction of the State Security.[548]

Interrogations of the more prominent protesters often took place day and night, with no opportunity to rest. Some of those interrogated later complained they had been brutally beaten and forced to confess to acts they had not committed.[549] Some were also pressured to give false testimony against other detained protesters.[550] Defendant Metoděj Stodůlka, for example, stated during his appeal hearing before the Regional Court that "this whole trial has been staged"[551] and that his co-defendant, who had incriminated Stodůlka by his statements, had privately confessed to him that he had "testified under the threat of being evicted from his apartment and sent to the uranium mines in Jáchymov."[552]

The atmosphere of day-and-night interrogations, as well as the interrogators' arrogant disregard of the accused's previous statements, was also described by the accused Josef Fencl:[553]

> I was interrogated for 7–10 days, mostly during the night, long into the morning hours. During the interrogation I was constantly told to "confess," but I didn't know what to confess to. [. . .] After some ten nights of this, I was demoralized by the constant orders to "confess"; my original statements were not taken into account because the interrogator said he wasn't interested. I was in such a state that I was ready to confess to anything as long as they would let me sleep. [. . .] When I saw how hopeless it was, as I said today for the record, I told the investigating officer to write down whatever he wanted and that I would sign it for him. The investigation went on as usual and the investigator wrote all the reports, which I signed even though I did not even read them, but I still had to write this: read, approved and signed.[554]

Other defendants voiced similar complaints regarding the course of the investigation and the false statements obtained from it.[555] On the other hand, a number of other persons did not mention any coercion during interrogations, and made complimentary observations regarding the interrogators' decent behavior to their cellmates.[556] Undue coercion was thus a widespread but by no means universal practice, and, considering the huge number of persons interrogated, it was probably directed only at selected key figures in the trials.

In custody, interrogators were often assisted by informants who reported on the behavior of their cellmates. Some of the detained protesters even consented to becoming State Security informants.[557] For their assistance, several of them were subsequently recommended for release without criminal charges.[558]

Some of the arrested protesters had not participated in any of the more radical forms of protest, yet they had little chance to prove their innocence. The investigators mistakenly saw the riots as the actions of a homogeneous whole and did not attempt any comprehensive reconstruction of events that would allow them to put the actions of specific individuals in the right context. The accused's mere presence on the square was often sufficient grounds for criminal charges and prosecution, without any examination as to whether the protests had any overt political content at the time or whether they had already escalated into violent riots. Moreover, if an interrogated person gave the names of witnesses who could prove their innocence, they risked that these persons could also be charged as protesters.[559] For example, Attorney JUDr. Josef Hegner, arrested during the protests, deliberately withheld the name of his friend, JUDr. Richard Weinfurter, from the investigators, and only dared to name him as a defense witness during the rehabilitation trial 16 years later.[560] Despite all this effort, preparation for the trial yielded surprisingly meager results. Out of the arrested protesters, who had been detained on very different occasions during the day, it was impossible to assemble a compact group whose members knew each other. Moreover, the detainees' background did not allow the authorities to imbue the trial with any credible political content.[561]

The Ministry of National Security left it entirely to the discretion of the Communist Party leadership to choose their own interpretation of the investigation results. On June 22, 1953, Minister Karol Bacílek submitted to Antonín Novotný, Secretary of the Central Committee of the Communist Party, a *Proposal for the public trial of the instigators of the anti-state provocation demonstration in Pilsen.* This document clearly reflected the investigators' inability to create a believable group of alleged organizers of the demonstrations. It therefore presented three distinct possibilities for the trial. In all of them, persons who did not know each other and whose political use in the trial was problematic were identified as the main instigators. In all cases, therefore, it was an emergency solution, and the organizers of the trial were well aware of it.[562]

The first proposal envisaged the conviction of thirteen of "the most active instigators and organizers of the anti-state demonstration, selected from the ranks of former active officials and members of anti-communist political parties, former private capitalists, followers of the American lifestyle, morally corrupt persons, and the like."[563] People on this list were a motley bunch of people who, for various reasons, were considered by the police to be staunch enemies of the regime and who were only connected to each other by their (often accidental) presence at the protests. This group included Emil Otradovec, former district secretary of the Czechoslovak Social Democratic Party in Tábor, who was supposed to represent the protesters' alleged connection to the former non-communist political left. Otradovec would be used to provide an indirect link to former Social Democratic deputies from Pilsen, Antonín Remeš and František Hatina. However, this plan could only be carried out much later, in 1954–1955 during the nationwide wave of trials against former Social Democratic officials.[564] The proposal also mentioned the name of Illja Nazarkevyč, son of a Ukrainian emigrant who came to Czechoslovakia during the First Republic and a proponent of the American way of life; Karel Schaffhauser (who had allegedly been disseminating pornography); former officials of the Pilsen branch of the Union of Friends of the USA, Josef Fencl and František Vorlovský; Jaroslav Žižka, an alleged American intelligence agent (who had previously emigrated to Germany); Rudolf Držka, former member of the French Foreign Legion; Anežka Krinesová, daughter of a rich farmer; and Josef Nečas, former member of the National Socialist Party.[565]

The second possible alternative envisaged the conviction of 10 protesters, mutually linked by their employment at the V. I. Lenin Factories and their complicity in the act of stealing and driving a National Security Corps car. The third proposed version of the trial envisaged the conviction of six employees of the Elektrotrakce Doudlevce subsidiary plant who had marched in the procession from the factory to Náměstí Republiky and then entered the City Hall.[566]

On June 23, 1953, however, the Political Secretariat of the Central Committee did not approve any of these proposals, for unspecified reasons, and opted for a larger number of separate criminal trials.[567] The result was a series of smaller, indirectly related trials that did not reveal any alleged cell of riot organizers, but contented themselves with punishing individual participants. These included a number of completely innocent persons who were not even active protesters. Moreover, the defendants' persons did not offer any clear clue as to how to politically interpret the protests. Thus, instead of a trial that could be used for propaganda purposes, the criminal proceedings turned into a sort of a mindless mass revenge against anyone who had been in any way involved in the protests.

The detainees were therefore not charged with the actual organization of the demonstrations at all, but only with crimes directly related to the course of the riots. The most frequent offenses were violence against public authorities (section 154 of the Criminal Code, breaking into the City hall); violence against a public official (section 177 of the Criminal Code, conflicts with SNB officers); damage to national property (section 245 of the Criminal Code; destruction of the equipment of the City hall and the Palace of Justice); sedition against the Republic (section 81 of the Criminal Code; verbal confrontations); assault against a group of people (sections 116 and 117 of the Criminal Code; beating up members of the Communist Party), advocating a crime (§ 169 of the Criminal Code; supporting other protesters), or interfering with the authority of a public official (§ 179 of the Criminal Code; disobeying the instructions of SNB officers).[568]

The Ministry also provided the party leadership with a list of 108 detained protesters whom it had no interest in prosecuting. These were mostly random bystanders or less active young protesters from working-class families. However, the Political Secretariat of the Communist Party Central Committee had all these cases re-examined.[569] In the end, only 61 people from this list were released without criminal charges.[570]

The preparation of the trials continued apace. At the beginning of July, criminal charges were filed with the Regional Prosecutor's Office in Pilsen. The main hearings in 14 group trials were held before the People's Court in Pilsen between July 13 and 22, 1953.[571] In the following months, these were followed by at least 29 additional individual criminal trials. These mainly concerned persons excluded from the group trials due to illness or other complications, as well as belatedly identified protesters.[572] Some of the hearings were conducted as closed sessions,[573] while a selected audience of industrial workers was invited to some of them.[574]

The court completely disregarded the previous misconduct of the investigators, even in cases where the affected persons had pointed it out. This concerned, in particular, the credibility of the prosecution's witnesses. In fact, the witnesses, many of whom were selected from among the other accused, were often not questioned at all during the trial and the court contented itself with reading out the relevant parts of the investigation reports. Moreover, these testimonies often failed to present even such basic information as the exact timing of the acts in question. The testimonies were often not verified by confronting the witness with the accused. Some defendants therefore requested that the witness specify the time when they were supposed to have committed the offense or identify the clothes they were wearing on that day.[575] However, these objections were routinely overruled by the court as without merit.[576]

In the sentencing, the court did not even require incontrovertible evidence that the defendants had actually committed the crimes in question. Even if some defendants failed to be convicted of anything other than passive observation of the protests, the court found them guilty of the crime of violence against public authorities.[577] The court justified its rulings in a rather convoluted manner, arguing that even the mere presence at protest sites should be viewed as active participation in the crimes committed there. This was both because of the scale of the demonstrations and because active protesters were allegedly bolstered in their actions by passive spectators. "Some defendants' defense attorneys argued a mere passive presence cannot be qualified as participation in violent acts or threats of violence. However, if one considers the extent of the rioting on the critical day at various places in Pilsen, then in the opinion of the court, even the mere presence of some of the accused at the places where the riots occurred qualifies as active participation in the rioting, since the active rioters were emboldened by the presence of presumed supporters."[578]

Similar offenses were assessed with varying degrees of severity, depending on the person accused. Persons of the wrong class background were often awarded punishments within the upper limit. Former tradesmen and members of non-communist political parties received inordinately stiff sentences. The court, on the other hand, accepted working-class origins as a mitigating circumstance, as well as the possession of a shock worker's book or other evidence of conscientious performance of work duties.[579] Furthermore, the impartiality of the judicial proceedings was perceptibly impaired by the fact that a number of the judges and prosecutors involved had been personally threatened during the protests by the crowd that had stormed the Palace of Justice. This led to a number of ironic situations. For example, one of the criminal trials was presided over by Judge Miroslav Tlapák, who had shot at the protesters through the door of his office on June 1, 1953. This fact was not considered an obstacle to an impartial criminal trial. Conversely, requests for defense counsel from a solicitors' firm in Pilsen were often refused because one of the arrested protesters, JUDr. Josef Hegner, was working for this firm.[580]

The court's verdicts and the public's reaction were continuously monitored by the Ministry of National Security, which intervened in the trials as necessary.[581] Ironically, this actually benefited some of the accused, as the ministry took a more lenient stance toward the protesters than local justice officials who had been directly affected by the protests. Preliminary guidelines for the sentencing were set by Minister of Justice Štefan Rais, and Minister of National Security Karol Bacílek, in a joint meeting with the presiding judges. These guidelines stipulated, among other things, that "in the case of underage persons who have merely been led astray, the court will either waive punishment or sentence the accused to time served."[582] However, the directives of the central authorities were not always followed. Representatives of the Ministry of National Security considered a number of verdicts to have been too harsh. Moreover, each court imposed widely varying sentences for similar offenses. These problems were repeatedly discussed at meetings between representatives of the two ministries and the presiding judges.[583]

The judgments were generally styled as a political manifesto rather than as accurate description of the defendants' acts. In particular, they stressed that only a minority of the population had been swayed into participating in the protests, and that the protesters were allegedly only a handful of reactionary elements—loafers, alcoholics, and criminals. The term *demonstration*, previously used in internal communication between the state authorities, was replaced in the judgments by the word *riot*. The protesters' actions were denigrated and verbally equated with senseless violence perpetrated by persons from the fringes of society. This misrepresentation was supported by the fact that among the hundreds of convicts, there were indeed several typical repeat offenders, and that the actions of the most radical protesters were indeed violent, although not entirely without purpose. Last but not least, the sentences extolled the universal benefits of the currency reform, without offering any concrete evidence.

In the vast majority of cases, the court's verdicts respected the wording of the indictment. Criminal charges were filed against at least 290 protesters and at least 268 of them were brought to trial. The People's Court in Pilsen found 242 people guilty. In contrast, only 25 persons were acquitted completely, and charges against one person were withdrawn.[584] The above figures are based on the sources found so far, but it cannot be excluded that there could have been many more protesters investigated or convicted.

The defendants received unconditional prison sentences of 403 years and 6 months in total, and suspended sentences of 1-year and 10-month imprisonment, respectively. The average sentence was a little over one and a half years' imprisonment. The highest sentence, 14-year imprisonment, was given to Pavel Katera, head of operations of the national enterprise Armstav, who was the only one of the detained protesters who had allegedly attempted to arm himself. The second highest sentence, 10-year imprisonment, was given to stagehand Jaroslav Treml, for leading a delegation of protesters to negotiate the release of prisoners at the Palace of Justice, and to worker Anežka Zámečková, for physically assaulting members of the People's Militias and members of the Communist Party. Among the convicted protesters were, for example, Jarolím Zenkl (relative of the former chairman of the National Socialist Party, Petr Zenkl), Jiřina Zahradníčková (née Pantoflíčková, daughter of the former director of the Škoda Works), Jaroslav Blavic (son of a former Lieutenant Colonel of the Czechoslovak Army, convicted of subversive activities), and Josef Vacek (former district secretary of the Social Democratic Party in Pilsen).[585]

Many of the convicted persons served their sentences in the uranium mines and were released from prison in poor health. There are also documented cases of deaths while serving a sentence.[586] Appeals and requests for clemency were mostly rejected. On the other hand, applications for parole were a much more feasible way to be released early, and in many cases the judicial authorities granted them. Many of sentences were reduced by the Presidential Amnesty of May 9, 1955. The majority of persons sentenced to long prison terms did not serve them in full. Regardless of the severity of the sentence or the actual time served, however, participation in the Pilsen demonstrations was a permanent stigma for the persons concerned, continuing to affect their lives in the form of negative cadre references.[587]

In addition to imprisonment, the sentences imposed a number of additional punishments. These included the loss of honorary civil rights, forfeiture of a part of one's property, prohibition of residence in the county or district, or forfeiture of a part of one's wages for a specified amount of time. A temporary or lifetime ban from practicing a profession could also be a very severe secondary punishment. Well-known Pilsen actor Bohumil Vávra, for example, was given a lifetime ban from the theater.[588] Vávra came from a traditional actors' family: his great-grandfather had been a tenor at the National Theater in Prague, and many of his relatives became renowned actors.[589] Vávra's efforts to obtain a pardon and be allowed return to the stage were hampered by negative references from his former colleagues. Especially vociferous in this regard was actor Josef Větrovec, chairman of the party's company organization, who had taken part in the communist rally in June 1953.[590] Vávra was not able to return to his profession until 1958.[591]

A large number of those convicted sought judicial rehabilitation in the 1960s and later in the 1990s. Only a few managed to get their sentences overturned during the Prague Spring of 1968–1969.[592] In the 1990s, after the Velvet Revolution, opportunities opened up for a general redress of past wrongs, but even then the rehabilitation process did not go smoothly.[593] The activities of the protesters in 1953–1954 were classified as criminal (not political) offenses, and rehabilitation in these cases could not therefore be granted automatically; each case had to be re-examined separately.[594] The judicial authorities focused their reassessment on procedural errors, particularly as regarded confessions and in witness statements.[595] Convictions were then overturned on the basis of these technicalities as unlawful, and criminal proceedings against the protesters were subsequently dismissed for lack of evidence, or those affected were acquitted on the same grounds. Even the post-November 1989 legal system did not generally call into question the criminal nature of the acts for which the protesters had previously been convicted; it merely reversed their convictions.[596] In some cases, the conviction was even only partially reversed.[597] This attitude on the part of the post-Soviet justice system understandably provoked a great deal of disillusionment among the affected persons.

AGE AND OCCUPATIONAL STRUCTURE OF THE PROTESTERS

The extensive collection of extant criminal files against the protesters enables us to determine which groups of the population were most heavily involved in the protests. Such an analysis has a possible pitfall, however. The persons prosecuted did not constitute a representative sample of the protesters, because the security forces selected the suspects to be prosecuted on the basis of their class origin and age. It is therefore necessary to correct the data regarding the age and occupational structure of the 290 persons against whom criminal charges were brought (sample A).[598] For comparison, we will use the set of 61 detained protesters who were released without prosecution at the suggestion of the security services (sample B).[599] Even after this control calculation, the data on the composition of the protesters will only be approximate, because even the mere arrest or denunciation of persons who subsequently became part of the two groups was far from a random selection that would generate a statistically relevant sample of protesters. Contrary to the testimony of participants, for example, there was a relatively small number of women among those arrested, since women presumably received less attention from the police than the male protesters. Moreover, the lists defined above do not distinguish between the different stages of the protests in the course of the day, even though the structure of the protesters was likely changing from hour to hour. Arrests on a larger scale only began in the afternoon and in the evening. The data obtained can therefore provide only a partial description of the situation and must be compared with other sources.

The average age of those prosecuted (sample A) was surprisingly low, at 29 years. However, 32.41% of them belonged to the youngest age category, under 20 years. If we also add the age group of persons between 21 and 25, we find that more than half of the prosecuted protesters (50.69%) were under 26 years of age. The third largest age group were protesters aged 26 to 30, and the number of protesters in higher age groups continued to decline.

This trend was even greater for those whom the police proposed to release without filing criminal charges (Sample B). The average age in this group was only 24 years, and protesters in the under-20 age category form a clear majority (52.46 %), with the 21–25 age group also being strongly represented.

We can therefore conclude that a high number of young people under the age of 25 did indeed participate in the protests, and that they probably represented the majority of the more active protesters. Among these young people, investigators tended to overlook people of working-class origin and focused their attention mainly on those members of the younger generation who admired the Western lifestyle or who came from families of former tradesmen and civil servants. These young people were commonly referred to by the pejorative term *loafer* (pásek). Many members of this subculture were already employed in blue-collar jobs in 1953, thus blending their alternative models of behavior with working-class traditions.[600]

The young age of the majority of the protesters was quite common in 1948–1953, both in June 1953 and in all the previous conflicts examined above. This can be largely attributed to general psychological factors. Young people are usually much less open to compromise than older generations, and need not consider family and career interests in their decisions. Both student (1948) and working-class youth (1953) thus acted as spokespersons for their social groups, which lacked the courage to protest themselves.

In addition to this, some generational aspects and, in particular, the standard of living of young workers without families also played a role in the June 1953 protests. Many of the protesters belonged to the emerging generation of industrial workers who, after February 1948, had enjoyed unprecedented social and financial security under the new regime and compared to the situation in the 1930s, had lost most of their existential fears (full employment, relatively high wages, national insurance).[601] On the other hand, their lifestyle often sharply contrasted with the official collectivist morality of the time, which promoted building efforts and uniform discipline.[602] Young people therefore found themselves in a highly contradictory reality, where social opportunities clashed with the disciplinary demands of the system. In many cases, they dealt with their unfulfilled expectations through non-conformist forms of behavior, rebellion against official authority, and sympathy for Western cultural models.[603] These attitudes of some of the working-class youth, already evident during the May 1949 demonstrations, manifested themselves fully during the Pilsen riots of June 1953.[604]

The two groups of protesters under study showed a rather unbalanced gender structure, in which men were significantly predominant, making up 79.31% (sample A) and 77.05% (sample B) of the persons identified. However, these figures probably do not correspond to what was happening on the streets, where, according to the surviving testimonies, women formed a significant part of the wider group of protesters, especially in the morning. Women were often quicker than men to react to the currency reform, as they were responsible for most of the day-to-day shopping in their households.[605] The exchange of money and price increases had an immediate impact on their daily schedules, as transport to work or the purchase of snacks had on the workers. It is likely, therefore, that far fewer women were arrested than men.

In terms of the social and professional structure, working-class protesters formed a clear majority, making up 64.48% (sample A) and 52.46% (sample B) of all persons on record. The overwhelming majority of them were employed in industrial plants, with only a small proportion working in smaller tradesmen's workshops. In addition, a large number of protesters from other occupational groups were also factory employees: clerks and apprentices accounted for 12.76% (sample A) and 14.75% (sample B) of the protesters, and 4.48% (sample A) and 8.2% (sample B), respectively. However, far fewer members of these groups participated in the process than workers. Factory foremen were only marginally involved in the protests, supporting the protesters more by deliberate inaction. Although the occupational group of foremen and service personnel accounted for 10% (sample A) and

8.2% (sample B) of the protesters, the vast majority of detainees belonged to service personnel (drivers, waitresses, conductors, etc.), rather than factory foremen (only 2.07% and 0%, respectively). A relatively small number of protesters in question were self-employed (tradesmen and small farmers), members of agricultural cooperatives, students, and pensioners. The number of housewives among the protesters was probably significantly higher than the recorded statistical data suggest.[606]

The occupational structure of protesters suggested for release without prosecution (sample B) included a higher proportion of apprentices and students compared to those against whom criminal charges were brought (sample A). It can therefore be assumed that the ranks of the protesters included a high number of members of these occupational groups who were not prosecuted because of their youth.

Accurate data regarding the occupational structure of the population of Pilsen in 1953 are unfortunately lacking. The most recent census was taken on March 1, 1950, and recorded the situation before the prohibition of small craftsmen, merchants, and private tradesmen. Despite these shortcomings, however, a comparison of the occupational structure of the protesters with that of the general population in 1950 clearly shows that the tendency to protest was particularly strong among workers, apprentices, factory foremen, service personnel, and low-ranking skilled workers. Their aggregate share of the number of gainfully employed protesters was 84.19% (sample A) and 82.35% (sample B), while their share of the overall gainfully employed population was only 64.25%. There were far fewer protest participants among clerks and senior specialists, on the other hand. Their share in the number of gainfully employed protesters was 13.6% (sample A) and 17.65% (sample B), respectively, while they constituted 29.22% of the city's gainfully employed population.[607]

Among the members of the two groups in question, a very high proportion was employed at the V. I. Lenin Factories, with workers at this enterprise accounting for 36.9% of Sample A and 40.98% of Sample B, respectively. During the morning protests, the proportion of employees of this enterprise among the protesters was probably even higher. Those employees and apprentices of the factory who went on strike therefore most likely constituted the largest group of protesters, as other extant sources seem to suggest.

The police also collected information about the detained protesters' or their families' past. Those persons whose former professional or political status was considered by the police to be the evidence of a reactionary mindset were more likely to be prosecuted. These background evaluations give us a rough idea of other aspects of the protesters' structure. The number of persons with an undesirable and desirable past differed significantly between the two samples examined. Negative past history was predominant in sample

A, whereas positive information was predominant in sample B. Obviously, a person's past could have both positive and negative aspects.

At least 21.03% of the prosecuted protesters (sample A) originally belonged to families of former tradesmen and private farmers, which may have been a part of their motivation to join the protests. At least 10.34% of the protesters belonged to families of former civil servants, military officers, or national administrators. At least 10% of the protesters were members of non-communist political parties before 1948. At least 8.28% of the persons prosecuted had personal or family experience of repression in the form of imprisonment or at least investigation for a political offense before June 1, 1953. Moreover, this total did not include numerous economic crimes, which may also have had a political overtone. The most frequently mentioned past transgressions in the criminal files were attempts to illegally cross the state border. In the opinion of the investigators, at least 7.24% of the prosecuted protesters had strong ties to Western countries or their culture (they could have relatives who lived in exile, or they could be regularly listening to foreign radio broadcasts). Only rarely did the negative aspects of the protesters' past include membership of a religious sect or suspicious activity during the Nazi occupation. Even though the frequent negative background information in sample A resulted not only from the structure of the protesters, but also from the overall approach of State Security investigators, the above figures suggest that a fairly significant amount of the protesters had, at least in theory, other relevant reasons for protesting than a mere disagreement with the currency reform.

In the case of the protesters suggested for release (sample B), all of the above aggravating circumstances were present to a much lesser extent. On the other hand, relatives of Communist Party members were significantly more numerous here than in Sample A (10%)—22.95% in total. A significant number of protesters were thus probably former or current members of the Communist Party or their relatives.

EXTRAJUDICIAL PERSECUTION OF THE PROTESTERS AT WORK AND SCHOOL

The persecution of protesters and sympathizers reached much wider proportions than the numbers of convicted persons would suggest. Many protesters suffered disciplinary repercussions in their workplaces. The situation at the V.I. Lenin Factories was again a good example. On June 11, 1953, in accordance with the directives of the Central Committee, the factory management decided that the protest participants would be treated as absentees—they would receive wages for the missed shift and their leave would be cut short.

As a rule, leave was reduced by three, six, or ten days, or by half of the total available days off.[608] The employees also had to return the bankbooks they had previously received as an award for exemplary performance.[609] Management also reassigned some protesters to inferior jobs within the plant. Clerical workers were reassigned to manual jobs, manual workers to machines, and assembly line workers were assigned to more difficult piece work.[610] The most flagrant cases ended in termination of employment. This mostly applied to those who had also been convicted by the court for participating in the protests.[611] Lists of the dismissed protesters were handed over by the factory management to the chairman of the Consolidated National Committee in Pilsen, who supervised their reassignment to appropriate jobs (street cleaning, brickworks, etc.).[612] In turn, loyal employees were rewarded. For example, former clerical workers who had been reassigned to manual labor in 1951 could return to their former positions if they spoke out against their fellow workers during the protests.[613]

The trade unions employed their own methods of punishment. A resolution of the presidium of the ZVIL factory council of July 2, 1953, laid down the methods of disciplinary action against four groups of workers: 1) Protesters who had been dismissed from the factory or taken into court custody were to be punished by expulsion from the Revolutionary Trade Union Movement. 2) Protest sympathizers from the ranks of officials of the shop councils and department secretaries were to be suspended from the trade union for one year. Those who were particularly aggressive during the protests inside or outside the factory were to receive the same punishment. 3) All workers who had left the factory during the demonstrations and were not included in Groups 1 and 2 were to be deprived of all benefits of trade union membership for a period of one year. These benefits included the right to medical treatment at a health spa, the right to recreation,[614] the right to canteen catering, the right to sports activities sponsored by the trade union,[615] the right to be allocated an apartment, and the right to an official certificate entitling them to certain benefits (e.g., a certificate for their children's admission to university). 4) All employees who had been involved in the protests in any way were to be deprived of all privileges in a similar way to Group 3, but only until 31 December 31, 1953. Signboards with the names of those punished were put up in all the factory workshops.[616] Those affected often had special notes written on their identity cards regarding their participation in the protests.[617]

The procedure for punishing protest sympathizers was coordinated by the KSČ Factory Committee, which set up a special commission tasked with investigating all known protesters.[618] Workshop investigation committees were set up in each workshop, consisting of the chairman of the shop council, the chairman of the base party organization, a representative of the department concerned, and a representative of the factory Personnel Department.[619] The so-called Comrades' trials were then conducted directly in the workplaces.[620] In July, the Factory Committee conducted a vetting of all communists in the factory. The vetting of all non-partisan employees was carried out by their trade union organizations.

Protesters were identified by checking the records of absences on June 1, 1953, based on police information or denunciations from their fellow workers.[621] Protesters were also invited to turn themselves in voluntarily, and were promised a more lenient consideration of their case in return. In some workshops, workers attempted to organize a collective denial of participation in the protests.[622] The higher party authorities therefore complained that "there is a kind of false solidarity among the workers; they try to conceal facts, and many know nothing and remember nothing."[623] In later years, workers in the workshops even advocated for their convicted coworkers to be released from prison on parole.[624]

Some workshop foremen initially tried to protect their subordinates from punishment and reported only those protesters whose absence was officially recorded at the factory gates. It was only after pressure from the factory council that they were forced to report the names of other known protesters.[625] Similar defensive attitudes also occurred during the background checks of the Communist Party members, with many communists covering up for protest sympathizers.[626] Even the workshop investigation committees showed certain resistant tendencies and often proposed only light punishments in the form of additional work commitments, contrary to the opinion of the Factory Commission. The situation got so out of hand that "in some commissions, the protesters even decide their own punishment, and simply give up some of their days off."[627] In some cases, the punishments were appealed against by the disciplined workers themselves, who usually offered an additional work commitment as voluntary punishment.[628]

Unfortunately, the investigation of the protests affected many innocent people at the V. I. Lenin Factories who had not been involved in the protests at all. In fact, punishments were handed out for a mere absence from the workplace, even in the person's presence at the protests could not be proven. Among those punished were numerous workers who took advantage of the general confusion on the day in question to conduct their personal affairs outside the factory. However, those workers who were not allowed into the factory for the afternoon shift of security measures during the siege of Gate 4 were also written up for unexcused absences. Many of the commuting workers who had arrived at the nearby station in the southern suburbs of Pilsen tried to avoid the places of violent conflict and took the nearest train back home.[629] However, even these persons were considered to be protest participants due to their absence from work.[630]

Punishments were also meted out by the commissions to those workers who were found to be temporarily absent from their designated workplace, even though they had not left the factory at all. This meant that apart from the participants of the protest meeting in the factory courtyard, workers who had been sent by the workshop managers to another part of the factory and merely observed the gathering of strikers on their way were also punished. A number of workers left their workshops out of curiosity when they heard the crowd breaking through Gate 4 and were subsequently pushed out of the factory along with this crowd.[631] Another group of those punished were employees who waved at the protesters from office windows, tried to clock off their absent colleagues, or verbally opposed critics of the protests.[632] The purges also targeted long-term "opponents of the regime and subversive elements"[633] who, although not directly involved in the protests, influenced the atmosphere in the workplace with their opinions. The Commission issued notices to the employees who had been reported announcing that due to their participation in the protests, they would be transferred to a more menial job, without thoroughly investigating the claims. The affected employees had to sign the notices to indicate their agreement. Only a select few refused to sign the document, even though many of them were completely innocent.[634] In keeping with long-term post-war practice, harsher punishments were given mainly to clerical workers, even though they did not form the core of the protesters. Workers' actions, on the other hand, were treated much more leniently.[635] The authorities were so inconsistent in their approach that while many innocent persons were punished with extreme severity, some convicted working-class protesters were even allowed to retain lower-level positions in the trade union movement.[636]

The workers' reassignment to inferior positions was often accompanied by a reduction in wages because they lacked the qualifications for their new job and were therefore underperforming. Their families had to cope with considerable social upheaval, compounded by the recent currency reform. The mother of clerical worker Miloslav Míka, for example, protested against her son's punishment by saying,

> No one asked why he went to protest on the first of June. As a citizen, he had the right to express his disagreement with the government's actions. In April 1953, he received a newlywed loan of 36,000 Kč for new furniture, and on June 1 he had to exchange this money at [a ratio of] 1:50, but the government still wants him to repay it at [a ratio of] 1:5, which means he will be burdened by debt for years to come, and he still won't be able to buy the furniture. To make things worse, you pay him 500–600 Kč a month to support a family of three, but you want him to work as hard as if he was making a fortune. You didn't care about him enough to assign him to a job where he could earn more. I regret

> that I raised my son to be honest and believe in justice. If I had taught him to cheat, he would be better off today. [. . .] You have made it all too clear that he is a clerk, and those are not to be trusted, and should be judged differently than manual workers. Why try to convince them if you can punish them, right? Did you ask those who were outside why they left? You punish without investigation, without finding out who is guilty, and you punish everyone differently.[637]

A particularly drastic means of punishment was the eviction of workers from company apartments, which took place from June 22 to July 23, 1953.[638] Jan Cimrhanzl, a member of the Communist Party, was evicted by the housing committee of the V. I. Lenin Factories to another place that was too small for his family, even though he was cleared of all charges by the Workshop Investigation Commission. In addition, his furniture was badly damaged by the rain during the move, as the moving trucks were not covered with tarpaulin and the handover of the new apartment assigned to him by the Consolidated National Committee in Pilsen was not arranged in time.[639] Václav Nachtmann, a member of the regional committee of the Defenders of Peace, a state-sponsored anti-colonial organization, was evicted from his company apartment on the grounds that on June 1, 1953, he had talked back to a member of the People's Militias who had loudly expressed his determination to shoot all the protesters.[640]

This chaotic, misguided investigation had a considerable social impact. By the end of August 1953, 238 employees (193 workers and 45 clerks) had been dismissed from the V. I. Lenin Factories. Two hundred and six clerical workers were transferred to manual jobs and 261 workers were transferred to menial positions.[641] Leave was cut short for 258 workers, 28 workers were given additional jobs as punishment, and 136 persons were expelled from the trade union. In total, 1,127 persons were punished at the factory[642] which meant that 1 in 27 factory employees faced some sort of sanction. The high level of petty persecution in the workplaces deepened the atmosphere of fear in the ranks of Pilsen society in the first months after the demonstrations, and was one of the main factors in the gradual stabilization of the situation in the region, along with the decline in social panic.

However, normal factory operations could only resume after the sanctions were lifted. Moreover, harsh blanket measures against the disgruntled workers were politically untenable in the long term.[643] The unfair, unsystematic nature of the disciplinary actions provoked considerable resentment even among many party members, which soon forced the KSČ Factory Committee to reevaluate its hitherto reckless approach. On July 21, 1953, the Committee ordered a review of the wage conditions of persons transferred to inferior jobs within the factory and offered them financial assistance if their wages were too low to support their families.[644] On September 18, 1953, company director František Brabec proposed to the Factory Committee that all disciplinary cases at the plant be reviewed. He also expressed the willingness to pardon those employees who performed well.[645] Following his suggestion, the Central Investigation Commission then referred 84 selected cases to the company's Personnel Department for review, to ascertain whether it was appropriate for these persons to return to their original jobs. At this point, the process of pardoning the punished employees was delayed only by the reluctance of some workshop party officials and the fact that their former positions were already filled by someone else. By the end of October 1953, 50 persons had been reassigned to their original jobs and no placements were yet available for another 30.[646] A number of hard-to-replace specialists also returned to their original positions later in 1953.[647] In 1954, several dozen employees' punishments were revoked on the suggestion of the workshop councils.[648]

The easing of pressure by the factory management on the erstwhile working-class protesters was probably the result of a change in tactics by the central party leadership. At a request from Moscow, it revised its hitherto harsh attitude toward the workers' unrest in July1953 and sought different (non-repressive) ways out of its growing social isolation. This development was well-illustrated by the fate of the government's Decree No. 52/1953 on measures against high employee turnover and absenteeism, which was adopted just after the demonstrations on June 3, 1953, and imposed considerably stricter punishments for missing shifts.[649] It was revoked almost immediately, on July 6, and maintaining good work morale remained the responsibility of the trade unions operating within the safe world of the industrial enterprises.[650]

In investigating the protests, authorities also paid increasing attention to the Pilsen schools, as the protesters were predominantly young people. Seven national and secondary school teachers were dismissed from their posts and 11 were given warnings.[651] These punishments were imposed mostly for publicly approving the demonstrations, often following a denunciation by a student.[652] In addition, a total of 5 students were expelled and banned from studying at all schools, 10 students were banned from studying at schools in Pilsen, 20 were suspended for one year, and 5 left their schools voluntarily. Seventeen students were expelled from the vocational schools.[653] Dozens more students received a reprimand or a C in deportment.[654] In addition to verbal support of the protests, the students' offenses often involved direct participation in the protests. The most active of these were four students at the local nursing school, who climbed out the window of their classroom to join the protests.[655] However, the students' reactions to the currency reform were generally quite varied. Some students, for example, tore pictures of Klement Gottwald and Joseph Vissarionovich Stalin out of their textbooks,[656] while others had agreed to come to school on June 2 without the pioneer scarves they would normally wear.[657] Some innocent children of arrested protesters received punishments at their schools.[658]

University students did not participate in the demonstrations to any great extent and were difficult to locate because the exam period was underway and universities were out of session. Punishments of university students directly related to the currency reform were therefore extremely rare. Two students were expelled from the University of Mechanical and Electrical Engineering in Pilsen for participating in the protests, and three others were expelled for other infractions.[659] At the Faculty of Medicine of Charles University in Pilsen, one student was expelled for voicing his support for the protests, and another student was arrested. A female student who had an affair with a convicted protester, Josef Fencl, was also threatened with punishment.[660] Despite the low number of protesters among university students, the Faculty of Medicine planned a preemptive expulsion of 18 students guilty of other political infractions in August 1953.[661]

After the protests of June 1, the Communist Party leadership also adopted a harsher approach toward non-conformist youth behavior, which it described as slacking off and hooliganism, and regarded such students as potential allies of the counter-revolution.[662]

STATISTICAL INVESTIGATION INTO THE CAUSES OF THE STRIKE AT THE V. I. LENIN FACTORIES

Following the investigation of the demonstrations, statistical surveys were compiled at the V. I. Lenin Factories regarding the distribution of protesters among the various plants of the factory. The accuracy of these summaries was affected by the repressive mechanism described above and was therefore far from perfect. The surveys only included the officially exposed protesters, and a large number of participants were therefore left unrecorded; on the other hand, they also recorded a number of completely innocent people who had not directly participated in the protests. Another shortcoming was the fact that the statistics did not include data from all departments. Nevertheless, the results of this survey represent a unique source of its kind, which provides at least a partial answer to the question of which factory departments demonstrated the greatest support of the protests. This also opens up the possibility of formulating hypotheses about the causes of this asymmetry and, consequently, about the causes of the strike itself.

According to official statistics, a total of 1,433 employees of the V. I. Lenin Factories joined the protests of June 1, 1953, which represented 5.46% of the total number of employees registered by the enterprise (26,269 persons).[663] The vast majority of the workers started the morning or afternoon shift, and therefore had the theoretical possibility of joining the demonstrations. In absolute numbers, the largest number of protesters came from the Elektrotrakce Doudlevce subsidiary plant (286 persons) and from the following departments: Engineering III (208 persons), Locomotive Works (152 persons), Steel Works (139 persons), Engineering I (116 persons), and Auxiliary Production (103 persons). Based on the percentage of the total number of personnel in the individual workplaces, we can further determine that the greatest inclination to join the protests was demonstrated by employees of the following departments: Research and Development (11.44%), Engineering III (11.11%), Locomotive Works (9.69%) Engineering I (7.62%), Auxiliary Production (7.57%), Elektrotrakce Doudlevce (7.5%), and Sales and Supply (7.08%). The bastions of the protests were therefore some of the largest departments, namely Elektrotrakce Doudlevce, Engineering III, Locomotive Works, and Engineering I. On the other hand, employees in other large departments, especially Steel Works and Vehicles, showed much less inclination to join the protests. The protesters found increased support in some of the smaller departments with a suitable occupational structure, characterized by an increased proportion of skilled workers, such as Research and Development or Sales and Supply.[664]

According to other data from the same source, a total of 1,484 workers took part in the demonstrations, including 1,266 workers (85.31%) and 218 clerks (14.69%). More than a quarter of the clerical workers (58 persons) came from the Engineering III department.[665] The protests were therefore predominantly a working-class matter. The factory kept separate statistics on apprentices. Of the 1,808 apprentices present on the morning shift, only 40 reportedly left the plant, while another 48 did not report for the afternoon shift.[666] Despite the young age of a large part of the protesters, the core of the protesters were not apprentices, but rather young employees of the factory.

Factory management tried to use the statistical data obtained to clarify the causes of the unrest in various departments. They assumed that the protesters mainly came from those workshops that had a large number of workers from formerly non-worker professions who had been involuntarily reassigned to manual labor in 1948–1953. Such workers made up 19.65% of the factory's workforce (5,161 persons).[667] It turned out that almost all of the departments where an above-average percentage of workers participated in the protests did indeed have a very high proportion of workers transferred to industrial production from other sectors of the economy.[668] The structure of the employees' original qualifications was probably one of the factors that influenced the emergence of unrest at the V. I. Lenin Factories. Indeed, among the detained protesters there were many factory workers with experience in other professions.[669] Moreover, the above statistics did not record a typologically similar group of young workers from non-worker families, who were also frequent supporters of the protests.[670]

The statistical surveys also suggested a possible link between the low proportion of Communist Party members in some departments and the tendency of employees in these departments to engage in protests. Indeed, most of the establishments that were strong supporters of the strike had a below-average number of Communist Party members in their ranks.[671]

The causes of unrest, however, were thought to lie mainly in the composition of the membership of the party organizations in the factory. In 1953, the KSČ Factory Committee registered a total of 12,173 members and candidates. Of these, however, only 8,986 (73.82%) were non-partisan before joining the Communist Party, unencumbered by an undesirable past. On the other hand, more than a quarter (26.18%) of the members were originally members of other political parties. The largest number of these were former supporters of the Czechoslovak Social Democratic Party—a total of 2,463 (20.23%) members—and the Czechoslovak National Socialist Party, with a total of 659 (5.71%) members. By contrast, only 215 (1.77%) members could boast that they had been members of the Communist Party since before May 1945, which was generally regarded as a guarantee of ideological stability.[672]

Within the party organization, former members of other political parties, especially former Social Democrats, clearly outnumbered the original pre-war communists. This reflected the traditionally strong position of Social Democrats in the region and in the factory itself before February 1948.[673] At the time of the aforementioned large strike at the Elektrotrakce Doudlevce subsidiary plant in 1950, Pilsen officials were already aware of the risk posed by the high number of former Social Democrats in the party ranks. However, due to the protracted crisis in the functioning of the party organizations, they were unable to rectify the situation. In June 1953, their fears were seemingly realized when the party apparatus at the factory completely failed during the protests. They came to believe that vestiges of Social Democratic thinking were the main cause of this failure.

The key ideological statement in this regard was made by Minister of Culture Václav Kopecký at a nationwide meeting of the chief secretaries of KSČ Regional Committees on June 11, 1953:

> I think that the events in Pilsen and Ostrava can be explained primarily by the composition of the Party there, namely the fact that after February 1948 the treacherous course adopted by Slánský and his band, and by the will of the then regional secretaries, who were all Slánský's men, tens of thousands of Social Democrats could infiltrate the Party ranks in the Pilsen and Ostrava regions, including die-hard right-wing elements, often known enemies and turncoats, reformists rotten to the bone, corrupted by the capitalists and involved in

> strikebreaking during the First Republic. [. . .] It was undeniably a great hazard that the right-wing social democratic elements and other elements could so easily become members of the Party and exploit their membership and their affiliation with the working class to gain influence, especially in the factories. [. . .] We have seen that those who used to kowtow to the capitalist exploiters before are more and more brazen in professing their obedience to our people's democratic government. [. . .] A very serious lesson should be drawn from the June events: we need to focus our struggle against the vestiges of social-democratic treachery, social-democratic destructive attitudes, social-democratic marauding and social-democratic reformism.[674]

This hypothesis, however, only partially justified the outbreak of the June strike at the V. I. Lenin Factories. In fact, no Social Democratic group was visibly active in the factory to incite or organize unrest. Thus, the influence of social democracy in Pilsen was exercised exclusively in terms of general working-class traditions and established thought stereotypes, not in the form of a specific Social Democratic movement. The young age of most of the protesters, made it virtually impossible to build on some direct pre-war experience. The theory of Social Democratic influence only explained the protesters' activities of themselves in an indirect way. Moreover, it also offered only a partial justification for the passive approach of the party and factory apparatus. Although the communist officials and foremen were mostly older in age than the protesters, their inaction during the strikes was mainly an expression of their disapproval of the currency reform, the arrogance of its implementation and its social consequences. Such attitudes did not in themselves indicate any direct connection with Social Democratic traditions, since they were visibly shared by the majority of communists who did not carry the stigma of former Social Democrats. Emphasizing Pilsen's Social Democratic past was therefore greatly overused by local officials, and often utilized as a universal catchphrase to justify their long-term failures.

In addition to the employees' professional background and the political history of the Communist Party members, other long-term factors had a great influence on the strike at the various departments of the V. I. Lenin Factories. These included the specific production conditions and the degree of antagonistic relationships at the workplace in question. It is worth noting, for example, that the departments which joined the June protests at the earliest opportunity and to the greatest extent were not able to meet the disproportionately high production targets in the first half of 1953. This was particularly true of the Engineering I and Engineering III departments.[675] Their workers were therefore subjected to increased pressure to perform better in the usual end-of-month rush, which occurred simultaneously with the announcement of the currency reform. In addition, they were greatly frustrated by the fact that as a result of the unfeasible and unrealistic plan they were not entitled to any bonuses.[676] The Engineering III department even had a reputation as a place where new recruits were sent as punishment.[677] In both cases, these were plants that had been severely affected by the restructuring of the company and the associated high turnover of staff in 1949–1953.

Many of the workplaces affected by the June 1 riots had shown an increased tendency to protest even in previous years. The Engineering I department, for example, had been the epicenter of rebellious sentiments during the fabric affair in 1949 and again during the panic buying in May 1953. In 1950, employees at the Elektrotrakce Doudlevce subsidiary plant had launched the biggest strike in the company to date, caused by the unfair distribution of bonuses, and more strike attempts occurred there in 1951. Both workplaces were therefore among the traditional sources of social conflict within the factory.

However, the stratification of the June strikes within the factory was also determined by certain temporary factors. For example, the geographical location of the workshops within the factory, namely their eventual position along the route of the workers' protest march, played a major role. Participation in protests was often determined by the conduct of local officials and the flexibility of their reactions to the outbreak of unrest. This factor was particularly evident in the steelworks. However, completely random factors could also play a significant role. For example, the supervising officials explained the outbreak of discontent among the workers at Engineering I by the fact that the workers there had not had any snacks on the morning of June 1 because they had all been bought out by their colleagues in the Steelworks department.[678] Odd as such an explanation may seem, it should not be underestimated, considering that snacks had been the cause of a strike that had broken out in the same plant on Tuesday, May 25, 1953. In the heated atmosphere of the currency reform, virtually anything could have provided the decisive impetus for the protests.

In general terms, workers at the V. I. Lenin Factories differed from the workers at other factories primarily by their greater self-confidence as employees of the traditionally dominant factory in the region, as well as by the fact that a large number of workers earned relatively high wages and had considerable savings. Employees of the plant reportedly exchanged as much as CZK 40,000–50,000, but there were instances of exchanges of more than CZK 200,000.[679] Some observers noted that it was the better paid workers who often left the workplace during protests.[680] More than any other enterprise, employees at the V. I. Lenin Factories had incurred considerable losses by the abolition of the rationing system, since most of them were entitled to preferential rations for hard workers and did not have to spend their wages on expensive goods on the open market. For these workers, then, the abolition of the restricted market meant a noticeable increase in their basic spending.[681] The fact that workers at the V. I. Lenin Factories possessed large amounts of money that had been devalued by the currency reform; that they were fully aware of their own importance within the country's political and economic system; the substantial overload caused by the implementation of the five-year economic plan; the factory's considerable isolation from the control mechanisms of the outside world; and the factory's unusually large traditional influence on the development of the region were probably the main reasons why a strike broke out at the V. I. Lenin Factories and why it inspired a significant part of the city's population to protest.[682]

FORCED EVICTION OF CERTAIN GROUPS IN PILSEN

The widespread extrajudicial persecution of the protesters was also accompanied by the forced eviction of selected groups of people from apartments in the city center. This was one of the most severe types of punishment, which greatly complicated the family lives of those affected and significantly affected the overall atmosphere in West Bohemian society.

Although the action itself was a retaliatory measure, triggered by the demonstrations of June 1, 1953, it was based on a longer-term tactical consideration. There had been a considerable, chronic housing shortage in the city throughout the post-war period, which was exacerbated after February 1948 by the increasing demands of the public authorities and the security forces, especially the army.[683] At the same time, the original social structure of the inhabitants of the city center was also becoming politically untenable. Only a small number of workers lived in the luxury apartments in downtown Pilsen, and there was a proportionately high concentration of former private tradesmen and supporters of non-communist political parties.[684]

This was especially important when riots broke out in the streets. In fact, the crowds of bystanders, made up of local residents, regularly boosted the protesters' morale (in both 1948 and 1953). The idea of a systematically organized change in the composition of the inner-city population had therefore emerged as far back as September 1948, following the previous protests. Its primary aim was to prevent a repetition of similar incidents. However, no large-scale population relocation was attempted at that time, presumably in fear of public disapproval; but in June 1953, a substantial number of people living in the streets around Náměstí Republiky and the Palace of Justice were again cheering protesters from the windows.[685] Shortly after the suppression of the protests, the communist officials therefore took up the earlier idea again. Amid the shock caused by the protests, it was quite easy to push through.[686]

For the reasons mentioned above, the forced eviction did not apply primarily to the protesters themselves, but to a wider circle of potential opposition who were about to lose not only their apartments but also strategically advantageous positions in the city center.[687] The vacated dwellings were to be given to families of ideologically conscious workers, militiamen, and security officers, whose members would help to handle any future unrest if the need arose. Preparations for these measures proceeded with extraordinary speed. As early as June 2, 1953, the relevant proposal was discussed by the KSČ Regional Committee, and the following day it was brought to the attention of the plenary session of the KSČ Municipal Committee.[688] On that occasion, chief secretary Josef Žák summed up the actual purpose of the operation with the following words: "We need to finally do something about the old, rotten city center, where the bourgeoisie still struts around while the workers have to live on the outskirts. We will evict the worst among them from Pilsen, and as far as their little friends are concerned, nothing prevents us from replacing them and installing party members, militiamen, non-partisan workers in the apartments downtown, so that the center of the city [will] become the mainstay of the working class; that even if 150 people storm the square, the wives of our comrades must be so many that they can beat them off with their hats."[689]

The evictions began almost immediately, in an emotionally charged mood. The first three families were moved as early as June 5.[690] The lists of persons proposed for eviction were given to the chairman of the Regional National Committee.[691] Meanwhile, the police hastily compiled their own lists of candidates, based on existing documents drawn up in preparation for a similar project in 1951–1952,[692] which had, however, never been implemented. This meant that only a minimum of those who were singled out for eviction had actually participated in the protests. Apart from verbal approval of protests or waving from windows at protesters, any other kind of suspicious activity registered by the police in previous years could have become grounds for eviction.[693] When assessing individual cases, the person's earnings in 1947 were also taken into account.[694]

The actual process of forced relocation of families to their new homes was organized by the Consolidated National Committee in Pilsen, both on legal and technical levels.[695] Evictions were carried out in a very unscrupulous manner. After receiving a notice from the Consolidated National Committee, the affected persons were given an impossibly short time to move out—usually 16 or 36 hours, respectively.[696] An appeal to the Regional National Committee did not grant an extension.[697] Families were often relocated to extremely remote areas, especially to the borderlands depopulated by the recent expulsion of the German population.[698] They were uprooted, cut off from their existing social ties, made to live in substandard conditions, and faced a lack of employment opportunities.[699]

In the initial stages of the operation, the Pilsen authorities had the full support of the national authorities.[700] Early in June, President Antonín Zápotocký actually called for a thorough purge of the large city centers.[701] The KSČ Regional Committee sent several optimistic reports to the Secretariat of the Central Committee, claiming that the evictions were proceeding peacefully, without any signs of resistance, and that "the majority of the population fully approves of this measure."[702]

In reality, a large part of the public was greatly outraged by the unleashing of such arbitrary terror. Critics of the evictions were particularly bolstered by the fact that the operation was marred by excesses that endangered even loyal sympathizers of the regime. Some police officers actually pushed for the eviction of certain families for purely personal reasons. Many families of party members and lower-ranking party officials were also affected by the operation.[703] Evictions were frequently carried out despite explicit protests from the workers' representative bodies in their respective enterprises.[704] Moreover, the reasons for eviction were often completely fabricated and were not verified by the officials responsible.[705] This generated an atmosphere of fear in which no one, not even the communists themselves, could be sure whether they would be end up being the victims the next day. The secretary of the KSČ Municipal Committee later assessed this unsustainable situation:

> It often involved Party members; for example, comrades from the National Security Corps were urging us to evict the railroad porter, who was a Party member and sat on the workshop council, just because his wife had participated in the protest. That is going too far. [. . .] There is no other way to proceed; we would end up creating an atmosphere of fear in Pilsen, where half the city would be worried that they would be next. [. . .] People must be made to see that the entire operation is directed against the bourgeoisie.[706]

Therefore, the central authorities gradually began to intervene in the implementation of the operation, trying to moderate the indiscriminate zeal of the local officials. For example, the Ministry of the Interior stopped the eviction of several families in the Blatná region.[707] At a national meeting of the secretaries of Regional Party Committees on June 11, 1953, President Antonín Zápotocký demanded that the evictions should not be carried out in a spontaneous but carefully planned manner:

> I agree that evictions are necessary, but giving people notices to move out within three days? I will never agree with that. There is not enough time to prepare, not if we are to provide the people with alternative housing. [. . .] I do believe that many people need to be evicted from Pilsen. But there must be some kind of a plan. It is not enough to evict them from the main square and settle

> them a few kilometers away from Pilsen. [. . .] It would be a serious mistake to close our eyes to blatant mistakes, and then try to fix those mistakes by excessive means.[708]

The Central Committee of the Communist Party soon began to see the entire operation as a problem that was compromising the political stability of the region.[709]

Due to the indignation of a large part of the population and the reticent attitude of the central authorities, the operation to clear the city of undesirable elements was never fully completed.[710] The main wave of evictions ended on July 16, 1953. At least 626 eviction proposals were discussed in Pilsen. In the end, only 204 families were evicted. Those affected were mostly former tradesmen and merchants who lived near the main protest sites.[711] Most of those affected successfully tried to avoid resettlement to remote parts of the country and moved in with their relatives or to their weekend cottages on the outskirts of the city.[712] Almost all of them were allowed to return to Pilsen in the following years.[713]

Like other forms of extrajudicial persecution, the eviction project clearly demonstrated that blanket repressions after June 1, 1953, had their limits, largely determined by their political feasibility. Repressions could not be applied against a vaguely defined group of people for an indefinite period of time, because it would impede the daily running of society and the national economy and, paradoxically, hinder the intended stabilization of the situation. Moreover, the strong arm policy was also criticized by Moscow, from where the so-called New Direction began to spread to Czechoslovakia in July 1953, encouraging a partial liberalization of the system.[714]

ASSIGNING PERSONAL RESPONSIBILITY IN THE PARTY AND SECURITY APPARATUS

From the Communist Party's point of view, the question of revitalizing the floundering local power apparatuses was crucial for stabilizing the political situation in the Pilsen region. Investigation into the causes of the protests therefore also focused on analyzing the misconduct of individual party authorities and possibilities for remedial action, including personnel changes in the key positions. It turned out, however, that the various levels of the party structure held completely different, often incompatible, views on the causes of the protests.

Even after the dispersal of the protests, the lower party authorities operating directly in the city, and especially the factory organizations at the V. I. Lenin Factories, still considered the currency reform announced by the central authorities to be the main source of problems. This was to a large extent the position adopted by the KSČ Municipal Committee. The Regional Committee, on the other hand, claimed that the crisis was caused by the Municipal Committee's neglect of political work and the low dedication of the members of basic organizations under its authority. The rural district organizations, on the other hand, saw the main shortcoming in the inability of the KSČ Regional and Municipal Committees to manage the crackdown on protesters in the heart of the region, which subsequently complicated the situation in other parts of West Bohemia. Finally, the Central Secretariat could not allow open criticism of its work, and therefore needed to find the culprit among the discordant cliques within the region. A conflict over the interpretation of the protests gradually broke out between the various levels of the apparatus, which included the struggle over who would be held responsible for the political failure of the currency reform.

The party authorities resumed their operation in Pilsen on Tuesday June 2, with a meeting of the KSČ Regional Committee discussing the instructions from the central authorities, delivered earlier that night.[715] The primary task was to reassure the disoriented communists from outside Pilsen. The meeting of the Regional Committee was therefore followed the next day by meetings of all the District Committees, at which an official explanation of the Pilsen protests as a reactionary putsch was given, which was then to be passed on to all the basic organizations.[716] However, the meetings did not go smoothly at all; critical voices pointed out the inability of the Regional Committee to prevent the protests in time. Numerous complaints were also voiced regarding the continuing information embargo on the demonstrations. District representatives pointed in particular to the fact that a number of false rumors about the Pilsen events were circulating in the countryside, needlessly fueled by the fact that the regional daily newspaper, *Pravda*, had not yet brought any news of the protests.[717]

At the insistence of the districts, the regional press agency therefore published an article on June 5 entitled *Pilsen Workers Deal with the Reactionaries*, which provided the uninformed communists in rural areas with the first official account of the riots.[718] Its publication was pushed through by chief secretary Jan Hlína, against the will of the other secretaries. However, the publication of reports on the protests, albeit clouded by ideological interpretation, was later reevaluated as a completely ill-advised move that only gave fodder to foreign propaganda.[719] Some Pilsen communists and militiamen also protested against the wording of the article because they disagreed with its claim that the workers had not understood the reactionary intentions of the protesters in time.[720] The whole case was even investigated by the Central Committee.[721] Jan Hlína was later forced to perform public self-criticism for printing the article.[722]

The most tumultuous of all the district meetings, however, was the meeting of the KSČ Municipal Committee in Pilsen, which was supervised by Ladislav Kopřiva, a representative of the central authorities.[723] Justified reservations about the currency reform still persisted among the participants. Only very seldom were they willing to perform the required self-criticism and to search for their alleged mistakes which had supposedly facilitated the outbreak of protests.[724] On the contrary, many debaters openly pointed out the misconduct of the higher party authorities, including the Central Committee of the Communist Party. Kopřiva was actually forced to defend the currency reform and the manner of its implementation. He argued, for example, that the reform could not have been announced to party members earlier because the supply system would have collapsed: "Do you think that our Party and government are made up of comrades who cannot think for themselves?"[725] He also assured those present that the supply of goods to the retail network would surely stabilize soon and declared that the temporary destitution of some residents was a minor sacrifice compared to the years of starvation in the era of the First Czechoslovak Republic (1918–1938): "We are convinced that a working man can last a day or two on bread alone."[726] Despite Kopřiva's forceful intervention, members of the Municipal Committee voiced a number of objections to the official interpretation of the protests at subsequent meetings.[727]

Membership meetings of the basic party organizations at the V. I. Lenin Factories, held on June 4, similarly rejected the required self-criticism. Here, too, the communists did not feel responsible for the outbreak of the Monday protests. They did not see the causes of the protests in their own insufficient political work, but in the irresponsible actions of their superiors. Voices were raised here that it was not right to reproach the lower-ranking factory officials "for they have long been pointing out that the Central Committee, the Regional Committee and the Factory Committee have become alienated from the masses."[728] Some corruption scandals were again discussed. Some of the employees actually felt that this alienation applied not only to the local political leaders, but in some cases also to the central party leadership. The wife of one worker, for example, said of President Antonín Zápotocký: "What has Zápotocký done for us? He has climbed up on the workers' backs. He's the only one who has enough to eat, while we will soon be going begging."[729]

However, debate about the causes of the protests was also taking place in the Prague central authorities. On June 11, 1953, a meeting was held of the department heads of the Secretariat of the Central Committee with the chief secretaries of all the Regional Committees, at which Antonín Zápotocký analyzed the situation and laid down the essential guidelines for further action. In particular, he called for the strengthening of the authority of the unified trade unions among the workers, for the prevention of all strikes and protests organized in an anarchist manner outside the trade union organization, and for the consistent education of young people. In doing so, he put forward the idea that working-class youth had been over-indulged by the post-1948 regime and therefore found it difficult to cope with the disillusionment over their standard of living as they moved into productive life. The most important programmatic point of his speech, however, was a scathing critique of the cult of the worker, which had hitherto been officially cultivated. He declared, for example: "Of course we rely on the working class, without whom we would not have been able to make our goals and ideals a reality. But we must not assume that workers should be given leeway in everything; we must not create a cult of the worker."[730]

In addition, Zápotocký announced to those present the upcoming vetting of all party members. The search for the culprits of the protests had now spread quite systematically into the party ranks.[731] Following this decision, the Organizing Secretariat of the Central Committee sent a five-member commission to Pilsen on June 17 to investigate the protests and the overall operation of the West Bohemian Party apparatus.[732] Unlike the Pilsen officials and ordinary party members, the Central Committee saw the fundamental fault not in the reform itself, but in the negligence and misconduct of the party authorities in the region.[733]

On June 27, 1953, the bureau of the KSČ Regional Committee launched a review of all party and mass organizations and security forces in the region.[734] Each operative had to submit a written report on their activities during the currency reform. On June 30, the Regional Committee bureau held a vetting session, at which all those present were positively vetted.[735] By July 13, 1953, all the members and candidates of the Regional Committee, with the exception of the chief of the Regional StB Administration, Matěj Bálek, had also passed the vetting.[736] Bálek failed to submit a report on his activities at the time of the protests and was removed from his post the following day; only his poor health saved him from prosecution for a long-term abuse of official authority.[737] Similarly, the bureau of the KSČ Municipal Committee vetted all its members on July 14.[738] At that time, there was still hope among the ranks of the Pilsen officials that the protests would not lead to any significant personnel changes. They were soon to be disabused of this notion.

Simultaneously with the vetting process, official documents describing the causes of the demonstrations were drawn up by the central authorities. At a meeting of the Organizing Secretariat of the Central Committee, held on August 3, 1953, Bruno Köhler presented the report of a special commission regarding the events in Pilsen, and a draft resolution by which the Central Committee was to take a definitive political stance toward the Pilsen protests. The meeting was attended by three members of the KSČ Regional Committee in Pilsen and two members of the KSČ Municipal Committee in Pilsen. Both documents were provisionally approved, but their final wording was still to be confirmed by the Political Secretariat of the Central Committee. The commission's report saw the main causes of the protests in the poor performance of all Pilsen communists (from the Regional Committee down to the basic organizations) both before and during the protests. In particular, it emphasized the following errors:

> 1) The helplessness and impotence of the [KSČ] Regional Committee and the [KSČ] Municipal Committee in Pilsen, which manifested itself in their opportunistic surrender to the reactionaries. 2) The complete disarray of the management and coordination of actions against the rioters; and the refusal of the [KSČ] Municipal Committee, some leading officials of the [KSČ] Regional Committee, State Security officers and the People's Militias to take responsibility for their decisions and actions. 3) Political recklessness and complacency about some of the economic achievements of the V. I. Lenin Factories; overestimation of these achievements; and, above all, underestimation of the activities of the class enemies and ignorance of the political situation at the plants. 4) Distrust of some leading functionaries toward low-ranking Party members, and lack of faith in the strength of the Party organization. 5)Shortcomings in ideological, political and organizational work in the Pilsen region.[739]

Although the central leadership welcomed the fact that there was no bloodshed in Pilsen, it nevertheless considered the actions of the Pilsen security forces to have been insufficiently forceful.[740] The report concluded that the main fault lay at the ideological level; namely, that the Pilsen communists had long regarded the demonstrations as workers' protests and not as a hostile putsch and had therefore not intervened against them.[741] Ironically, the Central Committee reproached the Pilsen officials for measures it had officially prescribed (the tactics of unarmed persuasion). In addition to the party apparatus, the report also reproached the Regional National Committee in Pilsen for its complete inaction, since its employees had not come to the aid of the attacked Consolidated National Committee.[742] Criticism was also leveled at trade union leaders and leaders of the Czechoslovak Youth Union at the V.I. Lenin Factories, who had failed to take action against the protesters and had in fact been long remiss in the ideological education of young workers.[743]

Based on this analysis, the resolution on the events of June 1, 1953, established the binding interpretation of the Pilsen demonstrations as an attempted counter-revolutionary coup, made possible by the failure of all the party authorities in the city. "In connection with the implementation of the currency reform and the abolition of the ration system on foodstuffs and industrial goods, a serious reactionary uprising took place in the city of Pilsen on 1 June of this year. The reactionaries, who understood very well and perhaps better than many Party members in Pilsen that the currency reform was another heavy blow against the capitalist elements and a great step towards the building of socialism in our country, took advantage of the unpreparedness of our Party in Pilsen to organize demonstrations, provocations and violent riots. The events in Pilsen need not have occurred at all if the higher Party authorities, the Regional and Municipal Committee in Pilsen, had acted accordingly, both on political and organizational levels, and if all the Party organizations and members in Pilsen had fulfilled their duties toward the Party."[744]

The resolution explained the failure of the local party apparatus by the alleged long-term shortcomings in ideological work in the region:

> The behavior of these comrades is rooted in a misunderstanding of the principles of democratic centralism and Party discipline, which has led to a serious undermining of the Party organizations' readiness to act. There have even been opinions that the Central Committee should have informed the entire membership of the upcoming currency reform earlier, which would have undermined the Central Committee's leading role and given the reactionaries an opportunity to find out about the Central Committee's action before it was launched.[745]

Because of these failures, the resolution demanded that extensive personnel changes be made in the Pilsen Party leadership: "It will be necessary to draw organizational consequences for those who are unwilling and unable to perform adequate self-criticism, and for those whose criticism and self-criticism does not help to correct their mistakes and improve their Party involvement, and to replace them with comrades who give better guarantees of the correct implementation of Party policy."[746] The document thus put a decisive end to the disputes over the possible causes of the protests and opened the way for the pacification of opposition sentiments in the Pilsen Communist Party, whose leaders had hitherto resisted more vigorous self-criticism and personnel changes, despite the ongoing party vetting process.

The resolution was subsequently submitted to the Political Secretariat of the Central Committee,[747] which approved a revised version of its text on August 26, 1953. The new version incorporated the original text regarding the Pilsen demonstrations into the context of the June events in Berlin[748] and sought to demonstrate that the protests were allegedly directed by an international reaction from abroad.[749] The resolution was intended to serve as a binding ideological interpretation of the protests and was therefore discussed within all the basic party organizations in the Pilsen region, as well as in Regional Committees throughout the country. Along with adopting this document, the Political Secretariat of the Central Committee also confirmed its intention to remove some of the leading Pilsen officials and replace them with experienced operatives from Prague and other regions.[750]

The requirements posed by the resolution were discussed in Pilsen at an extraordinary meeting of the Regional Committee bureau on August 31, 1953. The prescribed necessity to find scapegoats turned the long-standing personal aversion between Chief Secretary Jan Hlína and Secretary Václav Kolena into an open political struggle. Jan Hlína also attempted to cover up his undeniable personal responsibility for the failure to handle the protests by sharply criticizing the leading officials of the security forces, especially the regional staff of the People's Militias.[751] He falsely claimed that he had issued an order to deploy the People's Militias at the outbreak of the demonstrations, which his subordinates allegedly did not respect. He pressured the senior officers of the regional staff of the People's Militias by emphasizing their real and alleged personal misconduct not to protest against this distorted information.[752]

However, the self-criticism collectively presented by members of the bureau at a meeting of the extended plenary session of the KSČ Regional Committee, held on September 7, 1953, was rejected as insufficient.[753] In fact, officials from the districts and basic organizations demanded personnel changes in the leadership of the Regional and Municipal Committees. They also called for the punishment of the unpopular Miloslav Mudra, the dismissal of the director of the V. I. Lenin Factories, František Brabec, and replacement of the entire regional staff of the People's Militias. Some debaters even called for the punishment of Ladislav Kopřiva, who had come to Pilsen on 1 June 1 to oversee the operations on behalf of the central authorities but failed to make any contribution toward resolving the situation.[754]

There was no way around it. Pressure from both above and below forced the party leadership in Pilsen to make significant personnel changes. The KSČ Municipal Committee was particularly affected by these changes, perhaps not entirely rightfully. At a meeting of the Municipal Committee bureau on September 9, several leading officials resigned,[755] and this purge was subsequently approved the following day by the Regional Committee bureau under the supervision of representatives of the Central Committee, Miroslav Pastyřík, Josef Paleček, and Jaroslav Samek. Chief Secretary Josef Žák was dismissed from his post, as were other officials of the Municipal Committee, Josef Král, František Netolický, Josef Mainzer, Juliána Dolejšová, and Václav Myslík.[756]

The purge also affected the senior officials of the Regional Committee. A violent controversy between Chief Secretary Jan Hlína and Secretary Václav Kolena ended with both declaring that they refused to work together and that one of them had to be dismissed. Kolena was an experienced pre-war official and his authority rivaled that of the young chief secretary Jan Hlína. The disputes between them came to a head during the investigation into the causes of the Pilsen protests. Hlína accused Kolena of an overbearing, distrustful attitude toward other officials. More specifically, he accused him of failing to hand over all the sealed instructions regarding the currency reform (for the People's Militias) at the end of May.[757] Kolena, on the other hand, accused Hlína of having waited like a coward and relying on assistance from Prague during the protests, and of unfairly bringing their personal antipathy out in the open afterward.[758]

After a long discussion, the bureau of the KSČ Regional Committee resolved to recommend to the Central Committee that Jan Hlína remain in his position as chief secretary and that Václav Kolena resign from his positions as secretary and member of the Regional Committee bureau.[759] Kolena's removal was not justified by any specific misconduct during the protest, but rather by his long-term inability to maintain positive interpersonal relations within the regional secretariat that would allow for peaceful cooperation.[760] At the same time, Kolena was seen as an important enough scapegoat to allow other operatives of the Regional Committee to continue in their positions.[761]

Subsequently, the regional leadership also dismissed some chiefs of security forces based on Hlína's criticism. The Committee acknowledged the dismissal of Matěj Bálek, chief of the Regional StB Administration; chief of the regional staff of the People's Militias Václav Drozda and operations officer František Čala were relieved of their positions. All three had failed in their task of coordinating the activities of the security forces during the demonstrations. Josef Mainzer, chairman of the Consolidated National Committee, and Václav Schejbal, the chief of staff of the Civil Defence Department at the Consolidated National Committee in Pilsen, who had allowed the delegation of protesters inside the Civil Defense offices in the City Hall on June 1, 1953, were dismissed from the Consolidated National Committee.[762] Unlike in the Municipal Committee, only a minimum of personnel changes occurred at the V. I. Lenin Factories. Miloslav Kuběna, chairman of the Factory Committee of the Czechoslovak Youth Union, was removed from his post,[763] and substitute member Stanislav Bejm was expelled from the factory council for supporting the protests.[764]

The Regional Committee also sought to shift part of the responsibility for the riots to the director of the V. I. Lenin Factories, František Brabec, who had allegedly "violated state discipline in the matter of payment of advances [for wages]; failed to explain the importance of the currency reform to the workforce; and failed to ensure that the department managers took care to maintain order in the workplaces on 1 June 1953."[765] The generally unpopular Miloslav Mudra, former chief secretary of the KSČ District Committee at the Škoda Works and current director of the 7th Main administration of the Ministry of Heavy Engineering in Prague, also faced imminent punishment.

However, punishment of these two officials fell within the purview of the Central Committee and local officials had no direct say in it.[766] Brabec was eventually dismissed from his post in April 1954.[767]

The Central Secretariat installed its own operatives in some of the vacated posts in order to be more closely informed about the events in the problematic region. It appointed the Pilsen official Karel Pešek secretary of the KSČ Regional Committee,[768] while promoting Jaroslav Samek, a present operative of the central party apparatus, to the position of chief secretary of the KSČ Municipal Committee, and appointed Alois Tvardík, also an operative of the Secretariat of the Central Committee, to carry out organizational duties at the V. I. Lenin Factories.[769] The chairmanship of the Consolidated National Committee was taken over by Josef Smolák, former chief secretary of the KSČ District Committee in the Pilsen suburbs.[770] Matěj Bálek was replaced as head of the Regional StB Administration by his deputy, Captain Josef Jindřich.[771]

After these personnel changes in party leadership, self-criticism of the remaining officials in the region was finally accepted. It happened at a meeting of the extended plenary session of the Regional Committee on September 25 in the presence of representatives of the Central Committee, Antonín Novotný and Miroslav Pastyřík.[772] The final report of the Regional Committee on the fulfillment of the Central Committee's demands was subsequently discussed by the Organizational Secretariat of the Central Committee of the Communist Party on February 9, 1954.[773]

NOTES

1. Jiří Pernes, *Snahy o překonání politicko-hospodářské krize v Československu v roce 1953* (Brno: ÚSD AV ČR, 2000), 14; Karel Kaplan, *Československo v letech 1953–1966* (Prague: Státní pedagogické nakladatelství, 1992), 5; Jirásek and Šůla, *Velká peněžní loupež*, 126.

2. ABS, f. H, sv. H-193, report from KS StB in Prague, sent to the Ministry of National Security, June 24, 1953; *NA*, f. Měnová reforma, Events in ČKD Stalingrad and Aero Vysočany, 1953; Ibid., ÚRO information bulletin, June 1, 1953; Jirásek and Šůla, *Velká peněžní loupež*, 99–101.

3. Karel Kaplan and Jan Váchová, eds., *Perzekuce po měnové reformě v Československu v roce 1953* (Prague: ÚSD AV ČR, 1993), 185–196.

4. *ABS*, f. A2/1, sv. 1586, report to the Minister for Railroads, July 21, 1953; Jirásek and Šůla, *Velká peněžní loupež*, s. 110–118.

5. ABS, f. H, sv. H-193, report on the events in Bohumín, Orlová and Ostrava, June 22, 1953.

6. Ibid., report from KS StB in České Budějovice, sent to the Ministry of National Security, June 24, 1953; *NA*, f. Měnová reforma, progress report regarding

the currency reform, based on telephone reports from the regions to the ÚV KSČ in the morning hours of June 1, 1953; Jiří Petráš, "Peněžní reforma 1953," *Sborník Archivu ministerstva vnitra* 3, no. 1 (2005): 141–171.

7. ABS, f. A2/1, sv. 1586, report to Minister of National Security Karol Bacílek regarding the intervention in Strakonice–Vimperk, June 6, 1953; Ibid., sv. 250, Ministry of Interior advisory board, May 30, 1957; Jirásek and Šůla, *Velká peněžní loupež*, 122–124.

8. Cf. Hron, *Změny v oblasti mezd.*

9. Pernes, "Neznámý dokument o peněžní reformě," 175.

10. Průcha, *Hospodářské a sociální dějiny Československa*, 110–114; Jirásek and Šůla, *Velká peněžní loupež*, 23–45; Věra Něměčková, "Československá měnová reforma 1945: Elegantní řešení nebo krach?," in *Peněžní reformy a zvraty na území České republiky (po roce 1918)*, ed. Jiří Knapík (Opava: Slezská univerzita v Opavě, 2005), 78–93.

11. Průcha, *Hospodářské a sociální dějiny Československa*, 278–281.

12. Cf. Hron, *Změny v oblasti mezd.*

13. Jirásek and Šůla, *Velká peněžní loupež*, 16–23.

14. NA, f. MF Praha, Tajné – peněžní reforma 1953, kart. 11, report on the currency reform and its final account, undated; Musilová, *Měnová reforma 1953*, 45–95.

15. Jirásek and Šůla, *Velká peněžní loupež*, 66–76.

16. Currency Reform Act of May 30, 1953, No. 41/1953 Sb.

17. Kaplan and Váchová, *Perzekuce po měnové reformě*, s. 117–118.

18. Musilová, *Měnová reforma 1953*, s. 22.

19. *NA*, f. MF Praha, Sekretariát, sig. F 72d-III, směrnice ministra financí o způsobu provedení peněžní reformy, May 30, 1953.

20. Průcha, *Hospodářské a sociální dějiny Československa*, 285–288.

21. NA, f. MF Praha, Tajné – peněžní reforma 1953, kart. 11, report on the currency reform and its final account, undated; Musilová, *Měnová reforma 1953*, 24–33.

22. Pernes, "Neznámý dokument o peněžní reformě," 174.

23. Kaplan, *Sociální souvislosti krizí*, 13.

24. NA, f. 1261/0/44, kart. 14, official correspondence, 1953, report from the OV KSČ Mladá Boleslav, sent to the KV KSČ in Prague, May 21, 1953.

25. Jirásek and Šůla, *Velká peněžní loupež*, s. 46–51.

26. NA, f. MF Praha, Tajné – peněžní reforma 1953, kart. 11, changes in wage and pension payment dates, August 26, 1953.

27. SOA Pilsen, f. ZKNV Pilsen, kart. 147, report from the KS SNB in Pilsen, sent to the KNV in Pilsen, May 20, 1953; ABS, f. KS MV Pilsen, sv. V-1131 Pilsen, Jindřich Kutzman's statement, taken by the KS StB in Pilsen, June 22, 1953.

28. *SOA Pilsen*, f. PV KSČ Škoda, kart. 18, inv. č. 4, Minutes of the meeting of the presidium of PV KSČ Škoda 7. 1. 1951; AMP, f. MV KSČ Pilsen, kart. 14, Minutes of the meeting of the MV KSČ v Plzni May 11, 1953.

29. PA Škoda, f. ZVIL, ZVIL 1513 PV 1297, report on a trade survey, May 20, 1953.

30. SOA Pilsen, f. ZKNV Pilsen, kart. 147, report from the KS SNB in Pilsen, sent to the KNV in Pilsen, May 20, 1953.

31. PA Škoda, f. ZVIL, ZVIL 1513 PV 1297, report on a trade survey, May 20, 1953.

32. SOA Pilsen, f. KV KSČ Pilsen, kart. 451, inv. č. 3603, leaflet listing arguments in favor of the currency reform, end of May/beginning of June, 1953.

33. *NA*, f. MF Praha, Tajné – peněžní reforma 1953, kart. 21, report on sales trends, May 27, 1953; Jirásek and Šůla, *Velká peněžní loupež v Československu 1953 aneb 50:1*, 55–56.

34. SOA Pilsen, f. ZKNV Pilsen, kart. 147, report from the KS SNB in Pilsen, sent to the KNV in Pilsen, May 20, 1953.

35. NA, f. MF Praha, Tajné – peněžní reforma 1953, kart. 21, report on sales trends, May 27, 1953.

36. SOkA v Blovicích, f. OS Pilsen, zn. 1T 141/1953, main hearing court file, July 15, 1953.

37. AMP, f. MV KSČ Pilsen, inv. č. 42, kart. 14, Minutes of the meeting of the MV KSČ in Pilsen, September 9, 1953.

38. NA, f. MF Praha, Tajné – peněžní reforma 1953, kart. 21, report on sales trends, May 27,1953.

39. SOA Pilsen, f. KV KSČ Pilsen, kart. 29, inv. č. 100, minutes of the plenary session of KV KSČ, June 2, 1953.

40. Ibid., f. ZKNV Pilsen, kart. 147, report from the KS SNB in Pilsen, sent to the KNV in Pilsen, end of May, 1953

41. Ibid., f. KV KSČ Pilsen, kart. 29, inv. č. 99, minutes of the extraordinary plenary session of KV KSČ, May 30, 1953.

42. *NA*, f. ÚV KSČ – 1261/0/3, sv. 36, a. j. 334/4, Minutes of the meeting of the presidium of ÚV KSČ, June 29, 1953.

43. *SOA Pilsen*, f. KV KSČ Pilsen, kart. 449, inv. č. 3603, telegram from KV KSČ to ÚV KSČ No. 303, May 30, 1953.

44. Ibid., kart. 450, inv. č. 3603, instruction from ÚV KSČ to KV KSČ in Pilsen, May 30, 1953.

45. Ibid., kart. 449, inv. č. 3603, telegram from KV KSČ to ÚV KSČ No. 308, June 1, 1953, 3.05 a.m.

46. ABS, f. 310, sv. 310–72–29, instruction from ÚV KSČ on preparations for the currency reform, May 30, 1953.

47. SOA Pilsen, f. KV KSČ v Plzni, kart. 449, inv. č. 3603, telegram from KV KSČ to ÚV KSČ No. 305, May 31, 1953, 5:10 hod; Ibid., telegram from KV KSČ to ÚV KSČ No. 307 May 31, 1953, 5.20 p.m.

48. SOA Pilsen, f. KV KSČ v Plzni, kart. 449, inv. č. 3603, telegram from KV KSČ to ÚV KSČ No. 307 May 31, 1953, 5.20 p.m.

49. Ibid., telegram from KV KSČ to ÚV KSČ No. 305 May 31, 1953, 5:10 hod.; Ibid., telegram from KV KSČ to ÚV KSČ No. 307 May 31, 1953, 5.20 p.m.; NA, f. Měnová reforma, report on enforcing the decision of the Party and government in the Stod region, May 30–June 5, 1953, of June 9, 1953.

50. SOA Pilsen, f. KV KSČ Pilsen, kart. 449, inv. č. 3603, telegram from KV KSČ to ÚV KSČ No. 307 May 31, 1953, 5.20 p.m.

51. ABS, f. 305, sv. 305–403–3, report on the general mood among the local population in relation to the currency reform, beginning of June, 1953, p. 206.

52. *NA*, f. ÚV KSČ – 1261/0/22, sv. 60, a. j. 163/4, Minutes of the meeting of the ÚV KSČ political secretariat, July 17, 1953; SOA Pilsen, f. KV KSČ Pilsen, kart. 449, inv. č. 3603, telegram from KV KSČ to ÚV KSČ No. 308, June 1, 1953, 3.05 a.m.

53. Ibid., kart. 450, inv. č. 3603, report of the KSČ base organizations members' meetings in the Pilsen-City district, May 31, 1953.

54. Ibid., kart. 449, inv. č. 3603, telegram from KV KSČ to ÚV KSČ No. 314, June 1, 1953, 10.50 p.m.; Ibid., telegram from KV KSČ to ÚV KSČ No. 307 May 31, 1953, 17:20 hod.

55. Ibid., telegram from KV KSČ to ÚV KSČ No. 305 May 31, 1953, 5:10 hod.

56. Ibid., kart. 450, inv. č. 3603, report of the KSČ base organizations members' meetings in the Pilsen-City district, May 31, 1953.

57. Ibid., kart. 450, inv. č. 3603, letter from the KSČ organization at the College of Mechanical and Electrical Engineering in Pilsen to ÚV KSČ, June 20, 1953.

58. Ibid., kart. 449, inv. č. 3603, report of the KSČ factory organizations members' meeting in the ZVIL electric steel finishing plant, June 1, 1953; Ibid., kart. 108, inv. č. 800, Minutes of the meeting of the KV KSČ executive committee, June 5, 1953; AMP, f. MV KSČ Pilsen, kart. 42, Minutes of the meeting of the MV KSČ executive committee in Pilsen, June 8, 1953.

59. SOA Pilsen, f. KV KSČ Pilsen, kart. 452, inv. č. 3603, Minutes of the meeting of the officials of CZV KSČ in ZVIL in Pilsen, September 10, 1953.

60. SOA Pilsen, f. KV KSČ Pilsen, kart. 449, inv. č. 3603, telegram from KV KSČ to ÚV KSČ No. 307, May 31, 1953, 5.20 p.m.

61. *NA*, f. MF Praha, Tajné – peněžní reforma 1953, kart. 21, report on implementing the government's decision on moving the wages and salaries payment dates, May 25, 1953; Ibid., report on sales trends, May 25, 1953; SOA Pilsen, f. KV KSČ Pilsen, kart. 29, inv. č. 103, Minutes of the extended plenary session of KV KSČ, September 7, 1953; Ibid., kart. 449, inv. č. 3603, report of the department of industry and construction of the secretariat of KV KSČ in Pilsen, 1953; Ibid., kart. 451, inv. č. 3603, report on the vetting of the members of the KV KSČ Regional Audit Commission in Pilsen, July 15, 1953.

62. Ibid., f. PV KSČ Škoda Pilsen, kart. 21, inv. č. 8, complaint from the KSČ ETD factory organization, workshop crew XI, sent to ÚV KSČ, May 21, 1953.

63. Ibid., f. KV KSČ Pilsen, kart. 450, inv. č. 3603, minutes of the extraordinary meeting of MV KSČ executive committee, June 3, 1953; NA, f. Měnová reforma, ÚRO information bulletin, June 1, 1953; Jirásek and Šůla, *Velká peněžní loupež v Československu*, 76–79.

64. SOA Pilsen, f. KV KSČ Pilsen, kart. 450, inv. č. 3603, minutes of the extraordinary meeting of MV KSČ executive committee, June 3, 1953.

65. Ibid., kart. 449, inv. č. 3603, report of the department of industry and construction of the secretariat of KV KSČ in Pilsen, 1953; Ibid., telegram from KV KSČ to ÚV KSČ No. 307, May 31, 1953, 17:20 hod.; SOkA v Blovicích, f. OS Pilsen, zn. 3T 274/1954, court file of the main hearing at the People's Court in Pilsen, October 13, 1954.

66. SOA Pilsen, f. KV KSČ Pilsen, kart. 449, inv. č. 3603, telegram from KV KSČ to ÚV KSČ No. 307, May 31, 1953, 5.20 p.m.; Ibid., kart. 450, inv. č. 3603, minutes of the extraordinary meeting of MV KSČ, June 3, 1953.

67. Ibid., kart. 449, inv. č. 3603, telegram from KV KSČ to ÚV KSČ No. 313, June 1, 1953, 5.45 p.m.; Ibid., telegram from KV KSČ to ÚV KSČ No. 323, June 5, 1953, 7.40 a.m.

68. Ibid., telegram from KV KSČ to ÚV KSČ No. 313, June 1, 1953, 5.45 p.m.

69. Ibid., telegram from KV KSČ to ÚV KSČ No. 314, June 1, 1953, 10.50 p.m.; Ibid., kart. 450, inv. č. 3603, report on extraordinary members' meetings of KSČ factory organizations in the ZVIL in Pilsen, June 4, 1953.

70. ABS, f. 305, sv. 305–403–3, report on the general mood among the local population in relation to the currency reform, beginning of June, 1953; McDermott, "Lidový odpor v komunistickém Československu," 209; Plamper, "Beyond Binaries," 64–80.

71. ABS, f. 305, sv. 305–403–3, report on the general mood among the local population in relation to the currency reform, beginning of June, 1953.

72. SOA Pilsen, f. KV KSČ Pilsen, kart. 449, inv. č. 3603, telegram from KV KSČ to ÚV KSČ No. 313, June 1, 1953, 5.45 p.m.

73. Ibid., telegram from KV KSČ to ÚV KSČ No. 307, May 31, 1953, 5.20 p.m.

74. Ibid., telegram from KV KSČ to ÚV KSČ No. 305, May 31, 1953, 5.10 p.m.

75. Ibid., report of the KSČ factory organizations members' meeting in the ZVIL electric steel finishing plant, June 1, 1953; Ibid., telegram from KV KSČ to ÚV KSČ No. 308, June 1, 1953, 3.05 a.m.

76. ABS, f. 310, sv. 310–72–31, instruction from the chiefs of main StB and VB administrations to all chiefs of KS StB and KS VB, May 28, 1953; Jirásek and Šůla, *Velká peněžní loupež*, 59–64.

77. ABS, f. 310, sv. 310–72–29, instructions from ÚV KSČ sent to all KV KSČ, May 30, 1953; *SOA Pilsen*, f. KV KSČ Pilsen, kart. 450, inv. č. 3603, instruction from ÚV KSČ sent to KV KSČ in Pilsen for the regional LM command, May 30, 1953; Jirásek and Šůla, *Velká peněžní loupež*, 59–76.

78. VÚA, f. MNO, inv. č. 1999, kart. 344, sig. 44/1/3, č.j. 004500 NGŠ 1953, summary report on the army's involvement in implementing the resolution of the ÚV KSČ and the government regarding the currency reform and abolition of the rationing system, June 9, 1953; *NA*, f. MF Praha, Tajné – peněžní reforma 1953, kart. 19, list of secured warehouses, April 11, 1953; Bílek, "Československá armáda," 71; Jirásek a Šůla, *Velká peněžní loupež*, 23–45.

79. NA, f. ÚV KSČ – 1261/0/12, sv. 43, a. j. 231/1, Minutes of the meeting of the ÚV KSČ organizational secretariat, August 3, 1953.

80. *NA*, f. MF Praha, Tajné – peněžní reforma 1953, kart. 11, report on the currency reform and its final account, undated; Musilová, *Měnová reforma 1953*, 45–95.

81. AČNB, f. SBČS, sig. S VII/a, kart. 149, reports from the exchange centers, sent by the SBČS regional branch in Pilsen to SBČS headquarters, July 1953; Ibid., kart. 161, reports of the SBČS regional branch in Pilsen on closing down the exchange centers, August 31, 1953, and September 21, 1953; Ibid., f. SBČS Pilsen, sig. 820/7 PL, , reports of the SBČS regional branch in Pilsen to the central issue and cash

administration, July 29, 1953; NA, f. MV NA, inv. č. 169, kart. 258, currency reform, situational report from the Pilsen region to the Ministry of Interior, June 3, 1953.

82. SOA Pilsen, f. KV KSČ Pilsen, kart. 449, inv. č. 3603, evaluation of SNB's work in Pilsen, 1953.

83. Ibid., report of the LM department to the KV KSČ secretariat in Pilsen, 1953.

84. ABS, f. 310, sv. 310–28–3, instruction of Minister of National Security Karol Bacílek to chiefs of all StB regional administraitons, May 28, 1953; Ibid., 310–72–31, instruction from the chief of StB central administration to all chiefs of KS StB, May 30, 1953.

85. ABS, f. 310, sv. 310–72–31, telegram from KS StB in Olomouc to StB Central administration in Prague, May 31, 1953.

86. SOA Pilsen, f. ZKNV Pilsen, kart. 147, report from KS VB in Pilsen to the chairman of the KNV in Pilsen, June 2, 1953; Ibid., f. KV KSČ Pilsen, kart. 451, inv. č. 3603, report from the Antonín Vintr, KS VB chief in Pilsen, to KV KSČ, September 17, 1953.

87. Ibid., kart. 449, inv. č. 3603, report of the LM department to the KV KSČ secretariat in Pilsen, 1953.

88. PA Škoda, f. ZVIL, ZVIL 524 PŘ 2003, directive of the ZVIL general headquarters in Pilsen regarding the extraordinary measures in the factory during the currency exchange, May 31, 1953; Directive of the Finance Minister of May 30, 1953, No. 159/1953 Ú. l., on the method of implementation of the currency reform.

89. SOkA v Blovicích, f. OS Pilsen, zn. 1T 141/1953, main hearing court file, July 15, 1953, testimony of Zdeňka Juzíková.

90. PA Škoda, f. ZVIL, ZVIL 524 PŘ 2003, directive of the ZVIL general headquarters in Pilsen regarding the extraordinary measures in the factory during the currency exchange, May 31, 1953.

91. ABS, f. 310, sv. 310–72–29, instruction from ÚV KSČ on preparations for the currency reform, May 30, 1953.

92. SOA Pilsen, f. KV KSČ Pilsen, kart. 449, inv. č. 3603, report of the KSČ factory organizations members' meeting in the ZVIL electric steel finishing plant, June 1, 1953.

93. NA, f. ÚV KSČ – 1481, sv. 15, a. j. 110, Minutes of the nationwide meeting of chief secretaries of KV KSČ, heads of the departments of ÚV KSČ and chief officials of mass organizations, held on June 11, 1953; speech by Antonín Zápotocký.

94. SOA Pilsen, f. KV KSČ Pilsen, kart. 449, inv. č. 3603, implementation of the currency reform and implementing the Party and government resolution to abolish the ration system on foodstuffs and industrial goods in the Pilsen region, 1953.

95. NA, f. Měnová reforma, report on the events in Pilsen on July 1, 1953, July 1953.

96. SOA Pilsen, f. KV KSČ Pilsen, kart. 449, inv. č. 3603, telegram from KV KSČ to ÚV KSČ No. 314, June 1, 1953, 10.50 p.m.

97. Čestmír Císař, *Paměti: nejen o zákulisí pražského jara* (Prague: SinCon, 2005), 405–438.

98. SOA Pilsen, f. KV KSČ Pilsen, kart. 449, inv. č. 3603, summary report on the activities of KV KSČ members and candidates, drawn up for the meeting of KV

KSČ in Pilsen , August 15, 1953; Ibid., report on the activities of Čestmír Císař, June 1, 1953, from 1953.

99. Ibid., report of the department of industry and construction of the secretariat of KV KSČ in Pilsen, 1953; Ibid., kart. 450, inv. č. 3603, minutes of the extraordinary meeting of MV KSČ June 3, 1953; NA, f. ÚV KSČ – 1261/0/12, sv. 43, a. j. 231/1, Minutes of the meeting of the ÚV KSČ organizational secretariat, August 3, 1953; AMP, f. MV KSČ Pilsen, inv. č. 498, kart. 42, Minutes of the meeting of the MV KSČ executive committee in Pilsen July 14, 1953.

100. SOA Pilsen, f. KV KSČ Pilsen, kart. 451, inv. č. 3603, report on the activities of Robert Fürbach, July 4, 1953.

101. Ibid., f. ZKNV Pilsen, kart. 147, report of the KS VB in Pilsen to the chairman of the KNV in Pilsen, June 2, 1953; Ibid., f. KV KSČ Pilsen, kart. 450, inv. č. 3603, minutes of the extraordinary meeting of MV KSČ executive committee June 3, 1953.

102. Ibid., kart. 449, inv. č. 3603, telegram from KV KSČ to ÚV KSČ No. 314, June 1, 1953, 10.50 p.m.; Ibid., report on the activities of Robert Fürbach, July 4, 1953.

103. Ibid., kart. 451, inv. č. 3603, report on the activities of Robert Fürbach, July 4, 1953; PA Škoda, f. ZVIL, ZVIL 1515 PV 1287, minutes of the plenary session of ZR ZVIL 26. 8. 1953.

104. SOkA v Blovicích, f. OS Pilsen, zn. 1T 144/1953, main hearing court file, July 17, 1953, testimony of Antonín Meca.

105. SOA Pilsen, f. KV KSČ Pilsen, kart. 451, inv. č. 3603, report on the activities of Robert Fürbach, July 4, 1953; Ibid., kart. 449, inv. č. 3603, report on the activities of Robert Fürbach, July 4, 1953.

106. Ibid., telegram from KV KSČ to ÚV KSČ No. 310, June 1, 1953, 10.00 a.m.; Ibid., telegram from KV KSČ to ÚV KSČ No. 314, June 1, 1953, 10.50 p.m.

107. Ibid., kart. 450, inv. č. 3603, minutes of the extraordinary meeting of MV KSČ June 3, 1953.

108. Ibid., kart. 451, inv. č. 3603, report on the activities of Robert Fürbach, July 4, 1953.

109. PA Škoda, f. ZVIL, ZVIL 1074, supplement to the statement of employee Poláková, June 10, 1953.

110. ABS, f. KS MV Pilsen, sv. V-1131 Pilsen, Jindřich Kutzman's statement, taken by the KS StB in Pilsen, June 10, 1953.

111. PA Škoda, f. ZVIL, ZVIL 1455 PV 109, evaluation of the work of ZR ZVIL during the events of June 1, 1953, from 1953; Ibid., ZVIL 203, Petr Svoboda's statement, June 1953; ABS, f. KS MV Pilsen, sv. V-1131 Pilsen, Jindřich Kutzman's statement, taken by the KS StB in Pilsen, June 10, 1953; Skála, "Měnová reforma," 625.

112. SOA Pilsen, f. KV KSČ Pilsen, kart. 449, inv. č. 3603 implementation of the currency reform and implementing the Party and government resolution to abolish the ration system on foodstuffs and industrial goods in the Pilsen region, 1953.

113. SOA Pilsen, f. KV KSČ Pilsen, kart. 451, inv. č. 3603, report on the activities of Josef Žák, July 4, 1953; PA Škoda, f. ZVIL, ZVIL 203, Petr Svoboda's statement,

June 1953; SOkA v Blovicích, f. OS Pilsen, zn. 1T 136/1953, court file of the main hearing at the People's Court in Pilsen, July 13, 1953, testimony of Josef Hájek.

114. NA, f. Měnová reforma, report on the business trip of the employees of the State Planning Office to the ZVIL in Pilsen, June 1, 1953, from June 5, 1953.

115. SOA Pilsen, f. KV KSČ Pilsen, kart. 449, inv. č. 3603, telegram from KV KSČ to ÚV KSČ No. 314, June 1, 1953, 10.50 p.m.

116. SOkA v Blovicích, f. OS Pilsen, zn. 2T 157/1953, verdict of the People's Court in Pilsen, October 13, 1953; Ibid., zn. 2T 170/1953, Alfons Kroupa's statement, taken by the VB District Department in Pilsen, June 25, 1953; ABS, f. KS MV Pilsen, sv. V-1131 Pilsen, Jindřich Kutzman's statement, taken by the KS StB in Pilsen, June 4, 1953; Ibid., Jindřich Kutzman's statement, taken by the KS StB in Pilsen, June 10, 1953.

117. PA Škoda, f. ZVIL, ZVIL 1455 PV 109, evaluation of the work of ZR ZVIL during the events of June 1, 1953, from 1953.

118. SOA Pilsen, f. KV KSČ Pilsen, kart. 449, inv. č. 3603, report from the meeting of the KSČ factory organization, department Engineering II of the ZVIL, June 4, 1953.

119. SOkA v Blovicích, f. OS Pilsen, zn. 1T 139/1953, court file of the main hearing, July14, 1953, testimony of Miroslav Neužil.

120. NA, f. ÚV KSČ – 1261/0/12, sv. 43, a. j. 231/1, Minutes of the meeting of the ÚV KSČ organizational secretariat, August 3, 1953.

121. SOA Pilsen, f. KV KSČ Pilsen, kart. 449, inv. č. 3603, report of the 2nd department to the KV KSČ secretariat in Pilsen, 1953.

122. Ibid., kart. 450, inv. č. 3603, minutes of the extraordinary meeting of MV KSČ June 3, 1953.

123. SOA Pilsen, f. ZKNV Pilsen, kart. 147, report of the KS VB in Pilsen to the KNV chairman in Pilsen, June 2, 1953; Ibid., f. KV KSČ Pilsen, kart. 450, inv. č. 3603, minutes of the extraordinary meeting of MV KSČ executive committee, June 3, 1953.

124. Ibid., kart. 449, inv. č. 3603, report of the agricultural department of KV KSČ in Pilsen, 1953.

125. NA, f. ÚV KSČ – 1261/2/1, sv. 378, a. j. 2292, report on the survey of the Party members' work in Pilsen with regard to the events of June 1, 1953, from 1953.

126. SOkA v Blovicích, f. OS Pilsen, zn. 1T 153/1953, court file of the main hearing, July 22, 1953, testimony of Illja Nazarkevyč; Ilja Nazarkevyč, Illja, "Jsme národ Masarykův," *Plzeňský deník*, June 4, 1994, 3.

127. SOkA v Blovicích, f. OS Pilsen, zn. 1T 149/1953, court file of the main hearing, July 20, 1953, testimony of Bohumil Vaník.

128. SOA Pilsen, f. ZKNV Pilsen, kart. 147, report of the KS VB in Pilsen to the KNV chairman in Pilsen, June 2, 1953; Ibid., f. KV KSČ Pilsen, kart. 449, inv. č. 3603, telegram from KV KSČ sent by ÚV KSČ to the LM commander-in-chief's staff, June 1, 1953; Ibid., telegram from KV KSČ to ÚV KSČ No. 314, June 1, 1953, 10.50 p.m.; Ibid., report of the LM department to the KV KSČ secretariat in Pilsen, 1953; Ibid., kart. 451, inv. č. 3603, report on the activities of Josef Žák, July 4, 1953; NA, f. Měnová reforma, progress report regarding the currency reform, based

on telephone reports from the regions to the ÚV KSČ in the morning hours of June 1, 1953.

129. SOkA v Blovicích, f. OS Pilsen, zn. 1T 146/1953, Václav Engenvald's statement, taken by the KS MV 2, June 2, 1954; Ibid., zn. 1T 144/1953, court file of the main hearing, July 17, 1953, testimony of Antonín Meca.

130. PA Škoda, f. ZVIL, ZVIL 203, results of the investigation of employees who were not present in their workplace (assembly plant) on June 1, 1953, from 1953; SOkA v Blovicích, f. OS Pilsen, zn. 1T 136/1953, court file of the main hearing at the People's Court in Pilsen, July 13, 1953, testimony of Josef Hájek; Ibid., court file of the main hearing at the People's Court in Pilsen, July 13, 1953, testimony of Jaroslav Reichel.

131. PA Škoda, f. ZVIL, ZVIL 1455 PV 109, evaluation of the work of ZR ZVIL during the events of June 1, 1953, from 1953.

132. SOkA v Blovicích, f. OS Pilsen, zn. 1 T 149/1953, court file of the main hearing, July 20, 1953, testimony of Vojtěch Kasík.

133. Ibid., zn. 1T 174/1953, report of the interrogation of Ladislav Hobl at the VB Kozolupy district department, July 17, 1953.

134. SOA Pilsen, f. KV KSČ Pilsen, kart. 449, inv. č. 3603, telegram from KV KSČ to ÚV KSČ No. 311, June 1, 1953, 10.45 a.m.; VÚA, f. MNO, inv. č. 1999, kart. 344, sig. 44/1/3, č.j. 004500 NGŠ 1953, report of Lt. Col. Vojtěch Dolníček, deputy chief of the general staff, on the situation in Pilsen, May 30, – June 3, 1953, June 6, 1953.

135. Heumos, *Vyhrňme si rukávy*, 71; McDermott, "Lidový odpor v komunistickém Československu," 224.

136. SOA Pilsen, f. KV KSČ Pilsen, kart. 449, inv. č. 3603, telegram from KV KSČ to ÚV KSČ No. 309, June 1, 1953, 9:30 a.m.; Ibid., report on the activities of Alois Peiskar, June 1, 1953, from 1953.

137. Ibid., implementation of the currency reform and implementing the Party and government resolution to abolish the ration system on foodstuffs and industrial goods in the Pilsen region, 1953.

138. Ibid., telegram from KV KSČ to ÚV KSČ No. 311, June 1, 1953, 10:45 a.m.

139. AMP, f. MV KSČ Pilsen, kart. 42, Minutes of the meeting of the MV KSČ executive committee in Pilsen, July 14, 1953.

140. SOA Pilsen, f. KV KSČ Pilsen, kart. 450, inv. č. 3603, report of the extraordinary members' meeting of the ZO KSČ Osvobozená domácnost, June 4, 1953.

141. SOkA v Blovicích, f. OS Pilsen, zn. 1T 142/1953, court file of the main hearing, 16. 7. 1953, testimony of Marie Kreidlová; Ibid., zn. 1T 140/1953, verdict of the People's Court in Pilsen, July 14, 1953; Štěpánek, *Utajené povstání 1953*, 15.

142. SOkA v Blovicích, f. OS Pilsen, zn. 1T 151/1953, court file of the main hearing, 21. 1. 1953, testimony of Drahomír Bokr; Ibid., zn. 1T 136/1953, court file from the People's Court in Pilsen 8. 7. 1953, testimony of Eva Moravičová; Ibid., zn. 1T 144/1953, statement taken with Josef Hegner, June 5, 1953.

143. Martinovský, ed., *Dějiny Plzně v datech*, s. 296.

144. Ibid., s. 366–368.

145. Ibid., s. 429.

146. SOkA v Blovicích, f. OS Pilsen, zn. 1T 144/1953, court file of the main hearing, July 17, 1953, testimony of Josef Lhoták.

147. SOA Pilsen, f. ZKNV Pilsen, kart. 147, report of the JNV chairman in Pilsen to chairman of the KNV in Pilsen, June 1, 1953.

148. Ibid.

149. SOkA v Blovicích, f. OS Plzeň, zn. 1T 153/1953, court file of the main hearing, July 22, 1953, testimony of Josef Šilhánek.

150. Ibid., zn. 1T 142/1953, court file of the main hearing, July 16, 1953, testimony of Bohumil Blahovec.

151. Ibid., zn. 1T 144/1953, court file of the main hearing, July 17, 1953, testimony of Antonín Meca.

152. Ibid., zn. 1T 146/1953, court file of the main hearing, July 20, 1953, testimony of Jan Johánek.

153. Ibid., zn. 1T 144/1953, court file of the main hearing, July 17, 1953, testimony of Josef Popek.

154. Ibid., zn. 1T 136/1953, court file of the main hearing at the People's Court in Pilsen, July 13, 1953, testimony of Václav Jílek; Šlouf, "Byly Plzeňské demonstrace," 85–96.

155. SOA Pilsen, f. KV KSČ Pilsen, kart. 451, inv. č. 3603, report on the activities of Josef Žák, July 4, 1953; NA, f. ÚV KSČ – 1261/0/12, sv. 43, a. j. 231/1, Minutes of the meeting of the ÚV KSČ organizational secretariat, August 3, 1953.

156. SOkA v Blovicích, f. OS Pilsen, zn. 1T 139/1953, court file of the main hearing, July 14, 1953, testimony of Jaroslav Treml.

157. SOA Pilsen, f. KV KSČ Pilsen, kart. 451, inv. č. 3603, testimony of Jaroslav Heřman, from 1953.

158. Ibid., f. ZKNV Pilsen, kart. 147, report of the JNV chairman in Pilsen to chairman of the KNV in Pilsen, June 1, 1953.

159. SOkA v Blovicích, f. OS Pilsen, zn. 1T 144/1953, court file of the main hearing, July 17, 1953, testimony of Břetislava Štekla.

160. SOA Pilsen, f. ZKNV Pilsen, kart. 147, report of the JNV chairman in Pilsen to chairman of the KNV in Pilsen, June 1, 1953.

161. Ibid., f. KV KSČ Pilsen, kart. 449, inv. č. 3603, telegram from KV KSČ to ÚV KSČ No. 314, June 1, 1953, 10.50 p.m.

162. SOkA v Blovicích, f. OS Pilsen, zn. 1T 144/1953, Josef Hegner's statement, June 5, 1953.

163. Ibid., court file of the main hearing, July 17, 1953, testimony of Antonín Meca.

164. SOA Pilsen, f. KV KSČ Pilsen, kart. 450, inv. č. 3603, report of the extraordinary members' meeting of the ZO KSČ Osvobozená domácnost, June 4, 1953.

165. SOkA v Blovicích, f. OS Pilsen, zn. 1T 142/1953, court file of the main hearing, 16. 7. 1953, testimony of Bohumil Blahovec.

166. SOA Pilsen, f. ZKNV Pilsen, kart. 147, report of the JNV chairman in Pilsen to chairman of the KNV in Pilsen, June 1, 1953; Ibid., f. KV KSČ Pilsen, kart. 449, inv. č. 3603, telegram from KV KSČ to ÚV KSČ No. 314, June 1, 1953, 10.50 p.m.

167. SOkA v Blovicích, f. OS Pilsen, zn. 1T 144/1953, court file of the main hearing, July 17, 1953, testimony of Antonín Meca; Ibid., zn. 1T 136/1953, žaloba

okresního prokurátora Lidovému soudu in Pilsen 7. 7. 1953; Ibid., zn. 1T 148/1953, verdict of the People's Court in Pilsen July 21, 1953.

168. SOA Pilsen, f. KV KSČ Pilsen, kart. 450, inv. č. 3603, comments on the events in Pilsen, June 1, 1953, undated; NA, f. ÚV KSČ – 1261/0/12, sv. 43, a. j. 231/1, Minutes of the meeting of the ÚV KSČ organizational secretariat, August 3, 1953.

169. SOA Pilsen, f. ZKNV Pilsen, kart. 147, report of the JNV chairman in Pilsen to chairman of the KNV in Pilsen, June 1, 1953; Ibid., f. KV KSČ Pilsen, kart. 449, inv. č. 3603, telegram from KV KSČ to ÚV KSČ No. 314, June 1, 1953, 10.50 p.m.; SOkA v Blovicích, f. OS Pilsen, zn. 1T 144/1953, Josef Hegner's statement, June 5, 1953; Ibid., zn. 1T 140/1953, verdict of the People's Court in Pilsen, July 14, 1953.

170. Ibid., zn. 1T 146/1953, court file of the main hearing, July 20, 1953, testimony of Bohuslav Pikart.

171. SOA Pilsen, f. KV KSČ Pilsen, kart. 450, inv. č. 3603, minutes of the extraordinary meeting of MV KSČ executive committee June 3, 1953, speech by Josef Mainzer; Ibid., f. ZKNV Pilsen, kart. 147, report of the JNV chairman in Pilsen to chairman of the KNV in Pilsen, June 1, 1953; Ibid., f. KV KSČ Pilsen, kart. 451, inv. č. 3603, report on the activities of MP Ivo Skála, June 1, 1953, of June 9, 1953.

172. AMP, f. JNV Pilsen, kart. 117, vettings of the JNV employees, September 1, 1953.

173. SOA Pilsen, f. ZKNV Pilsen, kart. 147, report of the JNV chairman in Pilsen to chairman of the KNV in Pilsen, June 4, 1953.

174. Ibid., f. KV KSČ Pilsen, kart. 451, inv. č. 3603, report on the activities of MP Ivo Skála, June 1, 1953, of June 9, 1953; SOkA v Blovicích, f. OS Pilsen, zn. 1T 159/1953, Eva Hrůzová's statement, taken by the KS StB in Pilsen, June 1, 1953.

175. SOA Pilsen, f. KV KSČ Pilsen, kart. 451, inv. č. 3603, report on the activities of MP Ivo Skála, June 1, 1953, of June 9, 1953.

176. SOkA v Blovicích, f. OS Pilsen, zn. 1T 146/1953, court file of the main hearing, July 20, 1953, testimony of Bohuslav Pikart.

177. SOA Pilsen, f. KV KSČ Pilsen, kart. 451, inv. č. 3603, report on the activities of MP Ivo Skála, June 1, 1953, of June 9,1953.

178. SOkA v Blovicích, f. OS Pilsen, zn. 1T 139/1953, court file of the main hearing, July 14, 1953, testimony of Jaroslav Treml; Ibid., zn. 1T 153/1953, action of the District Prosecutor in Pilsen filed with the People's Court in Pilsen, July 18, 1953.

179. Ibid., zn. 1T 139/1953, court file of the main hearing, July 14, 1953, testimony of Jaroslav Treml.

180. ABS, f. A8/1, sv. 1218, report on the interrogation of Ludvík Rataj for the Ministry of Interior inspectorate, July 6, 1964.

181. SOkA v Blovicích, f. OS Pilsen, zn. 1T 153/1953, court file of the main hearing, July 22, 1953, testimony of Ilja Nazarkevyč.

182. NA, f. MV NA, inv. č. 169, kart. 258, report of Václav Schejbal, Civilian Defense commander with the JVN in Pilsen to the Ministry of Interior, June 1, 1953.

183. SOkA v Blovicích, f. OS Pilsen, zn. 1T 138/1953, court file of the main hearing, July 13, 1953, testimony of Karel Doležal; Ibid., zn. 1T 149/1953, court file of

the main hearing, July 20, 1953, testimony of Vojtěch Kasík; Ibid., zn. 1T 145/1953, court file of the main hearing, July 17, testimony of Jan Holeček.

184. Jirásek and Šůla, *Velká peněžní loupež*, 101–103; František Hykeš, "Dramatické události staré čtyřicet let," *Haló noviny*, June 2, 1993, 1–5.

185. SOA Pilsen, f. ZKNV Pilsen, kart. 147, report of the JNV chairman in Pilsen to chairman of the KNV in Pilsen, June 1, 1953.

186. SOkA v Blovicích, f. OS Pilsen, zn. 1T 149/1953, court file of the main hearing, July 20, 1953, testimony of Bohumil Vaník.

187. Ibid., court file of the main hearing, July 20, 1953, testimony of Vojtěch Kasík.

188. Ibid., zn. 1T 146/1953, court file of the main hearing, July 20, 1953, testimony of Libuše Rubášová; Ibid., zn. 1T 145/1953, court file of the main hearing, July 17, 1953, testimony of Jan Holeček; Šlouf, "Byly Plzeňské demonstrace," 85–96.

189. SOkA v Blovicích, f. OS Pilsen, zn. 1T 144/1953, Josef Hegner's statement, June 5, 1953.

190. Ibid., Josef Fencl's statement for the Ministry of Interior inspectorate, June 2, 1964; Ibid., f. A2/1, Ministry of Interior advisory board, May 30, 1957, report of the military counter-intelligence on the Pilsen protests, June 1953; SOkA v Blovicích, f. OS Pilsen, zn. 1T 151/1953, court file of the main hearing, January 21, 1953, testimony of František Moravec; Ibid., zn. 1T 159/1953, Eva Hrůzová's statement, taken by the KS StB in Pilsen, June 13, 1953; Ibid., zn. 1T 160/1953, Václav Brůha's statement, taken by the KS StB in Pilsen, June 8, 1956; Michaela Pánková, "První vzpoura proti vládě zla: Defenestrace Stalina a Gottwalda z Plzeňské radnice," *Lidová demokracie*, June 1, 1990, 3.

191. Ibid., zn. 1T 141/1953, action filed by the District Prosecutor in Pilsen, July 10, 1953; *ABS*, f. A8/1, sv. 1218, report from the interrogation of Jan Ulče for the Ministry of Interior inspectorate, July 51964.

192. SOA Pilsen, f. KV KSČ Pilsen, kart. 451, inv. č. 3603, minutes of the extraordinary meeting of the KV KSČ executive committee, September 10, 1953.

193. SOkA v Blovicích, f. OS Plzeň, zn. 1T 144/1953, court file of the main hearing, July 17, 1953, testimony of Josef Lhoták.

194. Ibid., zn. 1T 141/1953, verdict of the People's Court in Pilsen, July 14, 1953.

195. Ibid., zn. 1T 160/1953, court file of the main hearing, August 6, 1953, testimony of Josef Fencl.

196. Ibid., zn. 1T 153/1953, court file of the main hearing, July 22, 1953, testimonies of Josef Fous and Václav Oliberius.

197. Ibid., zn. 1T 144/1953, court file of the main hearing, July 17, 1953, testimony of Josef Popek; Ibid., zn. 1T 151/1953, court file of the main hearing, January 21, 1953, testimony of Drahomír Bokr.

198. Ibid., zn. 1T 144/1953, Josef Hegner's statement, June 5, 1953; Ibid., zn. 1T 149/1953, court file of the main hearing, July 20, 1953, testimony of Alois Kučera; Ibid., zn. 1T 142/1953, court file of the main hearing, July 16, 1953, testimony of Marie Kreidlová.

199. Ibid., zn. 1T 159/1953, Eva Hrůzová's statement, taken by the KS StB in Pilsen, June 1, 1953.

200. Ibid., zn. 1T 136/1953, court file of the main hearing at the People's Court in Pilsen, July 13, 1953, testimony of Bartoloměj Chudoba.

201. Ibid., court file of the main hearing at the People's Court in Pilsen, July 13, 1953, testimony of Václav Melka.

202. Ibid., court file of the main hearing at the People's Court in Pilsen, July 13, 1953, testimony of Margarita Kuráňová.

203. Ibid., zn. 1T 138/1953, court file of the main hearing, July 13, 1953, testimony of Bohumil Ulč.

204. Ibid., zn. 1T 149/1953, court file of the main hearing, July 20, 1953, testimony of Alois Kučera.

205. Ibid., zn. 1T 138/1953, court file of the main hearing, July 13, 1953, testimony of Libuše Dlouhá.

206. Ibid., zn. 1T 144/1953, court file of the main hearing, July 17, 1953, testimony of Josef Popek.

207. Ibid., zn. 1T 142/1953, court file of the main hearing, 16. 7. 1953, testimony of Rudolf Krüger.

208. Ibid., zn. 1T 149/1953, court file of the main hearing, July 20, 1953, testimony of Bohumil Vaník.

209. Ibid., court file of the main hearing, July 20, 1953, testimony of Miloslav Khek.

210. Ibid., zn. 1T 138/1953, court file of the main hearing, July 13, 1953, testimony of Oldřich Bartásek.

211. Ibid., zn. 1T 146/1953, court file of the main hearing, July 20, 1953, testimony of Vladimír Matoušek; Ibid., zn. 1T 149/1953, court file of the main hearing, July 20, 1953, testimony of Bohumil Vaník; ABS, f. A2/1, Ministry of Interior advisory board, May 30, 1957, report of the military counter-intelligence on the Pilsen protests, June 1953.

212. SOkA v Blovicích, f. OS Pilsen, zn. 1T 140/1953, action filed by the District Prosecutor, July 9, 1953; Ibid., zn. 1T 153/1953, court file of the main hearing, July 22, 1953, testimony of Václav Dobízl; Ibid., zn. 3T 148/1953, report from the interrogation of Josef Vacek at the District Prosecutor's office in Pilsen 17. 8. 1953.

213. SOA Pilsen, f. ZKNV Pilsen, kart. 147, report of the JNV chairman in Pilsen to chairman of the KNV in Pilsen, June 1, 1953.

214. SOkA v Blovicích, f. OS Pilsen, zn. 1T 139/1953, court file of the main hearing, July 14, 1953, testimonies of Jaroslav Voják and Josef Žežulka; Ibid., zn. 1T 143/1953, court file of the main hearing, July 16, 1953, testimony of Adolf Jílek; ABS, f. A8/1, sv. 1218, Josef Fencl's statement for the Ministry of Interior inspectorate, June 2, 1964; Ibid., Antonín Votava's statement for the Ministry of Interior inspectorate, July 7, 1964; Šlouf, "Byly Plzeňské demonstrace," 85–96.

215. SOkA v Blovicích, f. OS Pilsen, zn. 1T 139/1953, court file of the main hearing, July 14, 1953, testimony of Jaroslav Treml; Ibid., zn. 1T 145/1953, court file of the main hearing, July 17, 1953, testimony of Jan Holeček.

216. Ibid., zn. 1T 139/1953, court file of the main hearing, July 14, 1953, testimonies of Bohumil Pfeffer and Viktor Pospíšil.

217. Ibid., zn. 1T 143/1953, court file of the main hearing, 16. 7. 1953, testimony of Adolf Jílek; Ibid., zn. 1T 146/1953, court file of the main hearing, July 20, 1953,

testimony of Libuše Rubášová; ABS, f. A8/1, sv. 1218, Josef Fencl's statement for the Ministry of Interior inspectorate, June 2, 1964.

218. SOkA v Blovicích, f. OS Pilsen, zn. 1T 139/1953, court file of the main hearing, July 14, 1953, testimony of Josef Žežulka.

219. Ulč, *The Judge in a Communist State*, 122; Skála, "Měnová reforma," 628.

220. SOkA v Blovicích, f. OS Pilsen, zn. 1T 153/1953, court file of the main hearing, July 22, 1953, testimony of Jaroslav Mikulášek; Ibid., zn. 1T 149/1953, court file of the main hearing, July 20, 1953, testimony of Josef Kadlec; *ABS*, f. A8/1, sv. 1218, Josef Fencl's statement for the Ministry of Interior inspectorate, June 2, 1964; Šlouf, "Byly Plzeňské demonstrace," 85–96.

221. SOkA v Blovicích, f. OS Pilsen, zn. 1T 146/1953, court file of the main hearing, July 20, 1953, testimony of Libuše Rubášová; Ibid., zn. 1T 145/1953, court file of the main hearing, July 17, 1953, testimony of Libuše Fujová.

222. Ulč, *The Judge in a Communist State*, 119.

223. SOkA v Blovicích, f. OS Pilsen, zn. 1T 144/1953, reports on the damages and injuries suffered by security forces members during the protests of June 1, 1953 in Pilsen, July 1953.

224. Prokop Tomek, "Vývoj československého vězeňství v letech 1948–1989," in *Za demokracii a svobodu III*: *Třetí (protikomunistický) odboj*, ed. Lukáš Babka a Václav Weber (Hradec Králové: Univerzita Hradec Králové, 2002), 47.

225. SOkA v Blovicích, f. OS Pilsen, zn. 1T 159/1953, statement of SNB officer František Lausecker, taken by the KS StB in Pilsen, July 10, 1953.

226. Ibid., zn. 1T 140/1953, action filed by the District Prosecutor, July 9, 1953.

227. Ibid., zn. 1T 139/1953, court file of the main hearing, July 14, 1953, testimony of Jaroslav Treml.

228. Ibid., zn. 1T 153/1953, court file of the main hearing, July 22, 1953, testimonies of Ilja Nazarkevyč a Alexandr Slavík; ABS, f. KS MV Pilsen, V-868, testimony of Ilja Nazarkevyč.

229. SOkA v Blovicích, f. OS Plzeň, zn. 1T 148/1953, verdict of the People's Court in Pilsen, July 21, 1953.

230. Ibid., zn. 1T 136/1953, court file of the main hearing at the People's Court in Pilsen, July 13, 1953, testimony of Karel Giebitz; Ibid., zn. 1T 145/1953, court file of the main hearing, July 17, 1953, testimony of Jan Holeček; Ibid., zn. 1T 153/1953, court file of the main hearing, July 22, 1953, testimony of Roman Hron.

231. Ibid., zn. 1T 146/1953, court file of the main hearing, July 20, 1953, testimony of Václav Engenvald.

232. ABS, f. A2/1, Ministry of Interior advisory board, May 30, 1957, report of the military counter-intelligence on the Pilsen protests, June 1953; SOA Pilsen, f. KV KSČ Pilsen, kart. 451, inv. č. 3603, testimony of Jaroslav Heřman, from 1953.

233. Jirásek and Šůla, *Velká peněžní loupež*, 101–103; Ondřej Neff, "Oprátka pro Masaryka," *Mladá fronta*, March 3, 1990, 1–2.

234. AMP, f. MV KSČ Pilsen, inv. č. 498, kart. 42, Minutes of the meeting of the MV KSČ executive committee in Pilsen July 14, 1953, report on the activities of Josef Mainzer.

235. SOkA v Blovicích, f. OS Pilsen, zn. 1T 159/1953, Eva Hrůzová's statement, taken by the KS StB in Pilsen, 5. 6. 1953; Ibid., zn. 1T 138/1953, court file of the main hearing, July 13, 1953, testimony of Josef Jílek.

236. Ibid., zn. 1T 140/1953, action filed by the District Prosecutor, July 9, 1953; Ibid., verdict of the People's Court in Pilsen, July 14, 1953.

237. Ibid., zn. 1T 136/1953, court file of the main hearing at the People's Court in Pilsen, July 13, 1953, testiomonies of Václav Jílek and Josef Hájek; Ibid., zn. 1T 136/1953, court file of the main hearing, July 13, 1953, testimony of Jaroslav Reichl; Ibid., zn. 1T 149/1953, court file of the main hearing, July 20, 1953, testimony of Václav Malík.

238. SOA Pilsen, f. ZKNV Pilsen, kart. 147, report of the KS VB in Pilsen to the chairman of the KNV in Pilsen, June 2, 1953; Ibid., f. KV KSČ Pilsen, kart. 451, inv. č. 3603, report of the KS VB in Pilsen to the KV KSČ in Pilsen, June 2, 1953.

239. SOkA v Blovicích, f. OS Pilsen, zn. 1T 176/1953, verdict of the People's Court in Pilsen August 27, 1953.

240. Jirásek and Šůla, *Velká peněžní loupež*, 154.

241. SOkA v Blovicích, f. OS Pilsen, zn. 1T 149/1953, court file of the main hearing, July 20, 1953, testimony of Bohumil Vávra.

242. ABS, f. A2/1, Ministry of Interior advisory board, May 30, 1957, report of the military counter-intelligence on the Pilsen protests, June 1953.

243. SOA Pilsen, f. KV KSČ Pilsen, kart. 451, inv. č. 3603, report on the activities of Antonín Podzimek, June 1, 1953.

244. SOkA v Blovicích, f. OS Pilsen, zn. 1T 141/1953, court file of the main hearing, July 15, 1953, testimony of Zdeňka Juzíková.

245. Ibid., zn. 1T 144/1953, court file of the main hearing, July 17, 1953, testimony of Jaroslav Preis.

246. ABS, f. KS MV Pilsen, V-868, testimonies of Ilja Nazarkevyč; Ibid., V-881 Pilsen, testimonies of Jaroslav Satoria.

247. SOkA v Blovicích, f. OS Pilsen, zn. 3T 148/1953, report of the interrogation of Jindřich Kutzman at the District Prosecutor's Office in Pilsen 18. 8. 1953; ABS, f. KS MV Pilsen, sv. V-1131, Cecílie Kutzmanová's statement, taken by the KS StB in Pilsen June 23, 1953.

248. SOkA v Blovicích, f. OS Pilsen, zn. 1T 138/1953, court file of the main hearing, July 13, 1953, testimony of Vlasta Davidovičová.

249. Ibid., zn. 1T 148/1953, verdict of the People's Court in Pilsen, July 21, 1953; SOA Pilsen, f. KV KSČ Pilsen, kart. 450, inv. č. 3603, report of the extraordinary members' meeting of the ZO KSČ Osvobozená domácnost, June 4, 1953.

250. SOkA v Blovicích, f. OS Pilsen, zn. 1T 144/1953, court file of the main hearing, July 17, 1953, testimony of LM member LM František Umon.

251. Ibid., zn. 1T 146/1953, court file of the main hearing, July 20, 1953, testimony of Jaroslav Valentová.

252. SOA Pilsen, f. ZKNV Pilsen, kart. 147, report of the JNV chairman in Pilsen to chairman of the KNV in Pilsen, June 1, 1953.

253. VÚA, f. MNO, inv. č. 2032, kart. 349, sig. 44/10/1/1, č.j. 0012199 OS 1953, report on the situation in Pilsen on June 1, 1953, from Brig. Gen. Jan Knotek, sent to Minister of National Defence Alexej Čepička, June 2, 1953.

254. SOkA v Blovicích, f. OS Pilsen, zn. 1T 149/1953, court file of the main hearing, July 20, 1953, testimony of Alois Kučera.

255. SOA Pilsen, f. ZKNV Pilsen, kart. 147, report of the KS VB in Pilsen to the chairman of the KNV in Pilsen, June 2, 1953.

256. SOkA v Blovicích, f. OS Pilsen, zn. 1T 258/1953, verdict of the People's Court in Pilsen, December 29, 1953.

257. Ibid., zn. 1T 144/1953, court file of the main hearing, July 17, 1953, testimony of Anežka Krinesová and Helena Fišerová.

258. Ibid., zn. 1T 149/1953, court file of the main hearing, July 20, 1953, testimony of Alois Kučera; Ibid., zn. 1T 144/1953, court file of the main hearing, July 17, 1953, testimonies of Jaroslav Preis and Antonín Meca; Eva Šafránková, "*Ty jsi červnovej, viď?: 1. June 1953 v Plzni očima pamětníků*" (PhD diss., Západočeská univerzita v Plzni, 2005), 64.

259. SOkA v Blovicích, f. OS Pilsen, zn. 1T 146/1953, court file of the main hearing at the People's Court in Pilsen, July 20, 1953, testimony of Dagmar Volšanová.

260. Ibid., zn. 3T 175/1953, verdict of the People's Court in Pilsen 18. 12. 1953.

261. Boštík, ed., *Jak to bylo s osvobozením Plzně*, 44–60; Barbora Köpplová, ed., *Dějiny českých médií v datech, rozhlas, televize, mediální právo* (Prague: Karolinum, 2003), 57–58; Martinovský, ed., *Dějiny Plzně v datech*, 366–382; Eva Klausnerová, *Svobodná Pilsen hovoří: Příběhy vzepětí i pokoření Českého rozhlasu Pilsen* (Pilsen: NAVA, 2005), s. 200.

262. SOkA v Blovicích, f. OS Pilsen, zn. 1T 141/1953, copy of the main hearing court file, July 15, 1953, testimony of Karel Meluzina.

263. Ibid., zn. 1T 140/1953, verdict of the People's Court in Pilsen July 14, 1953; Karel Kasal, "Tahal Větrovce za nohu," *Plzeňský deník*, June 4, 1994, 3; Jindřich Rosendorf, "Utajené povstání," *Svobodné slovo*, May 29, 1993, 2.

264. VÚA, f. MNO, inv. č. 1999, kart. 344, sig. 44/1/3, č.j. 004500 NGŠ 1953, report of Lt. Col. Vojtěch Dolníček, deputy chief of the general staff, on the situation in Pilsen, May 30, – June 3, 1953, June 6, 1953; NA, f. MV NA, inv. č. 169, kart. 258, report to Prime Minister Viliam Široký, č. j. 20/53 PT, undated.

265. ABS, f. A2/1, Ministry of Interior advisory board, May 30, 1957, report of the military counter-intelligence on the Pilsen protests of June 1, 1953, undated; Ibid., report for the Minister of Interior, comparing several security forces reports, August 2, 1957; Štěpánek, *Utajené povstání 1953*, 35–36.

266. SOkA v Blovicích, f. OS Pilsen, zn. 1T 140/1953, verdict of the People's Court in Pilsen July 14, 1953; Kasal, "Tahal Větrovce za nohu," 3.

267. SOkA v Blovicích, f. OS Pilsen, zn. 1T 143/1953, court file of the main hearing, 16. 7. 1953, testimony of Karel Matheisl; Ibid., zn. 1T 141/1953, action filed by the District Prosecutor in Pilsen July 10, 1953; Ibid., zn. 1T 140/1953, verdict of the People's Court in Pilsen July 14, 1953; NA, f. Měnová reforma, report on the business trip of the employees of the State Planning Office to the ZVIL in Pilsen, June 1, 1953, from June 5, 1953.

268. SOkA v Blovicích, f. OS Pilsen, zn. 3T 132/1953, criminal charges filed by the VB District Department in Pilsen, sent to the District Prosecutors office in Pilsen 2, June 2, 1953; Ibid., Jan Dejl's statement, taken by the VB District Department in Pilsen, June 6, 1953; ABS, f. A2/1, Ministry of Interior advisory board, May 30, 1957, report of the military counter-intelligence on the Pilsen protests, June 1953.

269. SOkA v Blovicích, f. OS Pilsen, zn. 1T 144/1953, court file of the main hearing, July 17, 1953, testimony of Jaroslav Kopecký.

270. Ibid., zn. 1T 146/1953, court file of the main hearing, July 20, 1953, testimony of Jan Johánek.

271. NA, f. ÚV KSČ – 1261/0/12, sv. 43, a. j. 231/1, Minutes of the meeting of the ÚV KSČ organizational secretariat, August 3, 1953; SOkA v Blovicích, f. OS Pilsen, zn. 1T 144/1953, court file of the main hearing, July 17, 1953, testimony of Václav Bažant.

272. Ibid., zn. 1T 136/1953, court file of the main hearing at the People's Court in Pilsen, July 13, 1953, testimonies of Jaroslav Reichl a Eva Marovičová.

273. Ibid., zn. 1T 151/1953, verdict of the People's Court in Pilsen, July 21, 1953.

274. PA Škoda, f. ZVIL, ZVIL 203, list of employees who entered the factory carrying replacement IDs, June 1953.

275. SOkA v Blovicích, f. OS Pilsen, zn. 1T 149/1953, court file of the main hearing at the People's Court in Pilsen, July 20, 1953, testimony of Ladislav Šamberger; ABS, f. KS MV Pilsen, sv. V-1131 Pilsen, Jindřich Kutzman's statement, taken by the KS StB in Pilsen, June 4, 1953.

276. SOkA v Blovicích, f. OS Pilsen, zn. 1T 146/1953, court file of the main hearing, July 20, 1953, testimony of Vladimír Matoušek; Ibid., zn. 1T 144/1953, verdict of the People's Court in Pilsen, July 17, 1953.

277. Ibid., zn. 1T 149/1953, court file of the main hearing, July 20, 1953, testimony of Václav Krs.

278. Ibid., zn. 1T 144/1953, court file of the main hearing, July 17, 1953, testimony of Antonín Meca.

279. Ibid., zn. 1T 149/1953, court file of the main hearing, July 20, 1953, testimony of Jaroslav Blavic.

280. PA Škoda, f. ZVIL, ZVIL 1552 PV 1730, proposal to award a bonus to LM member Josef Beran, 24. 7. 1953.

281. SOkA v Blovicích, f. OS Pilsen, zn. 1T 258/1953, verdict of the People's Court in Pilsen, December 29, 1953.

282. Ibid., zn. 1T 146/1953, court file of the main hearing, July 20, 1953, testimony of Jan Johánek; Ibid., zn. 1T 169/1953, Václav Eliáš' testimony, taken by the VB District Department Pilsen 1, June 1, 1953; AMP, f. MV KSČ Pilsen, inv. č. 498, kart. 42, Minutes of the meeting of the MV KSČ executive committee in Pilsen, July 14, 1953.

283. SOkA v Blovicích, f. OS Pilsen, zn. 1T 146/1953, court file of the main hearing, July 20, 1953, testimony of Vladimír Matoušek; Ibid., zn. 1T 140/1953, verdict of the People's Court in Pilsen, July 14, 1953.

284. Ibid., zn. 1T 146/1953, court file of the main hearing, July 20, 1953, testimony of Anna Rosolová.

285. Ibid., zn. 1T 146/1953, criminal charges filed by KS StB in Pilsen to the Regional Prosecutor's Office in Pilsen 6. 7. 1953.

286. PA Škoda, f. ZVIL, ZVIL 1552 PV 1988, memorandum of the investigation commission regarding the punishment of Karel Křepínský, June 1953.

287. Ibid., lists of persons from Machine Shop IV punished for participating in the protests of 1 June 1953, June 13, 1953.

288. SOkA v Blovicích, f. OS Pilsen, zn. 1T 146/1953, court file of the main hearing, July 20, 1953, testimony of Josef Honzík.

289. Ibid., zn. 1T 149/1953, court file of the main hearing, July 20, 1953, testimony of Jaroslav Blavic; Ibid., zn. 1T 146/1953, court file of the main hearing, July 20, 1953, testimony of Anna Rosolová; Ibid., zn. 1T 140/1953, verdict of the People's Court in Pilsen, July 14, 1953.

290. Ibid., zn. 1T 149/1953, court file of the main hearing, July 20, 1953, testimony of Jaroslav Blavic; Ibid., zn. 1T 146/1953, court file of the main hearing, July 20, 1953, testimony of Anna Rosolová.

291. Ibid., zn. 1T 151/1953, court file of the main hearing, July 21, 1953, testimony of Jaroslav Staněk; Ibid., zn. 1T 145/1953, court file of the main hearing, July 17, 1953, testimony of Josef Havránek.

292. SOA Pilsen, f. KV KSČ Pilsen, kart. 29, inv. č. 100, minutes of the plenary session of KV KSČ, June 2, 1953.

293. Ibid., kart. 450, inv. č. 3603, minutes of the extraordinary meeting of MV KSČ June 3, 1953.

294. Ibid., report on the exchange of cash in the ZVIL Pilsen, June 1, 1953; Ibid., kart. 449, inv. č. 3603, telegram from KV KSČ to ÚV KSČ No. 314, June 1, 1953, 10.50 p.m.

295. SOkA v Blovicích, f. OS Pilsen, zn. 1T 136/1953, court file of the main hearing at the People's Court in Pilsen, July 13, 1953, testimony of Josef Štrunec.

296. Ibid., zn. 1T 146/1953, court file of the main hearing, July 20, 1953, testimony of Anna Rosolová.

297. ABS, f. Sekretariát ministra, Ministry of Interior advisory board, May 30, 1957, report of the military counter-intelligence on the Pilsen protests, June 1953.

298. SOkA v Blovicích, f. OS Pilsen, zn. 1T 136/1953, court file of the main hearing at the People's Court in Pilsen, July 13, 1953, testimony of Michael Baťa.

299. SOA Pilsen, f. KV KSČ Pilsen, kart. 450, inv. č. 3603, report from the interrogation of militiaman Jiří Hruška 5. 6. 1953.

300. SOkA v Blovicích, f. OS Pilsen, zn. 1T 138/1953, court file of the main hearing, July 13, 1953, testimony of Josef Nečas.

301. Ibid., zn. 1T 144/1953, court file of the main hearing, July 17, 1953, testimony of Václav Makrlík.

302. PA Škoda, f. ZVIL, ZVIL 1455 PV 109, evaluation of the work of ZR ZVIL during the events of June 1, 1953, z 30. 8. 1953.

303. SOkA v Blovicích, f. OS Pilsen, zn. 1T 144/1953, court file of the main hearing, July 17, 1953, testimony of Václav Makrlík; Ibid., zn. 1T 182/1953, Václav Telín's statement, taken by the VB District Department in Kozolupy, July 15, 1953.

304. Ibid., zn. 1T 138/1953, court file of the main hearing, July 13, 1953, testimony of Josef Nečas; Ibid., zn. 1T 145/1953, court file of the main hearing, July 17, 1953, testimony of Josef Havránek.

305. SOA Pilsen, f. KV KSČ Pilsen, kart. 451, inv. č. 3603, testimony of Jaroslav Heřman, from 1953; Ibid., report on the activities of Antonín Podzimek, June 1, 1953.

306. Ibid., f. ZKNV Pilsen, kart. 147, report of the KS VB in Pilsen to the chairman of the KNV in Pilsen, June 2, 1953; ABS, f. A2/1, sv. 250, Ministry of Interior advisory board, May 30, 1957, report of the military counter-intelligence on the Pilsen protests, June 1953; NA, f. ÚV KSČ – 1261/0/12, sv. 43, a. j. 231/1, Minutes of the meeting of the ÚV KSČ organizational secretariat, August 3, 1953; Ibid., f. ÚV KSČ – 1261/2/1, sv. 361, a. j. 2190, report of the members of a political volunteer team, sent on May 5–June 4, 1953 to assist the KV KSČ in Pilsen in spreading the proclamation of ÚV KSČ on that year's harvest season.

307. Martinovský, ed., *Dějiny Plzně v datech*, 453; Jirásek a Šůla, *Velká peněžní loupež*, 101–103.

308. VÚA, f. MNO, inv. č. 2032, kart. 349, sig. 44/10/1/1, č.j. 0012199 OS 1953, report on the situation in Pilsen, June 1, 1953, from Brig. Gen. Jan Knotek, sent to Minister of National Defence Alexej Čepička, June 2, 1953; Ibid., kart. 344, sig. 44/1/3, č.j. 004500 NGŠ 1953, summary report on the army's involvement in implementing the resolution of the ÚV KSČ and the government regarding the currency reform and abolition of the rationing system, June 9, 1953.

309. SOA Pilsen, f. KV KSČ Pilsen, kart. 450, inv. č. 3603, JNV report on the population structure in Pilsen, June 26, 1953; McDermott, "Lidový odpor v komunistickém Československu," 216–217.

310. *NA*, f. ÚV KSČ – 1261/0/12, sv. 43, a. j. 231/1, Minutes of the meeting of the ÚV KSČ organizational secretariat, August 3, 1953.

311. Petráš, "Peněžní reforma 1953," 141–171.

312. SOA Pilsen, f. ZKNV Pilsen, kart. 147, report of the KS VB in Pilsen to the chairman of the KNV in Pilsen, June 2, 1953.

313. SOkA v Blovicích, f. OS Pilsen, zn. 1T 136/1953, court file of the main hearing at the People's Court in Pilsen, July 13, 1953, testimony of Václav Melka.

314. Ibid., zn. 1T 144/1953, court file of the main hearing, July 17, 1953, testimony of witness Jiří Hruška; Ibid., zn. 1T 136/1953, court file of the main hearing at the People's Court in Pilsen, July 13, 1953, testimony of Michael Baťa.

315. SOA Pilsen, f. KV KSČ Pilsen, kart. 450, inv. č. 3603, report from the interrogation of Václav Huncl, June 8, 1953.

316. SOkA v Blovicích, f. OS Pilsen, zn. 1T 144/1953, court file of the main hearing, July 17, 1953, testimony of witness Jiří Hruška.

317. Ibid., zn. 1T 136/1953, court file of the main hearing at the People's Court in Pilsen, July 13, 1953, testimony of Václav Melka.

318. ABS, f. A2/1, sv. 250, Ministry of Interior advisory board, May 30, 1957, report of the military counter-intelligence on the Pilsen protests, June 1953.

319. SOkA v Blovicích, f. OS Pilsen, zn. 1T 139/1953, court file of the main hearing, July 14, 1953, testimony of Jaroslav Treml; Ibid., zn. 1T 136/1953, court file of

the main hearing at the People's Court in Pilsen, July 13, 1953, testimony of Karel Giebitz.

320. Ibid., zn. 1T 148/1953, verdict of the People's Court in Pilsen July 21, 1953; Hykeš, "Dramatické události," 1–5.

321. SOkA v Blovicích, f. OS Pilsen, zn. 1T 144/1953, court file of the main hearing, July 17, 1953, testimony of Josef Lhoták.

322. ABS, f. A2/1, sv. 250, Ministry of Interior advisory board, May 30, 1957, report of the military counter-intelligence on the Pilsen protests, June 1953; SOA Pilsen, f. KV KSČ Pilsen, kart. 450, inv. č. 3603, report from the interrogation of Václav Huncl, June 8, 1953.

323. Ibid., f. ZKNV Pilsen, kart. 147, report of the JNV chairman in Pilsen to chairman of the KNV in Pilsen June 4, 1953.

324. NA, f. ÚV KSČ – 1261/0/12, sv. 43, a. j. 231/1, Minutes of the meeting of the ÚV KSČ organizational secretariat, August 3, 1953.

325. SOA Pilsen, f. KV KSČ Pilsen, kart. 450, inv. č. 3603, report on the proceedings of ZO KSČ member meetings in the ČSD workshops in Pilsen, June 3, 1953.

326. Ibid., resolution of the ÚV KSČ regarding the events of 1 June 1953 in Pilsen.

327. ABS, f. A2/1, sv. 494, report on the situation in Pilsen during the currency reform, sent to KS StB, November 3, 1953.

328. PA Škoda, f. ZVIL, PV KSČ 1 271, Minutes of the meeting of the OV KSČ Škoda special commission regarding the case of Jan Zítek, Jan Danda and Jan Piller, May 10, 1951; ABS, f. 318, sv. 319–5–1, investigation of the complaints regarding the activities of Matěj Bálek in 1954.

329. ABS, f. A2/1, sv. 494, report on the situation in Pilsen during the currency reform, sent to KS StB, November 3, 1953.

330. SOA Pilsen, f. KV KSČ Pilsen, kart. 451, inv. č. 3603, minutes of the meeting of the LM regional staff, September 1, 1953; NA, f. ÚV KSČ – 1261/0/12, sv. 43, a. j. 231/1, Minutes of the meeting of the ÚV KSČ organizational secretariat, August 3, 1953.

331. SOA Pilsen, f. KV KSČ Pilsen, kart. 450, inv. č. 3603, complaint of the LM unit from the Pilsen Power Distribution Plant to KV KSČ in Pilsen, sent to ÚV KSČ, June 15, 1953.

332. NA, f. ÚV KSČ – 1261/0/12, sv. 43, a. j. 231/1, Minutes of the meeting of the ÚV KSČ organizational secretariat, August 3, 1953.

333. SOA Pilsen, f. KV KSČ Pilsen, kart. 449, inv. č. 3603, evaluation of SNB's work in Pilsen, 1953.

334. Ibid., kart. 451, inv. č. 3603, report on the activities of agricultural officer Jan Pelnář on June 1, 1953, from June 1953.

335. Ibid., kart. 450, inv. č. 3603, letter from the KSČ organization at the College of Mechanical and Electrical Engineering in Pilsen to ÚV KSČ, June 20, 1953.

336. Ibid., kart. 449, inv. č. 3603, report on the activities of Josef Mervart on June 1, 1953, from 1953.

337. SOkA v Blovicích, f. OS Pilsen, zn. 1T 144/1953, action filed by the District Prosecutor in Pilsen with the People's Court in Pilsen 11. 7. 1953.

338. SOA Pilsen, f. KV KSČ Pilsen, kart. 449, inv. č. 3603, report of the MV KSČ to the Party authorities dpt. of KV KSČ, July 24, 1953.

339. Ibid., report from the LM department to the KV KSČ secretariat, 1953.

340. Ibid., kart. 450, inv. č. 3603, complaint of the LM unit from the Pilsen Power Distribution Plant to KV KSČ in Pilsen, sent to ÚV KSČ, June 15, 1953.

341. ABS, f. A2/1, sv. 494, report on the situation in Pilsen during the currency reform, sent to KS StB, November 3, 1953.

342. Ibid., sv. 1631, report on the state of Party and political work at the na KS StB in Pilsen, September 25, 1953; SOA Pilsen, f. KV KSČ Pilsen, kart. 107, inv. č. 791, Minutes of the meeting of the KV KSČ executive committee 17. 4. 1953.

343. Ibid., kart. 450, inv. č. 3603, report from the interrogation of militiaman František Lešák, June 25, 1953.

344. Ibid., comments on the events in Pilsen on 1 June 1953, undated.

345. Ibid., kart. 449, inv. č. 3603, report of the department of industry and construction of the secretariat of KV KSČ in Pilsen, 1953; Ibid., implementation of the currency reform and implementing the Party and government resolution to abolish the ration system on foodstuffs and industrial goods in the Pilsen region; NA, f. ÚV KSČ – 1261/0/12, sv. 43, a. j. 231/1, Minutes of the meeting of the ÚV KSČ organizational secretariat, August 3, 1953.

346. SOA Pilsen, f. KV KSČ Pilsen, kart. 450, inv. č. 3603, report from the interrogation of Václav Huncl, July 10, 1953; Ibid., report from the interrogation of militiaman František Růžičky, June 26, 1953; Ibid., report from the interrogation of militiaman František Lešák, June 25, 1953.

347. Ibid., minutes of the extraordinary meeting of MV KSČ executive committee June 3, 1953.

348. NA, f. ÚV KSČ – 1261/0/12, sv. 43, a. j. 231/1, Minutes of the meeting of the ÚV KSČ organizational secretariat, August 3, 1953.

349. SOA Pilsen, f. KV KSČ Pilsen, kart. 451, inv. č. 3603, report on the activities of Matěj Bálek on June 1, 1953, from 1953.

350. Ibid., kart. 449, inv. č. 3603, vetting of the LM regional staff, July 7, 1953; Ibid., additional vetting of the LM regional staff, September 14, 1953.

351. Ibid., kart. 451, inv. č. 3603, minutes of the extraordinary meeting of the KV KSČ executive committee, September 10, 1953.

352. NA, f. Měnová reforma, special information report based on telephone conversations between the individual KV KSČ and the ÚV KSČ on 1 June 1953 between 8 a.m.–9.30 a.m., June 1, 1953.

353. SOA Pilsen, f. KV KSČ Pilsen, kart. 450, inv. č. 3603, complaint of the LM unit from the Pilsen Power Distribution Plant to KV KSČ in Pilsen, sent to ÚV KSČ, June 15, 1953.

354. Ibid., kart. 449, inv. č. 3603, telegram from the KV KSČ sent by the ÚV KSČ to the LM commander-in-chief's staff, June 1, 1953.

355. Ibid., report from the LM department to the KV KSČ secretariat, 1953.

356. Ibid., kart. 450, inv. č. 3603, complaint of the LM unit from the Pilsen Power Distribution Plant to KV KSČ in Pilsen, sent to ÚV KSČ, June 15, 1953.

357. Ibid., f. ZKNV Pilsen, kart. 147, report of the KS VB in Pilsen to the chairman of the KNV in Pilsen, June 2, 1953.

358. Ibid., f. KV KSČ Pilsen, kart. 449, inv. č. 3603, evaluation of SNB's work in Pilsen, 1953; Ibid., implementation of the currency reform and implementing the Party and government resolution to abolish the ration system on foodstuffs and industrial goods in the Pilsen region, 1953; NA, f. ÚV KSČ – 1261/0/12, sv. 43, a. j. 231/1, Minutes of the meeting of the ÚV KSČ organizational secretariat, August 3, 1953.

359. SOA Pilsen, f. KV KSČ Pilsen, kart. 451, inv. č. 3603, report on the activities of Matěj Bálek on June 1, 1953, from 1953.

360. Ibid., report of Antonín Vintr, chief of the KS VB in Pilsen, sent to the KV KSČ, September 17, 1953.

361. SOA Pilsen, f. ZKNV Pilsen, kart. 147, report of the KS VB in Pilsen to the chairman of the KNV in Pilsen, June 2, 1953.

362. AMP, f. MV KSČ Pilsen, inv. č. 494, kart. 42, Minutes of the meeting of the MV KSČ executive committee in Pilsen, June 23, 1953; Ibid., inv. č. 498, kart. 42, Minutes of the meeting of the MV KSČ executive committee in Pilsen, July 14, 1953, report on the activities of Josef Mainzer.

363. SOA Pilsen, f. KV KSČ Pilsen, kart. 451, inv. č. 3603, report of Antonín Vintr, chief of the KS VB in Pilsen, sent to the KV KSČ, September 17, 1953.

364. Ibid., kart. 449, inv. č. 3603, evaluation of SNB's work in Pilsen, 1953.

365. Ibid., f. ZKNV Pilsen, kart. 147, report of the KS VB in Pilsen to the chairman of the KNV in Pilsen, June 2, 1953.

366. SOA Pilsen, f. KV KSČ Pilsen, kart. 449, inv. č. 3603, report from the LM department to the KV KSČ secretariat, 1953.

367. Ibid., kart. 451, inv. č. 3603, report of Antonín Vintr, chief of the KS VB in Pilsen, sent to the KV KSČ, September 17, 1953.

368. Ibid., kart. 449, inv. č. 3603, evaluation of SNB's work in Pilsen, 1953.

369. ABS, f. A2/1, sv. 250, Ministry of Interior advisory board, May 30, 1957, report of the military counter-intelligence on the Pilsen protests, June 1953; VÚA, f. MNO, inv. č. 1999, kart. 344, sig. 44/1/3, č.j. 004500 NGŠ 1953, report of Lt. Col. Vojtěch Dolníček, deputy chief of the general staff, on the situation in Pilsen, May 30, – June 3, 1953, June 6, 1953.

370. ABS, f. A2/1, sv. 250, Ministry of Interior advisory board, May 30, 1957.

371. NA, f. Měnová reforma, report of the LM department of the ÚV KSČ secretariat, sent to Antonín Novotný, June 2, 1953; SOA Pilsen, f. KV KSČ Pilsen, kart. 451, inv. č. 3603, minutes of the extraordinary meeting of the KV KSČ executive committee, September 10, 1953.

372. Ibid., f. ZKNV Pilsen, kart. 147, report of the KS VB in Pilsen to the chairman of the KNV in Pilsen, June 2, 1953.

373. Ibid., f. KV KSČ Pilsen, kart. 449, inv. č. 3603, report from the LM department to the KV KSČ secretariat, 1953.

374. Ibid., kart. 451, inv. č. 3603, report on the activities of Matěj Bálek on June 1, 1953, from 1953.

375. Ibid., kart. 450, inv. č. 3603, report from the interrogation of Václav Huncla June 8, 1953; Ibid., complaint of the LM unit from the Pilsen Power Distribution Plant to KV KSČ in Pilsen, sent to ÚV KSČ, June 15, 1953.
376. ABS, f. A2/1, sv. 250, Ministry of Interior advisory board, May 30, 1957, report of the military counter-intelligence on the Pilsen protests, June 1953.
377. SOkA v Blovicích, f. OS Pilsen, zn. 1T 145/1953, court file of the main hearing, July 17, 1953, testimony of Libuše Fujové.
378. SOA Pilsen, f. KV KSČ Pilsen, kart. 450, inv. č. 3603, report from the interrogation of Václav Huncla June 8, 1953.
379. ABS, f. A2/1, sv. 250, Ministry of Interior advisory board, May 30, 1957, report of the military counter-intelligence on the Pilsen protests, June 1953.
380. SOA Pilsen, f. KV KSČ Pilsen, kart. 451, inv. č. 3603, report on the activities of Matěj Bálek on June 1, 1953, from 1953.
381. SOkA v Blovicích, f. OS Pilsen, zn. 1T 145/1953, court file of the main hearing, July 17, 1953, testimony of witness Václav Beránek.
382. ABS, f. A2/1, sv. 250, Ministry of Interior advisory board, May 30, 1957, report of the military counter-intelligence on the Pilsen protests, June 1953; SOA Pilsen, f. KV KSČ Pilsen, kart. 451, inv. č. 3603, report on the activities of Matěj Bálek on June 1, 1953, from 1953.
383. Ibid., f. ZKNV Pilsen, kart. 147, report of the KS VB in Pilsen to the chairman of the KNV in Pilsen, June 2, 1953.
384. Ibid., f. KV KSČ Pilsen, kart. 449, inv. č. 3603, telegram from KV KSČ to ÚV KSČ No. 314, June 1, 1953, 10.50 p.m.
385. AMP, f. MV KSČ Pilsen, kart. 42, minutes of the extraordinary meeting of MV KSČ in Pilsen July 17, 1953, report on the activities of Bedřich Perlík.
386. SOA Pilsen, f. KV KSČ Pilsen, kart. 451, inv. č. 3603, report on the vetting of the propaganda department of the KV KSČ secretariat, July 8–13, 1953.
387. Ibid., kart. 449, inv. č. 3603, implementation of the currency reform and implementing the Party and government resolution to abolish the ration system on foodstuffs and industrial goods in the Pilsen region, 1953; NA, f. ÚV KSČ – 1261/0/12, sv. 43, a. j. 231/1, Minutes of the meeting of the ÚV KSČ organizational secretariat, August 3, 1953.
388. SOA Pilsen, f. KV KSČ Pilsen, kart. 449, inv. č. 3603, report from the LM department to the KV KSČ secretariat, 1953; SOkA v Blovicích, f. OS Pilsen, zn. 1T 169/1953, statement of militiaman Josef Veverka, taken by the VB District Department in Pilsen, June 15, 1953.
389. NA, f. ÚV KSČ – 1261/0/12, sv. 43, a. j. 231/1, Minutes of the meeting of the ÚV KSČ organizational secretariat, August 3, 1953; Ibid., f. ÚV KSČ – 1261/2/1, sv. 378, a. j. 2292, report on the survey of the Party's work in Pilsen in connection with the events of 1 June 1953, from 1953.
390. ABS, f. A2/1, sv. 250, Ministry of Interior advisory board, May 30, 1957; AMP, f. MV KSČ Pilsen, kart. 42, minutes of the extraordinary meeting of MV KSČ in Pilsen, July 17, 1953, report on the activities of Bedřich Perlík; SOA Pilsen, f. KV KSČ Pilsen, kart. 449, inv. č. 3603, telegram from KV KSČ to ÚV KSČ No. 314, June 1, 1953, 10.50 p.m.

391. Ibid., report from the LM department to the KV KSČ secretariat, 1953.

392. Ibid., telegram from KV KSČ to ÚV KSČ No. 314, June 1, 1953, 10.50 p.m.

393. SOA Pilsen, f. KV KSČ Pilsen, kart. 450, inv. č. 3603, report from the interrogation of Václav Huncl, July 10, 1953.

394. Ibid., kart. 451, inv. č. 3603, report of Antonín Vintr, chief of the KS VB in Pilsen, sent to the KV KSČ, September 17, 1953.

395. SOkA v Blovicích, f. OS Pilsen, zn. 1T 151/1953, court file of the main hearing, July 21, 1953, testimony of Zdeňka Kocůmová.

396. Ibid., zn. 1T 148/1953, verdict of the People's Court in Pilsen July 21, 1953.

397. Ibid., zn. 1T 141/1953, copy of the main hearing court file, July 15, 1953, testimony of Zdeňka Juzíková; Ibid., zn. 1T 145/1953, court file of the main hearing, July 17, 1953, testimony of Jan Holeček.

398. Ibid., zn. 1T 141/1953, court file of the main hearing, July 15, 1953, testimony of Jarmila Škardová.

399. ABS, f. A2/1, sv. 250, Minutes of the meeting of the Ministry of Interior advisory board, May 30, 1957.

400. SOA Pilsen, f. ZKNV Pilsen, kart. 147, report of the KS VB in Pilsen to the chairman of the KNV in Pilsen, June 2, 1953.

401. ABS, f. A2/1, sv. 250, Ministry of Interior advisory board, May 30, 1957, report of the military counter-intelligence on the Pilsen protests, June 1953; SOkA v Blovicích, f. OS Pilsen, zn. 1T 142/1953, court file of the main hearing, 16. 7. 1953, testimony of Vladimíra Šimice.

402. ABS, f. A2/1, sv. 250, Ministry of Interior advisory board, May 30, 1957, report of the military counter-intelligence on the Pilsen protests, June 1953.

403. SOA Pilsen, f. KV KSČ Pilsen, kart. 449, inv. č. 3603, report from the LM department to the KV KSČ secretariat, 1953.

404. ABS, f. A2/1, sv. 250, Ministry of Interior advisory board, May 30, 1957.

405. SOA Pilsen, f. KV KSČ Pilsen, kart. 451, inv. č. 3603, report on the activities of MP Ivo Skála, June 1, 1953, z 9. 6. 1953.

406. ABS, f. A2/1, sv. 250, Ministry of Interior advisory board, May 30, 1957.

407. SOA Pilsen, f. ZKNV Pilsen, kart. 147, report of the KS VB in Pilsen to the chairman of the KNV in Pilsen, June 2, 1953; Ibid., f. KV KSČ Pilsen, kart. 451, inv. č. 3603, report of Antonín Vintr, chief of the KS VB in Pilsen, sent to the KV KSČ, September 17, 1953.

408. ABS, f. A2/1, sv. 250, Ministry of Interior advisory board, May 30, 1957, report of the military counter-intelligence on the Pilsen protests, June 1953.

409. SOA Pilsen, f. KV KSČ Pilsen, kart. 451, inv. č. 3603, report of Antonín Vintr, chief of the KS VB in Pilsen, sent to the KV KSČ, September 17, 1953; Ibid., f. ZKNV Pilsen, kart. 147, report of the JNV chairman in Pilsen to chairman of the KNV in Pilsen June 4, 1953; ABS, f. A2/1, sv. 250, Ministry of Interior advisory board, May 30, 1957, report of the military counter-intelligence on the Pilsen protests, June 1953; VÚA, f. MNO, inv. č. 1999, kart. 344, sig. 44/1/3, č.j. 004500 NGŠ 1953, summary report on the army's involvement in implementing the resolution of the ÚV KSČ and the government regarding the currency reform and abolition of the rationing system, June 9, 1953.

410. ABS, f. A2/1, sv. 250, Ministry of Interior advisory board, May 30, 1957, report of the military counter-intelligence on the Pilsen protests, June 1953.

411. NA, f. Měnová reforma, report of the LM department of the ÚV KSČ secretariat, sent to Antonín Novotný, June 2, 1953; SOA Pilsen, f. KV KSČ Pilsen, kart. 449, inv. č. 3603, report from the LM department to the KV KSČ secretariat, 1953; Ibid., f. ZKNV Pilsen, kart. 147, report of the KS VB in Pilsen to the chairman of the KNV in Pilsen, June 2, 1953.

412. Ibid., report of the JNV chairman in Pilsen to chairman of the KNV in Pilsen June 4, 1953; ABS, f. A2/1, sv. 250, Ministry of Interior advisory board, May 30, 1957, report of the military counter-intelligence on the Pilsen protests, June 1953; SOA Pilsen, f. KV KSČ Pilsen, kart. 449, inv. č. 3603, report from the LM department to the KV KSČ secretariat, 1953.

413. Ibid., kart. 451, inv. č. 3603, report on the activities of MP Ivo Skála, June 1, 1953, z 9. 6. 1953.

414. Ibid., zpráva ÚV KSČ zaslaná KV KSČ in Pilsen 2. 12. 1953.

415. ABS, f. A2/1, sv. 250, Minutes of the meeting of the Ministry of Interior advisory board, May 30, 1957.

416. Ibid., information for the Minister of Interior, August 2, 1957.

417. SOA Pilsen, f. KV KSČ Pilsen, kart. 451, inv. č. 3603, report of ÚV KSČ sent to KV KSČ in Pilsen, December 2, 1953; ABS, f. A2/1, sv. 250, Ministry of Interior advisory board, May 30, 1957, information for the Minister of Interior, August 2, 1957.

418. Ibid., f. A8/1, sv. 1218, report from the interrogation of Milan Moučka for the Ministry of Interior inspectorate, July 15, 1964.

419. Ibid., f. A2/1, sv. 494, list of persons proposed for release, June 1953.

420. SOkA v Blovicích, f. OS Pilsen, zn. 1T 136/1953, court file of the main hearing at the People's Court in Pilsen, July 13, 1953, testimony of Marie Dobiášová.

421. Ibid., zn. 1T 146/1953, verdict of the People's Court in Pilsen July 20, 1953.

422. NA, f. ÚV KSČ – 1481, sv. 15, a. j. 110, Minutes of the nationwide meeting of chief secretaries of KV KSČ, heads of the departments of ÚV KSČ and chief officials of mass organizations, held on June 11, 1953; speech by Antonín Zápotocký.

423. SOA Pilsen, f. ZKNV Pilsen, kart. 147, report of the KS VB in Pilsen to the chairman of the KNV in Pilsen, June 2, 1953.

424. ABS, f. A2/1, sv. 494, proposal for a public trial with the "instigators of the subversive , provocative protest in Pilsen, June 2, 1953; ABS, f. 310, sv. 310–68–4, proposal for a public trial, June 2, 1953; Jirásek and Šůla, *Velká peněžní loupež*, 130–135.

425. ABS, f. A2/1, sv. 250, Ministry of Interior advisory board, May 30, 1957, report of the military counter-intelligence on the Pilsen protests, June 1953.

426. SOA Pilsen, f. ZKNV Pilsen, kart. 147, report of the KS VB in Pilsen to the chairman of the KNV in Pilsen, June 2, 1953.

427. Ibid., report of the JNV chairman in Pilsen to chairman of the KNV in Pilsen June 4, 1953; *ABS*, f. A2/1, sv. 250, Ministry of Interior advisory board, May 30, 1957; Skála, "Měnová reforma," 624.

428. SOA Pilsen, f. ZKNV Pilsen, kart. 147, report of the KS VB in Pilsen to the chairman of the KNV in Pilsen, June 2, 1953.

429. ABS, f. A2/1, sv. 250, Ministry of Interior advisory board, May 30, 1957.

430. Ibid., f. 310, sv. 310–72–31, telegram of the StB chief administration to all KS StB June 8, 1953.

431. Ibid., f. A2/1, sv. 250, Ministry of Interior advisory board, May 30, 1957, report of the military counter-intelligence on the Pilsen protests, June 1953.

432. VÚA, f. MNO, inv. č. 2032, kart. 349, sig. 44/10/1/1, č.j. 0012199 OS 1953, report on the situation in Pilsen on June 1, 1953, from Brig. Gen. Jan Knotek, sent to Minister of National Defence Alexej Čepička, June 2, 195; Bílek, "Československá armáda," 77.

433. ABS, f. A2/1, sv. 250, Ministry of Interior advisory board, May 30, 1957, information for the Minister of Interior, August 2, 1957.

434. SOkA v Blovicích, f. OS Pilsen, zn. 1T 144/1953, reports on the damages and injuries suffered by security forces members during the protests of June 1, 1953 in Pilsen, July 1953.

435. SOA Pilsen, f. KV KSČ Pilsen, kart. 451, inv. č. 3603, minutes of the extraordinary meeting of the KV KSČ executive committee, September 10, 1953; NA, f. ÚV KSČ – 1261/0/12, sv. 43, a. j. 231/1, Minutes of the meeting of the ÚV KSČ organizational secretariat, August 3, 1953.

436. SOA Pilsen, f. KV KSČ Pilsen, kart. 451, inv. č. 3603, report on the activities of agricultural officer Jan Pelnář on June 1, 1953, from June 1953.

437. Ibid., kart. 450, inv. č. 3603, letter from the KSČ organization at the College of Mechanical and Electrical Engineering in Pilsen to ÚV KSČ, June 20, 1953.

438. NA, f. ÚV KSČ – 1261/0/12, sv. 43, a. j. 231/1, Minutes of the meeting of the ÚV KSČ organizational secretariat, August 3, 1953.

439. SOA Pilsen, f. KV KSČ Pilsen, kart. 450, inv. č. 3603, letter from the KSČ organization at the College of Mechanical and Electrical Engineering in Pilsen to ÚV KSČ, June 20, 1953; Ibid., kart. 449, inv. č. 3603, evaluation of SNB's work in Pilsen, 1953.

440. AMP, f. MV KSČ Pilsen, inv. č. 494, kart. 42, Minutes of the meeting of the MV KSČ executive committee in Pilsen 2June 3, 1953.

441. SOA Pilsen, f. KV KSČ Pilsen, kart. 451, inv. č. 3603, report on the activities of agricultural officer Jan Pelnář on June 1, 1953, from June 1953.

442. Ibid., kart. 450, inv. č. 3603, minutes of the extraordinary meeting of MV KSČ executive committee June 3, 1953.

443. Ibid., kart. 452, inv. č. 3603, Minutes of the meeting of the ZO KSČ committee of the ZVIL ROH factory organization in Pilsen, September 11, 1953.

444. Ibid., kart. 450, inv. č. 3603, minutes of the extraordinary meeting of MV KSČ June 3, 1953; Ibid., kart. 449, inv. č. 3603, implementation of the currency reform and implementing the Party and government resolution to abolish the ration system on foodstuffs and industrial goods in the Pilsen region, 1953.

445. Ibid., report on the activities of Comrade Chleborád, June 1, 1953, from 1953.

446. Ibid., kart. 451, inv. č. 3603, report on the activities of agricultural officer Jan Pelnář on June 1, 1953, from June 1953; Ibid., report on the activities of Václav Zíka, July 1, 1953.

447. Ibid., kart. 449, inv. č. 3603, report on the activities of KV KSČ employee Jan Kruml on June 1, 1953, from 1953; NA, f. ÚV KSČ – 1261/0/12, sv. 43, a. j. 231/1, Minutes of the meeting of the ÚV KSČ organizational secretariat, August 3, 1953.

448. AMP, f. MV KSČ Pilsen, inv. č. 498, kart. 42, Minutes of the meeting of the MV KSČ executive committee in Pilsen July 14, 1953; ABS, f. A2/1, sv. 250, Ministry of Interior advisory board, May 30, 1957, report of the military counter-intelligence on the Pilsen protests, June 1953.

449. SOA Pilsen, f. KV KSČ Pilsen, kart. 450, inv. č. 3603, minutes of the extraordinary meeting of MV KSČ executive committee June 3, 1953; Ibid., report on the exchange of cash at the ZVIL on June 1, 1953; NA, f. ÚV KSČ – 1261/0/12, sv. 43, a. j. 231/1, Minutes of the meeting of the ÚV KSČ organizational secretariat, August 3, 1953.

450. SOA Pilsen, f. KV KSČ Pilsen, kart. 450, inv. č. 3603, minutes of the extraordinary meeting of MV KSČ executive committee June 3, 1953.

451. NA, f. Měnová reforma, report for the delegates of the KSČ municipal conference in Pilsen, from 1954; Ibid., f. ÚV KSČ – 1261/2/31, a. j. 368, kart. 65, annual statistical report of the MV KSČ in Pilsen, 8. 3. 1954; Ibid., a. j. 369, kart. 65, monthly report of the MV KSČ in Pilsen, January–December 1953; Ibid., f. ÚV KSČ – 1261/0/12, sv. 43, a. j. 231/1, Minutes of the meeting of the ÚV KSČ organizational secretariat, August 3, 1953.

452. SOA Pilsen, f. KV KSČ Pilsen, kart. 450, inv. č. 3603, minutes of the extraordinary meeting of MV KSČ June 3, 1953; ABS, f. A2/1, sv. 250, Ministry of Interior advisory board, May 30, 1957, report of the military counter-intelligence on the Pilsen protests, June 1953; Skála, "Měnová reforma," 623.

453. SOA Pilsen, f. KV KSČ Pilsen, kart. 450, inv. č. 3603, report of the KV KSČ in Pilsen on the activities of Marie Majerová on June 1, 1953 from July 14, 1953.

454. Ibid., kart. 451, inv. č. 3603, report on the activities of agricultural officer Jan Pelnář on June 1, 1953, from June 1953.

455. Ibid., report on the vetting of the propaganda department of the KV KSČ secretariat, July 8–13, 1953.

456. AMP, f. MV KSČ Pilsen, inv. č. 498, kart. 42, Minutes of the meeting of the MV KSČ executive committee in Pilsen July 14, 1953, report on the activities of Václav Myslík.

457. SOkA v Blovicích, f. OS Pilsen, zn. 1T 144/1953, court file of the main hearing, July 17, 1953, testimony of Jaroslav Kopecký; Ibid., zn. 1T 146/1953, verdict of the People's Court in Pilsen, July 20, 1953.

458. Ibid., zn. 1T 142/1953, court file of the main hearing, 16. 7. 1953, testimony of Vladimír Šimic.

459. Ibid., zn. 1T 153/1953, court file of the main hearing, July 22, 1953, testimony of Josef Fous.

460. Štěpánek, *Utajené povstání 1953*, s. 48; AMP, f. OF Vladimír Havlic, kart. 2018, inv. č. 19/2 (31), letter from František Pražák to the Civic Forum in Pilsen, February 15, 1990.

461. SOkA v Blovicích, f. OS Pilsen, zn. 1T 146/1953, verdict of the People's Court in Pilsen July 20, 1953; "Mohutná manifestace souhlasu pracujících s provedením měnové reformy a se zrušením lístkového systému," *Pravda*, June 2, 1953, 1; Císař, *Paměti*, 405–438.

462. SOA Pilsen, f. ZKNV Pilsen, kart. 147, report of the KS VB in Pilsen to the chairman of the KNV in Pilsen, June 2, 1953.

463. Ibid., f. KV KSČ Pilsen, kart. 449, inv. č. 3603, telegram from KV KSČ to ÚV KSČ No. 314, June 1, 1953, 22:50.

464. Trapl, *Osudy sochy*, 3–5; Jan Plachta, *Pravda o T. G. Masarykovi* (Prague: Orbis, 1953).

465. Adam Skála, "June 1953 ve vzpomínkách Josef Hodka," *Minulostí západočeského kraje* 43, no. 1 (2008): 368.

466. SOA Pilsen, f. KV KSČ Pilsen, kart. 107, inv. č. 791, Minutes of the meeting of the KV KSČ executive committee 17. 4. 1953; Martinovský, ed., *Dějiny Plzně v datech*, 453.

467. SOA Pilsen, f. KV KSČ Pilsen, kart. 107, inv. č. 797, Minutes of the meeting of the KV KSČ executive committee 22. 5. 1953.

468. Ibid., kart. 451, inv. č. 3603, report on the activities of agricultural officer Jan Pelnář on June 1, 1953, from June 1953; AMP, f. OF Vladimír Havlic, kart. 2018, inv. č. 19/2 (3), letter from Václav Větrovec to Gustav Kural, January 10, 1990; Císař, *Paměti*, 405–438.

469. NA, f. ÚV KSČ – 1481, sv. 15, a. j. 110, Minutes of the nationwide meeting of chief secretaries of KV KSČ, heads of the departments of ÚV KSČ and chief officials of mass organizations, held on June 11, 1953, speech by Jan Hlína.

470. Brand, "Budeme rehabilitovat 1. June 1953," 3; Budilová, "Strhli pomník Plzeňští divadelníci," 2.

471. SOA Pilsen, f. KV KSČ Pilsen, kart. 451, inv. č. 3603, report on the activities of Josef Žák, July 4, 1953.

472. *AMP*, f. Národní výbor města Plzně, sig. 29 d 16, Minutes of the meeting of the JNV council in Pilsen, June 1, 1953; Ibid., f. OF Vladimír Havlic, kart. 2018, inv. č. 19/2 (10), memories of Taťána Kottová, February 7, 1990; SOA Pilsen, f. ZKNV Pilsen, kart. 147, report of the JNV chairman in Pilsen to chairman of the KNV in Pilsen June 4, 1953; AMP, f. MV KSČ Pilsen, kart. 42, minutes of the extraordinary meeting of MV KSČ in Pilsen, July 17, 1953; Martinovský, "A Novotný pak zkritizoval všechny," *Region Plzeňsko: Západočeské noviny*, June 3, 1993, 6; Havlic, *Památník národního osvobození v Plzni*, 69.

473. ABS, f. A2/1, sv. 250, Ministry of Interior advisory board, May 30, 1957, report of the military counter-intelligence on the Pilsen protests, June 1953; Zdeněk Štěpánek, "Co se odehrálo v Plzni před osmatřiceti lety?," *Škodovák*, May 31, 1991, 1; Štěpánek, *Utajené povstání 1953*, 48.

474. Martinovský, ed., *Dějiny Plzně v datech*, 454.

475. SOA Pilsen, f. KV KSČ Pilsen, kart. 29, inv. č. 100, minutes of the plenary session of KV KSČ, June 2, 1953; AMP, f. OF Vladimír Havlic, kart. 2018, inv. č. 19/2 (6), memories of Josef Smola, February 4, 1990.

476. Štěpánek, "Co se odehrálo v Plzni," 1; Štěpánek, *Utajené povstání 1953*, 50–51.

477. Hojda and Pokorný, *Pomníky a zapomníky*, 43; Knapík, *V zajetí moci*, 218.

478. AMP, f. OF Josef Brand, kart. 738, memories of Josef Brand, May 26, 1994.

479. Ibid., f. OF Vladimír Havlic, kart. 2018, inv. č. 19/2 (20), letter from Josef Větrovec to the Civic Forum in Pilsen, undated; Ibid., f. OF Josef Brand, kart. 738, letter from Josef Větrovec to the ZO KSČ of the J.K. Tyl theater, May 29, 1968.

480. Ibid., f. OF Vladimír Havlic, kart. 2018, inv. č. 19/2 (5), memories of Františka Seifertová, January 21, 1990; Ibid., inv. č. 19/2 (6), memories of Josef Smola, February 4, 1990; Ibid., inv. č. 19/2 (7), memories of Miroslav Kanta, February 5, 1990; Markéta Čekanová, "Díky klíčům od auta stanul v čele vzpoury," *Plzeňský deník*, June 1, 1998, 11; Budilová, "Strhli pomník Plzeňští divadelníci," 2; Štěpánek, *Utajené povstání 1953*, 50.

481. SOA Pilsen, f. KV KSČ Pilsen, kart. 451, inv. č. 3603, report on the activities of Robert Fürbach, July 4, 1953.

482. NA, f. Měnová reforma, ÚRO information bulletin, June 1, 1953; Ibid., f. MV NA, inv. č. 169, kart. 258, měnová reforma, report of Václav Schejbal, Civilian Defense commander with the JVN in Pilsen to the Ministry of Interior, June 1, 1953.

483. AMP, f. MV KSČ Pilsen, inv. č. 498, kart. 42, Minutes of the meeting of the MV KSČ executive committee in Pilsen, July 14, 1953; SOA Pilsen, f. KV KSČ Pilsen, kart. 449, inv. č. 3603, telegram from KV KSČ to ÚV KSČ No. 314, June 1, 1953, 10.50 p.m.; ABS, f. A2/1, sv. 250, Ministry of Interior advisory board, May 30, 1957, report of the military counter-intelligence on the Pilsen protests, June 1953.

484. SOA Pilsen, f. ZKNV Pilsen, kart. 147, report of the KS VB in Pilsen to the chairman of the KNV in Pilsen, June 2, 1953; Ibid., f. KV KSČ Pilsen, kart. 450, inv. č. 3603, telegram from the *Rudé právo* office in Pilsen to the *Rudé právo* office in Prague, June 2, 1953, 10:50 hod.

485. Ibid., f. KV ČSM Pilsen, inv. č. 34, kart. 37, report on the activities of Emilie Bobrovová; Ibid., report on the activities of Comrade Vrbová.

486. Ibid., inv. č. 19, kart. 20, evaluation of the events accompanying the currency reform and the abolition of the rationing system in Pilsen on 1 June 1953, June 19531953.

487. Ibid., f. KV KSČ Pilsen, kart. 449, inv. č. 3603, report from the exchange center at the Main Post Office in Pilsen, June 2, 1953; *NA*, f. MF Praha, Sekretariát, sig. F 72, situational report No. 3, June 1, 1953, 6 p.m. on the course of the currency reform, June 1, 1953.

488. *NA*, f. MF Praha, Tajné – peněžní reforma 1953, kart. 21, report on the review of the course of the currency reform, conducted by the Ministry of Finance in the Pilsen region, June 26, 1953; SOA Pilsen, f. KV KSČ Pilsen, kart. 449, inv. č. 3603, telegram from KV KSČ to ÚV KSČ No. 314, June 1, 1953, 10.50 p.m.; AČNB, f. SBČS, sig. S VII/a, kart. 161, telegram from the regional branch of the SBČS in Pilsen sent to the Prague headquarters, June 10, 1953; Ibid., kart. 149, reports

from the exchange centers, sent by the SBČS regional branch to the headquarters, July 1953.

489. SOA Pilsen, f. KV KSČ Pilsen, kart. 449, inv. č. 3603, telegram from KV KSČ to ÚV KSČ No. 313, June 1, 1953, 17:45 hod.

490. Ibid., report from the exchange center at the Main Post Office in Pilsen, June 2, 1953.

491. NA, f. MF Praha, Tajné – peněžní reforma 1953, kart. 12, number of exchange centers, undated; Ibid., f. MV NA, inv. č. 169, kart. 258, situational report from the Pilsen region sent to the Minister of Interior, June 3, 1953; SOA Pilsen, f. KV KSČ Pilsen, kart. 449, inv. č. 3603, telegram from ÚV KSČ to KV KSČ No. 482, June 1, 1953, 10 p.m.

492. Ibid., telegram from KV KSČ to ÚV KSČ No. 318, June 3, 1953, 12.55 a.m.; Ibid., report from the exchange center at the Main Post Office in Pilsen, June 2, 1953; Jirásek and Šůla, *Velká peněžní loupež*, 80–83.

493. SOA Pilsen, f. KV KSČ Pilsen, kart. 449, inv. č. 3603, telegram from KV KSČ to ÚV KSČ No. 324, June 5, 1953, 11.05 p.m.

494. Ibid., telegram from KV KSČ to ÚV KSČ No. 313, June 1, 1953, 5.45 p.m.

495. Ibid., telegram from KV KSČ to ÚV KSČ No. 323, June 5, 1953, 7.40 a.m.

496. PA Škoda, f. ZVIL, ZVIL 524 PŘ 2003, directive of the ZVIL headquarters in Pilsen on the extraordinary measures imposed in the factory during the currency exchange, May 31, 1953.

497. NA, f. ÚV KSČ – 1261/0/22, sv. 58, a. j. 157/13, Minutes of the meeting of the ÚV KSČ political secretariat, June 3, 1953; Ibid., f. MF Praha, Sekretariát, sig. F 72, settlement of wage and salary advances for the first half of May 1953, in case an advance exceeds half of the person's monthly earnings, June 1953; Ibid., minutes of the meeting of the economic ministers and ROH representatives with Deputy Prime Minister Jaromír Dolanský, June 3, 1953; Ibid., Tajné – peněžní reforma 1953, kart. 11, minutes of the meeting of chief officials charged with implementing the currency reform, June 2, 1953.

498. SOA Pilsen, f. KV KSČ Pilsen, kart. 451, inv. č. 3603, report of the KS VB in Pilsen, sent to the KV KSČ in Pilsen on 1 June 1953; PA Škoda, f. ZVIL, ZVIL 343 TS 90, decree of the ZVIL headquarters in Pilsen No. 24/1953, June 6, 1953.

499. Ibid., ZVIL 343 TS 90, decree of the ZVIL headquarters in Pilsen No. 27/1953, June 18, 1953.

500. Ibid., ZVIL 343 TS 90, decree of the ZVIL headquarters in Pilsen No. 24/1953, June 6, 1953; Government decree of 30 May 1953, No. 42/1953 Sb., on measures regarding wages, pensions and certain social benefits in connection with the abolition of the rationing system.

501. NA, f. MF Praha, Tajné – peněžní reforma 1953, kart. 12, report on the exchange of the old currency for new currency issued in 1953, and of the conversion of deposits in state savings banks, June 7, 1953; Ibid., Sekretariát, sig. F 72e, report on the exchange of the old currency for new currency issued in 1953, and of the conversion of deposits in state savings banks, undated.

502. Jirásek and Šůla, *Velká peněžní loupež*, 126.

503. SOA Pilsen, f. KV KSČ Pilsen, kart. 450, inv. č. 3603, telegram from *Rudé právo* Prague to *Rudé právo* Pilsen, June 2, 1953; Marie Faurová, "S radostí se zbavujeme přídělových lístků na zboží," *Pravda*, June 2, 1953, 1; "Nikomu nedovolíme, aby zkazil šťastný život našich dětí," *Pravda*, June 5, 1953, 2.

504. AČNB, f. SBČS Pilsen, sig. 1090/8 PL, dissolution of the regional commission for closing down the exchange centers in Pilsen, March 13, 1954.

505. *NA*, f. MF Praha, Sekretariát, sig. F 72a-II, report on the proceedings of the currency exchange by region, June 1, 1953; Ibid., Tajné – peněžní reforma 1953, kart. 18, population in the regions as of January 1, 1953.

506. Ibid., kart. 11, report on the currency reform and its final account, undated; Ibid., kart. 12, report on the exchange of the old currency for new currency issued in 1953, June 8, 1953; Ibid., Sekretariát, sig. F 72, report on the exchange of currency on June 1–4, 1953, from June 5, 1953; Musilová, *Měnová reforma 1953*, 88–89.

507. AČNB, f. SBČS Pilsen, sig. 820/7 PL, daily reports of exchange centers in Starý Plzenec, June 1953; Ibid., sig. 85/11 PL, daily reports of exchange centers in the Horšovský Týn district, June 1953.

508. PA Škoda, f. ROH, ROH 14 PV 33, outline of a report on the events in Pilsen on 1 June 1953, undated; SOA Pilsen, f. ZKNV Pilsen, kart. 147, report of the KS VB in Pilsen to the chairman of the KNV in Pilsen, June 4, 1953; Ibid., f. KV KSČ Pilsen, kart. 450, inv. č. 3603, minutes of the extraordinary meeting of MV KSČ executive committee June 3, 1953.

509. NA, f. MF Praha, Tajné – peněžní reforma 1953, kart. 11, report on the currency reform and its final account, undated.

510. Ibid., kart. 12, report on the exchange of the old currency for new currency issued in 1953, and of the conversion of deposits in state savings banks, June 7, 1953; Ibid., report on the conversion of deposits in state savings banks as of 1 June 1953, June 7, 1953.

511. Státník, *Sankční pracovní právo*, 142–162.

512. PA Škoda, f. ROH, ROH 14 PV 312, Minutes of the meeting of the presidium of ZR ZVIL in Pilsen, September 29, 1953; SOA Pilsen, f. KV KSČ Pilsen, kart. 450, inv. č. 3603, telegram from KV KSČ No. 372 to ÚV KSČ, September 29, 1953, 4. 30 p.m.; "Dny radosti a vděčnosti v Plzeňském kraji," *Pravda*, October 2, 1953, 1.

513. Pernes, *Snahy o překonání*, 16–26; McDermott, "Lidový odpor v komunistickém Československu," 229–230.

514. Vladimár Nálevka, *Studená válka* (Prague: Triton, 2003), 54–72.

515. Knapík, *V zajetí moci*, 219–221.

516. Průcha, *Hospodářské a sociální dějiny Československa*, 612–623; Jakub Rákosník, *Sovětizace sociálního státu: Lidově demokratický režim a sociální práva občanů v Československu 1945–1960* (Prague: Univerzita Karlova 2010), 445.

517. Muriel Blaive, *Promarněná příležitost: Československo a rok 1956* (Prague: Prostor, 2001), 302–308.

518. Kaplan, *Sociální souvislosti krizí*, 14–23.

519. SOA Pilsen, f. KV KSČ Pilsen, kart. 450, inv. č. 3603, report of members' meetings of KSČ base organizations in the Pilsen-City district, May 31, 1953; Ibid.,

kart. 449, inv. č. 3603, telegram from KV KSČ to ÚV KSČ No. 313, June 1, 1953, 5.45 p.m.

520. Ibid., f. ZKNV Pilsen, kart. 147, report of the KS VB in Pilsen to the chairman of the KNV in Pilsen, June 2, 1953; Ibid., f. KV KSČ Pilsen, kart. 449, inv. č. 3603, telegram from the KV KSČ sent by the ÚV KSČ to the LM commander-in-chief's staff, June 1, 1953; Ibid., telegram from KV KSČ to ÚV KSČ No. 314, June 1, 1953, 10.50 p.m.; Ibid., report from the LM department to the KV KSČ secretariat, 1953; *NA*, f. Měnová reforma, progress report regarding the currency reform, based on telephone reports from the regions to the ÚV KSČ in the morning hours of June 1, 1953; McDermott, "Lidový odpor v komunistickém Československu," 225.

521. SOA Pilsen, f. KV KSČ Pilsen, kart. 449, inv. č. 3603, telegram from KV KSČ to ÚV KSČ No. 314, June 1, 1953, 10.50 p.m.; Ibid., kart. 450, inv. č. 3603, report on extraordinary members' meetings of KSČ factory organizations in the ZVIL in Pilsen, June 4, 1953; ABS, f. 305, sv. 305–403–3, report on the sentiments among the population regarding the currency reform, beginning of June, 1953.

522. SOkA v Blovicích, f. OS Pilsen, zn. 1T 144/1953, court file of the main hearing, July 17, 1953, testimony of Josef Popek; Ibid., zn. 1T 151/1953, court file of the main hearing, January 21, 1953, testimony of Drahomíra Bokr; Ibid., zn. 1T 153/1953, court file of the main hearing, July 22, 1953, testimonies of Josef Fous and Václav Oliberius; Ibid., zn. 1T 144/1953, Josef Hegner's statement, June 5, 1953; Ibid., zn. 1T 149/1953, court file of the main hearing, July 20, 1953, testimony of Alois Kučera; Ibid., zn. 1T 142/1953, court file of the main hearing, 16. 7. 1953, testimony of Marie Kreidlová.

523. PA Škoda, f. ZVIL, ZVIL 1455 PV 109, evaluation of the work of ZR ZVIL during the events of June 1, 1953, from 1953.

524. SOA Pilsen, f. KV KSČ Pilsen, kart. 29, inv. č. 100, minutes of the plenary session of KV KSČ, June 2, 1953.

525. Ibid., f. PV KSČ Škoda, kart. 4, inv. č. 3, minutes of the plenary session of PV KSČ Škoda 11. 8. 1953; Ibid., f. KV KSČ Pilsen, kart. 449, inv. č. 3603, report from the member's meeting at ZO KSČ Machine Shop I in ZVIL, June 4, 1953; Ibid., telegram from KV KSČ to ÚV KSČ No. 319 z June 3, 1953, 1:55 a.m.; Ibid., kart. 450, inv. č. 3603, report on the political situation in ZVIL in Pilsen, June 2, 1953.

526. PA Škoda, f. ZVIL, ZVIL 1455 PV 45, resolution of the employees of the Machine Shop III department, June 6, 1953.

527. SOA Pilsen, f. KV KSČ Pilsen, kart. 450, inv. č. 3603, resolutions from factories, sent to the KV KSČ and ÚV KSČ, June 1953.

528. VÚA, f. MNO, inv. č. 1999, kart. 344, sig. 44/1/3, č.j. 004500 NGŠ 1953, report of Lt. Col. Vojtěch Dolníček, deputy chief of the general staff, on the situation in Pilsen, May 30, – June 3, 1953, June 6, 1953; SOA Pilsen, f. KV KSČ Pilsen, kart. 449, inv. č. 3603, telegram from KV KSČ to ÚV KSČ No. 316 z, June 2, 1953, 8:50 a.m.; NA, f. MV NA, inv. č. 169, kart. 258, report from the Ministry of Interior secretariat to Prime Minister Viliamu Široký, č. j. 20/53 PT, June 2, 1953.

529. SOA Pilsen, f. KV KSČ Pilsen, kart. 449, inv. č. 3603, telegram from KV KSČ to ÚV KSČ No. 319 z June 3, 1953, 1:55 a.m.; PA Škoda, f. ZVIL, ZVIL 203

Osob 2, lists of absences from work at individual workplaces of the ZVIL in Pilsen on 1 June 1953, June 1953.

530. SOA Pilsen, f. KV KSČ Pilsen, kart. 449, inv. č. 3603, telegram from KV KSČ to ÚV KSČ No. 321, June 3, 1953, 8.45 p.m.; Ibid., telegram from KV KSČ to ÚV KSČ No. 324, June 5, 1953, 11.05 p.m.

531. SOA Pilsen, f. KV KSČ Pilsen, kart. 449, inv. č. 3603, report from the member's meeting of the ZO KSČ in Machine Shop I of the ZVIL, June 4, 1953; Ibid., report from the member's meeting of the ZO KSČ in Machine Shop IV of the ZVIL, June 4, 1953.

532. Ibid., kart. 451, inv. č. 3603, report from the KS VB in Pilsen sent to the KV KSČ in Pilsen, June 7, 1953.

533. SOA Pilsen, f. KV KSČ Pilsen, kart. 450, inv. č. 3603, minutes of the extraordinary meeting of MV KSČ, June 3, 1953.

534. NA, f. ÚV KSČ – 1261/0/22, sv. 58, a. j. 157/13, Minutes of the meeting of the ÚV KSČ political secretariat, June 3, 1953.

535. NA, f. ÚV KSČ – 1261/0/12, sv. 43, a. j. 231/1, Minutes of the meeting of the ÚV KSČ organizational secretariat, August 3, 1953.

536. SOA Pilsen, f. KV KSČ Pilsen, kart. 449, inv. č. 3603, telegram from KV KSČ to ÚV KSČ No. 315 z, June 2, 1953, 2.35 a.m.

537. SOA Pilsen, f. ZKNV Pilsen, kart. 147, report of the KS VB in Pilsen to the chairman of the KNV in Pilsen, June 2, 1953; Ibid., f. KV KSČ Pilsen, kart. 449, inv. č. 3603, telegram from KV KSČ to ÚV KSČ No. 315 z, June 2, 1953, 2.35 a.m.

538. NA, f. Měnová reforma, reports from the regions sent to the ÚV KSČ, June 3, 1953; Jirásek and Šůla, *Velká peněžní loupež*, 105–118.

539. ABS, f. 305, sv. 305–403–3, report on the sentiments among the population regarding the currency reform, beginning of June, 1953.

540. Štěpánek, *Utajené povstání 1953*, 60–75; Pernes, "Neznámý dokument o peněžní reformě," 185; Jan Kumpera, "Pilsen na stránkách New York Times 1945 a 1953," in *Sborník Pedagogické fakulty Západočeské univerzity v Plzni: Dějepis XVI* (Prague: Státní pedagogicé nakladatelství, 1995), 113–120.

541. SOkA v Blovicích, f. OS Pilsen, zn. 1T 191/1953, verdict of the People's Court z 1. 10. 1953; Ibid., zn. 3T 122/1953; SOA Pilsen, f. KV KSČ Pilsen, kart. 451, inv. č. 3603, report from the KS VB in Pilsen sent to the KV KSČ in Pilsen, June 8, 1953.

542. Zdeněk Štěpánek, "Jako když hodíte kámen do vody," *Škodovák*, May 31, 1991, 2.

543. SOA Pilsen, f. ZKNV Pilsen, kart. 147, report of the JNV chairman in Pilsen to chairman of the KNV in Pilsen June 4, 1953.

544. Ibid., f. KV KSČ Pilsen, kart. 29, inv. č. 100, minutes of the plenary session of KV KSČ, June 2, 1953.

545. Ibid., kart. 450, inv. č. 3603, minutes of the extraordinary meeting of MV KSČ June 3, 1953.

546. ABS, f. A2/1, sv. 250, Ministry of Interior advisory board, May 30, 1957, report of the military counter-intelligence on the Pilsen protests, June 1953; SOA

Pilsen, f. KV KSČ Pilsen, kart. 29, inv. č. 100, minutes of the plenary session of KV KSČ, June 2, 1953.

547. ABS, f. A8/1, sv. 1218, report from the interrogation of Milan Moučka for the Ministry of Interior inspectorate, July 15, 1964.

548. Ibid., f. A2/1, sv. 494, report on the situation in Pilsen during the currency reform, sent to KS StB, November 3, 1953.

549. SOkA v Blovicích, f. OS Pilsen, zn. 1T 136/1953, request of Václav Melka for retrial, May 19, 1955; Ibid., zn. 1T 176/1953, letter from Božena Potočiarová, wife of Antonín Potočiar, to the President, October 16, 1953; Ibid., zn. 3T 132/1953, appellate proceedings file with the Regional Court in Pilsen, October 2, 1953.

550. Ibid., zn. 1T 139/1953, requests of Jaroslav Treml for retrial, October 25, 1953 and March 21, 1954.

551. Ibid., zn. 3T 132/1953, appellate proceedings file with the Regional Court in Pilsen, October 23, 1953.

552. Ibid., appellate proceedings file with the Regional Court in Pilsen, November 13, 1953.

553. Ibid., zn. 1T 160/1953, Josef Fencl's statement, taken in the Ostrov nad Ohří prison, June 5, 1956.

554. ABS, f. A8/1, sv. 1218, Josef Fencl's statement for the Ministry of Interior inspectorate, June 2, 1964; Šlouf, "Byly Plzeňské demonstrace," 85–96.

555. SOkA v Blovicích, f. OS Pilsen, zn. 3T 148/1953, report of the interrogation of witness Jiří Hruška at the District Prosecutor's Office in Pilsen 18. 8. 1953; Ibid., zn. 3T 148/1953, court file of the main hearing, September 10, 1953, testimony of Jindřich Kutzman; Nazarkevyč, "Jsme národ Masarykův," 3.

556. ABS, f. KS MV Pilsen, sv. V-1131 Pilsen, agent's report from KS StB in Pilsen, July 291953.

557. SOkA v Blovicích, f. OS Pilsen, zn. 1T 159/1953, agent's report from Eva Hrůzová regarding Anna Karnoldová, June 6, 1953.

558. ABS, f. A2/1, sv. 494, list of 108 persons proposed for release, June 1953.

559. SOkA v Blovicích, f. OS Pilsen, zn. 1T 144/1953, Josef Hegner's statement, June 5, 1953.

560. Ibid., Josefem Hegner's statement, taken at the District Prosecutor's Office in Pilsen-City, July 2, 1969.

561. ABS, f. A2/1, sv. 494, report on the situation in Pilsen during the currency reform, sent to KS StB, November 3, 1953.

562. Ibid., proposal for a public trial with the "instigators of the subversive , provocative protest in Pilsen," June 2, 1953; Ibid., f. 310, sv. 310–68–4, proposal for a public trial 2, June 2, 1953.

563. Ibid..

564. Ibid., f. A2/1, sv. 494, report on the situation in Pilsen during the currency reform, sent to KS StB, November 3, 1953; Ibid., f. KS MV Pilsen, sv. V-1310.

565. Ibid., f. A2/1, sv. 494, proposal for a public trial with the "instigators of the subversive , provocative protest in Pilsen," June 2, 1953; Ibid., f. 310, sv. 310–68–4, proposal for a public trial 2, June 2, 1953.

566. Ibid.

567. Ibid., f. A2/1, sv. 494, report for Deputy Minister of National Security Antonín Prchala, July 6, 1953; *NA*, f. ÚV KSČ – 1261/0/22, sv. 60, a. j. 160/18, Minutes of the meeting of the ÚV KSČ political secretariat, June 23, 1953.

568. Criminal Code of 12 July 1950, No. 86/1950 Sb.

569. ABS, f. A2/1, sv. 494, report for Deputy Minister of National Security Antonín Prchala, July 6, 1953; NA, ÚV KSČ – 1261/0/22, sv. 60, a. j. 160/18, Minutes of the meeting of the ÚV KSČ political secretariat, June 23, 1953.

570. ABS, f. A2/1, sv. 494, list of 108 persons proposed for release, June 1953.

571. These included the followig criminal cases tried by the People's Court in Pilsen: 1T 136/1953 (Václav Melka et al.), 1T 138/1953 (Josef Nečas et al.), 1T 139/1953 (Jaroslav Treml et al.), 1T 140/1953 (Karel Schaffhauser et al.), 1T 141/1953 (Anežka Zámečková et al.), 1T 142/1953 (Rudolf Krüger et al.), 1T 143/1953 (Adolf Jílek a spol), 1T 144/1953 (Anežka Krinesová et al.), 1T 145/1953 (Jan Holeček et al.), 1T 146/1953 (Bohuslav Pikart et al.), 1T 148/1953 (Pavel Katera et al.), 1T 149/1953 (Gustav Moravec et al.), 1T 151/1953 (František Moravec et al.), 1T 153/1953 (Emil Otradovec et al.).

572. These included the followig criminal cases tried by the People's Court in Pilsen: 1T 157/1953 (Miroslav Kanta), 1T 158/1953 (Vladimír Šimice), 1T 159/1953 (Eva Hrůzová), 1T 160/1953 (Josef Fencl), 1T 163/1953 (Bohumil Malotín), 1T 164/1953 (Karel Kodym), 1T 166/1953 (Václav Černý, Jaroslav Forst), 1T 169/1953 (Václav Eliáš, Václav Eliáš), 1T 170/1953 (Alfons a Anna Kroupovi), 1T 174/1953 (Ladislav Hobl), 1T 176/1953 (Antonín Potočiar), 1T 182/1953 (František Duchoň), 1T 234/1953 (Jaroslav Satoria), 1T 258/1953 (Rudolf Držka), 1T 259/1953 (František Prchal), 2T 157/1953 (Václav Vrzal), 2T 161/1953 (Miloslav Höll), 2T 180/1953 (Jaroslav Žižka), 3T 132/1953 (Metoděj Stodůlka, František Eret), 3T 133/1953 (Alžběta Taušová), 3T 147/1953 (Václav Soukup), 3T 148/1953 (Josef Vacek, Jindřich Kutzman), 3T 158/1953 (Jaroslav Schlichta), 3T 175/1953 (Karel Šindler), 3T 186/1953 (František Vorlovský), Ml 31/53 (Jaroslav Vlček), 1T 6/1954 (Julie Hrůzová), 1T 39/1954 (Ewald Fail), 3T 274/54 (Miloslav Vokáč).

573. ABS, f. A2/1, sv. 1586, reports on the main hearings in each separate trial, sent to Minister of National Security Karol Bacílek, July 1953.

574. PA Škoda, f. ROH, ROH 14 PV 61, Minutes of the meeting of the presidium of ZR ZVIL in Pilsen July 20, 1953.

575. Ibid., zn. 1T 136/1953, file from the People's Court in Pilsen, July 8, 1953, request of Jaroslav Drnec.

576. Ibid., zn. 1T 144/1953, court file of the main hearing, July 17, 1953, testimony of Josef Bůžek.

577. Ibid., Supreme Court verdict, zn. 3Tz 1/1969 z 30. 1. 1969.

578. Ibid., zn. 1T 149/1953, verdict of July 20, 1953.

579. Ibid., zn. 1T 146/1953, verdict of the Regional Court in Prague, September 30, 1953, zn. 1To 53/1953.

580. Štěpánek, *Utajené povstání 1953*, 63.

581. ABS, f. A2/1, sv. 1586, reports on the main hearings in each separate trial, sent to Minister of National Security Karolu Bacílek, July 1953.

582. Ibid., report from the KS StB in Pilsen, July 1953.

583. Ibid., reports on trial proceedings, sent to Minister of National Security Karol Bacílek, July 16, 1953 3.

584. Skála, "Měnová reforma," 606; Jirásek and Šůla, *Velká peněžní loupež*, 134.

585. Baťková, *Plzeňské povstání*, 140–168.

586. Baťková, *Plzeňské povstání*, s. 169.

587. Skála, "Měnová reforma," 607.

588. SOkA v Blovicích, f. OS Pilsen, zn. 1T 149/1953, verdict of July 20, 1953.

589. Ibid., request of Bohumil Vávra, sent to the People's Court in Pilsen, January 2, 1955.

590. Ibid., letter from the ZO KSČ of the Regional Theater in Pilsen to the People's Court in Pilsen, June 14, 1956, signed by Josef Větrovec; Ibid., letter from the director of the Regional Theater in Pilsen to the People's Court in Pilsen, May 28, 1956; AMP, f. OF Vladimír Havlic, kart. 2018, inv. č. 19/2 (24), letter from Miroslav Šubrt to the Civic Forum in Pilsen, January 16, 1990.

591. SOkA v Blovicích, f. OS Pilsen, zn. 1T 149/1953, report on the closed hearing of the Regional Court in Pilsen, July 19, 1956; Ibid., memorandum of the Ministry of Justice, sent to the People's Court in Pilsen, September 24, , 1956; Ibid., decision of the District Court in Prague 1, February 18, 1971.

592. Act No. 82/1968 Sb., of 25 July 1968, on Judicial Rehabilitation; Act. No. 70/1970 Sb., of 8 July 1970, amending and supplementing the Act. No. 82/1968 Sb., on Judicial Rehabilitation; SOkA v Blovicích, f. OS Pilsen, zn. 1T 144/1953, rozsudek Nejvyššího soudu zn. 3Tz 1/1969 z 30. 1. 1969.

593. Act No. 82/1968 Sb., of 23 April 1990, on Judicial Rehabilitation; Act. No. 47/1991 Sb., of 30 January 1991, amending and supplementing the Act. No. 119/1990 Sb., on Judicial Rehabilitation; Act. No. 198/1993 Sb., of 9 July 1993 on Illegality of the Communist Regime.

594. Štěpánek, *Utajené povstání 1953*, 66.

595. SOkA v Blovicích, f. OS Pilsen, zn. 1T 146/1953, verdictof the Supreme Court of the Czech Republic, January 21, 1992, zn. 3Tz 58/1991.

596. Ibid., zn. 1T 142/1953, verdictof the Supreme Court of the Czech Republic, January 21, 1992, zn. 3Tz 59/1991; Ibid., verdict of the District Court in Pilsen-City, February 9, 1993, zn. 3T 151/92.

597. Ibid., zn. 1T 234/1953, verdict of the District Court in Pilsen-City, December 4, 1990.

598. See the files referenced in footnotes 1071 and 1072 of this text.

599. See the list rferenced in footnote 1070 of this text.

600. VÚA, f. MNO, inv. č. 1999, kart. 344, sig. 44/1/3, č.j. 004500 NGŠ 1953, report of Lt. Col. Vojtěch Dolníček, deputy chief of the general staff, on the situation in Pilsen, May 30, – June 3, 1953, June 6, 1953.

601. Cf. Rákosník, *Sovětizace sociálního státu*; Kalinová, *Společenské proměny*.

602. ABS, f. KS MV Pilsen, V-868 Pilsen; Ibid., V-881 Pilsen.

603. SOkA v Blovicích, f. OS Pilsen, zn. T I 568/49.

604. *NA*, f. ÚV KSČ – 1481, sv. 15, a. j. 110, Minutes of the nationwide meeting of chief secretaries of KV KSČ, heads of the departments of ÚV KSČ and chief officials of mass organizations, held on June 11, 1953; speech by Antonín Zápotocký.

605. McDermott, "Lidový odpor v komunistickém Československu," 221.

606. *Sčítání lidu v Republice československé ke dni 1. března 1950, díl 2: Věkové složení a povolání obyvatelstva* (Prague: Státní úřad statistický, 1958), 6–21.

607. *Sčítání lidu a soupis domů a bytů v Republice československé ke dni 1. března 1950, díl 1: Nejdůležitější výsledky sčítání lidu a soupis domů a bytů za kraje, okresy a města* (Prague: Státní úřad statistický, 1957), 55.

608. PA Škoda, f. ZVIL, ZVIL 1552 PV 1988, lists of persons from Machine Shop IV punished for participating in the protests of 1 June 1953, z 1June 3, 1953; NA, f. ÚV KSČ – 1481, sv. 15, a. j. 110, Minutes of the nationwide meeting of chief secretaries of KV KSČ, heads of the departments of ÚV KSČ and chief officials of mass organizations, held on June 11, 1953; speech by Antonín Zápotocký.

609. PA Škoda, f. ZVIL, ZVIL 1552 PV 1988, employee requests for waiver of punishment for participation in the protests, 1954.

610. Ibid., ZVIL 1455 PV 109, announcement of extraordinary measures, June 1, 1953.

611. Ibid., copies of requests for the approval of an employee's dismissal sent to the JNV in Pilsen, from 1953.

612. AMP, f. MV KSČ Pilsen, kart. 42, Minutes of the meeting of the MV KSČ executive committee in Pilsen June 8, 1953.

613. PA Škoda, f. ZVIL, ZVIL 1455 PV 109, announcement of extraordinary measures, June 1, 1953.

614. Ibid., f. ROH, ROH 14 PV 34, Minutes of the meeting of the presidium of ZR ZVIL in Pilsen, June 15, 1953.

615. Ibid., ROH 14 PV 312, Minutes of the meeting of the presidium of ZR ZVIL in Pilsen September 9, 1953.

616. Ibid., ROH 16 ETD 35, resolution of the presidium of ZR ZVIL in Pilsen, July 2, 1953.

617. Kaplan and Váchová, *Perzekuce po měnové reformě*, 43.

618. PA Škoda, f. ZVIL, ZVIL 459 PŘ 813, resolution of CZV KSČ in the ZVIL in Pilsen, June 30, 1953.

619. NA, f. ÚV KSČ – 1261/0/12, sv. 43, a. j. 231/1, Minutes of the meeting of the ÚV KSČ organizational secretariat, August 3, 1953.

620. PA Škoda, f. ROH, ROH 14 PV 61, Minutes of the meeting of the presidium of ZR ZVIL in Pilsen 2, June 2, 1953.

621. Ibid., f. ZVIL, ZVIL 203 Osob 2, lists of absences from work at individual workplaces of the ZVIL in Pilsen on 1 June 1953, June 1953; Ibid., ZVIL 203 OS 302, lists of ZVIL employees sent by KS StB in Pilsen, from 1953.

622. SOkA v Blovicích, f. OS Pilsen, zn. 1T 39/1954, action filed by the District Prosecutor in Pilsen with the People's Court in Pilsen, February 3, 1954.

623. NA, f. ÚV KSČ – 1261/0/12, sv. 43, a. j. 231/1, Minutes of the meeting of the ÚV KSČ organizational secretariat, August 3, 1953.

624. SOkA v Blovicích, f. OS Pilsen, zn. 1T 139/1953, employee evaluation of František Hataj by the ROH workshop council in Machine Shop I, August 18, 1954.

625. PA Škoda, f. ZVIL, ZVIL 203 Os 303, report of the ZVIL investigation commission on investigation in the Construction and Investment departments, June 2, 1953.

626. SOA Pilsen, f. PV KSČ Škoda, kart. 4, inv. č. 3, minutes of the plenary session of PV KSČ Škoda, November 10, 1953.

627. PA Škoda, f. ZVIL, ZVIL 1552 PV 1988, notice of the investigation commission regarding the punishment of Stanislav Pech, June 1953; Ibid., lists of persons from Machine Shop IV punished for participating in the protests of 1 June 1953, June 13, 1953; NA, f. ÚV KSČ – 1261/0/12, sv. 43, a. j. 231/1, Minutes of the meeting of the ÚV KSČ organizational secretariat, August 3, 1953.

628. PA Škoda, f. ZVIL, ZVIL 1552 PV 1988, notice of the investigation commission regarding the change of punishment of Václav Frauz, June 15, 1953.

629. Ibid., report of the testimonies of Jaroslav Karas, written by the investigation commission, June 1, 1953.

630. Ibid., ZVIL 203 Osob 2, supplement to the list of employees who had left their departments on June 1 without permission, June 8, 1953.

631. Ibid., ZVIL 1552 PV 1988, lists of persons from Machine Shop IV punished for participating in the protests of 1 June 1953, 1953; Ibid., ZVIL 1552 PV 1988, notice of the investigation commission regarding the punishment of Karel Křepínský, June 1953.

632. Ibid., ZVIL 1474 ŘED 84, complaint lodged by Jaroslav Trol, September 16, 1953.

633. Ibid., f. ROH, ROH 16 ETD 35, lists of persons from plants 60 to 67 punished for participating in the protests of 1 June 1953, undated.

634. Ibid., f. ZVIL, ZVIL 1474 ŘED 84, complaint lodged by Jaroslav Trol, September 16, 1953.

635. SOA Pilsen, f. PV KSČ Škoda, kart. 4, inv. č. 3, minutes of the plenary session of PV KSČ Škoda, November 10, 1953.

636. PA Škoda, f. ZVIL, ZVIL 1455 PV 109, Minutes of the meeting of the factory committee and the section secretaries, September 17, 1953.

637. Ibid., complaint lodged by Ms. Míková, sent to the ZR ZVIL in Pilsen, November 6, 1953.

638. Ibid., ZVIL 203, schedule of shifts for ZVIL employees assisting in evictions, from 1953.

639. Ibid., ZVIL 1455 PV 303, complaint lodged by Jan Cimrhanzl regarding the course of his eviction from the company apartment, September 15, 1953.

640. Ibid., ZVIL 1455 PV 109, complaint lodged by Ing. Václav Nachtmann, sent to the ZR ZVIL in Pilsen, August 14, 1953.

641. Ibid., list of employees reassigned to worker professions, from 1953.

642. Ibid., ZVIL 203 PŘ 1674, notice for the ZVIL director, August 26, 1953; SOA Pilsen, f. KV KSČ Pilsen, kart. 449, inv. č. 3603, report on the implementation of the ÚV KSČ resolution regarding the events in Pilsen on 1 June 1953, undated; PA Škoda, f. ZVIL, ZVIL 203, list of dismissed or reassigned clerical workers, from 1953; Ibid., f. ROH, ROH 14 PV 34, Minutes of the meeting of the presidium of ZR ZVIL in Pilsen, June 26, 1953; McDermott, "Lidový odpor v komunistickém Československu," 222.

643. Kaplan and Váchová, *Perzekuce po měnové reformě*, 43–129.

644. SOA Pilsen, f. PV KSČ Škoda, kart. 4, inv. č. 3, minutes of the plenary session of PV KSČ Škoda, July 21, 1953.

645. PA Škoda, f. ZVIL, ZVIL 203 PŘ 1674, proposal of director František Brabec, sent to CZV KSČ ZVIL in Pilsen, September18, 1953.

646. Ibid., ZVIL 203 Osob 256, notice for the ZVIL director, October 30, 1953.

647. Ibid., ZVIL 1455 PV 109, request of the Machine Shop II workshop council, sent to ZR ZVIL, September 15, 1953; Ibid., report from the ZVIL personnel records department, sent to ZR ZVIL, October 6, 1953.

648. Ibid., ZVIL 1513 PV 1441, ZR ZVIL decision on "pardoning" employees punished for participating in the protests, 1954; Ibid., ZVIL 1074 ŘED 84, ZR ZVIL decision on "pardoning" employees punished for participating in the protests, 1954; Ibid., ZVIL 1515 PV 1287, Minutes of the meeting of ZR and the review board of workshop council chairmen, December 23, 1953.

649. VOA, f. ÚRO – P, kart. 16, inv. č. 179, draft directive for implementing the government decree introducing measures against high employee turnover and absenteeism, June 1953.

650. Ibid., inv. č. 181, minutes of the extraordinary meeting of the presidium of ÚRO, July 6, 1953; Státník, *Sankční pracovní právo*, s. 142–162.

651. SOA Pilsen, f. KV KSČ Pilsen, kart. 450, inv. č. 3603, report "June 1 in Schools," July 13, 1953.

652. NA, f. ÚV KSČ – 1261/0/12, sv. 43, a. j. 231/1, Minutes of the meeting of the ÚV KSČ organizational secretariat, August 3, 1953.

653. SOA Pilsen, f. KV KSČ Pilsen, kart. 449, inv. č. 3603, report on the implementation of the ÚV KSČ resolution regarding the events in Pilsen on 1 June 1953, undated; Ibid., kart. 450, inv. č. 3603, report "June 1 in Schools," July 13, 1953; Skála, "Měnová reforma," 603.

654. SOA Pilsen, f. KV KSČ Pilsen, kart. 450, inv. č. 3603, report "June 1 in Schools," July 13, 1953.

655. Ibid., report from the Vocational College of Social and Health Work in Pilsen, undated.

656. Ibid., report from the school organizations members' meetings, June 4, 1953.

657. Ibid., kart. 451, inv. č. 3603, report on the vetting of the staff of the economic administration department of the KV KSČ secretariat, July 8, 1953, statement of Barbora Šebánková.

658. Ibid., kart. 450, inv. č. 3603, report "June 1 in Schools," July 13, 1953.

659. Ibid., letter from the KSČ organization at the College of Mechanical and Electrical Engineering in Pilsen to ÚV KSČ, June 20, 1953.

660. Ibid., report from the KSČ organization at the Pilsen Medical School, July 4, 1953.

661. NA, f. ÚV KSČ – 1261/0/12, sv. 43, a. j. 231/1, Minutes of the meeting of the ÚV KSČ organizational secretariat, August 3, 1953.

662. Ibid., f. ÚV KSČ – 1481, sv. 15, a. j. 110, Minutes of the nationwide meeting of chief secretaries of KV KSČ, heads of the departments of ÚV KSČ and chief officials of mass organizations, held on June 11, 1953; speech byVáclav Kopecký. Matěj Kotalík, "'Páskové' a 'chuligáni' proti režimu?: Na okraj tradičních konceptů odboje a rezistence," in *Odboj a odpor proti komunistickému režimu v Československu a střední Evropě* (Prague: ÚSTR, 2010), 225–232.

663. SOA Pilsen, f. KV KSČ Pilsen, kart. 450, inv. č. 3603, list of industrial enterprises with more than 500 employees in the Pilsen region, 1953.

664. Ibid., ZVIL employee structure, 1953; *NA*, f. ÚV KSČ – 1261/0/12, sv. 43, a. j. 231/1, Minutes of the meeting of the ÚV KSČ organizational secretariat, August 3, 1953.

665. PA Škoda, f. ZVIL, ZVIL 203, list of departments, from 1953; Ibid., f. ROH, ROH 14 PV 346, Minutes of the meeting of the presidium of ZR ZVIL in Pilsen 1, June 1, 1953.

666. Ibid., f. ZVIL, ZVIL 204 458, notice to the director, June 3, 1953.

667. SOA Pilsen, f. KV KSČ Pilsen, kart. 449, inv. č. 3603, implementation of the currency reform and implementing the Party and government resolution to abolish the ration system on foodstuffs and industrial goods in the Pilsen region, 1953; Kaplan, *Sociální souvislosti krizí*, 9.

668. SOA Pilsen, f. KV KSČ Pilsen, kart. 450, inv. č. 3603, ZVIL employee structure, 1953; NA, f. ÚV KSČ – 1261/0/12, sv. 43, a. j. 231/1, Minutes of the meeting of the ÚV KSČ organizational secretariat, August 3, 1953.

669. SOkA v Blovicích, f. OS Pilsen, zn. 2T 157/1953, verdict of the People's Court in Pilsen, November 13, 1953; Ibid., zn. 2T 170/1953, Alfons Kroupa's statement, taken by the VB District Department in Pilsen 25. 6. 1953; ABS, f. KS MV Pilsen, sv. V-1131 Pilsen, Jindřich Kutzman's statement, taken by the KS StB in Pilsen, June 4, 1953; Ibid., Jindřich Kutzman's statement, taken by the KS StB in Pilsen, 10. 6. 1953.

670. Ibid., sv. V-868 Pilsen; Ibid., sv. V-881 Pilsen.

671. *NA*, f. ÚV KSČ – 1261/0/12, sv. 43, a. j. 231/1, Minutes of the meeting of the ÚV KSČ organizational secretariat, August 3, 1953.

672. SOA Pilsen, f. KV KSČ Pilsen, kart. 450, inv. č. 3603, list of members and candidates of the MV KSČ in Pilsen, 1953; NA, f. ÚV KSČ – 1261/0/12, sv. 43, a. j. 231/1, Minutes of the meeting of the ÚV KSČ organizational secretariat, August 3, 1953.

673. Cf. Šlouf, "Rivalita komunistické strany a sociální demokracie," 113–137; Šlajs, Václav, *Růže z Pekla: O historii a osobnostech sociální demokracie na Plzeňsku a v Plzeňském kraji 1878–2006* (Pilsen: Krajský výkonný výbor ČSSD, 2006).

674. NA, f. ÚV KSČ – 1481, sv. 15, a. j. 110, Minutes of the nationwide meeting of chief secretaries of KV KSČ, heads of the departments of ÚV KSČ and chief officials of mass organizations, held on June 11, 1953; speech byVáclav Kopecký.

675. SOA Pilsen, f. PV KSČ Škoda, kart. 4, inv. č. 3, minutes of the plenary session of PV KSČ Škoda, July 7, 1953; AMP, f. MV KSČ Pilsen, kart. 42, Minutes of the meeting of the MV KSČ executive committee in Pilsen, June 25, 1953.

676. SOA Pilsen, f. PV KSČ Škoda, kart. 1, inv. č. 2, PV KSČ Škoda conference, March 29, 1953; Ibid., kart. 18, inv. č. 4, Minutes of the meeting of the presidium of PV KSČ Škoda, May 15, 1951.

677. PA Škoda, f. ZVIL, ZVIL 1458 PV 59, Minutes of the meeting of ZR, ZVIL 1, June 1, 1953; Ibid., f. ROH, ROH 14 PV 61, Minutes of the meeting of the presidium of ZR ZVIL in Pilsen, January 14, 1953.

678. SOA Pilsen, f. KV KSČ Pilsen, kart. 29, inv. č. 100, minutes of the plenary session of KV KSČ, June 2, 1953.

679. PA Škoda, f. ROH, ROH 14 PV 33, outline of a report on the events in Pilsen on 1 June 1953, undated; SOA Pilsen, f. ZKNV Pilsen, kart. 147, report of the KS VB in Pilsen to the chairman of the KNV in Pilsen, June 4, 1953; Ibid., f. KV KSČ Pilsen, kart. 450, inv. č. 3603, minutes of the extraordinary meeting of MV KSČ executive committee, June 3, 1953; NA, f. MF Praha, Tajné – peněžní reforma 1953, kart. 11, report on the exchange and conversion of currency undated.

680. SOA Pilsen, f. KV KSČ Pilsen, kart. 449, inv. č. 3603, report from the member's meeting of the ZO KSČ in Machine Shop I in ZVIL, June 4, 1953.

681. PA Škoda, f. ROH, ROH 13 669, Minutes of the meeting of ZR, 2, June 2, 1951.

682. Heumos, *Vyhrňme si rukávy*, 66.

683. Adam Skála, "Pokusy o hromadné vystěhovávání Plzeňských obyvatel po roce 1948," *Minulostí západočeského kraje* 47, č. 1 (2012): 187–245.

684. Vladimír Bricha, *V první linii* (Pilsen: Západočeský KV KSČ v Plzni, 1968), 39.

685. SOA Pilsen, f. KV KSČ Pilsen, kart. 450, inv. č. 3603, minutes of the extraordinary meeting of MV KSČ, June 3, 1953; SOkA v Blovicích, f. OS Pilsen, zn. 1T 159/1953, report on the investigation conducted by KS StB in Pilsen, June 1, 1953.

686. NA, f. ÚV KSČ – 1481, sv. 15, a. j. 110, Minutes of the nationwide meeting of chief secretaries of KV KSČ, heads of the departments of ÚV KSČ and chief officials of mass organizations, held on June 11, 1953; speech byJan Hlína.

687. SOA Pilsen, f. KV KSČ Pilsen, kart. 449, inv. č. 3603, implementation of the currency reform and implementing the Party and government resolution to abolish the ration system on foodstuffs and industrial goods in the Pilsen region, 1953.

688. Ibid., kart. 29, inv. č. 100, minutes of the plenary session of KV KSČ, June 2, 1953.

689. Ibid., kart. 450, inv. č. 3603, minutes of the extraordinary meeting of MV KSČ June 3, 1953.

690. Ibid., kart. 451, inv. č. 3603, reports of the KS VB in Pilsen sent to the KV KSČ in Pilsen on June 6, 1953, June 8, 1953, June 2, 1953 and June 1, 1953; Adam Skála, "‚A bude se vám tam bydlet jako v Tatrách': Nucené vystěhování Plzeňských občanů do obce Úterý v roce 1953," in *Sborník k poctě Evy a Karla Waskových, západočeských archivářů*, ed. Marie Wasková (Pilsen: M. Wasková, 2011), 314.

691. SOA Pilsen, f. KV KSČ Pilsen, kart. 108, inv. č. 804, Minutes of the meeting of the KV KSČ executive committee, June 24, 1953.

692. Skála, "Pokusy o hromadné vystěhovávání," 187–245.

693. Neff, "Oprátka pro Masaryka," 1–2.

694. Skála, "A bude se vám tam bydlet," 314.

695. SOkA v Blovicích, f. OS Pilsen, zn. 1T 136/1953, JNV's notice of eviction of Jaroslav Modrý from his apartment, June 6, 1953.

696. Skála, "A bude se vám tam bydlet," 315–316.

697. SOkA v Blovicích, f. OS Pilsen, zn. 1T 136/1953, JNV's notice of eviction of Jaroslav Modrý from his apartment, June 6, 1953.

698. SOA Pilsen, f. KV KSČ Pilsen, kart. 108, inv. č. 810, Minutes of the meeting of the KV KSČ executive committee, July 17, 1953.

699. Skála, ",A bude se vám tam bydlet," 315–316.

700. SOA Pilsen, f. KV KSČ Pilsen, kart. 449, inv. č. 3603, telegram from ÚV KSČ to KV KSČ No. 482, June 1, 1953, 10 p.m.

701. NA, f. ÚV KSČ – 1481, sv. 15, a. j. 110, Minutes of the nationwide meeting of chief secretaries of KV KSČ, heads of the departments of ÚV KSČ and chief officials of mass organizations, held on June 11, 1953; speech by Antonín Zápotocký; Jirásek and Šůla, *Velká peněžní loupež*, 136–140.

702. SOA Pilsen, f. KV KSČ Pilsen, kart. 451, inv. č. 3603, report of the KS VB in Pilsen, sent to the KV KSČ in Pilsen on 1 June 1953.

703. Ibid., kart. 449, inv. č. 3603, report on the implementation of the ÚV KSČ resolution regarding the events in Pilsen on 1 June 1953, undated

704. Ibid., f. ZKNV Pilsen, kart. 147, report from KS VB in Pilsen to the KNV in Pilsen, June 13, 1953.

705. Skála, "Pokusy o hromadné vystěhovávání," 187–245.

706. AMP, f. MV KSČ Pilsen, kart. 14, Minutes of the meeting of the MV KSČ in Pilsen, July 13, 1953.

707. SOA Pilsen, f. KV KSČ Pilsen, kart. 450, inv. č. 3603, report from the Blatná district, July 25, 1953.

708. NA, f. ÚV KSČ – 1481, sv. 15, a. j. 110, Minutes of the nationwide meeting of chief secretaries of KV KSČ, heads of the departments of ÚV KSČ and chief officials of mass organizations, held on June 11, 1953; speech by Antonín Zápotocký; Hykeš, "Dramatické události," 1–5.

709. NA, f. ÚV KSČ – 1261/2/1, sv. 361, a. j. 2190, report on the inspection trip to Pilsen on October 14–16 1953.

710. SOA Pilsen, f. KV KSČ Pilsen, kart. 449, inv. č. 3603, report on the implementation of the ÚV KSČ resolution regarding the events in Pilsen on 1 June 1953, undated.

711. Skála, "Pokusy o hromadné vystěhovávání," 187–245.

712. SOA Pilsen, f. KV KSČ Pilsen, kart. 108, inv. č. 808, Minutes of the meeting of the KV KSČ executive committee, July 10, 1953.

713. Skála, "Pokusy o hromadné vystěhovávání," 187–245.

714. Pernes, *Snahy o překonání*, s. 16–26.

715. SOA Pilsen, f. KV KSČ Pilsen, kart. 449, inv. č. 3603, telegram from ÚV KSČ to KV KSČ No. 482, June 1, 1953, 10 p.m.; Ibid., kart. 29, inv. č. 100, minutes of the plenary session of KV KSČ, June 2, 1953.

716. Ibid., kart. 108, inv. č. 800, Minutes of the meeting of the KV KSČ executive committee, June 5, 1953; Ibid., kart. 449, inv. č. 3603, telegram from KV KSČ to ÚV KSČ No. 319, June 3, 1953, 1.55 a.m.

717. Ibid., telegram from KV KSČ to ÚV KSČ No. 322, June 4, 1953, 4.45 a.m.; Ibid., telegram from KV KSČ to ÚV KSČ No. 323, June 5, 1953, 7:40 a.m.

718. "Pilsenští pracující se vypořádají s reakcí," *Pravda*, June 5, 1953, 1–2; Baťková, *Plzeňské povstání*, s. 177–186.

719. Kumera, "Pilsen na stránkách," 113–120.

720. SOA Pilsen, f. KV KSČ Pilsen, kart. 450, inv. č. 3603, complaint of the LM unit from the Pilsen Power Distribution Plant to KV KSČ in Pilsen, sent to ÚV KSČ, June 15, 1953.

721. NA, f. ÚV KSČ – 1261/0/12, sv. 39, a. j. 223/42, Minutes of the meeting of the ÚV KSČ organizational secretariat, June 17, 1953.

722. SOA Pilsen, f. KV KSČ Pilsen, kart. 451, inv. č. 3603, minutes of the extraordinary meeting of the KV KSČ executive committee, September 10, 1953; Skála, "Měnová reforma 1. června," 629.

723. SOA Pilsen, f. KV KSČ Pilsen, kart. 450, inv. č. 3603, minutes of the extraordinary meeting of MV KSČ executive committee, June 3, 1953.

724. Ibid., vetting of members of party authorities following the currency reform, July 1953; AMP, f. MV KSČ Pilsen, inv. č. 42, kart. 14, Minutes of the meeting of the MV KSČ in Pilsen, September 9, 1953.

725. SOA Pilsen, f. KV KSČ Pilsen, kart. 450, inv. č. 3603, minutes of the extraordinary meeting of MV KSČ, June 3, 1953, speech by Ladislav Kopřiva.

726. Ibid.

727. AMP, f. MV KSČ Pilsen, inv. č. 494, kart. 42, Minutes of the meeting of the MV KSČ executive committee in Pilsen, June 23, 1953.

728. SOA Pilsen, f. KV KSČ Pilsen, kart. 449, inv. č. 3603, telegram from KV KSČ to ÚV KSČ No. 323 z 5. 6. 1953, 7:40 a.m.

729. Ibid.

730. NA, f. ÚV KSČ – 1481, sv. 15, a. j. 110, Minutes of the nationwide meeting of chief secretaries of KV KSČ, heads of the departments of ÚV KSČ and chief officials of mass organizations, held on June 11, 1953; speech by Antonín Zápotocký.

731. SOA Pilsen, f. KV KSČ Pilsen, kart. 108, inv. č. 802, Minutes of the meeting of the extended KV KSČ executive committee, June 16, 1953.

732. NA, f. ÚV KSČ – 1261/0/12, sv. 39, a. j. 223/31, Minutes of the meeting of the ÚV KSČ organizational secretariat, June 17, 1953; Ibid., sv. 40, a. j. 224/43, Minutes of the meeting of the ÚV KSČ organizational secretariat, June 2, 1953.

733. Karel Kaplan, *Československo v letech 1953–1966* (Prague: Státní pedagogické nakladatelství, 1992), 6–13.

734. SOA Pilsen, f. KV KSČ Pilsen, kart. 108, inv. č. 805, Minutes of the meeting of the KV KSČ executive committee, June 27, 1953.

735. Ibid., inv. č. 806, Minutes of the meeting of the KV KSČ executive committee, June 30, 1953; Ibid., inv. č. 807, Minutes of the meeting of the KV KSČ executive committee, July 3, 1953.

736. Ibid., inv. č. 809, Minutes of the meeting of the KV KSČ executive committee, July 13, 1953; Ibid., kart. 450, inv. č. 3603, telegram from KV KSČ in Pilsen č. 337 to ÚV KSČ, August 6, 1953, 4.15 p.m.

737. ABS, f. A8/1, sv. 41, report on the results of investigation of Matěj Bálek's case, May 22, 1954; Ibid., f. 319, sv. 319–5–1, investigation of complaints lodged against Matěj Bálek in 1954.

738. AMP, f. MV KSČ Pilsen, inv. č. 498, kart. 42, Minutes of the meeting of the MV KSČ executive committee in Pilsen, July 14, 1953.

739. NA, f. ÚV KSČ – 1261/0/12, sv. 43, a. j. 231/1, Minutes of the meeting of the ÚV KSČ organizational secretariat, August 3, 1953.

740. SOA Pilsen, f. KV KSČ Pilsen, kart. 451, inv. č. 3603, minutes of the meeting of the LM regional staff September 1, 1953, statement by Jan Hlína.

741. Ibid., kart. 449, inv. č. 3603, implementation of the currency reform and implementing the Party and government resolution to abolish the ration system on foodstuffs and industrial goods in the Pilsen region, 1953.

742. NA, f. ÚV KSČ – 1261/0/12, sv. 43, a. j. 231/1, Minutes of the meeting of the ÚV KSČ organizational secretariat, August 3, 1953.

743. SOA Pilsen, f. KV KSČ Pilsen, kart. 449, inv. č. 3603, implementation of the currency reform and implementing the Party and government resolution to abolish the ration system on foodstuffs and industrial goods in the Pilsen region, 1953.

744. NA, f. ÚV KSČ – 1261/0/12, sv. 43, a. j. 231/1, Minutes of the meeting of the ÚV KSČ organizational secretariat, August 3, 1953; SOA Pilsen, f. KV KSČ Pilsen, kart. 109, inv. č. 813, Minutes of the meeting of the KV KSČ executive committee, August 7, 1953.

745. NA, f. ÚV KSČ – 1261/0/12, sv. 43, a. j. 231/1, Minutes of the meeting of the ÚV KSČ organizational secretariat, August 3, 1953; SOA Pilsen, f. KV KSČ Pilsen, kart. 109, inv. č. 813, Minutes of the meeting of the KV KSČ executive committee, August 7, 1953.

746. NA, f. ÚV KSČ – 1261/0/12, sv. 43, a. j. 231/1, Minutes of the meeting of the ÚV KSČ organizational secretariat, August 3, 1953; SOA Pilsen, f. KV KSČ Pilsen, kart. 109, inv. č. 813, Minutes of the meeting of the KV KSČ executive committee, August 7, 1953.

747. NA, f. ÚV KSČ – 1261/0/22, sv. 62, a. j. 167/13, Minutes of the meeting of the ÚV KSČ political secretariat, August 5, 1953.

748. Cf. Koop, *Der 17. Juni 1953.*

749. NA, f. ÚV KSČ – 1261/0/22, sv. 63, a. j. 171/4, Minutes of the meeting of the ÚV KSČ political secretariat, August 26, 1953; SOA Pilsen, f. KV KSČ Pilsen, kart. 450, inv. č. 3603, resolution of the ÚV KSČ regarding the events of 1 June 1953 in Pilsen.

750. NA, f. ÚV KSČ – 1261/0/22, sv. 63, a. j. 171/4, Minutes of the meeting of the ÚV KSČ political secretariat, August 26, 19531953.

751. SOA Pilsen, f. KV KSČ Pilsen, kart. 109, inv. č. 817, Minutes of the meeting of the KV KSČ executive committee, August 31, 1953.

752. SOA Pilsen, f. KV KSČ Pilsen, kart. 449, inv. č. 3603, vetting of the LM regional staff, July 7, 1953; Ibid., additional vetting of the LM regional staff, September 14, 1953; Ibid., kart. 451, inv. č. 3603, minutes of the meeting of the LM regional staff, September 1, 1953.

753. Ibid., kart. 29, inv. č. 103, Minutes of the extended plenary session of KV KSČ, September 7, 1953; NA, f. ÚV KSČ – 1261/0/2 sv. 12, a. j. 198, information bulletin 60/II from September 11,, 1953.

754. SOA Pilsen, f. KV KSČ Pilsen, kart. 450, inv. č. 3603, report on discussing the President's talk and the resolution of the ÚV KSČ regarding the events of 1 June 1953 in Pilsen at meetings of the OV KSČ executive committees, September 1953;

Ibid., kart. 452, inv. č. 3603, Minutes of the meeting of the officials of CZV KSČ in ZVIL in Pilsen, September 10, 1953; Ibid., report from the meeting of KSČ street organization officials in Pilsen, September 11, 1953; AMP, f. MV KSČ Pilsen, inv. č. 494, kart. 42, Minutes of the meeting of the MV KSČ executive committee in Pilsen, June 23, 1953.

755. Ibid., inv. č. 42, kart. 14, Minutes of the meeting of the MV KSČ in Pilsen, September 9, 1953; SOA Pilsen, f. KV KSČ Pilsen, kart. 452, inv. č. 3603, report of the meeting of the MV KSČ executive committee in Pilsen, September 9, 1953; Skála, "Měnová reforma 1. června," s. 605.

756. SOA Pilsen, f. KV KSČ Pilsen, kart. 109, inv. č. 820, minutes of the extraordinary meeting of the KV KSČ executive committee, September 10, 1953; Ibid., kart. 449, inv. č. 3603, report on the implementation of the ÚV KSČ resolution regarding the events of 1 June 1953 in Pilsen, undated.

757. Ibid., kart. 451, inv. č. 3603, minutes of the extraordinary meeting of the KV KSČ executive committee, September 10, 1953; Ibid., additional vetting of the LM regional staff, September 14, 1953.

758. Ibid., kart. 29, inv. č. 103, Minutes of the extended plenary session of the KV KSČ, September 7, 1953, contribution by Jan Hlína.

759. Ibid., kart. 451, inv. č. 3603, minutes of the extended plenary session of the KV KSČ executive committee, September 10, 1953.

760. Ibid., kart. 449, inv. č. 3603, KV KSČ resolution on personnel changes, September 24, 1953.

761. Ibid., kart. 109, inv. č. 822, Minutes of the meeting of the KV KSČ executive committee September 17, 1953; Ibid., inv. č. 824, Minutes of the meeting of the KV KSČ executive committee September 25, 1953; Ibid., kart. 451, inv. č. 3603, report from the ZO KSČ at ZVIL Machine Shop IV, June 12, 1953.

762. Ibid., minutes of the extraordinary meeting of the KV KSČ executive committee, September 10, 1953; Ibid., kart. 449, inv. č. 3603, report on the implementation of the ÚV KSČ resolution regarding the events of 1 June 1953 in Pilsen, undated; Ibid., KV KSČ resolution on personnel changes, September 24, 1953.

763. Ibid., kart. 450, inv. č. 3603, vetting of members of party authorities following the currency reform, July 1953; Ibid., kart. 29, inv. č. 102, minutes of the plenary session of KV KSČ 14. 8. 1953, talk by Jan Hlína.

764. PA Škoda, f. ROH, ROH 14 PV 33, minutes of the plenary session of ZR ZVIL, June 11, 1953; Ibid., 1515 PV 1287, minutes of the plenary session of ZR ZVI, August 26, 1953, vetting of Stanislav Bejm.

765. SOA Pilsen, f. KV KSČ Pilsen, kart. 451, inv. č. 3603, draft resolution of the KV KSČ in Pilsen regarding the resolution of the ÚV KSČ political secretariat on the events of 1 June 1953, September 1953.

766. Ibid., kart. 109, inv. č. 822, Minutes of the meeting of the KV KSČ executive committee, September 17, 1953; Ibid., inv. č. 824, Minutes of the meeting of the KV KSČ executive committee, September 25, 1953.

767. PA Škoda, f. Personální spisy zaměstnanců, č. 11855–A, František Brabec; NA, f. ÚV KSČ – 1261/0/12, sv. 77, a. j. 200/7, Minutes of the meeting of the ÚV KSČ organizational secretariat, March 1, 1954.

768. Ibid., f. ÚV KSČ – 1261/0/22, sv. 65, a. j. 178/18a, Minutes of the meeting of the ÚV KSČ political secretariat, October 5, 1953.

769. Ibid., f. ÚV KSČ – 1261/0/12, sv. 45, a. j. 239/1, Minutes of the meeting of the ÚV KSČ organizational secretariat, September 24, 1953.

770. SOA Pilsen, f. KV KSČ Pilsen, kart. 109, inv. č. 824, Minutes of the meeting of the KV KSČ executive committee, September 25, 1953; Ibid., kart. 449, inv. č. 3603, KV KSČ resolution on personnel changes, September 24, 1953.

771. ABS, f. A2/1, sv. 494, report on the situation in Pilsen during the currency reform, sent to KS StB, November 3, 1953.

772. SOA Pilsen, f. KV KSČ Pilsen, kart. 29, inv. č. 104, Minutes of the meeting of the rozšířeného pléna KV KSČ, September 25, 1953; Ibid., kart. 109, inv. č. 824, Minutes of the meeting of the KV KSČ executive committee, September 25, 1953; Ibid., kart. 449, inv. č. 3603, report on the implementation of the ÚV KSČ resolution regarding the events of 1 June 1953 in Pilsen, undated; NA, f. ÚV KSČ – 1261/0/2 sv. 12, a. j. 206, information bulletin 68/II, October 7, 1953.

773. Ibid., f. ÚV KSČ – 1261/0/12, sv. 56, a. j. 260/2, Minutes of the meeting of the ÚV KSČ organizational secretariat, February 9, 1954.

Conclusion

Although the Pilsen revolt of June 1,1953, was an immediate and spontaneous reaction of the population to the announcement of the so-called currency reform, its course clearly mirrored some of the longer-term social conflicts that had gradually accumulated in the region during the post-war period. As a result, the revolt assumed the form of an unusually dynamic and polymorphous protest that changed its form and structure of its participants several times during the day. With some exaggeration, we may even state that at least three parallel, interrelated, but completely incommensurable protests took place in the city on that day. Different parts of society (individual social movements) reacted to the currency reform in very different ways, each utilizing a different culture of protest. Their actions were motivated by different social conflicts, drew on different cultural contexts, used different forms of resistance, and offered different ways out of the situation.

The first of the key conflicts broke out within the Communist Party itself. It was caused not only by the social impact of the currency reform but also by the arrogant manner of its announcement and the lack of consideration for the privileges of party members. The majority of the membership base and lower officials therefore adopted a position of passive resistance, thereby virtually preventing the proper implementation of the reform. At the same time, however, they claimed to remain loyal to the system. This loyal passive resistance led to the failure of the party's basic functions and, to some extent, failure of the security apparatus, even before the exchange of currency had begun. The authority of the national leadership temporarily collapsed. This created a power vacuum which opened the way for activities of other segments of society.

The specific forms of party protest were discussion and inaction. The communists drew ideological inspiration from their previous experience with political trials against top party officials (e.g., against Hanuš Lomský), during which the membership base was systematically incited to voice their criticism and suspicion of the higher authorities. In the Pilsen regional environment, this kind of resistance was a seamless continuation of the stormy debates about intra-party democracy and the struggles against the so-called local dictators that had been raging on and off since at least May 1948, when the West Bohemian Party apparatus went through a crisis caused by the pro-American demonstrations. The causes of this phenomenon lay mainly in the mass growth of the Communist Party after World War II, when a huge number of new members joined the party (especially in the Pilsen region) who were not mentally prepared for the post-war enforcement of the principles of the so-called democratic centralism. The post-war self-presentation of the Communist Party was far removed from the actual internal conditions in the 1950s.

The second conflict occurred between industrial workers and the state leadership. Workers had long been a privileged social group, able to defend their social and economic interests through boycotts or strikes. Their protests were generally considered legitimate within the system. At the same time, workers were characterized by their detachment from politics and only a token loyalty toward the regime. The currency reform therefore resulted in widespread, socially motivated strike activities. While the most radical section of the workers was not content to protest inside the factory premises and eventually took to the streets of the city to express its outrage, for various reasons the vast majority did not cross this symbolic line. Nevertheless, the workers' strikes unintentionally made way for the outbreak of political protests and even lent them the necessary legitimacy in the initial phase.

The main form of resistance among the workers was work stoppage. The actions of the workers in the Pilsen industrial plants continued the tradition of workers' protests that had been present in the public space throughout the post-war period and which had become increasingly widespread, especially during the implementation of the first Five-Year Plan in 1949–1953. The strength and self-confidence of the Pilsen workers' resistance was based on the national importance of Pilsen's largest industrial enterprise, the V. I. Lenin Factories, which formed the backbone of the restructuring of the national economy during the Five-Year Plan.

The third conflict stemmed from the conviction of a part of society that Czechoslovakia should maintain cultural and political ties both with Eastern and Western countries, and to strive to maintain greater continuity with the pre-February political order. In the Pilsen region, this alternative opinion was greatly bolstered by the fact that the city had been liberated by the American army at the end of the Second World War. In addition to sympathizers of former non-communist political parties and persons affected by the forced post-war transformation of the social structure of society, it was the young people in Pilsen who became proponents of pro-Western attitudes. Initially, inspiration from the American lifestyle resonated mainly among students, but during the 1950s this trend also shifted to the industrial plants, where a large number of young people from non-working-class families took up positions as workers. This group of young manual workers thus combined the social benefits of their profession with non-conformist, pro-Western cultural attitudes and dealt with this inner contradiction by rebelling against the disciplinary demands of the system. From the autumn of 1948 onward, public protests by this segment of society were generally seen as illegitimate, and security forces learned to prevent their occurrence. The revival of protests in June 1953 was only made possible thanks to the simultaneous passive resistance of Communist Party members and strikes by other industrial workers.

The cultural and political protest took the form of public demonstrations. The protesters drew from their experience during the pro-American demonstrations in May 1948, and the riots during the memorial service for former president Edvard Benes in September 1948. In June 1953, the area around the former foundation stone of the U.S. Army Monument, as well as the National Liberation Monument with the statue of first Czechoslovak president Tomáš Garrigue Masaryk, again became the symbols of their protest activities.

From the above classification of the different branches of resistance, it is clear that the Pilsen revolt was a hybrid form of protest that mirrored a wide range of social conflicts. Several different groups of the population with different methods and intentions expressed their opposition to the currency reform independently of each other. The passive resistance of the communists could be seen as a timid continuation of a series of attempts to democratize the mechanisms of party management, which, in the longer term, indirectly foreshadowed some aspects of the so-called revival process of the Prague Spring of 1968. The workers' strikes represented the culmination of previous socially motivated conflicts in the factories and led to a deepening of the consumerist mode of stabilizing the Czechoslovak state socialist regime in the following decades. Finally, the anti-government demonstrations were a component within a more general post-war effort by a section of society to revise the country's dominant orientation toward Eastern cultural and political models, which was only completed under very different circumstances after November 1989.

For the reasons given above, the June riots in Pilsen cannot be classified as an attempt to dismantle the state socialist regime. During some phases of the demonstrations, anti-government and sometimes even anti-communist positions were articulated, but these were only maintained by a small group of people and cannot be applied to the entirety of the protest participants, let alone the entire local population. The various slogans chanted by the protesting crowd did not constitute any coherent political program and were largely the product of heightened emotions. Anti-Soviet or anti-socialist attitudes were not heard at all. Moreover, the demonstrations themselves were more in the nature of a protest promoting alternative values in the public space than an attempt at a coup d'état. At the same time, however, the Pilsen revolt was not merely a reflection of workers' social unrest motivated by the currency reform. The strikes by industrial workers were only one aspect of a multilayered conflict at the time. Moreover, some impulses beyond the scope of traditional social protest were already resonating among the workers in 1953. Particularly symptomatic in this respect was the affinity of some young workers toward Western culture.

The Pilsen revolt therefore appears more as a spontaneous confluence of several individual, mutually incompatible protests, through which different parts of society reacted to the currency reform, using different cultural traditions. In the course of the protests, they each brought their own alternative authorities into the public space through which they assessed the then untenable social situation. These included the moral models of the First Republic, the Western notions of democracy, as well as socialist ideology, traditions of the labor movement, and the doctrine of class struggle. The partial demands of each group functioned as appeals for innovating the existing system, with some of the articulated conflicts able to be resolved by the regime (raising the workers' living standard, granting privileges to supporters of the regime at the expense of prominent figures of past eras), while others were probably incompatible with its preservation (free elections, Western cultural influences, intra-party democracy).

The currency reform merely temporarily cemented all of the above traditional forms of protest into one fluid whole. The connective tissue of this apparent fusion was social panic. People were entering the process of currency exchange after a two-week supply crisis, which raised legitimate fears of a collapse of the retail network. At the same time, they were not sufficiently informed about the level of their future wages. They were also distrustful of the new pricing system, in which they could only actively participate after the cash exchange. However, the exchange process itself became an ordeal due to the chaotic operation of the exchange centers. Moreover, households lost a substantial part of their financial reserves, and some were about to lose the significant social benefits of the dual market. The sum of all these factors meant that for several days people faced an unprecedented loss of basic life securities. The various forms of moral indignation arising from the various long-term social conflicts were therefore joined by an immediate general outrage stemming from the social consequences of the reform and the authoritarian and slapdash manner of its implementation.

The extreme level of frustration, anger, and panic meant that the June demonstrations and strikes displayed an unusually high degree of aggression compared to previous incidents. At the same time, physical violence was mainly employed during the initial phase of the protests, and the security forces were only able to respond to it after much hesitation. For the first time in Pilsen's post-1948 history, riots and attempted lynchings were used as forms of collective protest, even though they had not previously been a part of any of the revived protest traditions. This was the only entirely new aspect of the June revolt.

In addition to the diverse range of subjective motives for protest, some factors weakening the defenses of the state socialist regime also had a significant impact on the resulting form of social unrest. Among the most significant of these was the long-standing dysfunction of the network of party organizations, which had already manifested itself in the years 1949–1953 by the extreme passivity of the membership base and lower-level officials and in the formalistic manner in which tasks were carried out. Moreover, the deficiencies in this pillar of the system were compounded by the internal party show trials of 1951–1952 and the deaths of the official representatives and guarantors of the post-1948 political regime, Klement Gottwald and Joseph Vissarionovich Stalin, in March 1953. By June 1953, the Communist Party leadership was struggling not only with the widespread distrust of the low-ranking members toward their superiors, which it had often previously helped to foment for its own purposes, but also with the political weakness and instability of both of its command centers, in Prague and in Moscow. The protests therefore caught the Communist Party in a precarious period of transition.

At the same time, there were autonomous spaces within the system that largely escaped the control mechanisms of the Prague and regional party bodies. Party and security leaders were therefore ill-informed about social tensions in the factories and underestimated the strength of the workers' collective resistance to the currency reform. Closely related to this factor was another ideological aspect. The working class was a central concept in the official discourse and constituted the basic instrument for legitimizing the post-1948 regime. Because of this, the party leadership had to tolerate workers' strikes as legitimate, at least on a general level, and treat them differently from protests by other social groups. Within the specific environment of the industrial plants, different rules had long operated than in the outside world. In June 1953, this long-standing practice caused the regional and central party authorities to hesitate to employ forceful intervention against the emerging protests in Pilsen. Instead, they opted for a strategy of verbal persuasion and sending unarmed riot police units into the streets. In doing so, they unwittingly allowed for the protests to escalate and contributed to the destabilization of the local security authorities, who were unable to carry out their unrealistic orders.

From the perspective of the power apparatuses, the currency reform itself represented an extremely difficult task that would have significantly overburdened all political, administrative, and security structures of any regime. Because of the necessary secrecy surrounding the preparation of the event, party officials, public administration, and the police only had a few days to stage a publicity campaign, set up the cash exchange points, conduct inventories in the shops, and ensure the security of the exchange centers. This hasty procedure caused the local party apparatus to virtually collapse even during the preparatory promotional campaign, compounded significantly by resistant tendencies within its membership base. At the crucial moment on Monday morning, key party and administrative offices were left seriously understaffed (due to the need to carry out reform-related duties) and most of the security forces were deployed at the exchange centers. This created a significant shortage of available riot police forces, which was exacerbated in West Bohemia by the army's last-minute withdrawal of promised reinforcements, which subsequently had to be replaced by the Public Security and People's Militias reserves. The protests therefore reached exceptional proportions in Pilsen because there was not a sufficient force present in the city to be deployed against them immediately. The crisis situation was finally resolved by the regional commanders calling in troops from other regions. By merely announcing the reform, the Communist Party leadership had thus unwittingly thrown its power apparatus into a situation in which it was neither able nor willing to perform its basic functions.

The collapse of the local security structures was further caused by the personal misconduct of some regional commanding officers who underestimated the risks and were not present at their posts at the time of the outbreak of the riots. The poor coordination of the operations of the various security forces, combined with the reluctance of some of their members to intervene against the protesting crowd, created complete chaos in Pilsen. This was eventually overcome only when officers from Prague took command of the entire operation.

The June revolt in Pilsen thus benefited from the overall weakening of the Communist Party, which was going through a sensitive period of leadership renewal. Moreover, the currency reform overburdened the party and security apparatuses, which could not withstand the combined pressure of the passive resistance of their personnel and the public unrest. The unrealistic instructions of the party leadership, which initially tried to respect the legitimacy of workers' protests, also contributed to the destabilization. The result was a total collapse of local party and security structures, which created a temporary state of anarchy and lawlessness in West Bohemia and fundamentally shook the authority of state and party institutions. This temporary power vacuum had a comparably significant impact on the overall development of the revolt as the activities of the protesting population itself. The characteristic feature of the social atmosphere at the time was therefore not so much the strikes and demonstrations themselves, which only involved a fraction of the population, but primarily the lack of an adequate response on the part of the low-ranking communists and members of the security forces. It was their inaction that was the real indicator of the depth of the ongoing crisis.

The destabilization of the local pillars of power was only temporary and conditional, having been caused by the overload of the apparatuses during the implementation of the currency reform, and by the passive resistance of their staff. At the same time, the opposition of this segment of society to the currency reform stemmed from considerably different reasons than those voiced by the protesters; and in general, the party apparatus maintained its loyalty to the state socialist regime. A significant contributing factor was the temporary reluctance to address problems caused by someone else (the party leadership) and that the central authorities had not deigned to consult even formally beforehand. It did not therefore constitute a permanent obstruction. The afternoon intervention of the central authorities led to the restoration of order in Pilsen relatively quickly. The activities of the local apparatuses were resumed, and in the following weeks and months their normal operations were restored.

Social conditions in the West Bohemian region did not differ much from those in other parts of the country during the 1950s, and the reaction of the local population to the currency reform of 1953 did not deviate from the general nationwide trends. The Pilsen revolt began with a social protest similar to those that occurred in many other places. Its uniqueness, however, lay in the fact that it gradually escalated, and became radicalized and politicized.

The main reason for the extraordinary development of the Pilsen riots was the specific social position of the workers at the V. I. Lenin Factories. The enterprise was one of the fundamental pillars of the Five-Year Economic Plan. In 1949–1953, it was a major contributor to the nationwide increase in heavy industry production and served as a reservoir of workers' cadres for the politically motivated personnel changes within the state apparatus. Two contradictory phenomena were present here, to a much greater extent than in other industrial plants: on the one hand, the high social prestige of members of the working class under the state socialist regime, and on the other hand, the disorganization of the work process caused by the restructuring of production programs and the hectic execution of the plan. The factory employees were well aware of their supra-regional economic importance and the traditional influence of the company on the social climate in the West Bohemian metropolis. This lent them much higher self-confidence that consequently gave them the courage to incite the protests. In addition, increasing pressure on performance and inadequate working conditions had long contributed to a tense atmosphere within the factory. The high financial losses caused by the reform, which far exceeded the average losses in society as a whole, were also a significant incentive for the factory workers to protest. In fact, a large proportion of the local workers were paid above-average wages, which allowed them to amass considerable savings after 1945. The reform also deprived the workers of the social benefits of the hard-worker's allowance and completely wiped out their wartime savings (tied deposits).

Collective resistance to the reform was also fostered by the structure of the factory's workforce, which had been created over the previous years by the outflow of the original workforce into political or administrative positions and the simultaneous recruitment of workers from former non-worker professions. In June 1953, these new groups of employees constituted more than one-quarter of the total staff in some departments and brought different life experiences to the resulting conflict. Similar infiltration was also evident in the ranks of the workers' youth, who often came from families of clerks and tradesmen, adopted non-conformist lifestyles, rebelled against authority, and in some cases were even inspired by Western cultural models. This section of working-class youth combined the self-confidence of a traditional factory environment with a cultural revolt against the system.

To a certain extent, the development of protests at the V. I. Lenin Factories was influenced by the fact that the enterprise was one of the important bastions of social democracy in the interwar period. This manifested itself above all in long-standing stereotypes of thought and models of action, such as the right to strike or collective solidarity. Thus, while the ideals of social democracy in June 1953 indirectly reinforced the more general traditions cultivated in the workers' milieu, they remained largely unspoken and were not embodied in any clearly defined movement. The Communist Party had long overestimated their danger in the region and had searched in vain for larger resistance groups of this political orientation. It was particularly concerned about the high number of former social democrats within its own party. However, the passive resistance of the party apparatus against the currency reform was much more based on post-war inspiration and was not explicitly social democratic in nature.

The Pilsen revolt was also bolstered by the cultural and political impact of the liberation of the city by the U.S. army in May 1945. Sympathy for Western culture and lifestyle was already widespread among the local youth in 1945–1948 and later penetrated into the working-class milieu. Many of the young protesters in June 1953 therefore believed that in the changing international situation, American diplomacy or American troops might intervene on behalf of the protesting population of Pilsen. Similar illusions about the special relationship of the Western superpower to the Pilsen region then emboldened some parts of the protesting crowd.

The course of the Pilsen revolt in many ways foreshadowed the well-known events in the German Democratic Republic that immediately followed on June 16–17, 1953. The main driving force behind the German protests was the conflict between industrial workers and the government, which stemmed from the militarization of the East German economy during the Cold War and the stagnating living standard of the population. The concrete impetus was the outrage of construction workers triggered by increased performance targets. These were by no means the first protests of this kind in Germany. Here, too, the resistance of the workers, initially perceived as legitimate, was taken up by other segments of society. As in West Bohemia, political slogans began to be heard at the German demonstrations in addition to social demands. However, their themes differed considerably, with calls for the departure of the Soviet occupation troops and for the reunification of Germany. In this respect, the situation in the German Democratic Republic as a former defeated state of the Second World War was different from that in Czechoslovakia, where the protests did not carry an anti-Soviet aspect and their participants did not mobilize and integrate through nationalist sentiments.

The Berlin Revolt was also significantly bolstered by the interest of the world public, which was incomparably higher compared to the Czechoslovak incident. Moreover, in Germany, the West was able to intervene much more effectively at the epicenter of events due to the easy physical and informational permeability of the border between East and West Berlin. The population of East Germany, for example, was immediately informed about the conflict through West German radio broadcasts, with no language barrier. The scale of the protests was therefore also different. Apart from Berlin, 700 other places were involved in the revolt and the total number of participants reached several hundred thousand. Unlike in West Bohemia, the protests also forced the intervention of Soviet tanks and resulted in several dozen casualties and several thousand arrests. In this respect it was an event of a completely different magnitude compared to the Pilsen revolt. In terms of the typology of protests, however, the two incidents are closely related.

The attitudes of the Communist Party leadership toward the Pilsen riots underwent a similar dynamic change as the protests themselves. Initially, officials on the regional and central levels viewed the incident as a justified social protest by the workers and tried to calm it down through non-violent methods of persuasion. Only after the events in the streets began to radicalize did they gradually reassess the situation, and in the afternoon, they finally decided to officially label the protests as an attempt at counter-revolution. With this redefinition of the conflict, all branches of the protest were retroactively politicized. Loyal forms of resistance to reform were no longer possible. The party leadership chose to deal with the incident primarily on a political, social, and cultural level, and the various calls for regime innovation were either ignored or dismissed as hostile. The revolt, which did not form a unified whole in terms of the subjective motives of its protagonists and was a kind of social communication rather than an attempt at a power coup, thus collectively functioned as an anti-communist uprising within the system.

The political level of conflict resolution was maintained in the first phase of the subsequent process of the stabilization of the conditions in West Bohemia. The local communist officials who had been beaten and publicly shamed during the demonstrations initially acted under the influence of their heightened emotions. Their frustration was reflected in strong and theatrical gestures, such as the tearing down of the statue of President Tomáš Garrigue Masaryk in Pilsen. However, it also influenced the chosen form of repressive measures. Instead of punishing the real culprits, a widespread vendetta was unleashed in Pilsen against anyone who was in any way involved in the protests. At the same time, judicial trials, workplace persecutions, and eviction of the city's inhabitants were directed not only against the protesters themselves, but also against their alleged supporters, who were mistakenly identified as members of the former bourgeois classes. The strong-arm policy carried over into the ideological sphere, and an integral part of this was a large-scale campaign against the social democratic and Masarykian tradition and against the adoption of Western cultural models. In 1954–1955, this escalated propaganda campaign eventually resulted in a series of political trials against former representatives of Social Democracy. The Communist Party leadership thus failed to understand the complex structure of the articulated social conflicts, misjudged the protests as a homogeneous whole, focused its retaliation on largely fictitious targets, and a substantial part of the causes of the crisis completely escaped its attention.

The unusually extensive application of repressive measures led to a relatively rapid suppression of the protests. However, other factors also played a significant role in the suppression of public unrest. Among the most important of these was the decline in social panic caused by the completion of the currency exchange; the payment of the first wage advances in the new currency; and the resumption of the proper functioning of the retail network. The most difficult phase of the reform, associated with extreme social insecurity, was thus overcome and the population could begin to adjust to a new, more stable reality. The immediate sense of existential threat, which had been one of the most effective mobilizing tools of the revolt, was gradually fading. Last but not least, the internal ambivalence of the resistance to the currency reform was also decisive for the relatively smooth end of the protests. After the revolt was labeled an anti-state act, proponents of loyal forms of resistance were unable to continue the protests. Therefore, they subsequently approved the reform, placed the political responsibility for the public unrest on members of alleged reactionary circles, and declared themselves victims of misguided enemy propaganda. Czechoslovak society was no more united or cohesive in June 1953 than it was during the parliamentary elections in May 1946 or during the government crisis in February 1948.

At the same time, however, the opposition of the Czechoslovak population to the currency reform drew the attention of the Soviet Party leadership to the weaknesses of the existing economic and social policy, which threatened the stability of the whole system. The Pilsen revolt therefore strengthened reform tendencies in the Soviet Union, which resulted in the so-called New Course policy, aimed, among other things, at reviving the growth of the population's living standard (lowering prices, expanding the range of goods, changing the structure of investment). These facts then retroactively influenced the second phase of the resolution of the Pilsen revolt. From the outset, the emotional reactions of the West Bohemian communist officials were corrected by the more conceptual intentions of the central authorities. From July 1953 onward, the echoes of the so-called New Course, coming to Czechoslovakia from the Soviet Union, began to interfere with these efforts. The emphasis therefore shifted from political repressions to the stabilization of social conditions and the improvement of living standards. Widespread persecution was eased in favor of the restoration of everyday life in society and the practical running of the national economy. Although the party leadership had not yet fully acknowledged the complex roots of the conflict, the changes introduced represented a realistic solution to at least some of the social problems.

At the same time, the key issue of the party leadership's social isolation (both within society and within the party itself) was coming to the fore. Communist Party leaders realized that the long-standing passivity of the basic organizations had deprived the party of its only direct channel of communication with society and attempted to remedy this situation. However, the personnel changes in key regional positions, the vetting of all party members, the propaganda campaign against competing ideologies, and even ostentatious official public rallies did not do much for fostering independent initiative among rank-and-file communists. Indeed, this repertoire of traditional instruments of internal party politics only counteracted the consequences and did not cure the actual causes of disinterest in political activity. Significant liberalization of the party network management, which was probably the only thing that could have improved the atmosphere within the lower organizational levels in the long term, was not even considered.

The moral damage done to the party by the currency reform was long-lasting, and the wrongs committed during the subsequent repression remained a hot topic in some places as late as 1968. Nevertheless, the reform did not mark a major turning point in the relationship of Czechoslovak (or Pilsen) society to the state socialist regime. In fact, the general decline in the population's trust in the party leadership was compensated in the following years by an increase in the rate of growth of the living standard (personal consumption). The currency reform thus paradoxically marked both a significant upheaval and the beginning of stabilization in the development of the system.

The immediate impact of the revolt on the atmosphere in society was also twofold. The wave of widespread persecution temporarily created a climate of fear in the region in which even many staunch sympathizers of the regime could not be sure whether they would become targets of sanctions. A strong lesson in this regard was also taught to Pilsen's leading officials, who had to assume personal responsibility for failures caused by the government policy in which they had no part. On the other hand, the revolt, together with the reluctant introduction of some features of the so-called New Course, raised the hopes of many citizens for the future liberalization of the system. In July, the decline in international tension resulted in the end of the Korean War. The announcement of elections for National Committees and the National Assembly for 1954 elicited a considerable public response, and even activated some of the supporters of the political opposition who had been biding their time until then. Although no major changes were ultimately made, the social climate of late 1953 differed from that of the previous period more in the hopes placed in future political and social developments than in the fears of repression.

Czechoslovak exile propaganda reacted strongly to the Pilsen revolt and the end of the Korean War, shifting the focus of the ideological struggle against the state socialist regime away from military and political issues and toward a comparison of the economic and social conditions of the two systems. The appeals sent to Czechoslovakia in the following years were addressed not so much to anti-communist resistance fighters or the political opposition, but rather to industrial workers and in some cases even to trade union officials.

The Pilsen revolt did not in itself mark a major historical breakthrough on a national or regional scale. However, it was both a significant product and catalyst of a more general process of change in the international political constellation, which was manifested in Czechoslovakia by the gradual fading of the Stalinist era, associated with the heated phase of the Cold War, and the slow emergence of new peaceful solutions. It constituted only one of the stops on a longer journey from excessive armaments to rational disinvestment in the military, from wartime priorities to meeting at least the basic social needs of society, from public political processes to their reluctant revision, and from permanent revolution to more sophisticated (consumerist) forms of stabilizing the state socialist regime. However, these tendencies only became fully manifest in the longer term and were related to other factors, such as the death of Joseph Vissarionovich Stalin and the de-escalation of the Cold War.

The events of the Czechoslovak currency reform reflected the general revolutionary chaos that had dominated the political scene and the economic party apparatus in the previous years. The Pilsen protests against the reform, alongside the much more powerful Berlin revolt, occurred at a time when possibilities were slowly opening in Moscow for the gradual adaptation of the system to the new conditions. While the coming era was not free from oppression and injustice, it did provide a more stable and predictable environment for the majority of society. At the same time, the era of intense mutual delineation of the positions of the various social, cultural, and political factions in Czechoslovak society, which had been an accompanying feature of the first destructive phase of the 1948–1953 revolution, was coming to an end. As a result, the collective protests of individual social movements, which had culminated in the Pilsen revolt, receded into the background in the following years, and only became more widespread again in the late 1960s.

List of Archive Fonds and Abbreviations

Archiv bezpečnostních složek v Praze (ABS)
(Security Services Archive in Prague)

304: Různé bezpečnostní spisy po roce 1945 (various security files after 1945)
305: Ústředna Státní bezpečnosti (State Security Headquarters)
310: Velitelství Státní bezpečnosti (State Security Command)
319: Vytříděné spisy sekretariátu ministra vnitra (Assorted files of the Ministry of Interior Secretariat)
A2/1: Sekretariát ministra vnitra (Ministry of Interior Secretariat)
A8/1: Inspekce ministra vnitra (Ministry of Interior Inspectorate)
H: Historický fond státní bezpečnosti (State Security historic fonds)
KS MV Plzeň: Krajská správa ministerstva vnitra v Plzni (Regional Administration of the Ministry of Interior in Pilsen)

Archiv České národní banky v Praze (AČNB)
(Czech National Bank Archive)

SBČS: Státní banka československá (Czechoslovak State Bank)
SBČS Plzeň: Státní banka československá – pobočka Plzeň (Czechoslovak State Bank – Pilsen branch)

Archiv města Plzně (AMP) *(Archive of the City of Pilsen)*

JNV Plzeň: Jednotný národní výbor v Plzni – bezpečnostní referát (Consolidated National Committee in Pilsen – security department)

MV KSČ Plzeň: Městský výbor Komunistické strany Československa v Plzni (Municipal Committee of the Communist Party of Czechoslovakia)
NV Plzeň: Národní výbor v Plzni (National Committee in Pilsen)
OA Plzeň: Obchodní akademie v Plzni (Secondary Business School in Pilsen)
OF Josef Brand: Osobní fond Josef Brand (Josef Brand personal fonds)
OF Vladimír Havlic: Osobní fond Vladimír Havlic (Vladimír Havlic personal fonds)
SG Plzeň: Státní gymnázium v Plzni (State Secondary School in Pilsen)
ÚNV Plzeň: Ústřední národní výbor statutárního města Plzně – bezpečnostní referát (Central National Committee of the Statutory City of Pilsen – security department)

Národní archiv v Praze (NA) *(National Archives in Prague)*

MF Praha: Ministerstvo financí v Praze (Ministry of Finance in Prague)
MV NA: Ministerstvo vnitra – Noskův archiv (Ministry of Interior – The Nosek Archive)
SP USA: Svaz přátel USA (Association of Friends of the USA)
StS Praha: Státní soud v Praze (State Court in Prague)
ÚPV-T: Úřad předsednictva vlády – tajné spisy (Prime Minister's Office – classified files)
ÚV ČSM: Ústřední výbor Československého svazu mládeže v Praze (Central Committee of the Czechoslovak Youth Union in Prague)
ÚV KSČ – 1261/0/2: Ústřední výbor Komunistické strany Československa – Bulletiny (Central Committee of the Communist Party of Czechoslovakia – Bulletins)
ÚV KSČ – 1261/0/3: Ústřední výbor Komunistické strany Československa – Předsednictvo (Central Committee of the Communist Party of Czechoslovakia – Presidium)
ÚV KSČ – 1261/0/12: Ústřední výbor Komunistické strany Československa – Organizační sekretariát (Central Committee of the Communist Party of Czechoslovakia – Organizational secretariat)
ÚV KSČ – 1261/0/22: Ústřední výbor Komunistické strany Československa –Politický sekretariát (Central Committee of the Communist Party of Czechoslovakia – Political secretariat)
ÚV KSČ – 1261/0/32: Ústřední výbor Komunistické strany Československa –Generální sekretariát (Central Committee of the Communist Party of Czechoslovakia – General Secretariat)
ÚV KSČ – 1261/0/44: Ústřední výbor Komunistické strany Československa – Kancelář prvního tajemníka Antonína Novotného (Central Committee

of the Communist Party of Czechoslovakia – Office of Chief Secretary Antonín Novotný)

ÚV KSČ – 1261/2/1: Ústřední výbor Komunistické strany Československa – Oddělení stranických orgánů – I. oddělení (Central Committee of the Communist Party of Czechoslovakia – Party Authorities Division – department I)

ÚV KSČ – 1261/2/5: Ústřední výbor Komunistické strany Československa – Organizační oddělení, Marie Švermová (Central Committee of the Communist Party of Czechoslovakia – Organizational division, Marie Švermová)

ÚV KSČ – 1261/2/28: Ústřední výbor Komunistické strany Československa – Oddělení masových organizací (Central Committee of the Communist Party of Czechoslovakia – Mass Organizations Division)

ÚV KSČ – 1261/2/31: Ústřední výbor Komunistické strany Československa – Oddělení stranických orgánů, agendy stranická statistika a informace (Central Committee of the Communist Party of Czechoslovakia – Party Authorities Division, party statistic agenda)

ÚV KSČ – 1481: Ústřední výbor Komunistické strany Československa – Celostátní porady a konference (Central Committee of the Communist Party of Czechoslovakia – Nationwide meetings and conferences)

Měnová reforma: Měnová reforma (tematický soubor dokumentů předkládaný badatelům) (Currency reform [specialized set of documents available to researchers])

Podnikový archiv Škoda (PA Škoda) *Škoda Company Archive*

Relocated to the State Regional Archive in Pilsen during the writing of this text.

Personální spisy zaměstnanců: Personální spisy zaměstnanců (Employee personnel files)

Plzeň: závod Plzeň (Pilsen plant)

ROH: Revoluční odborové hnutí (Revolutionary Trade Union Movement)

ZVIL: The Vladimir Ilyich Lenin Factories in Pilsen

Státní oblastní archiv v Plzni (SOA v Plzni)
(State Regional Archive in Pilsen)

KS Plzeň: Krajský soud v Plzni (Regional Court in Pilsen)

KV ČSM Plzeň: Československý svaz mládeže – Krajský výbor v Plzni (Czechoslovak Youth Union – Regional Committee in Pilsen)

KV KSČ Plzeň: Západočeský krajský výbor Komunistické strany Československa v Plzni (West Bohemia Regional Committee of the Communist Party of Czechoslovakia)
KV NF Plzeň: Krajský výbor Národní fronty v Plzni (Regional Committee of the National Front in Pilsen)
PA Škoda: Dokumenty bývalého Podnikového archivu Škoda (Documents from the former Škoda Company Archive)
PŘ Plzeň: Policejní ředitelství v Plzni (Police Headquarters in Pilsen)
PV KSČ Škoda: Podnikový výbor Komunistické strany Československa Škoda Plzeň (Škoda Plzeň Company Committee of the Communist Party of Czechoslovakia)
SZ Plzeň: Státní zastupitelství v Plzni (State Prosecutor's Office in Pilsen)
ZKNV Plzeň: Západočeský krajský národní výbor v Plzni, tajné spisy (West Bohemia Regional National Committee in Pilsen, classified files)

Státní okresní archiv Plzeň-jih se sídlem v Blovicích (SOkA v Blovicích)
(State District Archive Pilsen-South in Blovice)

OS Plzeň: Okresní soud v Plzni (District Court in Pilsen)

Vojenský ústřední archiv v Praze (VÚA)
(Central Military Archive in Prague)

MNO: Ministerstvo národní obrany (Ministry of National Defence)

Všeodborový archiv v Praze (VOA)
(General Union Archive in Prague)

KOR: Sbírka krajské odborové rady (Collection of the Regional Union Council)
KOVO: Odborový svaz zaměstnanců kovovýroby (Metalworking Trade Union)
ÚRO – ORG: Ústřední rada odborů – Organizační oddělení (Central Council of Unions – Organizational department)
ÚRO – P: Ústřední rada odborů – Předsednictvo (Central Council of Unions – Presidium)

Bibliography

Abrams, Bradley Francis. *The Struggle for the Soul of the Nation: Czech Culture and the Rise of Communism*. Lanham: Rowman and Littlefield, 2004.

Babka, Lukáš, and Veber, Václav, eds. *Za demokracii a svobodu III: Třetí (protikomunistický) odboj*. Hradec Králové: Univerzita Hradec Králové 2002.

Bárta, Milan. "Podíl československé bezpečnosti na přípravě a provedení měnové reformy v roce 1953." *Securitas imperii* 24, no. 2 (2014): 52–81.

Bartošek, Karel, and Pichlík, Karel. *Američané v západních Čechách v roce 1945*. Prague: Mladá fronta, 1953.

Bartošek, Karel, and Pichlík, Karel. *Hanebná role amerických okupantů v západních Čechách v roce 1945*. Prague: Svoboda, 1951.

Baťková, Helena. "*Plzeňské povstání 1953 a jeho důsledky*." PhD diss., Univerzita Karlova v Praze, 2002.

Bauerová, Marie. "*Škodovy závody v letech 1945–1949*." PhD diss., Universita Karlova v Praze, 1974.

Bauerová, Marie. "Vznik revolučních orgánů dělnické třídy ve Škodových závodech v roce 1945." *Zpravodaj komise pro dějiny závodů v ČSSR* 5, no. 1 (1978): 13–33.

Berger, Peter, and Luckmann, Thomas. *Sociální konstrukce reality: Pojednání o sociologii vědění*. Brno: Centrum pro studium demokracie a kultury, 1999.

Bílek, Jiří. "Československá armáda a měnová reforma v roce 1953." *Historie a vojenství* 44, no. 1 (1995): 66–91.

Blaive, Muriel. *Promarněná příležitost: Československo a rok 1956*. Prague: Prostor, 2001.

Boštík, Jan, ed. *Jak to bylo s osvobozením Plzně?: Protifašistický odboj v Plzni za druhé světové války a květnové povstání Plzeňanů v roce 1945*. Prague: Orego, 2012.

Brand, Josef. "Budeme rehabilitovat 1. červen 1953?: Pokus o rekonstrukci událostí kolem měnové reformy v Plzni." *Pravda*, May 29, 1968.

Brenner, Christiane. *Mezi Východem a Západem: České politické rozpravy 1945–1948*. Prague: Argo, 2015.

Brichta, Vladimír, ed. *Dějiny Plzně III: Od roku 1918 do roku 1948*. Pilsen: Západočeské nakladatelství, 1982.

Brichta, Vladimír. "*Komunistická strana Československa a Československá strana sociálnědemokratická na Plzeňsku v období uskutečňování Košického vládního programu a voleb do Ústavodárného národního shromáždění*." PhD diss., Univerzita Karlova v Plzni, 1965.

Brichta, Vladimír, Bělohlávek, Miloslav, and Groser, Hynek. *Plzeň 1945–1970*. Pilsen: Západočeské nakladatelství, 1971.

Brichta, Vladimír. "Pokus o 'antiúnor' v Plzni roku 1953." *Minulostí západočeského kraje* 14, no. 1 (1978): 65–70.

Brichta, Vladimír. *V první linii*, Pilsen: Západočeský KV KSČ, 1968.

Budilová, Věra. "Strhli pomník plzeňští divadelníci? Pravda o stržení Masarykova pomníku v Plzni." *Rudé právo*, June 9, 1968.

Císař, Čestmír. *Paměti: nejen o zákulisí Pražského jara*. Prague: SinCon, 2005.

Connelly, John. *Zotročená univerzita: Sovětizace vysokého školství ve východním Německu, v českých zemích a v Polsku v letech 1945–1948*. Prague: Karolinum, 2008.

Cuhra, Jaroslav, and Veber, Václav, eds. *Za svobodu a demokracii. Odpor proti komunistické moci I*. Prague: Karolinum, 1999.

Černá, Marie, and Cuhra, Jaroslav, eds. *Prověrky a jejich místo v komunistickém vládnutí: Československo 1948–1989*. Prague: ÚSD AV ČR, 2012.

Černý, Václav. *Paměti III. 1945–1972*. Brno: Atlantis, 1992.

Dale, Gareth. *Popular Protest in East Germany, 1945–1989*. New York: Routledge, 2005.

Diani, Mario, and McAdam, Doug, eds. *Social Movements and Networks: Relations Aapproaches to Collective Action*. Oxford: Oxford University Press, 2003.

Dlouhý, Martin, and Fiala, Petr. *Úvod do teorie her*. Prague: Oeconomica, 2009.

Eisenhammer, Miroslav. "Mzdová hladina zaměstnanců Škodových závodů v Plzni v době druhé světové války." *Historie a vojenství* 5, no. 1 (2001): 128–143.

Eisenhammer, Miroslav. "Škody způsobené městu Plzni nálety v době druhé světové války." *Západočeský sborník historický* 5, no. 1 (1999): 267–307.

Fischer, Jan, and Eis, Zdeněk. *Americká okupace západních Čech v roce 1945*. Prague: Naše Vojsko, 1953.

Goodwin, Jeff, and Jasper, James. "Emotions and Social Movements." In *Handbook of the Sociology of Emotions*, edited by Jan Stets and Jonathan Turner. New York: New York University, 2007, pp. 611–635.

Habermas, Jürgen. *Strukturální přeměna veřejnosti: Zkoumání jedné kategorie občanské společnosti*. Pragie: Filosofia, 2000.

Havelka, Miloš. "Česká kultura a politika před různými horizonty generační zkušenosti." In *Nezapomenuté historie: Sborník k 70. narozeninám Františka Svátka*, edited by Zbyněk Machát, Ondřej Slačálek and Milan Znoj. Brno: Doplněk, 2007, pp. 98–117.

Havlic, Vladimír. *Památník národního osvobození v Plzni: Z materiálů archivu historie a obnovy památníku*. Pilsen: Karel Veselý, 1999.

Heath, Joseph, and Potter, Andrew. *Kup si svou revoltu*. Prague: Rybka, 2012.

Hellbeck, Jochen. *Revolution on My Mind: Writing a Diary under Stalin*. Cambridge: Harvard University Press, 2006.

Heumos, Peter. *"Vyhrňme si rukávy, než se kola zastaví!": Dělníci a státní socialismus v Československu*. Prague: ÚSD AV ČR, 2006.

Hojda, Zdeněk, and Pokorný, Jiří. *Pomníky a zapomníky*. Prague: Paseka, 1996.

Horák, Pavel. *Bohumil Laušman politický životopis: Riskantní hry sociálnědemokratického lídra*. Prague: Mladá fronta, 2012.

Hrabic, Pavel, and Hrabic, Zdeněk. *Vila pana prezidenta: Historie rodinného sídla Edvarda Beneše v letech 1929–2001*. Prague: Nakladatelství Erika, 2005.

Hron, Jan. *Změny v oblasti mezd v období 1945–1953*. Prague: Ekonomický ústav ČSAV, 1968.

Janáček, František. *Čtení o Škodovce*. Pilsen: Škoda Plzeň, 1978.

Janáček, František, ed. *Největší zbrojovka monarchie: Škodovka v dějinách, dějiny ve Škodovce 1859–1918*. Prague: Novinář, 1990.

Janák, Dušan. "Zapomenutá stávka. O stávce ve Slezských bavlnářských závodech ve Frýdku v srpnu 1948." *Slezský sborník* 114, no. 1 (2016): 115–143.

Janák, Dušan, and Kokoška, Stanislav, eds. *Průmyslové dělnictvo v českých zemích v letech 1938–1948*. Prague: ÚSD AV ČR, 2019.

Jarausch, Konrad, ed. *Dictatorship as Experience: Towards a Socio-Cultural History of the GDR*. New York: Oxford University Press, 1999.

Jasper, James. *The Art of Moral Protest: Culture, Biography and Creativity in Social Movements*. Chicago: Chicago University Press, 1997.

Jech, Karel. *Soumrak selského stavu 1945–1960*. Prague: ÚSD AV ČR 2001.

Jílek, Tomáš, ed. *Národní odboj a politické, kulturní a vojenské aspekty osvobození Plzně a Západních Čech americkou armádou*. Pilsen: Západočeská univerzita, 1996.

Jirásek, Zdeněk, and Šůla, Jaroslav. *Velká peněžní loupež v Československu 1953 aneb 50:1*. Prague: Svítání 1992.

Jíša, Václav. *Škodovy závody 1859–1965*. Prague: Práce, 1969.

Jukl, Eduard. "Plzeňští leninovci v boji za splnění úkolů první pětiletky a rozvinutí výstavby socialismu v Československu (1949–1953)." In *K dějinám závodů V. I. Lenina Plzeň*, edited by Eduard Jukl. Pilsen: Krajské nakladatelství v Plzni, 1964, pp. 7–104.

Jukl, Eduard. "Z kroniky bojů plzeňských leninovců za obnovu svého závodu a za upevnění lidově demokratického zřízení." In *K dějinám závodů V. I. Lenina Plzeň*, edited by Eduard Jukl. Pilsen: Krajské nakladatelství v Plzni, 1962, pp. 23–90.

Kalinová, Lenka. *Společenské proměny v čase socialistického experimentu: K sociálním dějinám v letech 1945–1969*. Prague: Academia, 2007.

Kaplan, Karel. *Československo v letech 1953–1966*. Prague: Státní pedagogické nakladatelství, 1992.

Kaplan, Karel. *Československo v RVHP 1949–1956*. Prague: ÚSD AV ČR, 1995.

Kaplan, Karel. *Nekrvavá revoluce*. Prague: Mladá fronta, 1993.

Kaplan, Karel. *Pět kapitol o únoru*. Brno: Doplněk, 1997.

Kaplan, Karel. *Poslední rok prezidenta: Edvard Beneš v roce 1948*. Prague: ÚSD AV ČR, 1993.

Kaplan, Karel. *Sociální demokracie po únoru 1948*. Brno: Doplněk, 2011.

Kaplan, Karel. *Sociální souvislosti krizí komunistického režimu 1953–1957 a 1968–1975*. Prague: ÚSD AV ČR, 1993.

Kaplan, Karel. *Tábory nucené práce v Československu v letech 1948–1954*. Prague: ÚSD AV ČR, 1992.

Kaplan, Karel, and Váchová, Jana. *Perzekuce po měnové reformě v Československu v roce 1953*. Prague: ÚSD AV ČR, 1993.

Karlický, Vladimír, ed. *Svět okřídleného šípu: Koncern Škoda Plzeň 1918–1945*. Pilsen: Paseka, 1999.

Keller, Jan. *Sociologie konfliktu*. Brno: Masarykova univerzita v Brně, 1990.

Klausnerová, Eva. *Svobodná Plzeň hovoří: Příběhy vzepětí i pokoření Českého rozhlasu Plzeň*. Pilsen: NAVA, 2005.

Kotkin, Stephen. *Magnetic Mountain: Stalinism As a Civilization*. California: University of California Press, 1997.

Knapík, Jiří, ed. *Peněžní reformy a zvraty na území České republiky (po roce 1918): Sborník příspěvků ze stejnojmenné konference Slezské univerzity v Opavě*. Opava: Slezská univerzita v Opavě, 2005.

Knapík, Jiří. *V zajetí moci: Kulturní politika, její systém a aktéři 1948–1956*. Prague: Libri, 2006.

Kocian, Jiří. *Československá strana národně socialistická v letech 1945–1948, organizace, program, politika*. Brno: Doplněk, 2002.

Kokoška, Stanislav. *Praha v květnu 1945: Historie jednoho povstání*. Prague: Nakladatelství Lidové noviny, 2005.

Koop, Volker. *Der 17. Juni 1953: Legende und Wirklichkeit*. Berlin: Siedler, 2003.

Köpplová, Barbora, ed. *Dějiny českých médií v datech: Rozhlas, televize, mediální právo*, Prague: Karolinum, 2003.

Konečný, Stanislav. *Vzbouření a veřejné násilí v Poličce 23. září 1949, aneb Jak Poličští bránili děkana Jaroslava Daňka*. Litomyšl: Státní okresní archiv Svitavy se sídlem v Litomyšli, 2005.

Kotalík, Matěj. "'Páskové' a 'chuligáni' proti režimu?: Na okraj tradičních konceptů odboje a rezistence." In *Odboj a odpor proti komunistickému režimu v Československu a střední Evropě*. Prague: ÚSTR, 2010, pp. 225–232.

Křesťan, Jiří. *Zdeněk Nejedlý: politik a vědec v osamění*. Prague: Paseka, 2012.

Kumpera, Jan. "Plzeň na stránkách New York Times 1945 a 1953." In *Sborník Pedagogické fakulty Západočeské univerzity v Plzni: Dějepis XVI*. Prague: Státní pedagogicé nakladatelství, 1995, pp. 113–120.

Kusák, Alexej. *Kultura a politika v Československu 1945–1956*. Prague: Torst, 1998.

Laštovka, Vojtěch. *Boj pracujícího lidu Plzeňska proti fašistickým okupantům*. Pilsen: Krajské nakladatelství v Plzni, 1959.

Laštovka, Vojtěch, Brichta, Vladimír, and Šůma, Vladimír. *Tři kapitoly z dějin boje revolučního hnutí západních Čech proti reformismu*. Pilsen: Západočeské nakladatelství, 1971.

Le Bon, Gustave. *Psychologie davů*. Prague: Samcovo knihkupectví, 1946.

Lendvai, Paul. *One Day That Shook the Communist World: The 1956 Hungarian Uprising and its Legacy*. Princeton: Princeton University Press, 2008.

Lesák, Josef. *Studentský průvod na Hrad v únoru 1948*. Prague: Společnost Edvarda Beneše, 1995.

Lindenberger, Thomas, ed. *Herrschaft und Eigen-Sinn in der Diktatur. Studien zur Gesellschaftsgeschichte der DDR*. Cologne: Böhlau, 1999.

Machcewicz, Paweł. *Rebellious Satellite: Poland 1956*. Stanford: Stanford University Press, 2009.

Maňák, Jiří. *Komunisté na pochodu k moci: Vývoj početnosti a struktury KSČ v období 1945–1948*. Prague: ÚSD AV ČR, 1995.

Matějka, Ondřej. "'Jsou to berani, ale můžeme je využít': Čeští evangelíci a komunistický režim 1948–1956." *Soudobé dějiny* 14, no. 2 (2007): 305–340.

Marada, Radim. *Kultura protestu a politizace každodennosti*. Brno: Centrum pro studium demokracie a kultury, 2003.

Marek, Pavel. *České živnostnictvo 1945–1960: Likvidace živnostníků, řemeslníků a obchodníků v českých zemích*. Brno: Doplněk, 2006.

Marek, Pavel. "Protikomunistické demonstrace v Československu v roce 1953." *Securitas imperii* 24, no. 2 (2014): 9–34.

Martinovský, Ivan. "A Novotný pak zkritizoval všechny." *Region Plzeňsko: Západočeské noviny*, June 3, 1993.

Martinovský, Ivan, ed. *Dějiny Plzně v datech: Od prvních stop osídlení až po současnost*. Prague: Nakladatelství Lidové noviny, 2004.

Mayerová, Francoise. "Vězení jako minulost, odboj jako paměť." *Soudobé dějiny*, no. 1 (2002): 42–64.

McDermott, Kevin. "Lidový odpor v komunistickém Československu: Plzeňské povstání v červnu 1953." *Minulostí západočeského kraje* 46, no. 1 (2011): 206–231.

McDermott, Kevin. "Popular Resistance in Communist Czechoslovakia: The Plzeň Uprising, June 1953." *Contemporary European History* 19, no. 4 (2010): 287–307.

Melucci, Alberto. *Nomads of the Present: Social Movements and Individual Needs in Contemporary Society*. Philadelphia: Temple University Press, 1989.

Merton, Robert. *Studie ze sociologické teorie*. Prague: Sociologické nakladatelství, 2000.

Michňák, Josef, and Niklíček, Ladislav. *Příspěvek k historii mládežnického hnutí v ČSSR (Boj za jednotu mládeže v letech 1945–1949)*. Prague: Mladá fronta, 1962.

Millington, Richard. *State, Society and Memories of the Uprising of 17 June 1953 in the GDR*. Basingstoke: Palgrave Macmillan, 2014.

Mommsen, Wolfgang. "Social Conditioning and Social Relevance of Historical Judgments." *History and Theory* 17, no. 4 (1978): 19–35.

Möbius, Regine. *Panzer gegen die Freiheit: Zeitzeugen des 17. Juni 1953 berichten*. Leipzig: Evangelische Verlagsanstalt, 2003.

Musilová, Dana. *Měnová reforma 1953 a její sociální důsledky*. Prague: ÚSD AV ČR, 1993.

Nakonečný, Milan. *Sociální psychologie*. Prague: Academia 2009.

Nálevka, Vladimír. *Studená válka*. Prague: Triton, 2003.

Navrátil, Antonín. "Průvod vysokoškoláků na Hrad 25. února 1948." In *Vysokoškoláci za svobodu*, edited by Zdeňka Onyskowová. Prague, Ústav pro informace a vzdělávání, 1998, pp. 26–27.

Nedvěd, Jaroslav. *Cesta ke sloučení sociální demokracie s komunistickou stranou v roce 1948*. Prague: Academia, 1968.

Neff, Ondřej. "Oprátka pro Masaryka." *Mladá fronta*, March 3, 1990, 1–2.

Němečková, Věra. "Československá měnová reforma 1945: Elegantní řešení nebo krach?" In *Peněžní reformy a zvraty na území České republiky (po roce 1918)*, edited by Jiří Knapík. Opava: Slezská univerzita v Opavě, 2005, pp. 78–93.

Olivová, Věra, and Šubrtová, Alena. *Tryzna za Edvarda Beneše 1998*. Prague: Společnost Edvarda Beneše, 1998.

Olšanová, Marie. *Únor 1948 na Plzeňsku: Dokumenty ke 20. výročí Února*. Pilsen: KV KSČ, 1968.

Ostermann, Christian, ed. *Uprising in East Germany, 1953: The Cold War, the German Question and the First Major Upheaval Behind the Iron Curtain*. Budapest: Central European University Press, 2001.

Pachta, Jan. *Pravda o T. G. Masarykovi*. Prague: Orbis, 1953.

Paczkowski, Andrzej. *Půl století dějin Polska 1939–1989*. Prague: Academia, 2000.

Pasák, Tomáš. "Demonstrace 28. října v Praze." *Pražský sborník historický* 14, no. 1 (1981): 120–147.

Pasák, Tomáš. "Pražská protifašistická demonstrace českého studentstva v listopadu 1939 a její důsledky." *Pražský sborník historický* 18, no. 1 (1985): 65–97.

Pecka, Jindřich. *Na demarkační čáře: Americká armáda v Čechách v roce 1945*. Prague: ÚSD AV ČR, 1995.

Pejčoch, Ivo. *Protikomunistické puče*. Cheb: Svět křídel, 2011.

Pejčoch, Ivo, and Tomek, Prokop. *Agenti-chodci na popravišti*. Cheb: Svět křídel, 2010.

Pelant, Jan, and Bystrický, Vladimír. *Únor 1948 v západních Čechách, faksimilia dokumentů*. Pilsen: Státní oblastní archiv v Plzni, 1978.

Pernes, Jiří. "Aféra majora Šoffra. Střetnutí vysokoškolských studentů a dělníků Zbrojovky v Brně v únoru 1946." In *Acta contemporanea. K pětašedesátinám Viléma Prečana*, edited by Jindřich Pecka. Praha: ÚSD AV ČR, 1998, pp. 295–318.

Pernes, Jiří. *Brno 1951: Příspěvek k dějinám protikomunistického odporu na Moravě*. Prague: ÚSD AV ČR, 1997.

Pernes, Jiří. "Neznámý dokument o peněžní reformě v Československu v roce 1953." In *Po stopách nedávné historie: Sborník k 75. narozeninám doc. Karla Kaplana*, edited by Jiří Pernes. Brno: Prius, 2003, s. 169–190.

Pernes, Jiří. *Snahy o překonání politicko-hospodářské krize v Československu v roce 1953*. Brno: ÚSD AV ČR, 2000.

Pešťák, Michael. "Stalinův pomník v Plzni." *Ročenka Státního oblastního archivu v Plzni* 1, no. 1 (2007): s. 88–90.

Petráš, Jiří. "Peněžní reforma 1953." *Sborník Archivu ministerstva vnitra* 3, no. 1 (2005): 141–171.

Pichlík, Karel, and Bartošek, Karel. *Z dějin dělnického hnutí na Plzeňsku: O úloze pravicových sociálních demokratů*. Prague: Státní nakladatelství politické literatury, 1954.

Pik, Luděk. *Dvě stě milionů vteřin: Reportáž a povídky*. Pilsen: E. Kosnar, 1946.

Plamper, Jan. "Beyond Binaries: Popular Opinion in Stalinism." In *Popular Opinion in Totalitarian Regimes: Fascism, Nazism, Communism*, edited by Paul Corner. Oxford: Oxford University Press, 2009, pp. 64–80.

Pousta, Zdeněk. "Smuteční pochod za demokracii." In *Stránkami soudobých dějin: Sborník prací k pětašedesátinám historika Karla Kaplana*, edited by Karel Jech. Prague: ÚSD AV ČR, 1993, pp. 198–207.

Prokš, Petr. *Politické programy Českoslovanské a Československé sociálně demokratické strany dělnické 1878–1948*. Prague: Historický ústav AV ČR, 1999.

Průcha, Václav, ed. *Hospodářské a sociální dějiny Československa 1918–1992. II. díl*. Brno: Doplněk, 2009.

Pullmann, Michal. "Sociální dějiny a totalitněhistorické vyprávění." *Soudobé Dějiny*, no. 3 (2008): s. 703–717.

Rákosník, Jakub. *Sovětizace sociálního státu: Lidově demokratický režim a sociální práva občanů v Československu 1945–1960*. Prague: Vydavatelství Filosofické fakulty Univerzity Karlovy v Praze, 2010.

Randák, Jan. "Socialističtí hrdinové a škodovák František Zýka." In *Hrdinství a zbabělost v české politické kultuře 19. a 20. Století*, edited by Jan Randák and Petr Koura. Prague: Dokořán, 2008, pp. 390–410.

Richthofen, Esther. *Bringing Culture to the Masses: Control, Compromise and Participation in the GDR*. New York: Berghahn, 2009.

Rokosová, Šárka. "Zásah jednotek SNB proti studentům 25. 2. 1948." *Securitas imperii* 12, no. 2 (2005): 41–52.

Rupnik, Jacques. *Dějiny Komunistické strany Československa od počátků do převzetí moci*. Prague: Academia, 2002.

Růžička, Karel. *ROH v boji o rozšíření moci dělnické třídy*. Prague: Práce, 1963.

Řeháček, Karel. "Plzeňští studenti a 1. červen 1953." In *Naše měna je pevná. Plzeň a měnová reforma 1953*, edited by Miroslav Breitfelder. Pilsen: Západočeská univerzita v Plzni, 2014, pp. 64–76.

Scott, James. *Domination and the Arts of Resistance: Hidden Transcripts*. New Haven: Yale University Press, 1990.

Sčítání lidu a soupis domů a bytů v Republice československé ke dni 1. března 1950, díl 1: Nejdůležitější výsledky sčítání lidu a soupis domů a bytů za kraje, okresy a města, Prague: Státní úřad statistický, 1957.

Sčítání lidu v Republice československé ke dni 1. března 1950, díl 2: Věkové složení a povolání obyvatelstva. Prague: Státní úřad statistický, 1958.

Skála, Adam. "'A bude se vám tam bydlet jako v Tatrách': Nucené vystěhování plzeňských občanů do obce Útery v roce 1953." In *Sborník k poctě Evy a Karla Waskových, západočeských archivářů*, edited by Marie Wasková. Pilsen: M. Wasková, 2011, pp. 315–316.

Skála, Adam. "Akce K – likvidace mužských řeholních domů v Plzni (1950)." *Minulostí západočeského kraje* 41, no. 1 (2006): 295–400.

Skála, Adam, ed. *Dějiny města Plzně 3 (1918–1990)*. Pilsen: Statutární město Plzeň, 2018.

Skála, Adam. "Červen 1953 ve vzpomínkách Josefa Hodka." *Minulostí západočeského kraje* 43, no. 1 (2008): 364–369.

Skála, Adam. "Měnová reforma 1. června 1953 v Plzni v hlášení mocenských orgánů." *Minulostí západočeského kraje* 42, no. 2 (2007): 592–630.

Skála, Adam. "Pokusy o hromadné vystěhovávání plzeňských obyvatel po roce 1948." *Minulostí západočeského kraje* 47, no. 1 (2012): 187–245.

Smula, Johann. "The Party and the Proletariat: Škoda 1948–53." *Cold War History* 6, no. 2 (2006): 153–75.

Sommer, Vítězslav. *Angažované dějepisectví: Stranická historiografie mezi stalinismem a reformním komunismem (1950–1970)*. Prague: Lidové noviny, 2011.

Staněk, Tomáš. *Poválečné "excesy" v českých zemích v roce 1945 a jejich vyšetřování*. Prague: ÚSD AV ČR, 2005.

Státník, Dalibor. *Sankční pracovní právo v padesátých letech*. Prague: ÚSD AV ČR, 1994.

Stibbe, Matthew. "The SED, German Communism and the June 19953 Uprising: New Trends and New Research." In *Revolution and Resistance in Eastern Europe: Challenges to Communist Rule*, edited by Kevin McDermott and Matthew Stibbe. Oxford: Berg, 2006, pp. 37–55.

Šafránková, Eva. "*Ty jsi červnovej?: 1953 očima pamětníků*." PhD diss., Západočeská univerzita v Plzni, 2005.

Šlajs, Václav. *Růže z Pekla: O historii a osobnostech sociální demokracie na Plzeňsku a v Plzeňském kraji 1878–2006*. Pilsen: Krajský výkonný výbor ČSSD, 2006.

Šlouf, Jakub. "Byly plzeňské demonstrace v červnu 1953 vyprovokovány spolupracovníkem StB?: Životní příběh kamelota Josefa Fencla (1909–1979)." In *České, slovenské a československé dějiny 20. století VI*, edited by Sylva Sklenářová. Ústí nad Orlicí: Oftis, 2012, pp. 85–96.

Šlouf, Jakub. "Krajské vedení KSČ na Plzeňsku v letech 1945–1948." *Minulostí západočeského kraje* 44, no. 1 (2009): 261–352.

Šlouf, Jakub. "KSČ na Plzeňsku v letech 1945–1948: Početnost a struktura členské základny." *Minulostí západočeského kraje* 42, no. 1 (2007): 337–432.

Šlouf, Jakub. "'Nechceme svaz mládeže, když má rudé otěže!': Politický život pražských a plzeňských středoškoláků v letech 1945–1948." *Soudobé dějiny*, no. 4 (2011): 627–668.

Šlouf, Jakub. "Obraz myšlení západočeských středoškoláků na stránkách nezávislého časopisu Studentský hlasatel (1946–1947) ." In *Sborník k poctě Evy a Karla Waskových, západočeských archivářů*, edited by Marie Wasková. Pilsen: M. Wasková 2011, pp. 290–295.

Šlouf, Jakub. "Okradená strana: Protesty členské základy KSČ proti měnové reformě v roce 1953." *Securitas Imperii* 32, no. 1 (2018): 250–285.

Šlouf, Jakub. *Podvedená strana: Zrod masového komunistického hnutí na Plzeňsku, jeho disciplinace, centralizace a byrokratizace (1945–1948)*. Pilsen: Západočeská univerzita v Plzni, 2016.

Šlouf, Jakub. "'Pojďte si s námi koupit svačinu za 500 Kč!': Plzeňské demonstrace 1. června 1953 jako důsledek dočasné ztráty každodenních životních jistot obyvatelstva v průběhu tzv. měnové reformy." In: *Naše měna je pevná. Plzeň a měnová reforma 1953*, edited by Miroslav Breitfelder. Pilsen: Západočeská univerzita v Plzni, 2014, pp. 29–36.

Šlouf, Jakub. "Proamerické demonstrace v Plzni 5.–6. května 1948: 'Nesneseme v republice štvaní proti Americe!'." In *Třetí odboj: Kapitoly z dějin protikomunistické rezistence v Československu v padesátých letech 20. století*, edited by Václav Veber. Prague: ÚSTR, 2010, pp. 83–103.

Šlouf, Jakub. "Rivalita komunistické strany a sociální demokracie na Plzeňsku v letech 1945–1948: Poválečné dědictví prvorepublikových tradic." In *Bolševismus, komunismus a radikální socialismus v Československu VI*, edited by Zdeněk Kárník and Jiří Kocian. Prague: ÚSD AV ČR, 2012, pp. 113–137.

Šlouf, Jakub. "Rozvrat lokálního stranického a bezpečnostního aparátu v průběhu plzeňských demonstrací 1. června 1953." In: *Osm let po válce: Rok 1953 v Československu*, edited by Jiří Petráš and Libor Svoboda. Prague: ÚSTR, 2014, pp. 295–305.

Šlouf, Jakub. *Spřízněni měnou: Genealogie plzeňské revolty 1. června 1953*. Prague: Univerzita Karlova v Praze, 2016.

Štěpánek, Zdeněk. *Utajené povstání 1953*. Prague: Michael, 1993.

Švermová, Marie. *Vzpomínky*. Prague: Futura, 2008.

Tigrid Pavel. *Dnešek je váš, zítřek je náš: Dělnické revolty v komunistických zemích*. Cologne: Index, 1982.

Tomeš, Josef. *Průkopníci a pokračovatelé: Osobnosti v dějinách české sociální demokracie 1878–2005*. Prague: Československá strana sociálně demokratická, 2005.

Tomek, Prokop. *Letákové operace Svobodné Evropy 1951–1956*. Cheb: Svět křídel, 2014.

Touraine, Alain. *Thinking Differently*. Cambridge: Polity Press, 2009.

Trapl, Miloš. *Osudy sochy*. Prostějov: Městský úřad Prostějov, 1999.

Trapl, Miloš. *Prostějovský "Černý pátek" 10. dubna 1953*. Prostějov: Městský úřad Prostějov, 1998.

Tůma, Oldřich. "Protirežimní demonstrace v Praze." In: *Opozice a odpor proti komunistickému režimu v Československu 1969–1989*, edited by Petr Blažek. Prague: Dokořán, 2005, pp. 140–157.

Ulč, Otto. *The Judge in a Communist State: A View From Within*. Columbus: Ohio University Press, 1972.

Vilímek, Tomáš, and Tůma, Oldřich, eds. *Projevy a podoby protirežimní rezistence v komunistickém Československu 1948–1989*. Prague: ÚSD AV ČR, 2018.

Vojtěchovský, Ondřej. *Z Prahy proti Titovi: Jugoslávská prosovětská emigrace v Československu*. Prague: Univerzita Karlova v Praze, 2012.

Veber, Václav. *Osudové únorové dny 1948*. Prague: Lidové noviny, 2008.

Vošahlíková, Pavla. *Československá sociální demokracie a Národní fronta*. Prague: Academia, 1985.

Welzer, Harald, ed. *"Můj děda nebyl nácek": Nacismus a holocaust v rodinné paměti*. Prague: Argo, 2010.

Žáček, Pavel. "'Drtina v Plzni: Pokus o organizování reakční mocenské akce', prověřování jedné fámy na pozadí reorganizace ministerstva vnitra v letech 1947–1948." *Paměť a dějiny*, no. 1 (2008): 60–75.

Name Index

About the Author

Dr. **Jakub Šlouf** obtained his PhD in 2015 at the Faculty of Arts of Charles University in Prague, and joined the Institute for the Study of Totalitarian Regimes Czech Republic as a researcher the same year. Since 2018, he also has worked as an archivist in the National Archives in Prague. His research is focused on public protests in state socialist dictatorships, the history of industrial workers, and the development of the lower organizational structures of the communist movement. His books include *Spřízněni měnou: Genealogie plzeňské revolty 1. června 1953 [Kindred by Currency: Origins and Development of the Pilsen Revolt of 1 June 1953]* (2016), *Nervová vlákna diktatury: Regionální elity a komunikace uvnitř KSČ v letech 1945–1956 [The Neural Network of a Dictatorship: Regional Elites and Commnunication within the Communist Party of Czechoslovakia in the years 1945–1956]* (2019), *Mimořádný lidový soud v Praze 1945–1948: Retribuce jako služební úkol na hraně možností i profesní cti zaměstnanců justice [Extraordinary People's Court in Prague, 1945–1948: Retribution as a Challenge Testing the Personal and Professional Boundaries of Judicial Employees]* (2020), and *Praha v červnu 1953: Dělnická revolta proti měnové reformě, vyjednávání v továrnách a strukturální proměna dělnické třídy [June 1953 in Prague: The Worker's Revolt Against the Currency Reform, Bargaining in Factories, and the Structural Transformation of the Working Class]* (2021). He is a member of the Czech National Archives Editorial Board and member of the editorial board of the *Securitas Imperii* journal.

www.ingramcontent.com/pod-product-compliance
Ingram Content Group UK Ltd.
Pitfield, Milton Keynes, MK11 3LW, UK
UKHW020839290926
15470UKWH00004B/1443

9 781793 646453